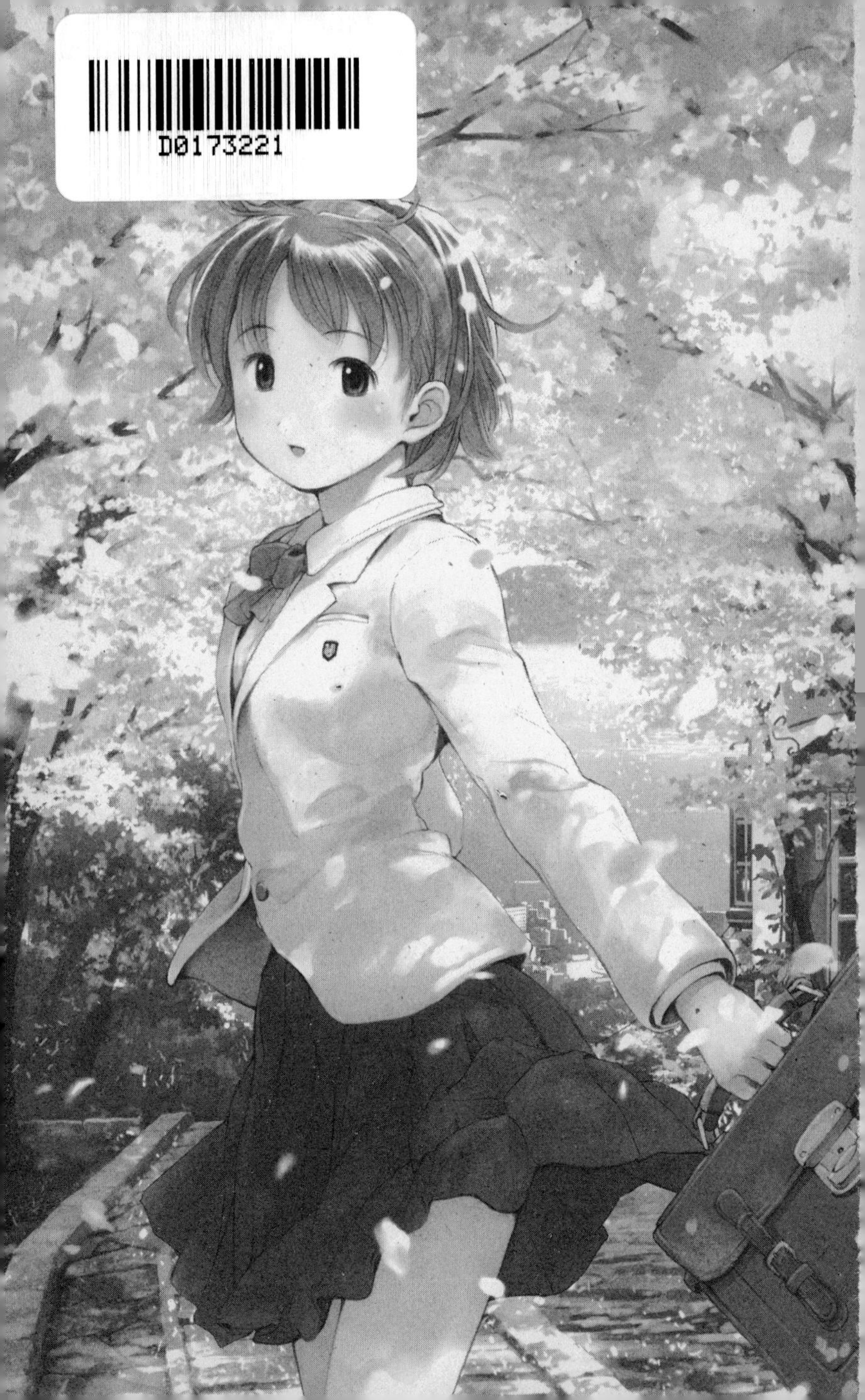

SOMEDAY's DREAMERS
SPELLBOUND™

Volume 1

Story by Norie Yamada
Art by Kumichi Yoshizuki

HAMBURG // LONDON // LOS ANGELES // TOKYO

Someday's Dreamers: Spellbound Vol. 1
Story By Norie Yamada
Art By Kumichi Yoshizuki

Translation - Jeremiah Bourque
English Adaptation - Hope Donovan
Retouch and Lettering - Bowen Park
Cover Design - Jose Macasocol, Jr.

Editor - Paul Morrissey
Digital Imaging Manager - Chris Buford
Pre-Production Supervisor - Erika Terriquez
Art Director - Anne Marie Horne
Production Manager - Liz Brizzi
Managing Editor - Vy Nguyen
VP of Production - Ron Klamert
Editor-in-Chief - Rob Tokar
Publisher - Mike Kiley
President and C.O.O. - John Parker
C.E.O. and Chief Creative Officer - Stuart Levy

A TOKYOPOP® Manga

TOKYOPOP Inc.
5900 Wilshire Blvd. Suite 2000
Los Angeles, CA 90036

E-mail: info@TOKYOPOP.com
Come visit us online at www.TOKYOPOP.com

MAHOUTSUKAI NI TAISETSUNA KOTO TAIYOU
TO KAZE NO SAKAMICHI Volume 1
©NORIE YAMADA/KUMICHI YOSHIZUKI 2004
First published in Japan in 2004 by KADOKAWA SHOTEN
PUBLISHING CO., LTD., Tokyo.
English translation rights arranged
with KADOKAWA SHOTEN PUBLISHING CO., LTD., Tokyo
through TUTTLE–MORI AGENCY, INC., Tokyo.
English text copyright © 2006 TOKYOPOP Inc.

ISBN: 1-59816-642-5

First TOKYOPOP printing: December 2006
10 9 8 7 6 5 4 3 2 1
Printed in the USA

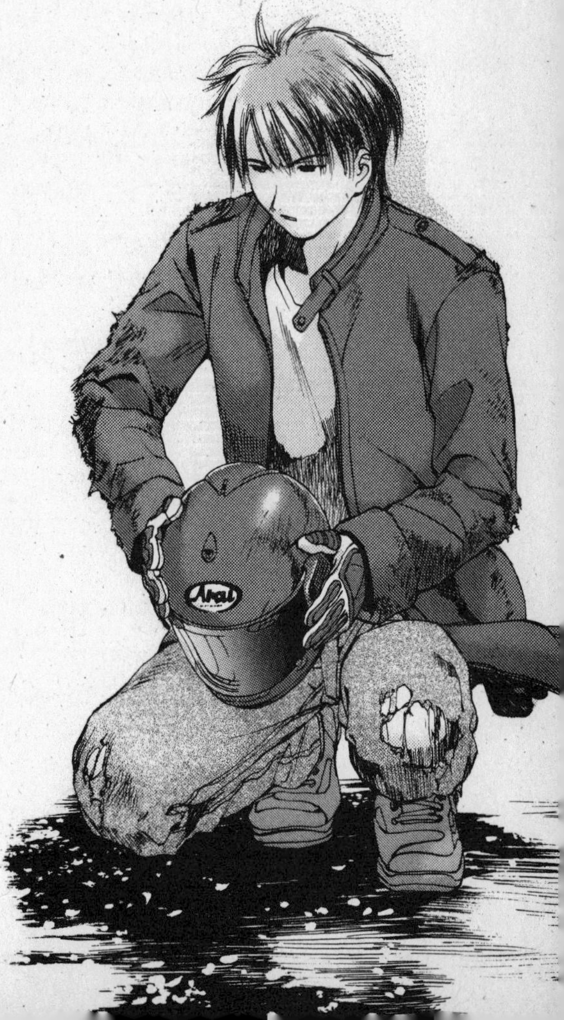
Arai

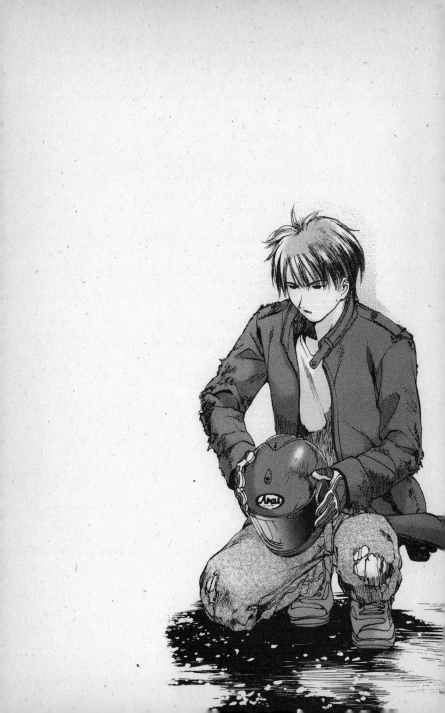

SOMEDAY'S DREAMERS
SPELLBOUND™

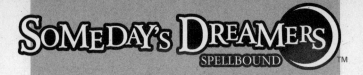

CONTENTS:

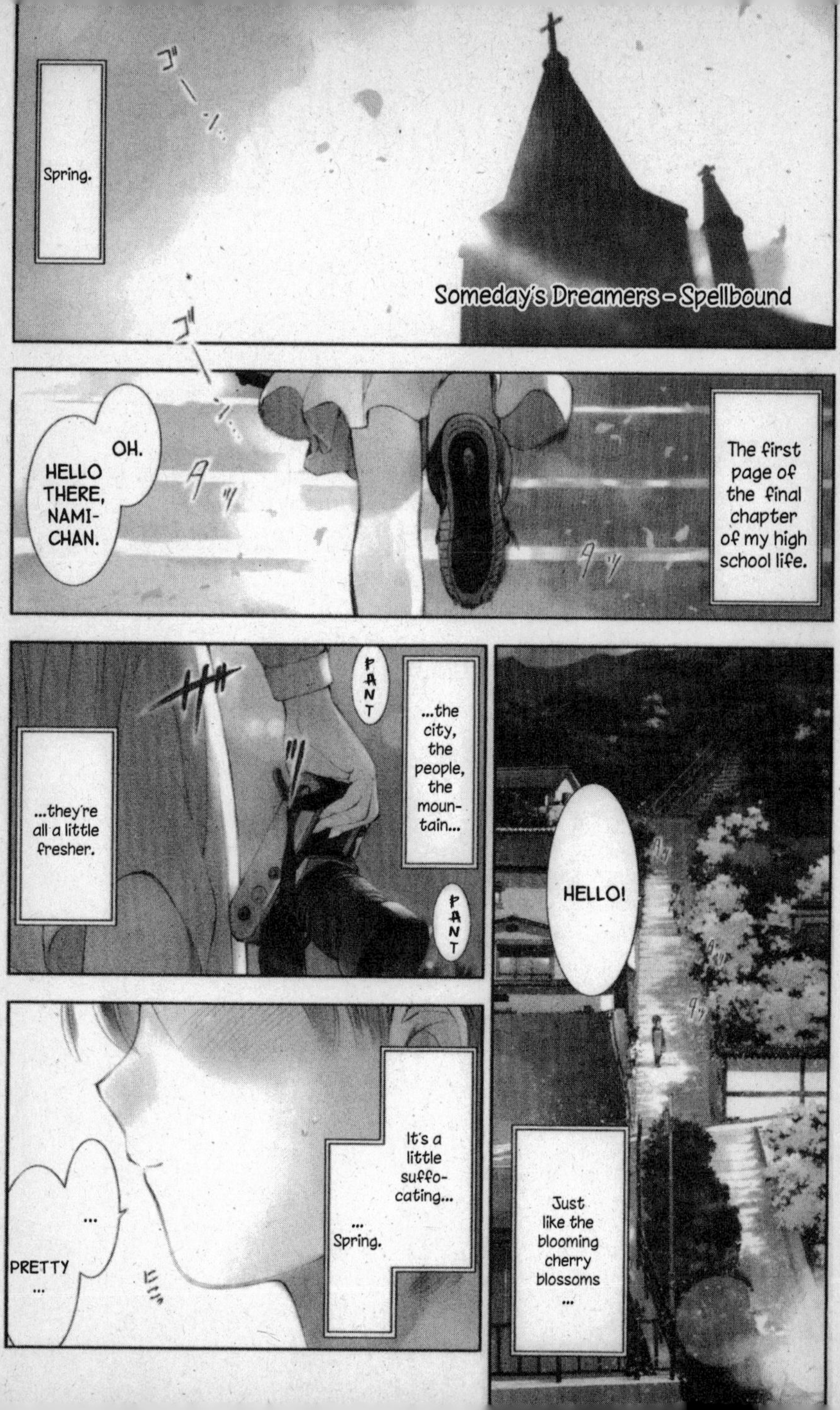
Spring.
Someday's Dreamers - Spellbound
The first page of the final chapter of my high school life.
OH. HELLO THERE, NAMI-CHAN.
HELLO!
Just like the blooming cherry blossoms ...
...the city, the people, the mountain...
PANT
PANT
...they're all a little fresher.
It's a little suffocating...
... Spring.
...
PRETTY ...

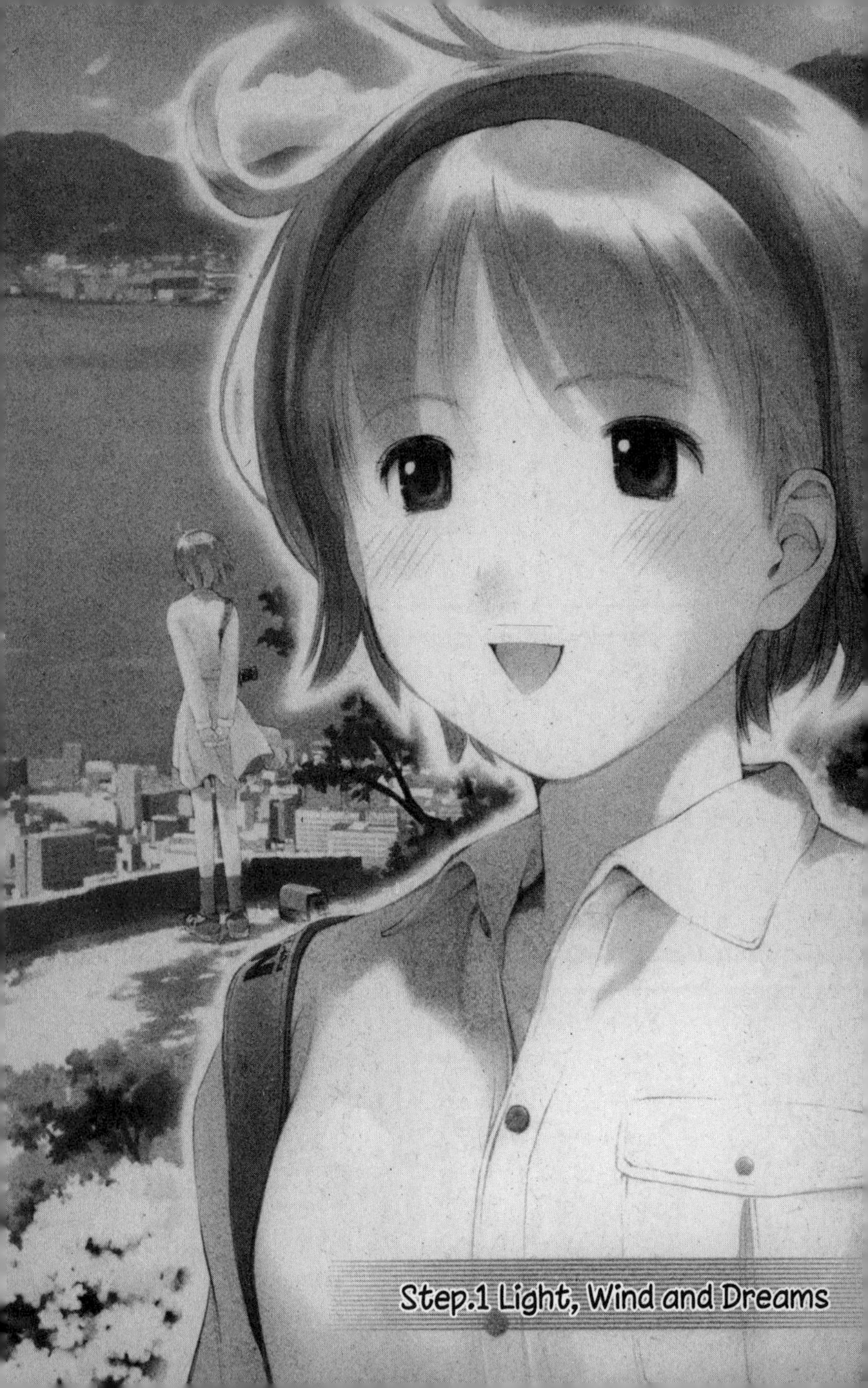
Step.1 Light, Wind and Dreams

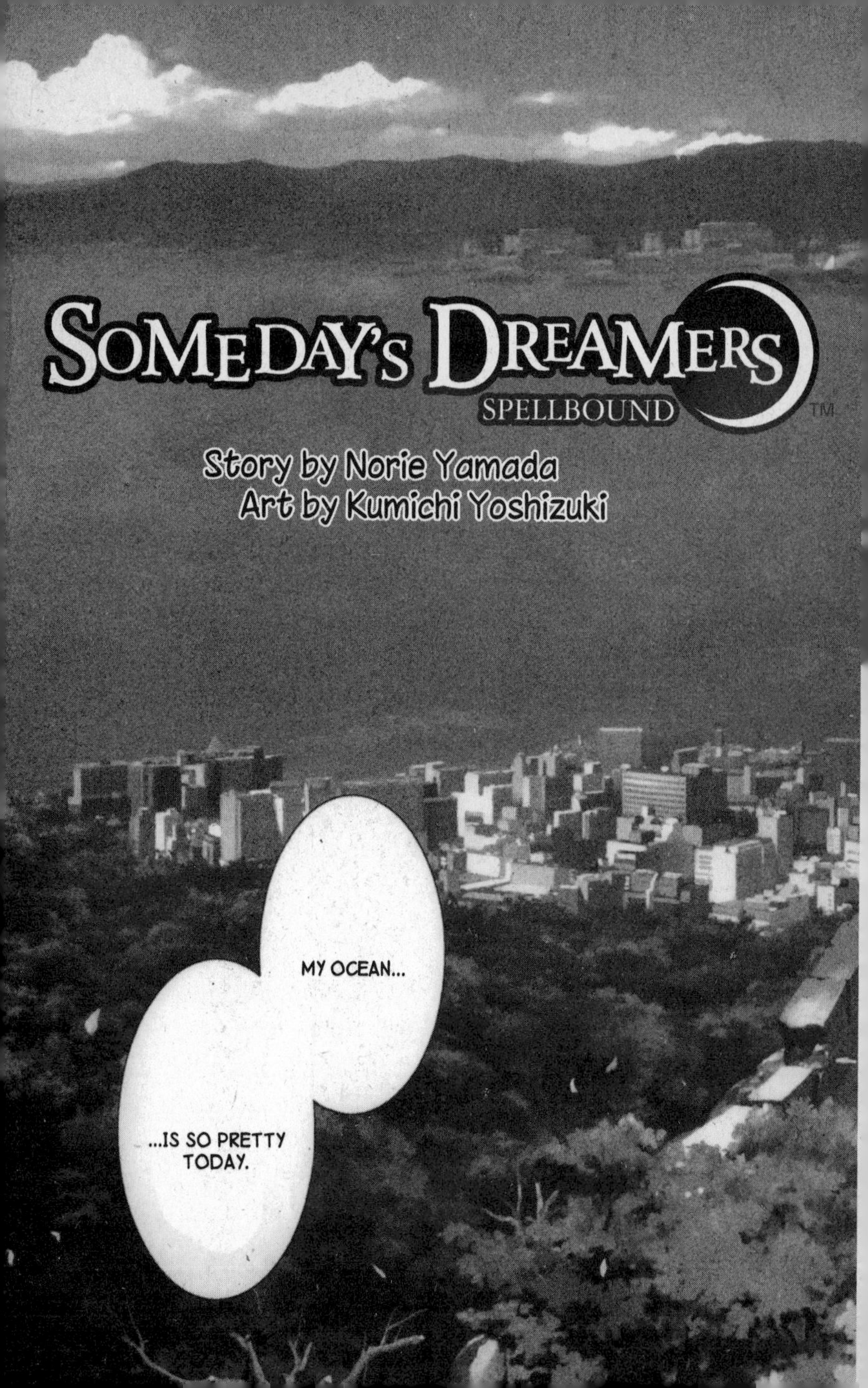
SOMEDAY'S DREAMERS
SPELLBOUND
TM
Story by Norie Yamada
Art by Kumichi Yoshizuki
MY OCEAN...
...IS SO PRETTY TODAY.

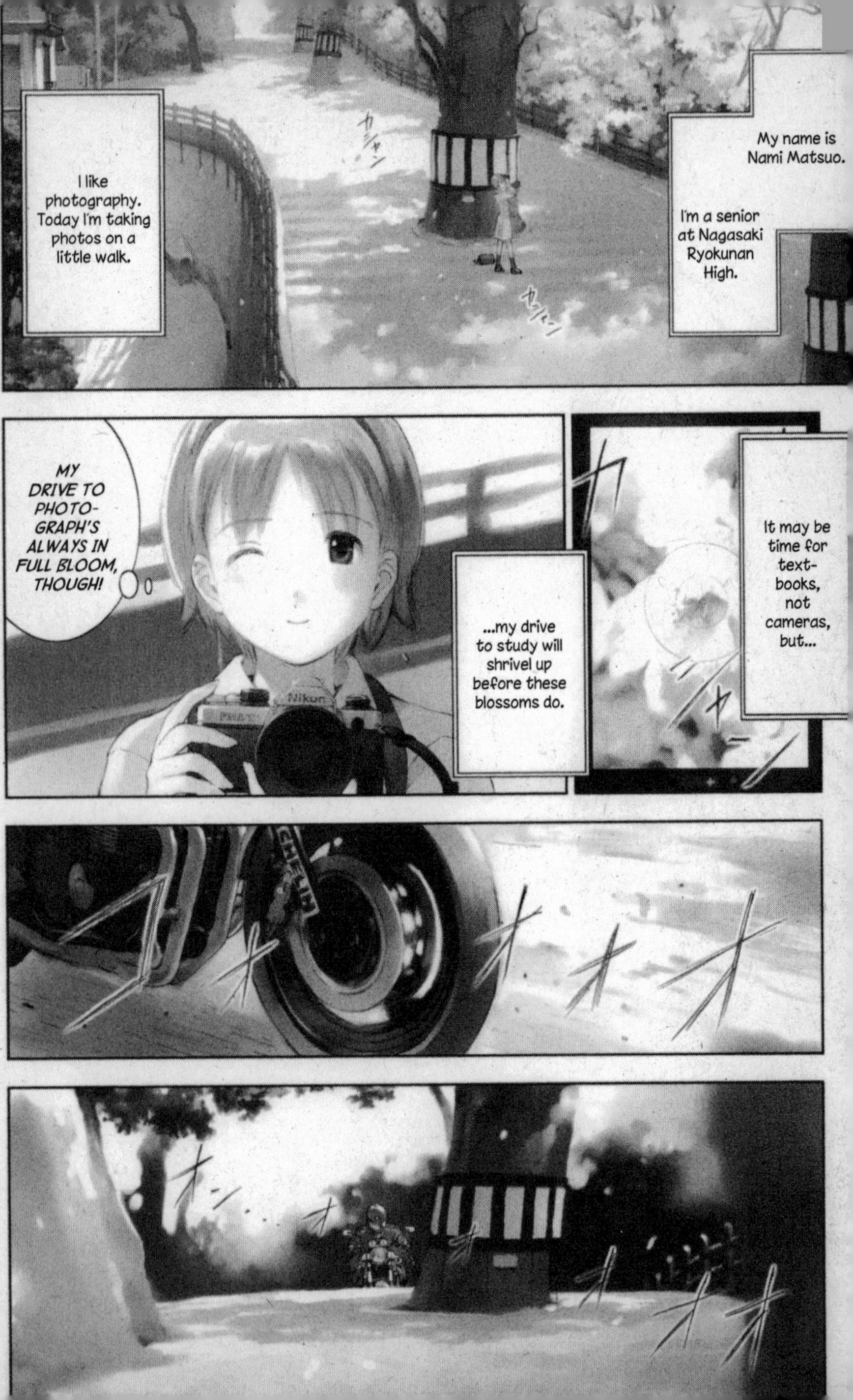
My name is Nami Matsuo.
I'm a senior at Nagasaki Ryokunan High.
I like photography. Today I'm taking photos on a little walk.
It may be time for text-books, not cameras, but...
...my drive to study will shrivel up before these blossoms do.
MY DRIVE TO PHOTO-GRAPH'S ALWAYS IN FULL BLOOM, THOUGH!

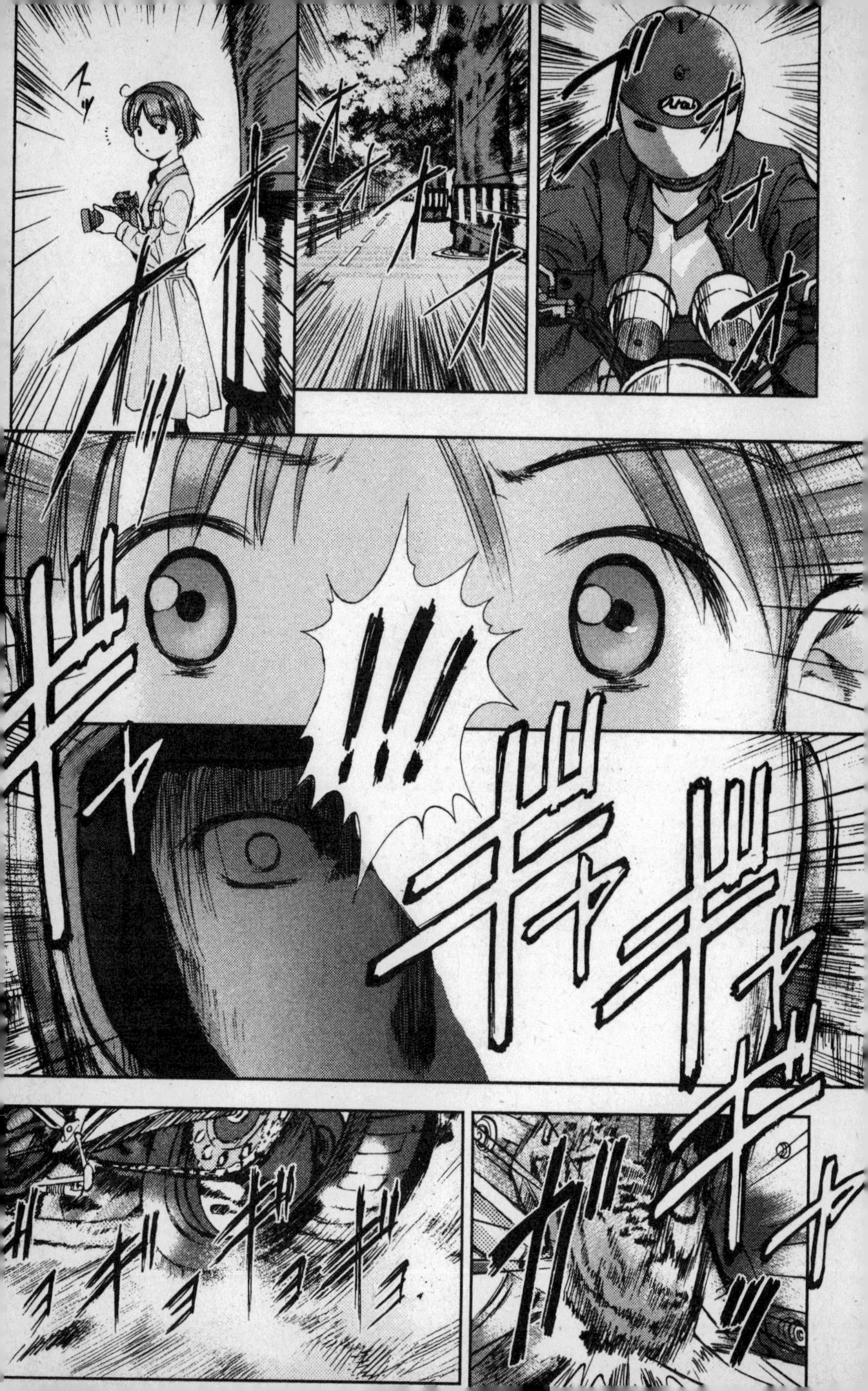
ブオオオオ
スッ
!!!
ギャギャギャ

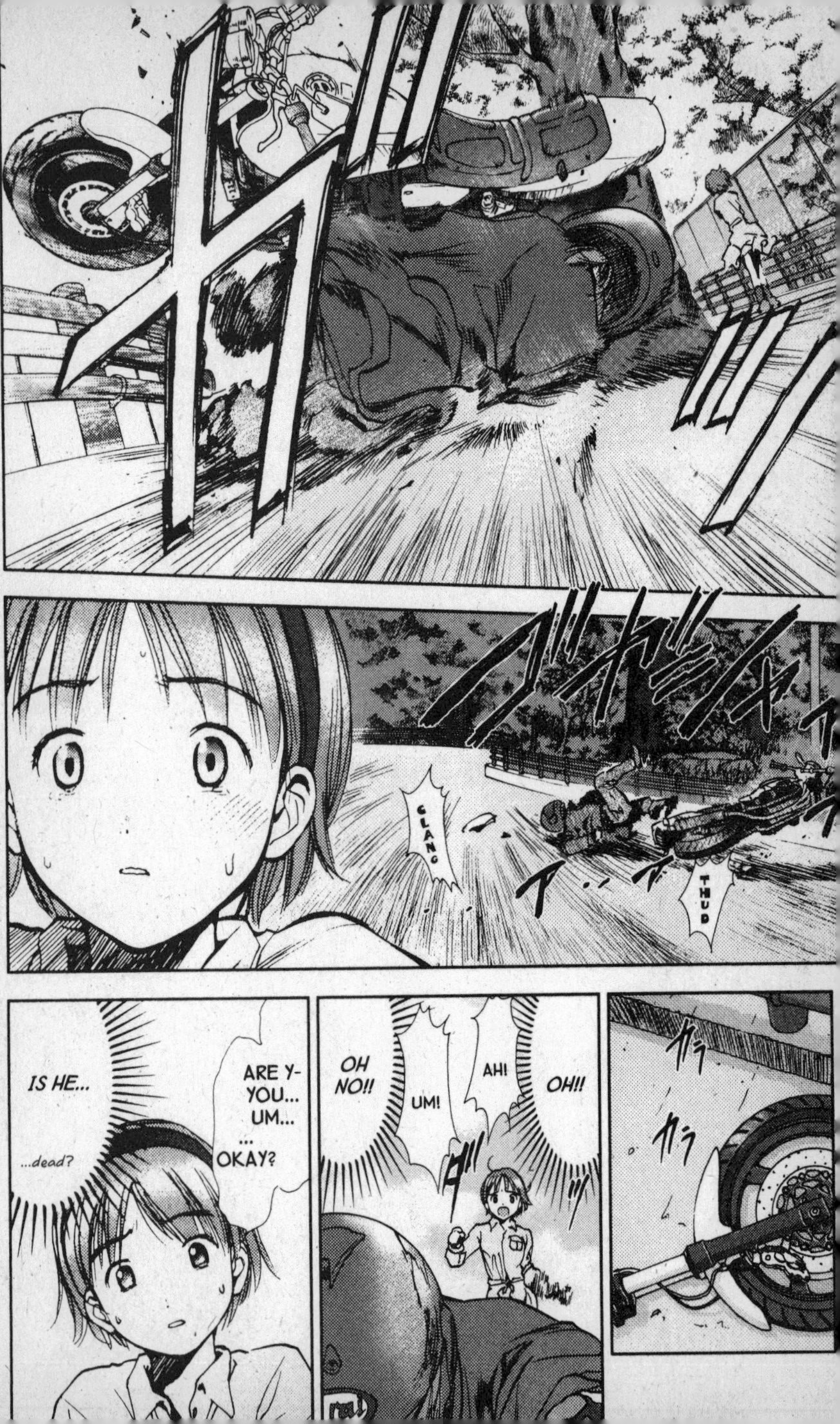
THUD
CLANG
OH!!
AH!
UM!
OH NO!!
ARE Y-YOU... UM... ...OKAY?
IS HE...
...dead?

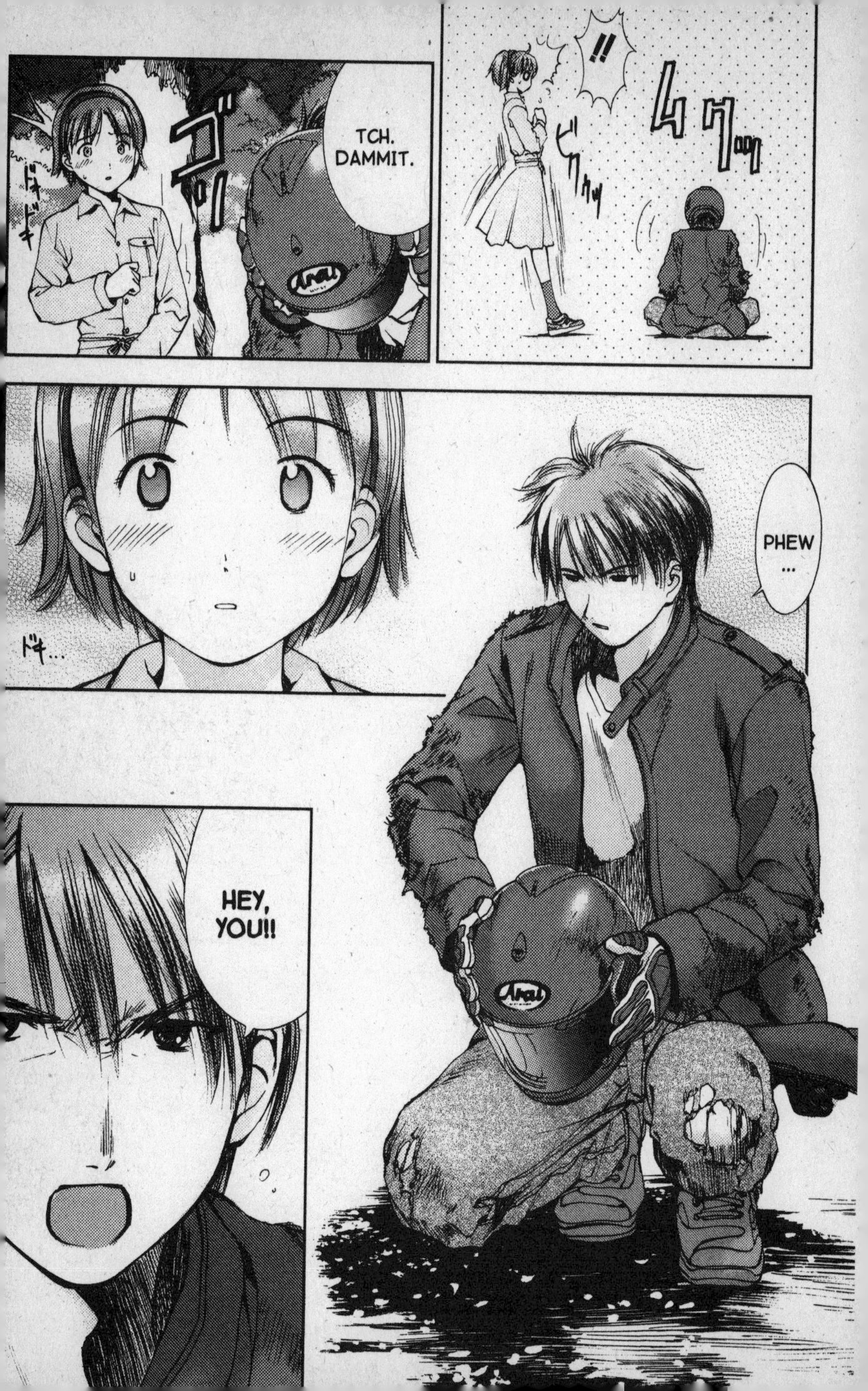
!!
TCH. DAMMIT.
PHEW ...
ドキ…
HEY, YOU!!

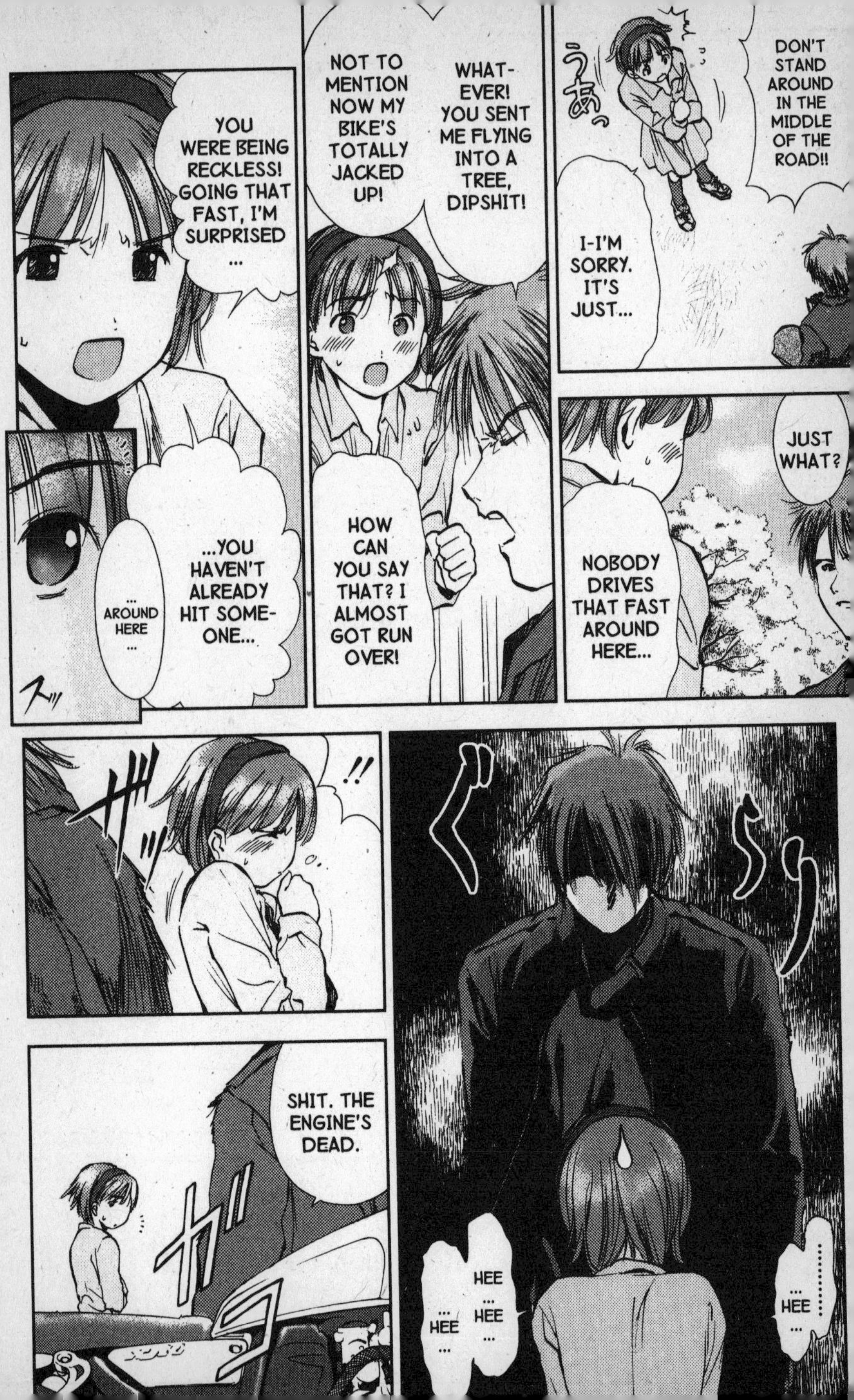
DON'T STAND AROUND IN THE MIDDLE OF THE ROAD!!
I-I'M SORRY. IT'S JUST...
JUST WHAT?
NOBODY DRIVES THAT FAST AROUND HERE...
WHAT-EVER! YOU SENT ME FLYING INTO A TREE, DIPSHIT!
NOT TO MENTION NOW MY BIKE'S TOTALLY JACKED UP!
HOW CAN YOU SAY THAT? I ALMOST GOT RUN OVER!
YOU WERE BEING RECKLESS! GOING THAT FAST, I'M SURPRISED ...
...YOU HAVEN'T ALREADY HIT SOME-ONE...
... AROUND HERE ...
......
... HEE ...
HEE ... HEE ...
... HEE ...
!!
SHIT. THE ENGINE'S DEAD.

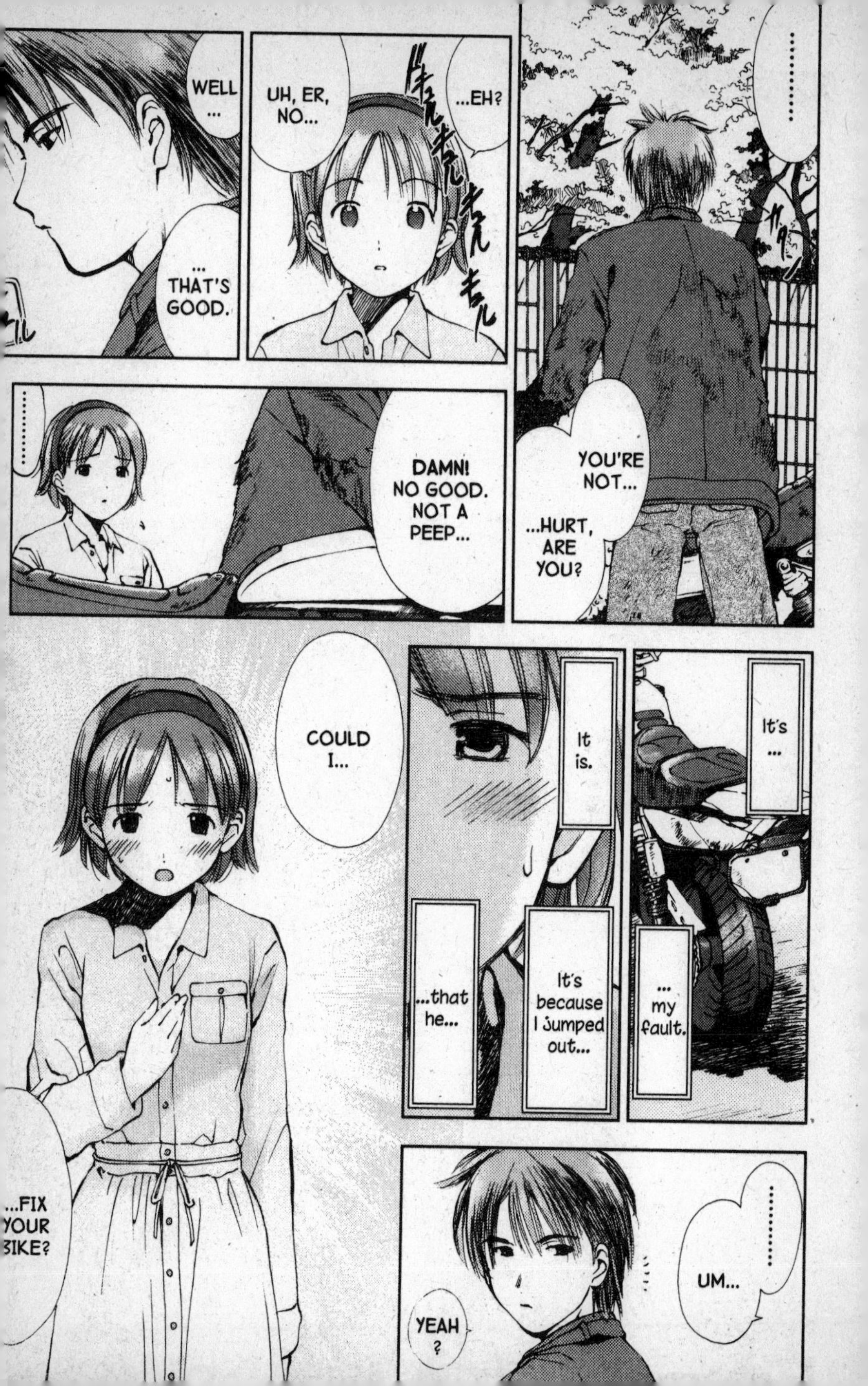
....
YOU'RE NOT...
...HURT, ARE YOU?
...EH?
UH, ER, NO...
WELL ...
... THAT'S GOOD.
DAMN! NO GOOD. NOT A PEEP...
....
It's ...
... my fault.
It is.
It's because I jumped out...
...that he...
....
UM...
YEAH?
COULD I...
...FIX YOUR BIKE?

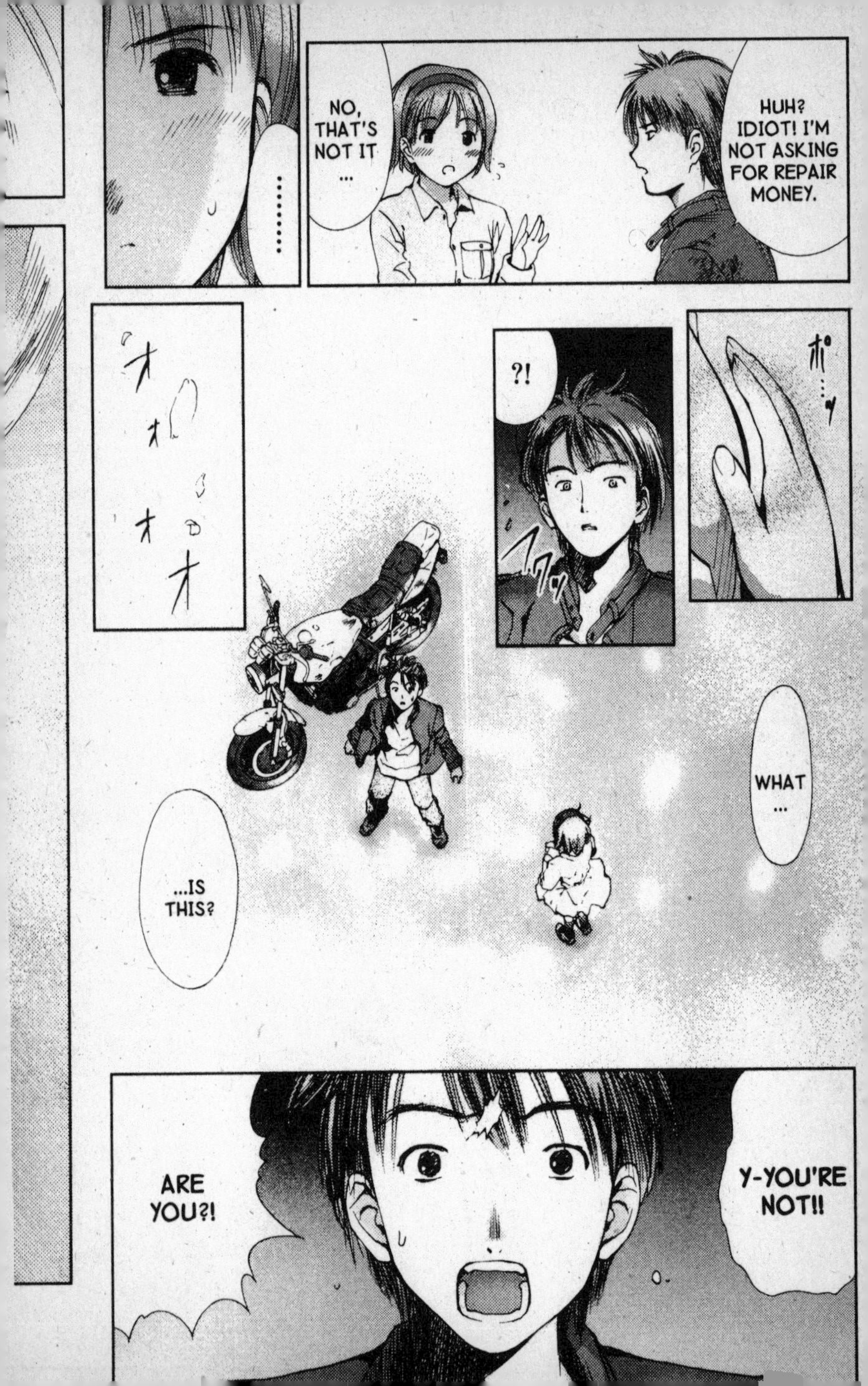

HUH? IDIOT! I'M NOT ASKING FOR REPAIR MONEY.
NO, THAT'S NOT IT ...
......
ポ…ッ
?!
WHAT ...
...IS THIS?
Y-YOU'RE NOT!!
ARE YOU?!

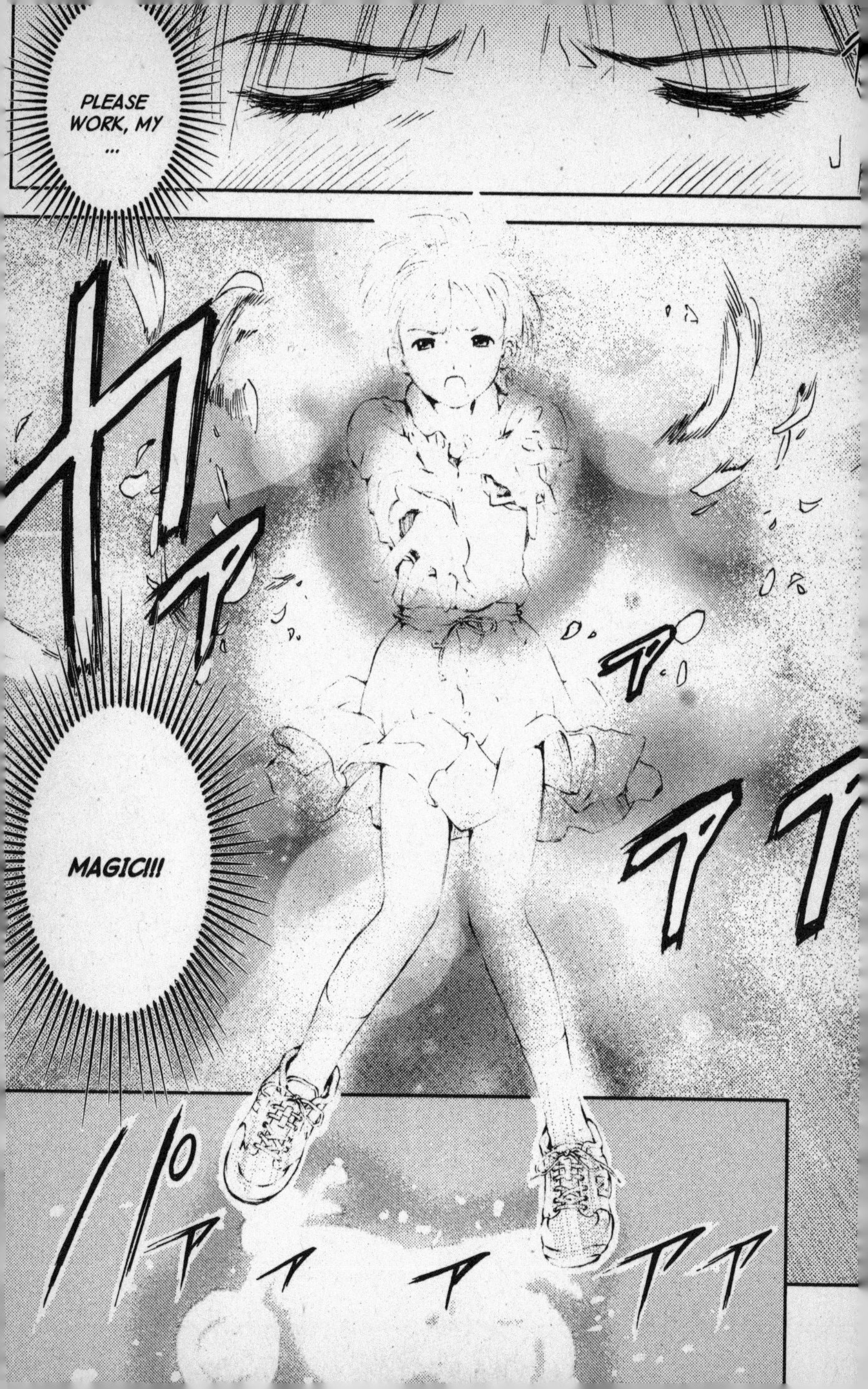
PLEASE WORK, MY ...
MAGIC!!!

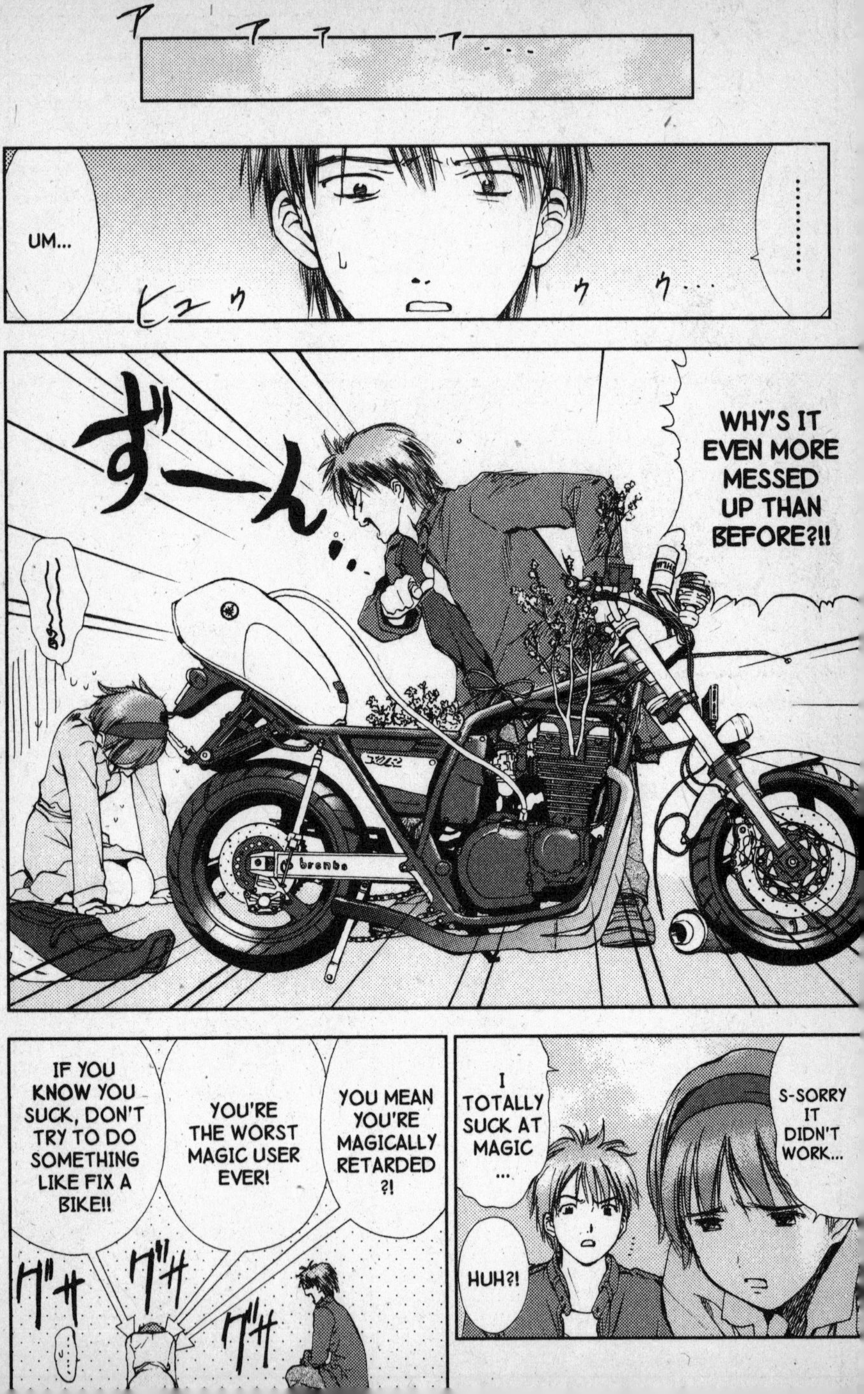
アアアア...
......
UM...
ヒュウウウ...
WHY'S IT EVEN MORE MESSED UP THAN BEFORE?!!
ずーん...
S-SORRY IT DIDN'T WORK...
I TOTALLY SUCK AT MAGIC...
HUH?!
YOU MEAN YOU'RE MAGICALLY RETARDED?!
YOU'RE THE WORST MAGIC USER EVER!
IF YOU KNOW YOU SUCK, DON'T TRY TO DO SOMETHING LIKE FIX A BIKE!!
グサ
グサ
グサ

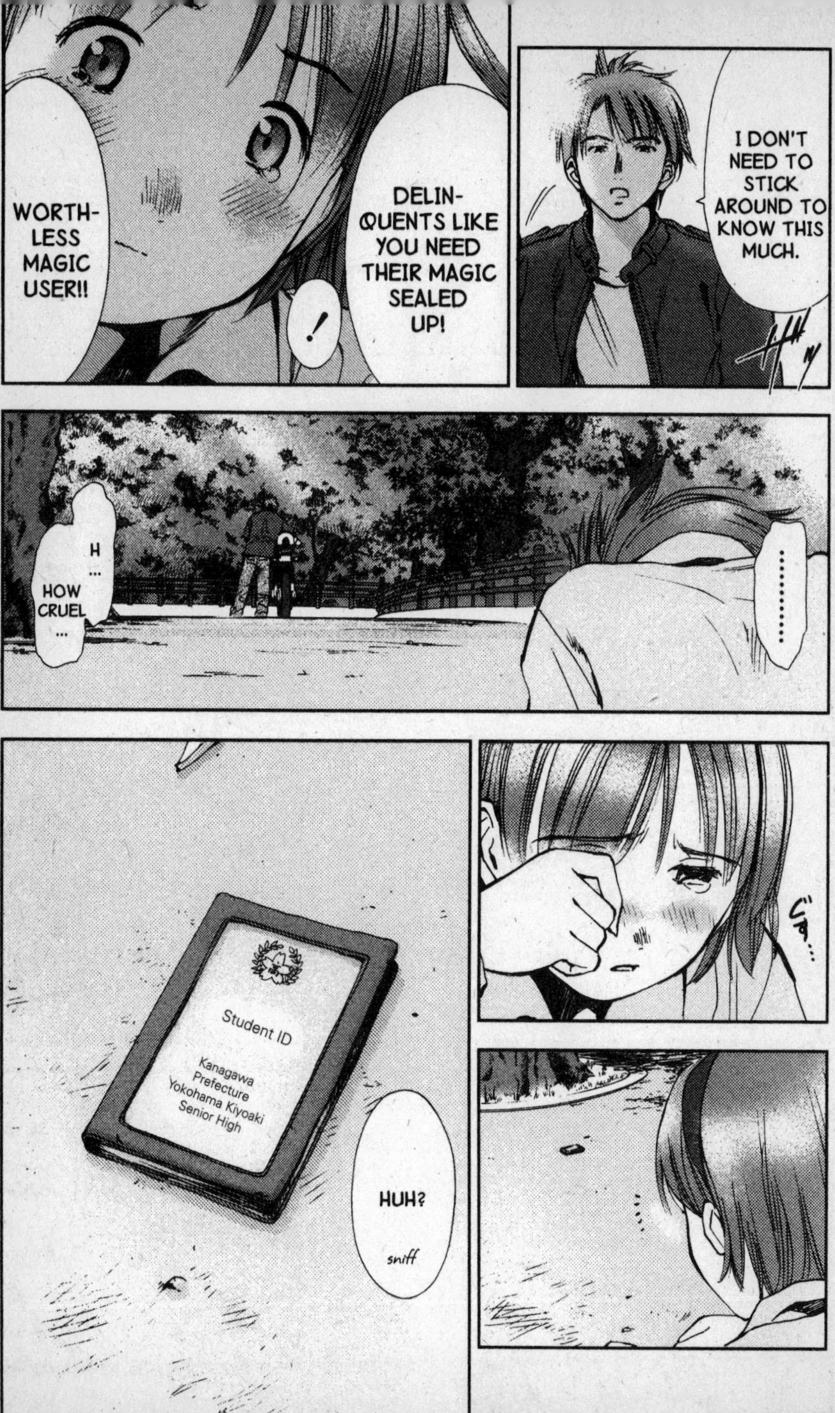
I DON'T NEED TO STICK AROUND TO KNOW THIS MUCH.
DELIN-QUENTS LIKE YOU NEED THEIR MAGIC SEALED UP!
!
WORTH-LESS MAGIC USER!!
……
H… HOW CRUEL…
じす…
…
HUH?
sniff
Student ID
Kanagawa Prefecture Yokohama Kiyoaki Senior High

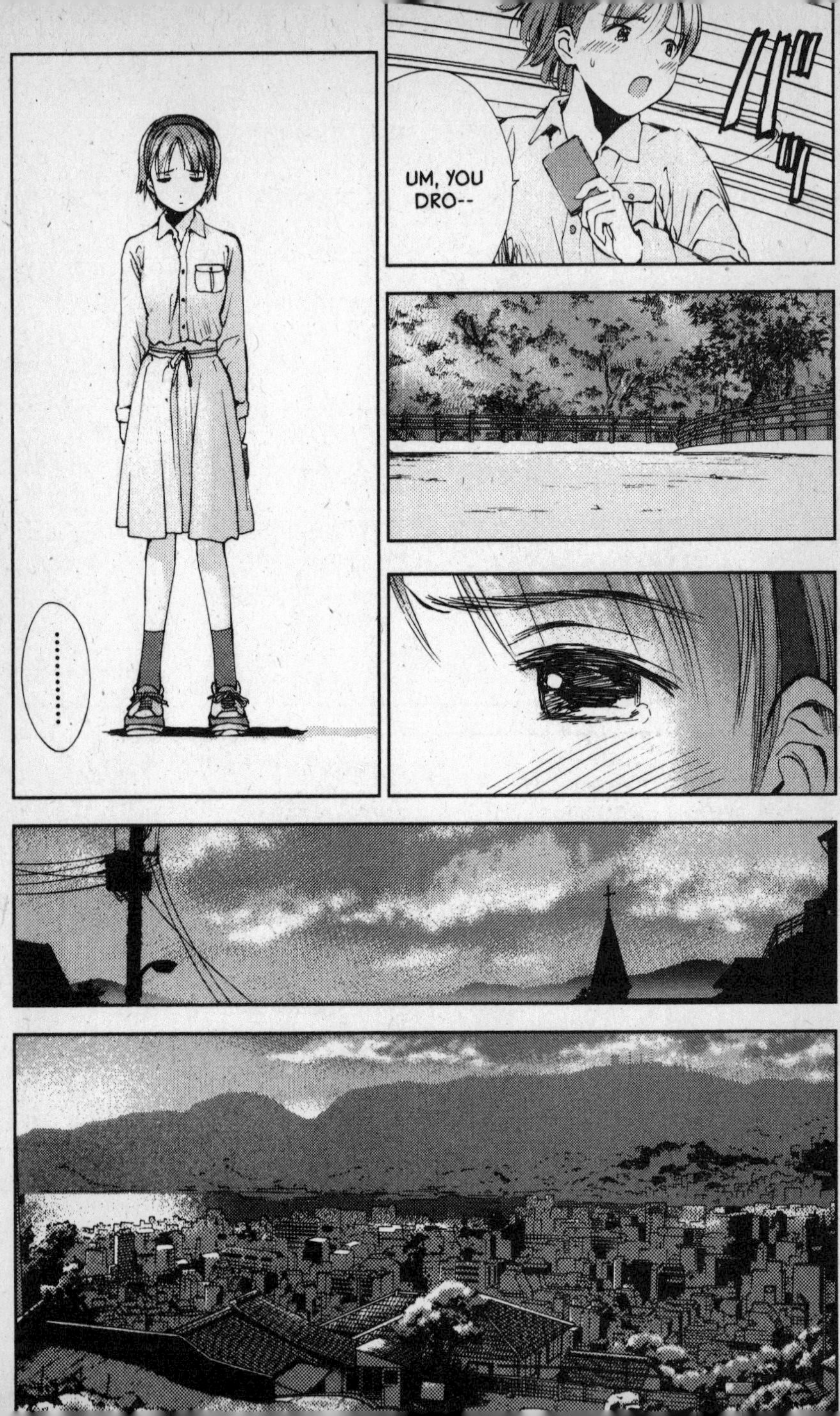
バッ
UM, YOU DRO--
....

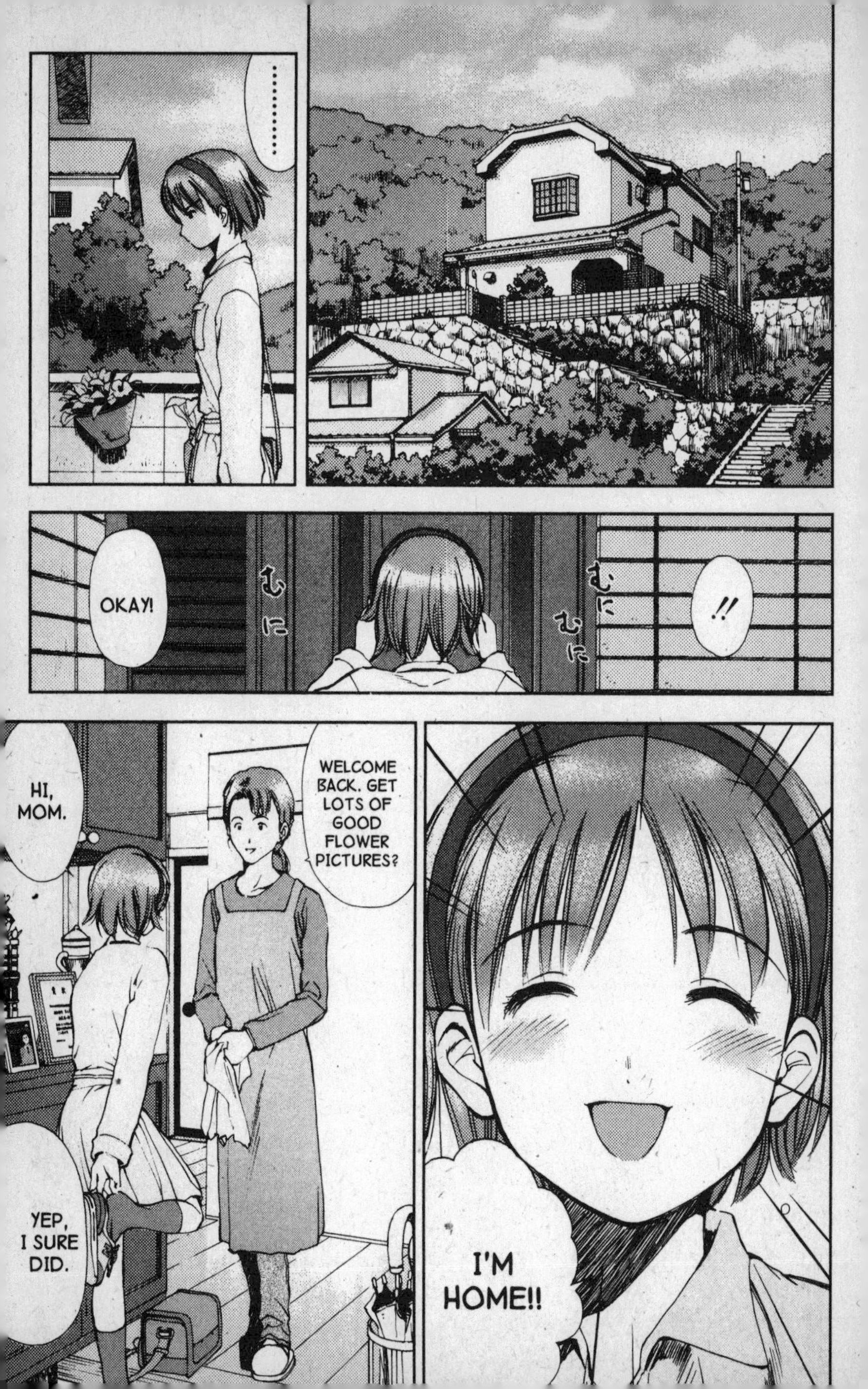
……
!!
むに
むに
むに
OKAY!
I'M HOME!!
WELCOME BACK. GET LOTS OF GOOD FLOWER PICTURES?
HI, MOM.
YEP, I SURE DID.

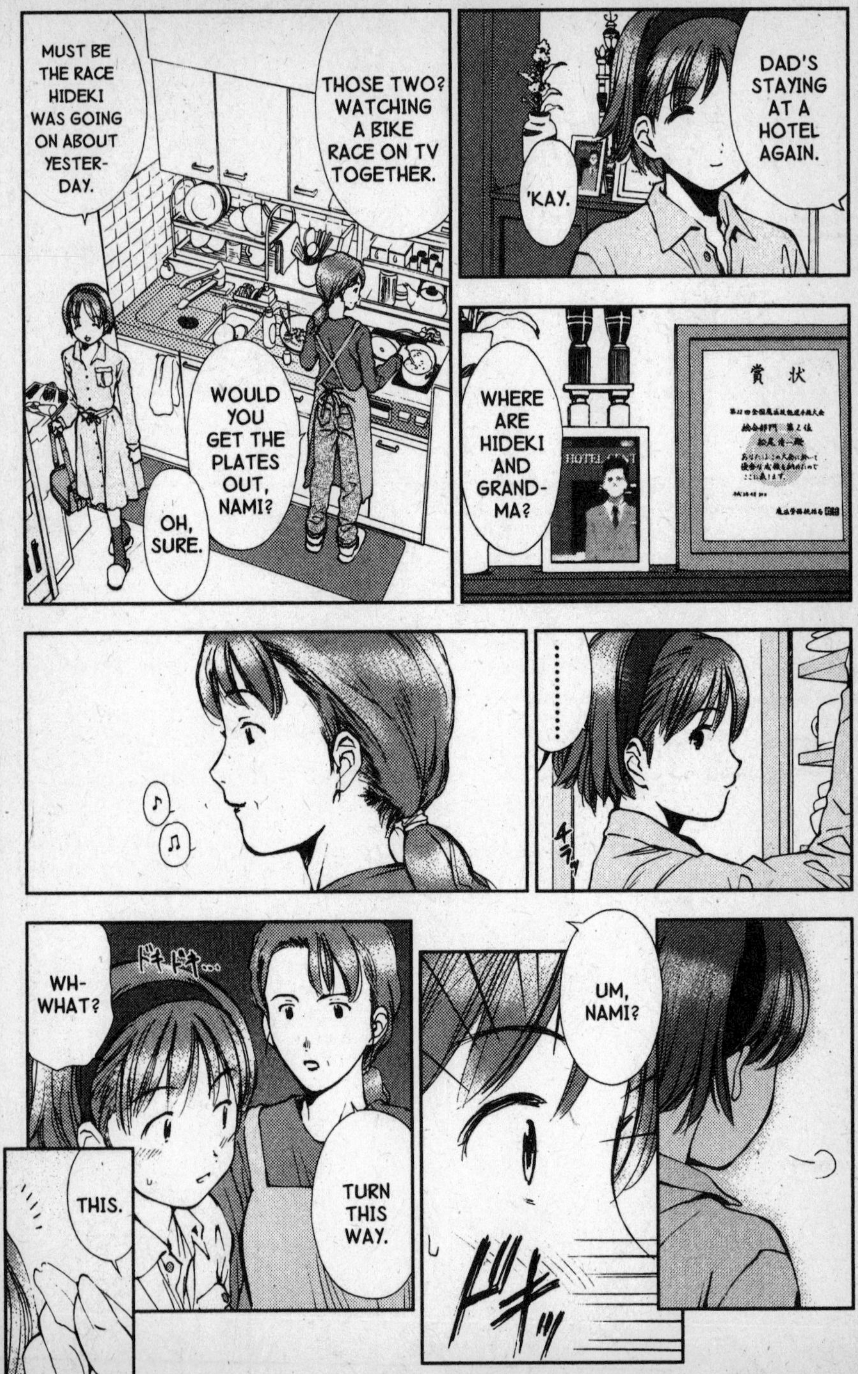
DAD'S STAYING AT A HOTEL AGAIN.
'KAY.
WHERE ARE HIDEKI AND GRAND-MA?
賞状
THOSE TWO? WATCHING A BIKE RACE ON TV TOGETHER.
MUST BE THE RACE HIDEKI WAS GOING ON ABOUT YESTER-DAY.
WOULD YOU GET THE PLATES OUT, NAMI?
OH, SURE.
......
UM, NAMI?
ドキッ
ドキドキ…
WH-WHAT?
TURN THIS WAY.
THIS.

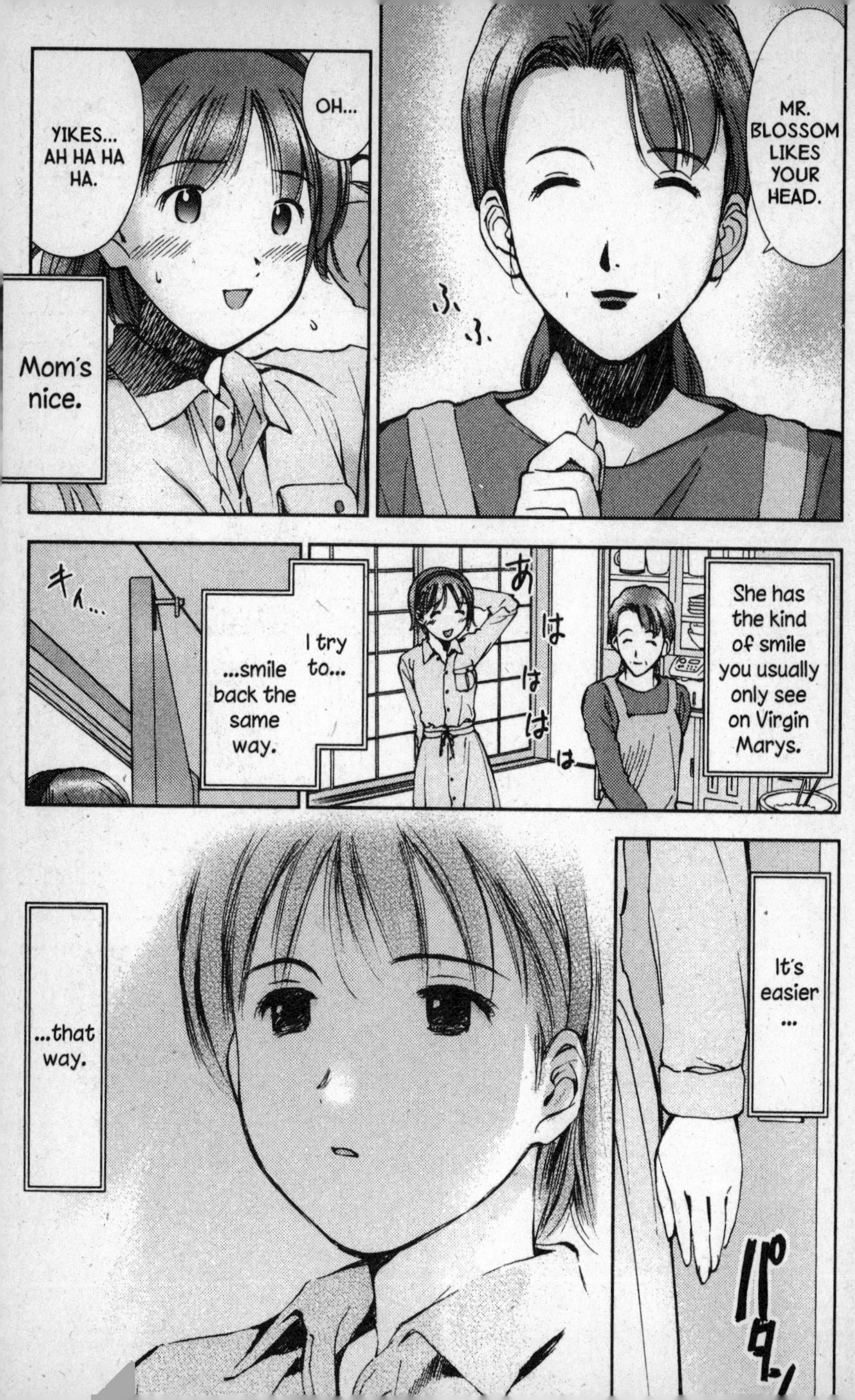
MR. BLOSSOM LIKES YOUR HEAD.
ふふ
OH...
YIKES... AH HA HA HA.
Mom's nice.
She has the kind of smile you usually only see on Virgin Marys.
あははは
I try to...
...smile back the same way.
キィ...
It's easier...
...that way.
パタ

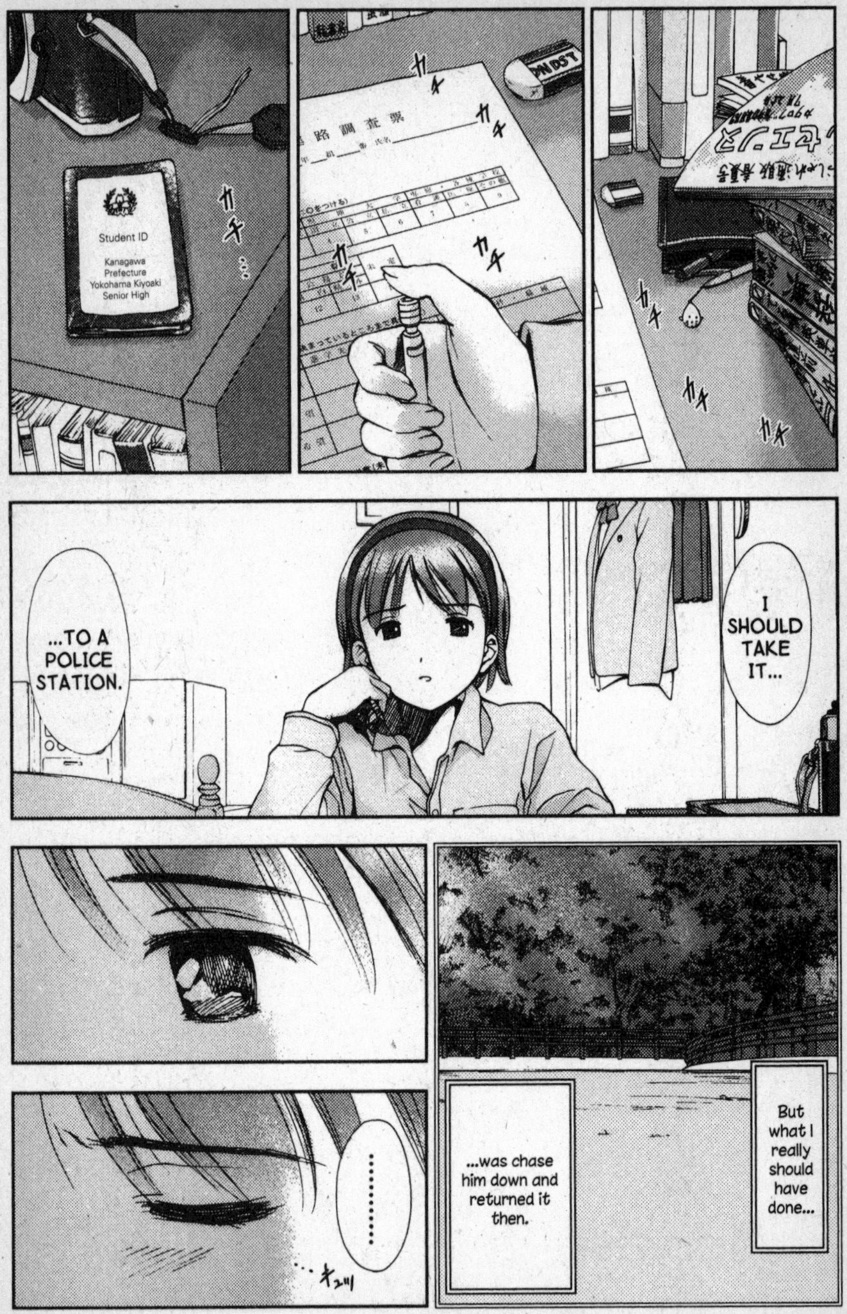
カチ
カチ
Student ID
Kanagawa Prefecture Yokohama Kiyoaki Senior High
カチ...
I SHOULD TAKE IT...
...TO A POLICE STATION.
But what I really should have done...
...was chase him down and returned it then.
......
...キュッ

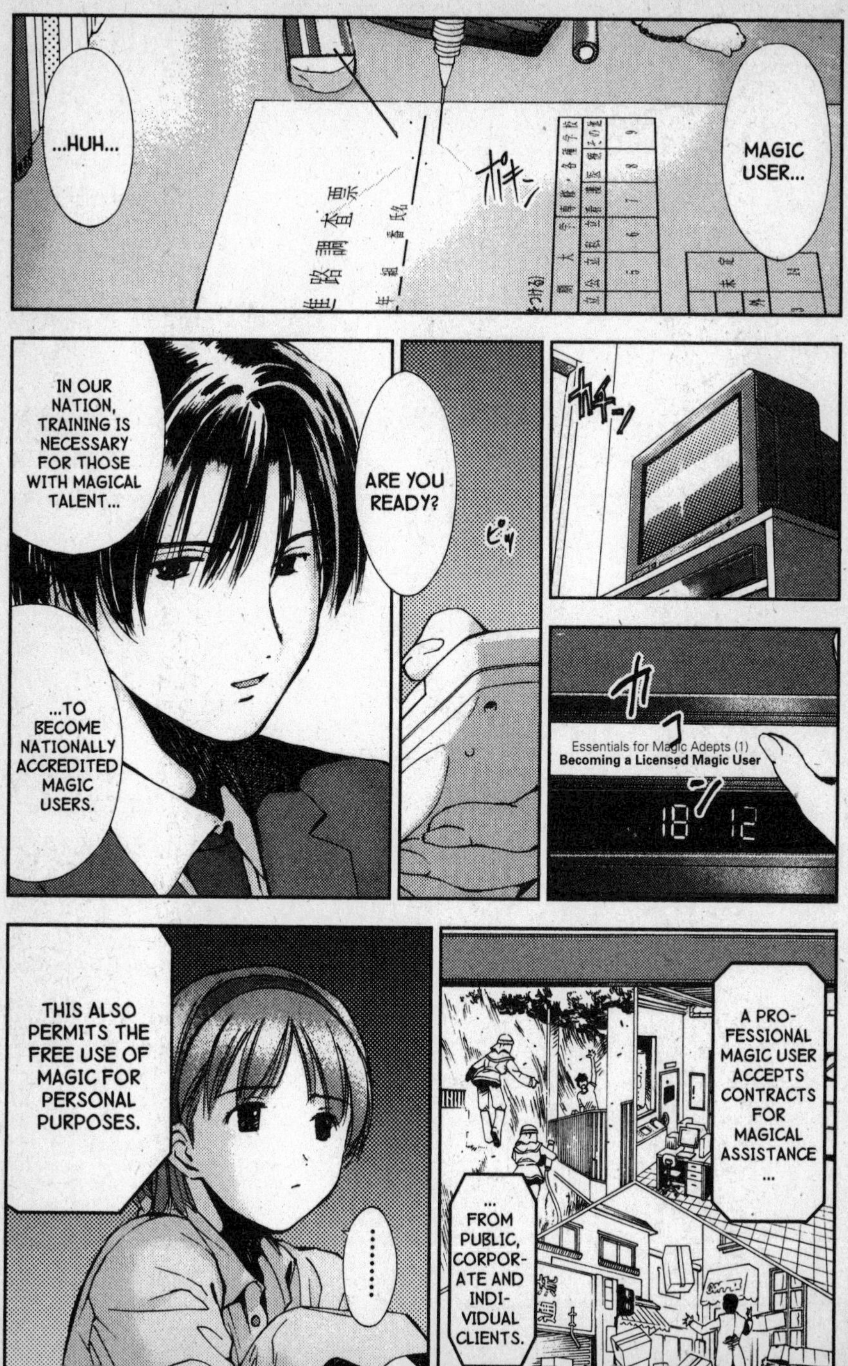
MAGIC USER...
...HUH...
Essentials for Magic Adepts (1)
Becoming a Licensed Magic User
18 12
ARE YOU READY?
IN OUR NATION, TRAINING IS NECESSARY FOR THOSE WITH MAGICAL TALENT...
...TO BECOME NATIONALLY ACCREDITED MAGIC USERS.
A PRO-FESSIONAL MAGIC USER ACCEPTS CONTRACTS FOR MAGICAL ASSISTANCE ...
... FROM PUBLIC, CORPOR-ATE AND INDI-VIDUAL CLIENTS.
THIS ALSO PERMITS THE FREE USE OF MAGIC FOR PERSONAL PURPOSES.
......

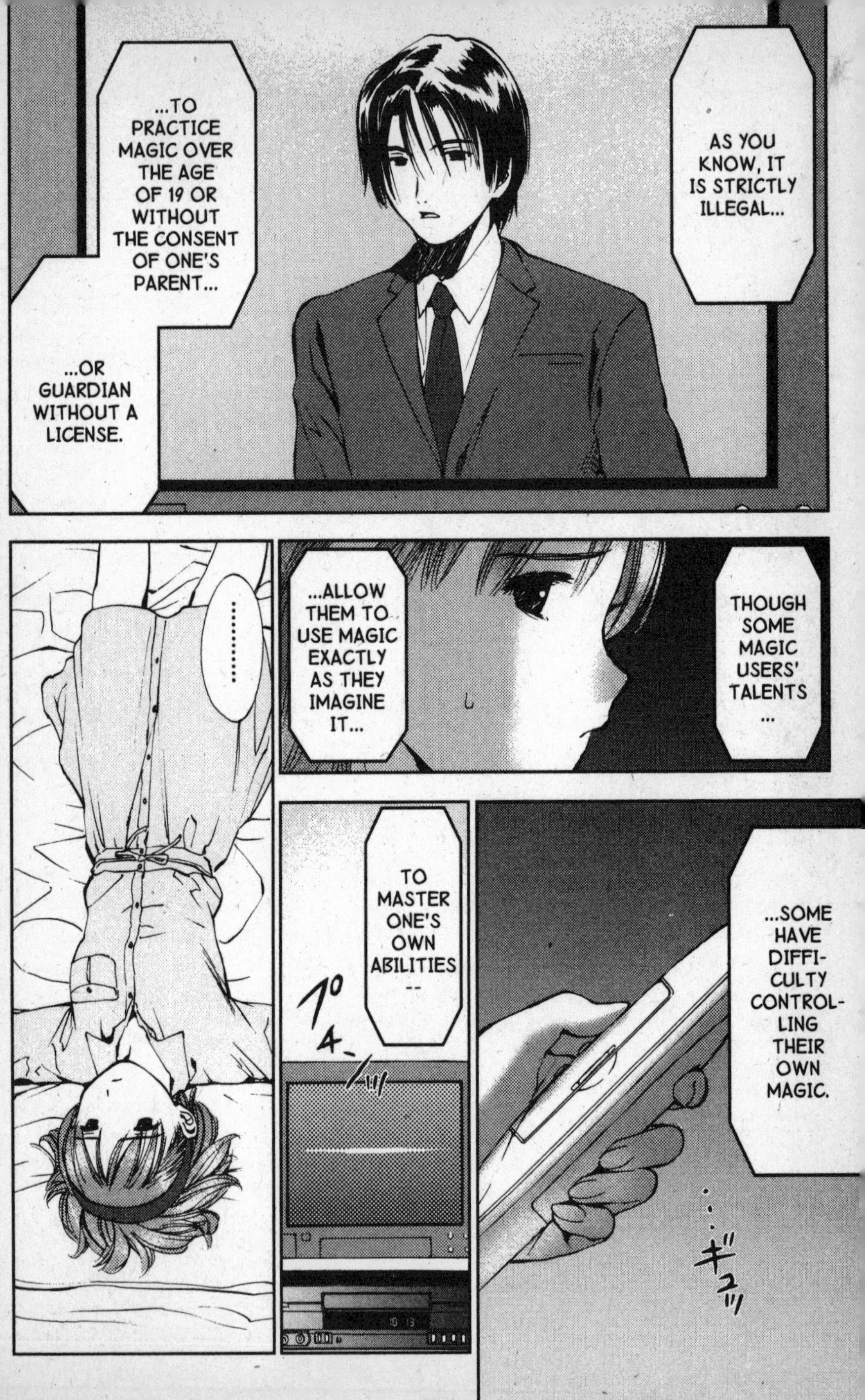
AS YOU KNOW, IT IS STRICTLY ILLEGAL...
...TO PRACTICE MAGIC OVER THE AGE OF 19 OR WITHOUT THE CONSENT OF ONE'S PARENT...
...OR GUARDIAN WITHOUT A LICENSE.
THOUGH SOME MAGIC USERS' TALENTS ...
...ALLOW THEM TO USE MAGIC EXACTLY AS THEY IMAGINE IT...
...SOME HAVE DIFFICULTY CONTROLLING THEIR OWN MAGIC.
...ギュッ
TO MASTER ONE'S OWN ABILITIES --
....

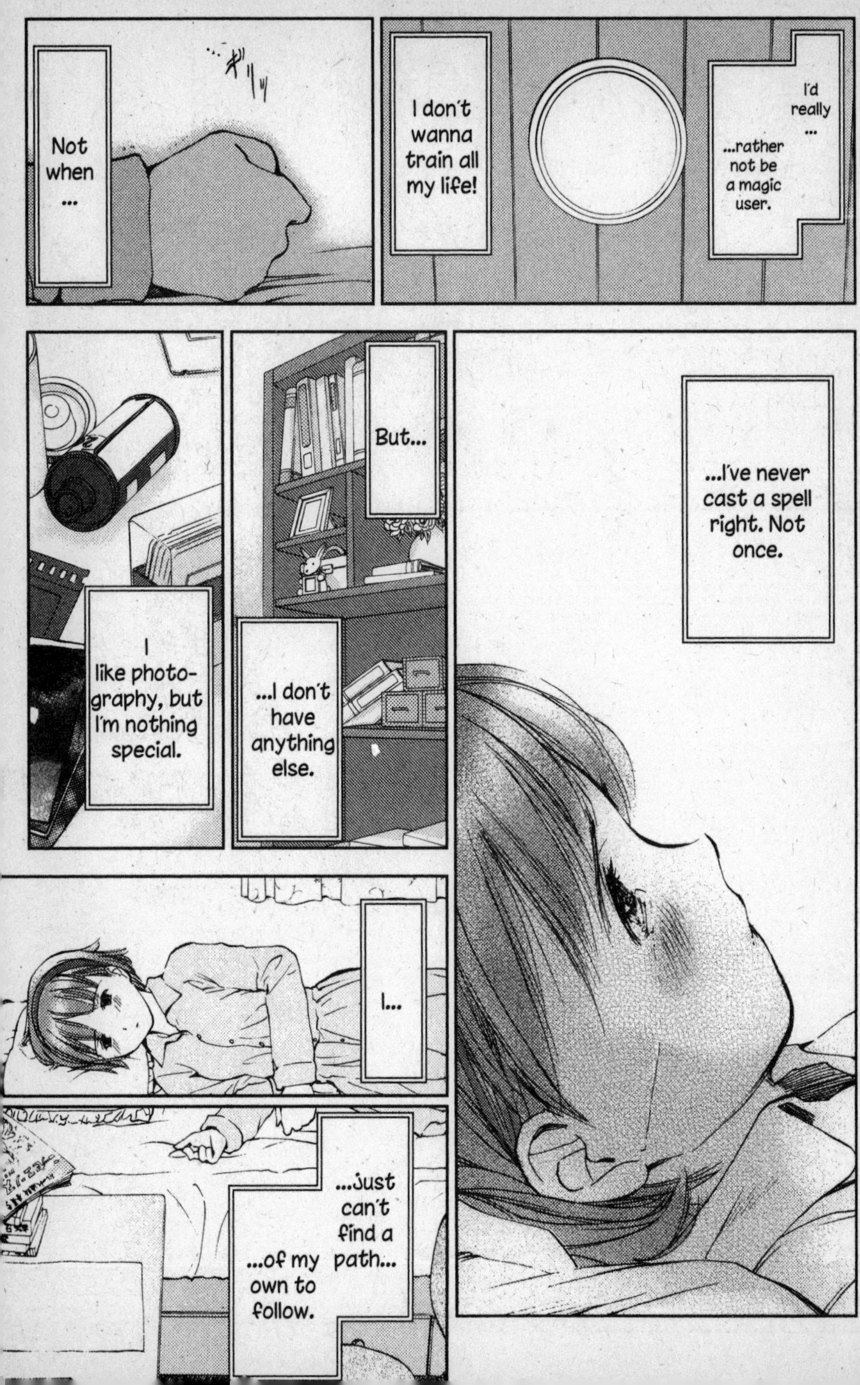
I'd really...
...rather not be a magic user.
I don't wanna train all my life!
ギリッ
Not when...
...I've never cast a spell right. Not once.
But...
...I don't have anything else.
I like photography, but I'm nothing special.
I...
...just can't find a path...
...of my own to follow.

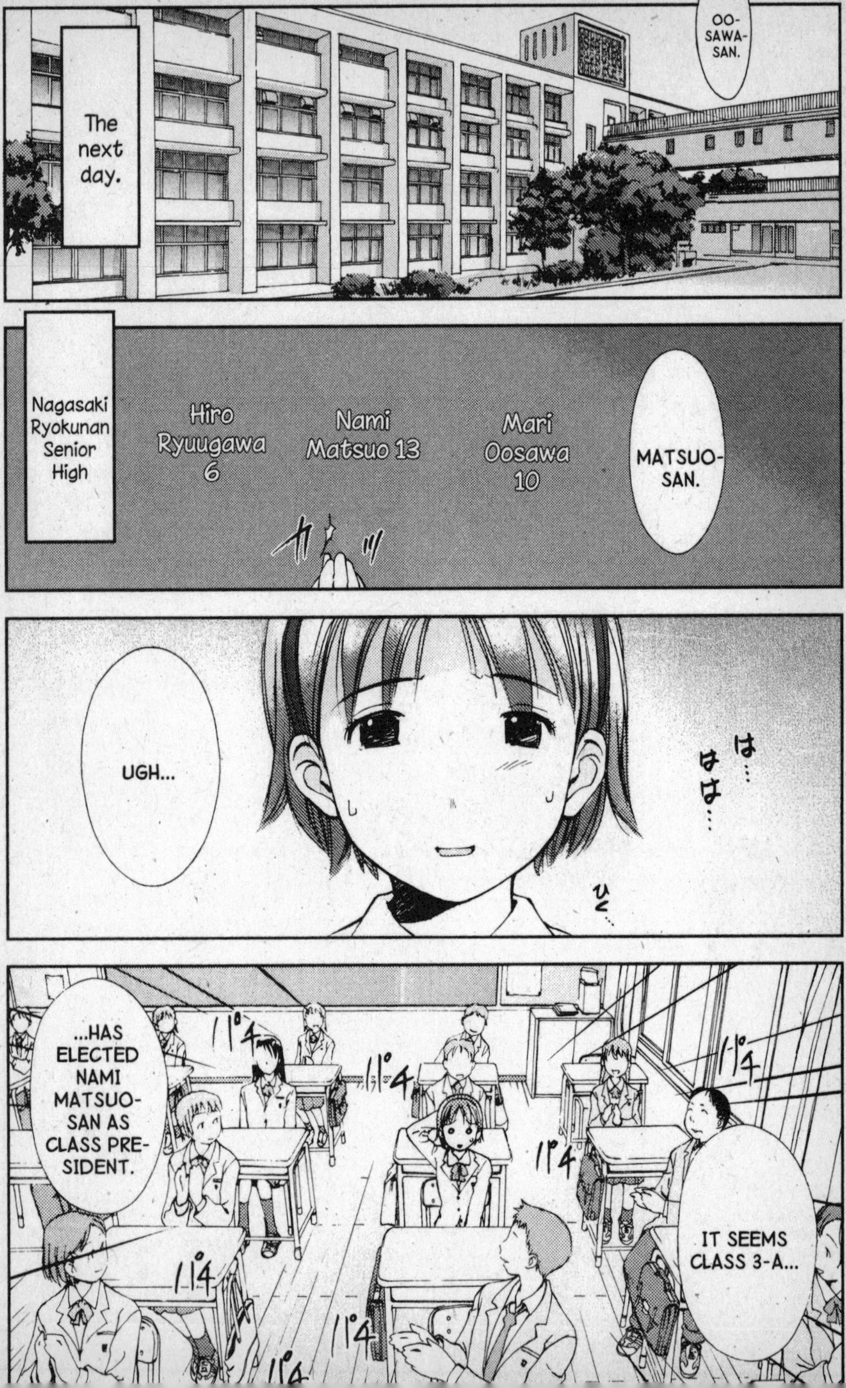
OO-SAWA-SAN.
The next day.
MATSUO-SAN.
Mari Oosawa 10
Nami Matsuo 13
Hiro Ryuugawa 6
Nagasaki Ryokunan Senior High
カッ
は… はは…
ひく…
UGH...
IT SEEMS CLASS 3-A...
...HAS ELECTED NAMI MATSUO-SAN AS CLASS PRESIDENT.

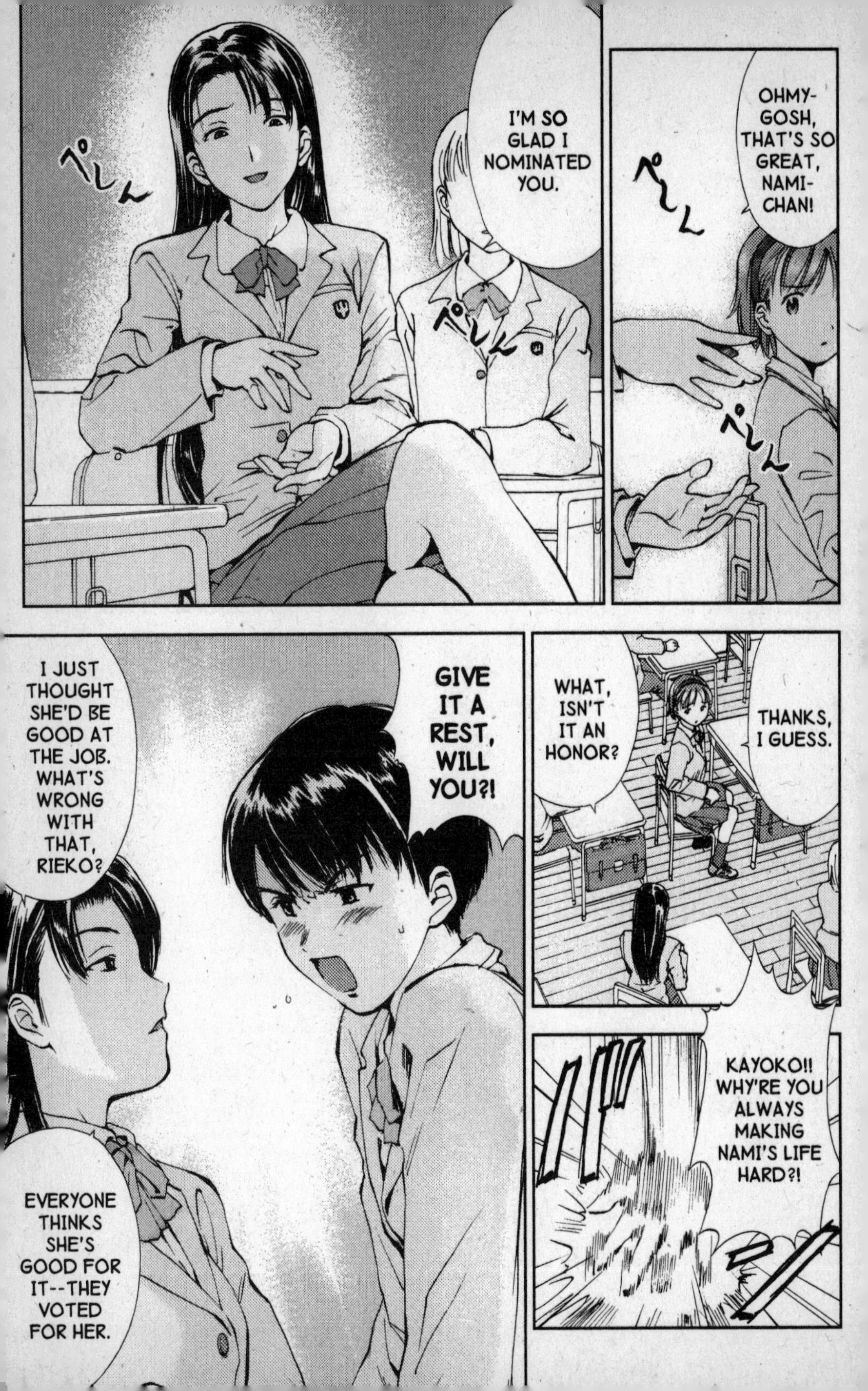
OHMY-GOSH, THAT'S SO GREAT, NAMI-CHAN!
ぺ～しん
ぺしん
I'M SO GLAD I NOMINATED YOU.
ぺしん
ぺしん
THANKS, I GUESS.
WHAT, ISN'T IT AN HONOR?
KAYOKO!! WHY'RE YOU ALWAYS MAKING NAMI'S LIFE HARD?!
GIVE IT A REST, WILL YOU?!
I JUST THOUGHT SHE'D BE GOOD AT THE JOB. WHAT'S WRONG WITH THAT, RIEKO?
EVERYONE THINKS SHE'S GOOD FOR IT--THEY VOTED FOR HER.

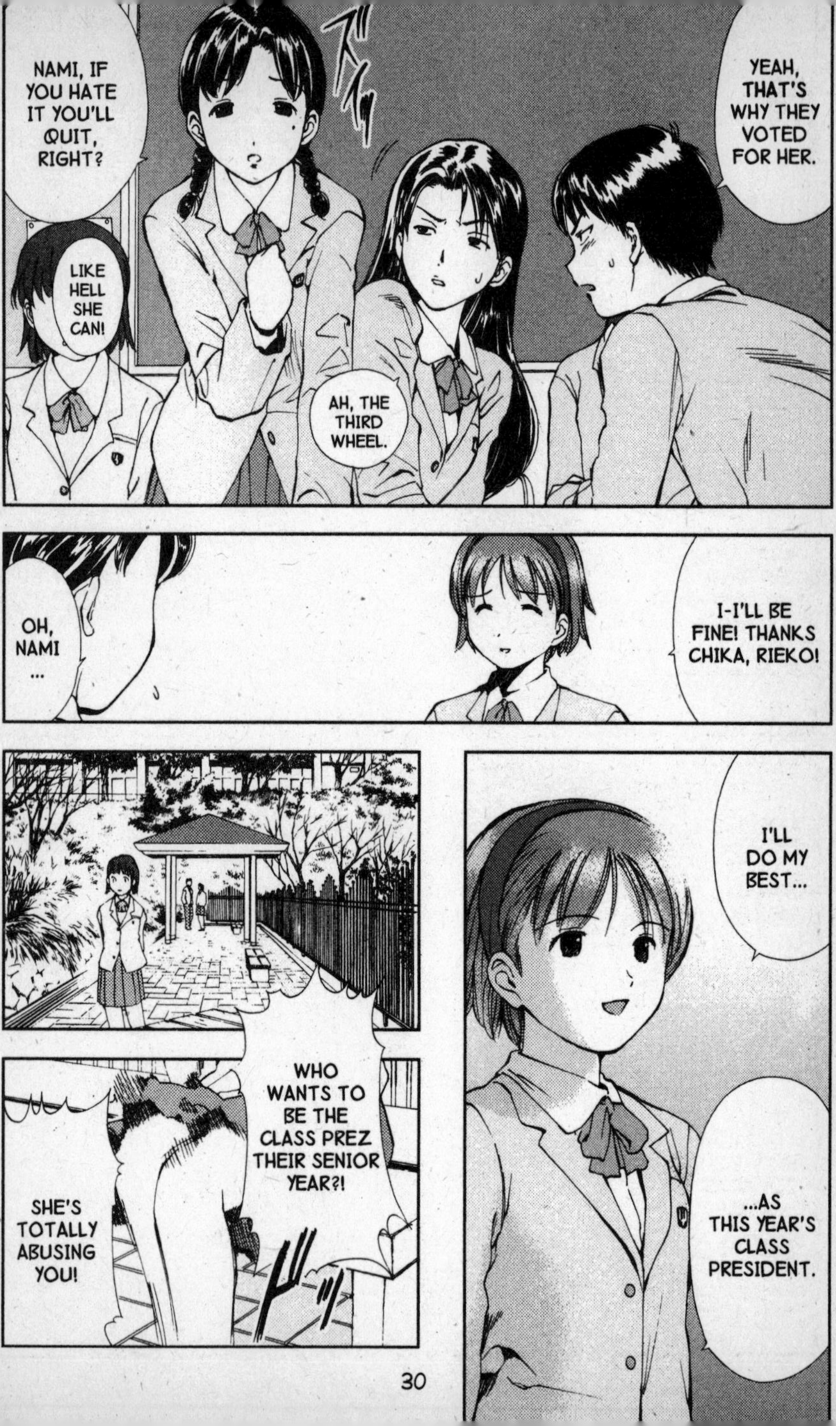
YEAH, THAT'S WHY THEY VOTED FOR HER.
NAMI, IF YOU HATE IT YOU'LL QUIT, RIGHT?
LIKE HELL SHE CAN!
AH, THE THIRD WHEEL.
I-I'LL BE FINE! THANKS CHIKA, RIEKO!
OH, NAMI ...
I'LL DO MY BEST...
...AS THIS YEAR'S CLASS PRESIDENT.
WHO WANTS TO BE THE CLASS PREZ THEIR SENIOR YEAR?!
SHE'S TOTALLY ABUSING YOU!

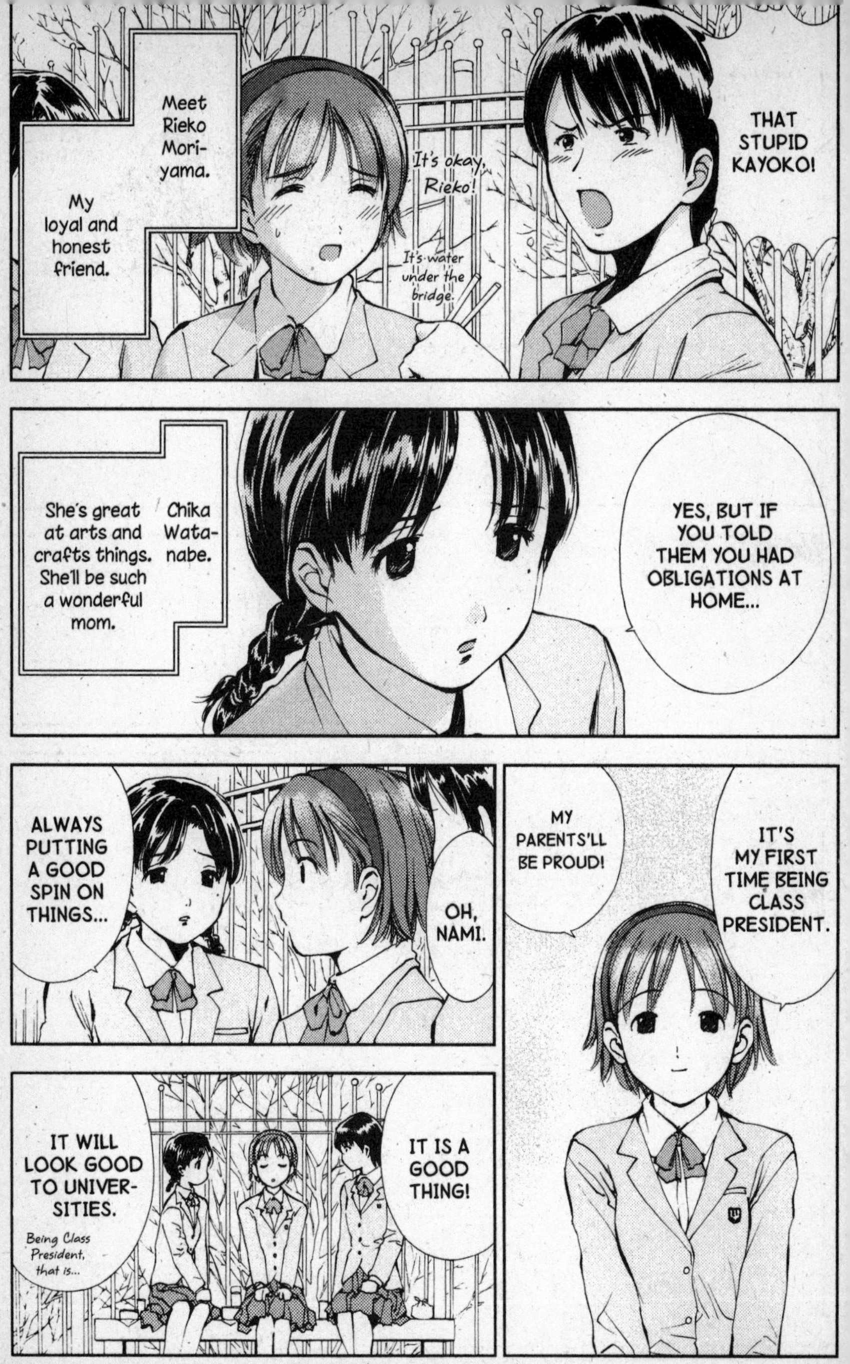
THAT STUPID KAYOKO!
It's okay, Rieko!
It's water under the bridge.
Meet Rieko Mori-yama.
My loyal and honest friend.
YES, BUT IF YOU TOLD THEM YOU HAD OBLIGATIONS AT HOME...
Chika Wata-nabe.
She's great at arts and crafts things. She'll be such a wonderful mom.
IT'S MY FIRST TIME BEING CLASS PRESIDENT.
MY PARENTS'LL BE PROUD!
OH, NAMI.
ALWAYS PUTTING A GOOD SPIN ON THINGS...
IT IS A GOOD THING!
IT WILL LOOK GOOD TO UNIVER-SITIES.
Being Class President, that is...

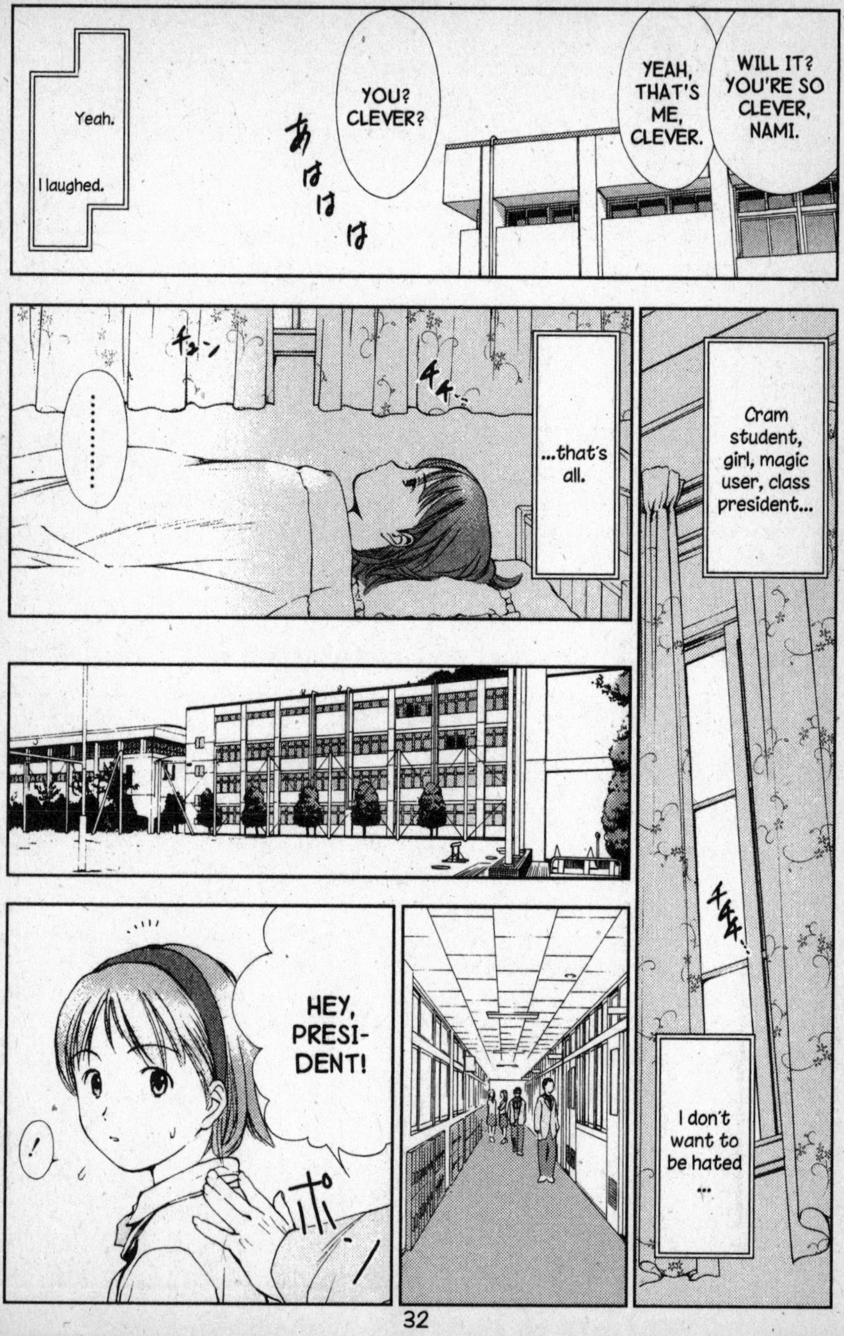
WILL IT? YOU'RE SO CLEVER, NAMI.
YEAH, THAT'S ME, CLEVER.
YOU? CLEVER?
あははは
Yeah.
I laughed.
Cram student, girl, magic user, class president...
チチチ...
I don't want to be hated...
...that's all.
チチ...
チュン
......
HEY, PRESIDENT!
ポン
!

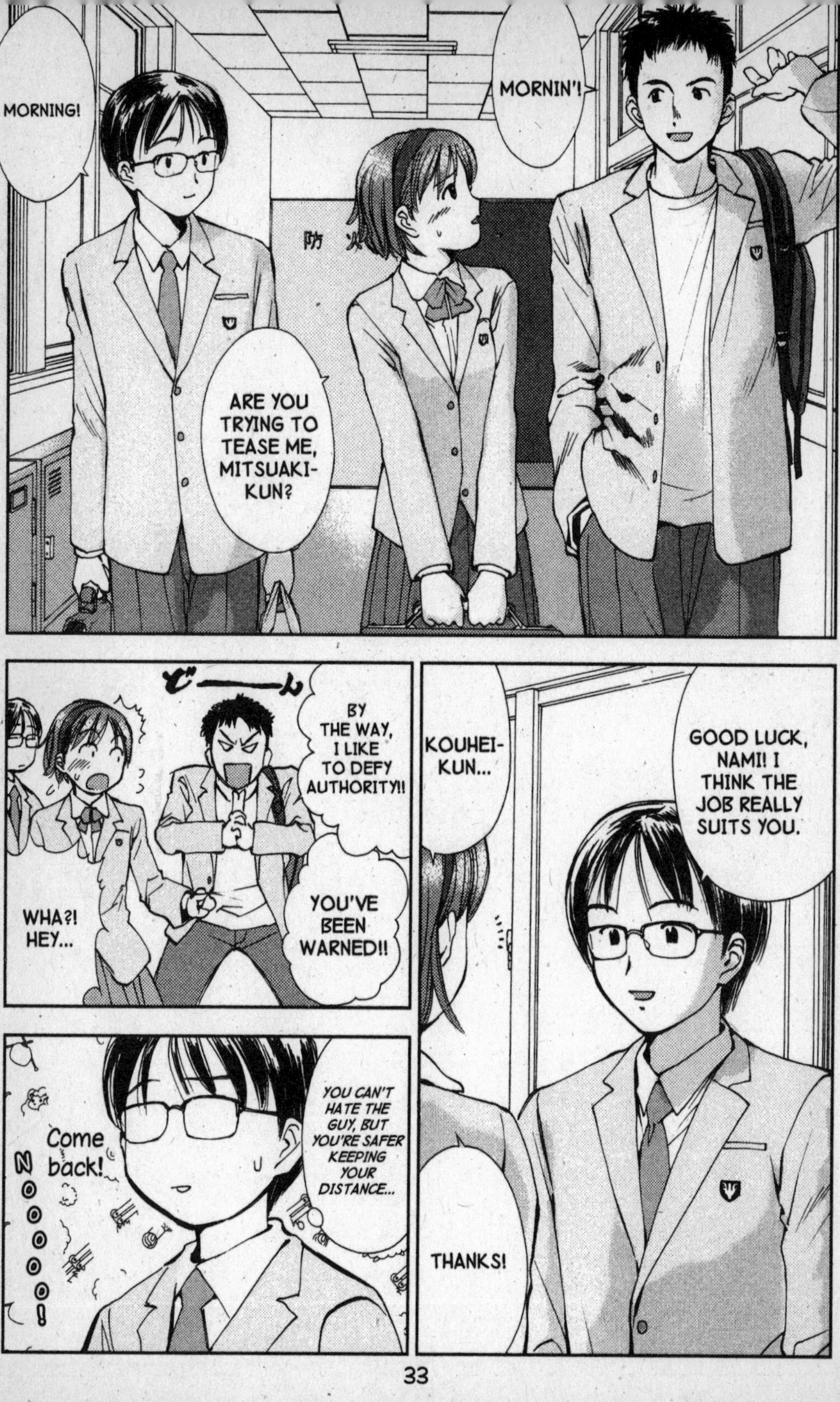
MORNIN'!
MORNING!
ARE YOU TRYING TO TEASE ME, MITSUAKI-KUN?
GOOD LUCK, NAMI! I THINK THE JOB REALLY SUITS YOU.
KOUHEI-KUN...
THANKS!
で——ん
BY THE WAY, I LIKE TO DEFY AUTHORITY!!
YOU'VE BEEN WARNED!!
WHA?! HEY...
YOU CAN'T HATE THE GUY, BUT YOU'RE SAFER KEEPING YOUR DISTANCE...
Come back!
Nooooooo!

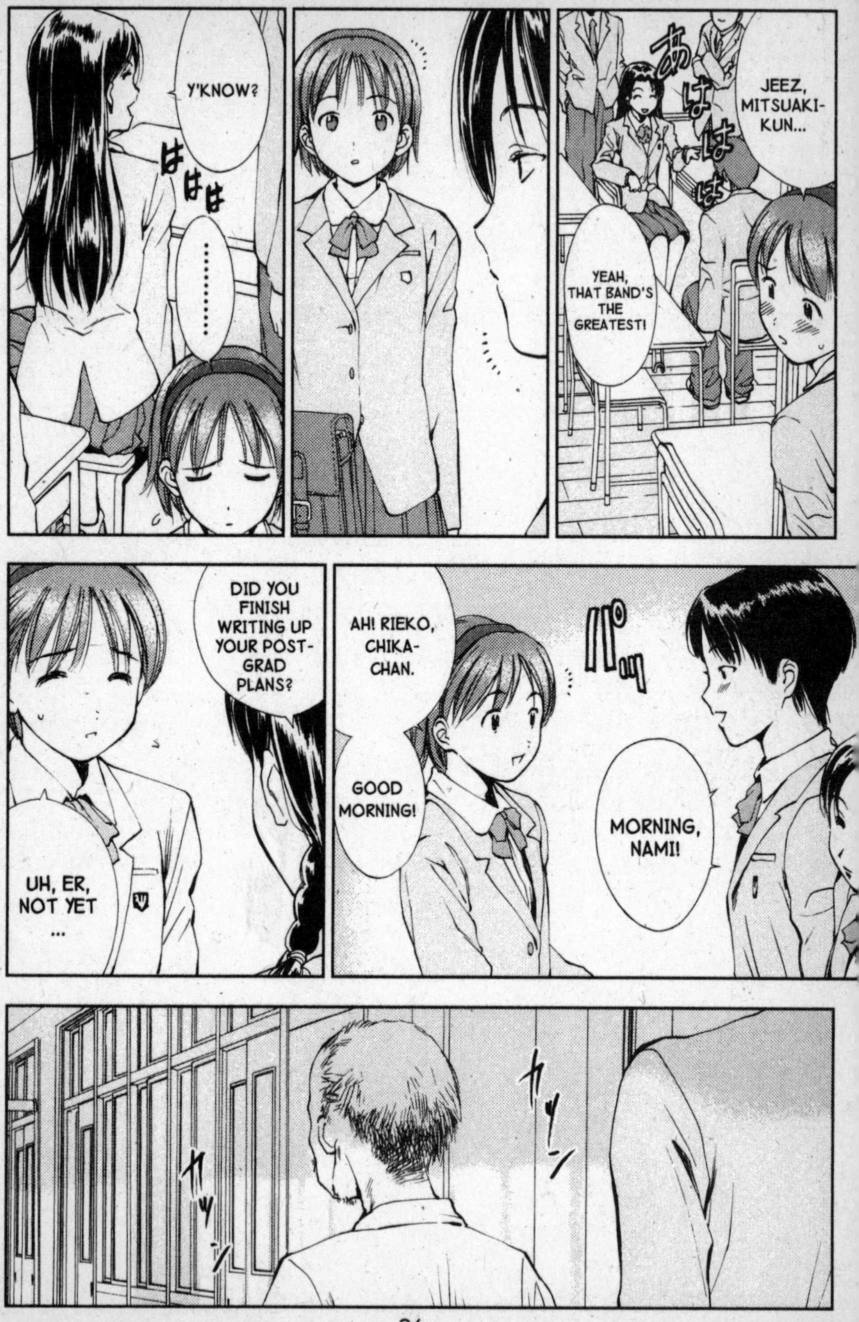
JEEZ, MITSUAKI-KUN...
あははは
YEAH, THAT BAND'S THE GREATEST!
Y'KNOW?
ははは
......
パッ
MORNING, NAMI!
AH! RIEKO, CHIKA-CHAN.
GOOD MORNING!
DID YOU FINISH WRITING UP YOUR POST-GRAD PLANS?
UH, ER, NOT YET ...
カツーン
カツーン

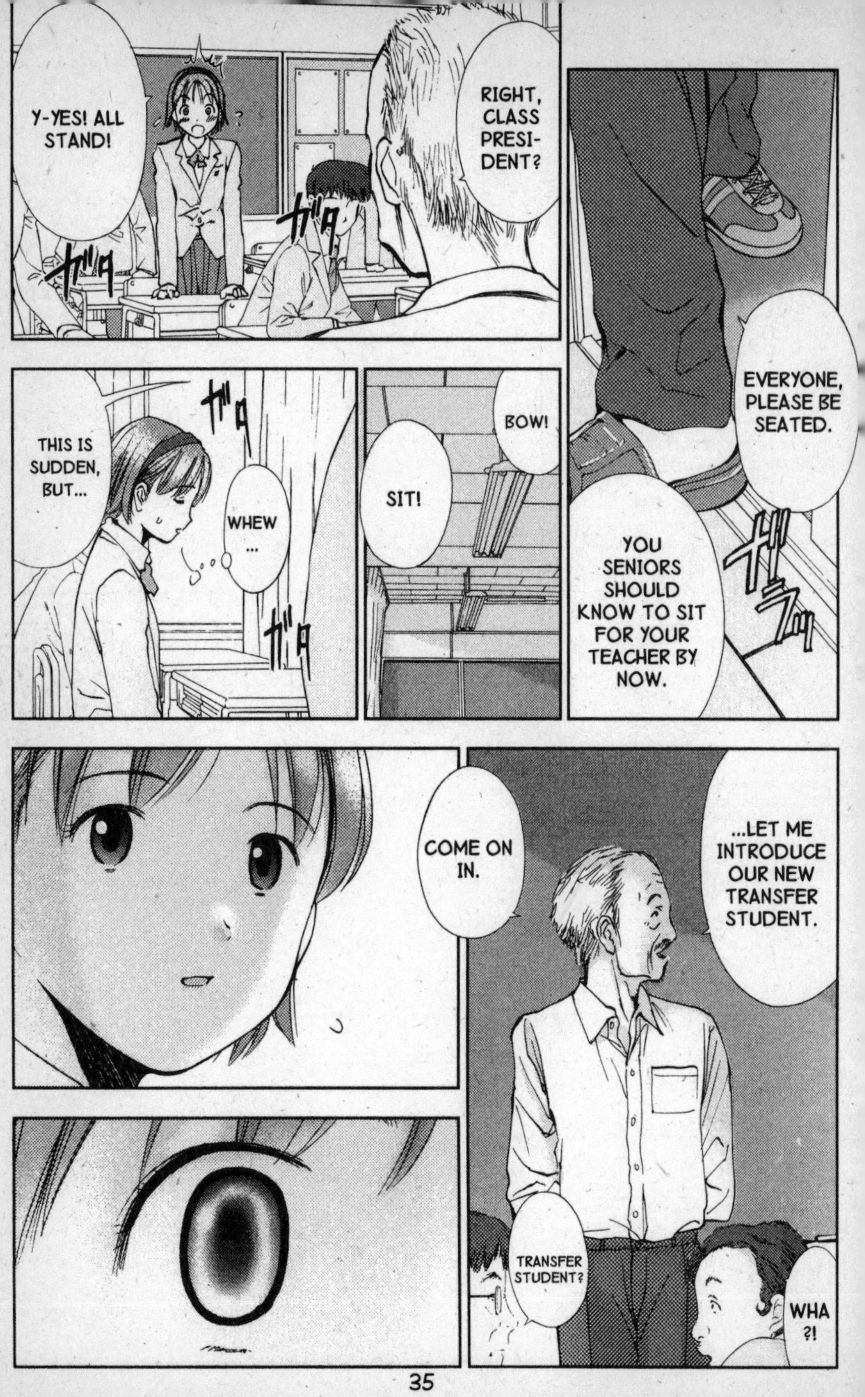
EVERYONE, PLEASE BE SEATED.
ガラッ
YOU SENIORS SHOULD KNOW TO SIT FOR YOUR TEACHER BY NOW.
RIGHT, CLASS PRESIDENT?
ガタ
Y-YES! ALL STAND!
ガタ
BOW!
SIT!
ガタ
THIS IS SUDDEN, BUT...
WHEW ...
ガタ
...LET ME INTRODUCE OUR NEW TRANSFER STUDENT.
COME ON IN.
WHA ?!
TRANSFER STUDENT?

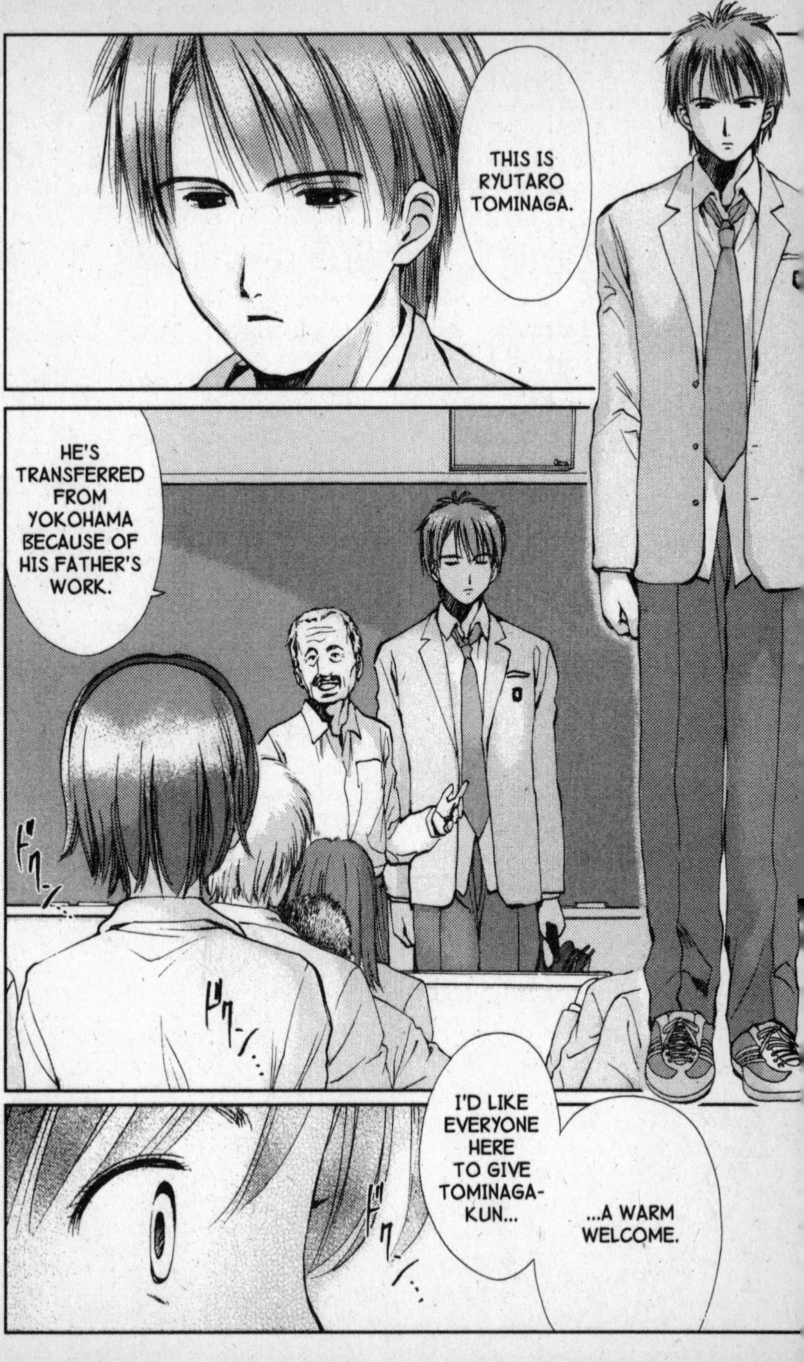
THIS IS RYUTARO TOMINAGA.
HE'S TRANSFERRED FROM YOKOHAMA BECAUSE OF HIS FATHER'S WORK.
I'D LIKE EVERYONE HERE TO GIVE TOMINAGA-KUN...
...A WARM WELCOME.

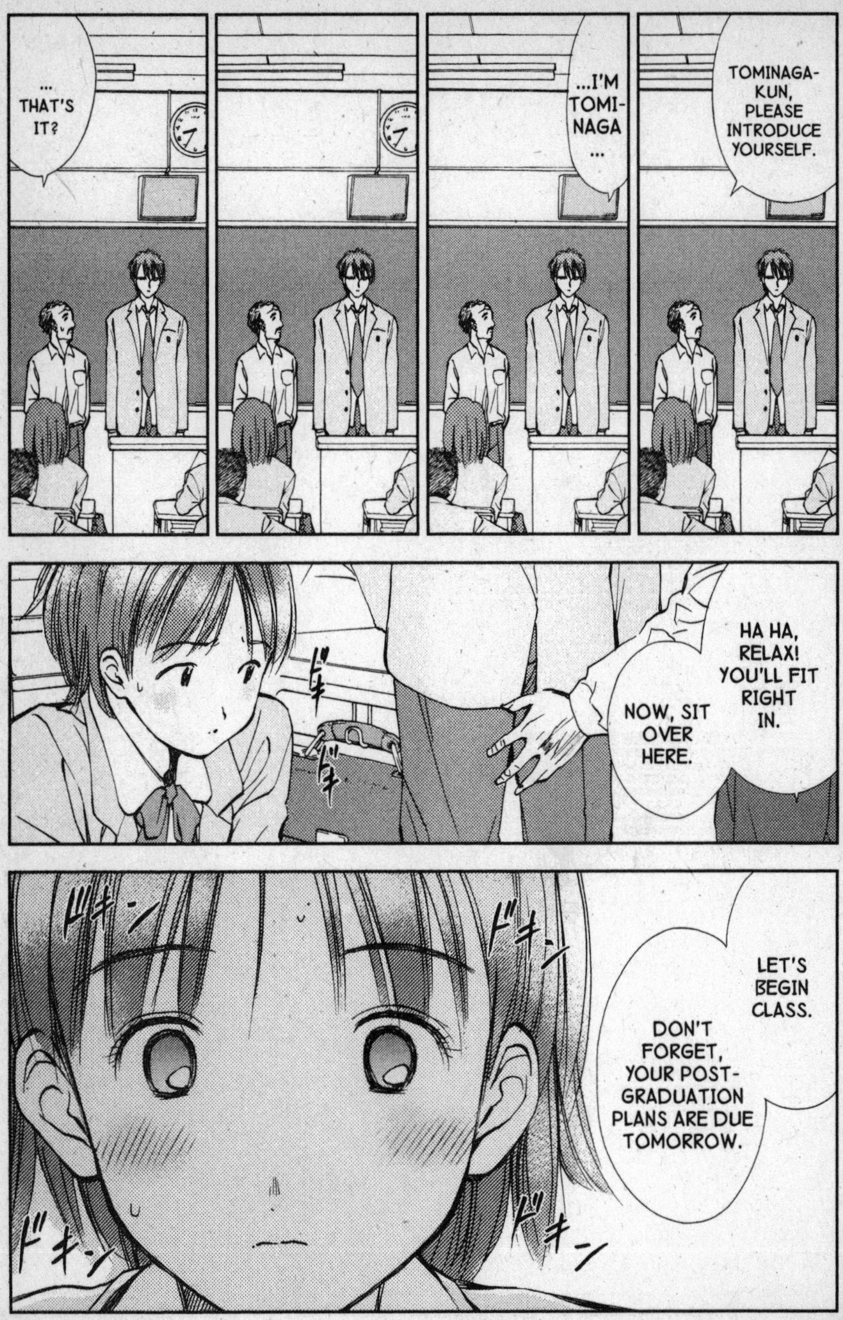
TOMINAGA-KUN, PLEASE INTRODUCE YOURSELF.
...I'M TOMINAGA...
... THAT'S IT?
HA HA, RELAX! YOU'LL FIT RIGHT IN.
NOW, SIT OVER HERE.
ドキ
ドキ
LET'S BEGIN CLASS.
DON'T FORGET, YOUR POST-GRADUATION PLANS ARE DUE TOMORROW.
ドキン
ドキン
ドキン
ドキン

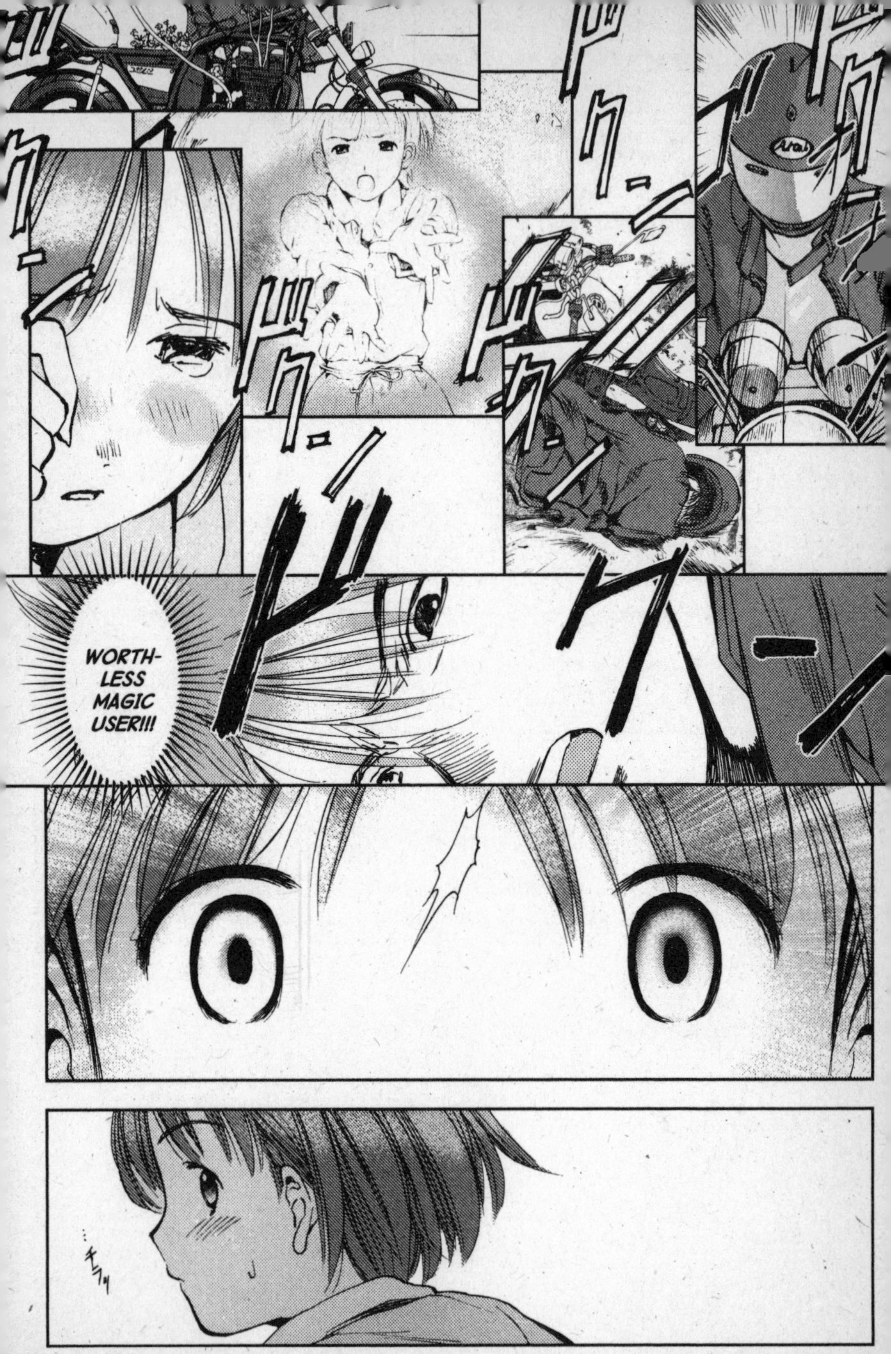
WORTH-LESS MAGIC USER!!!

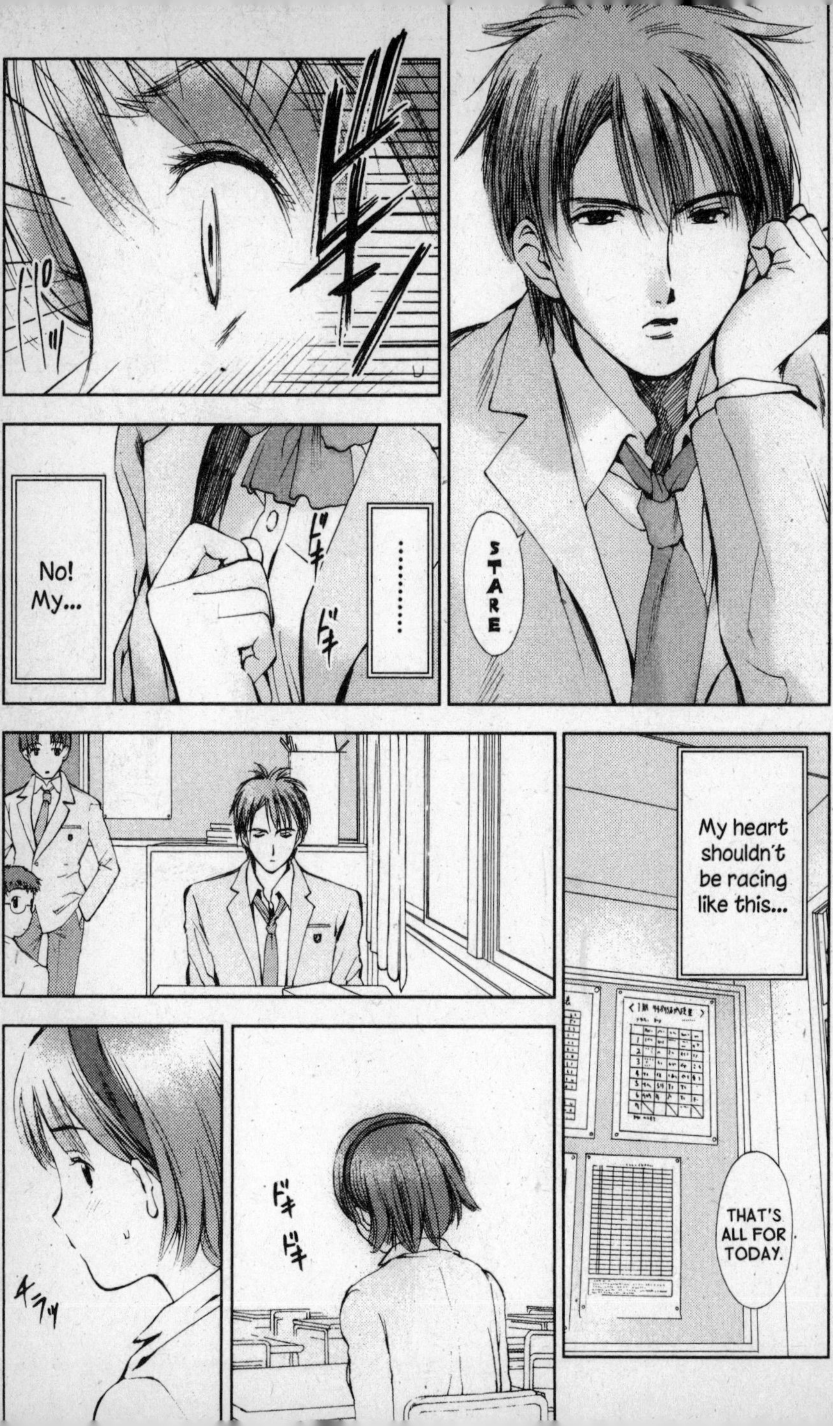
STARE
....
No! My...
My heart shouldn't be racing like this...
THAT'S ALL FOR TODAY.

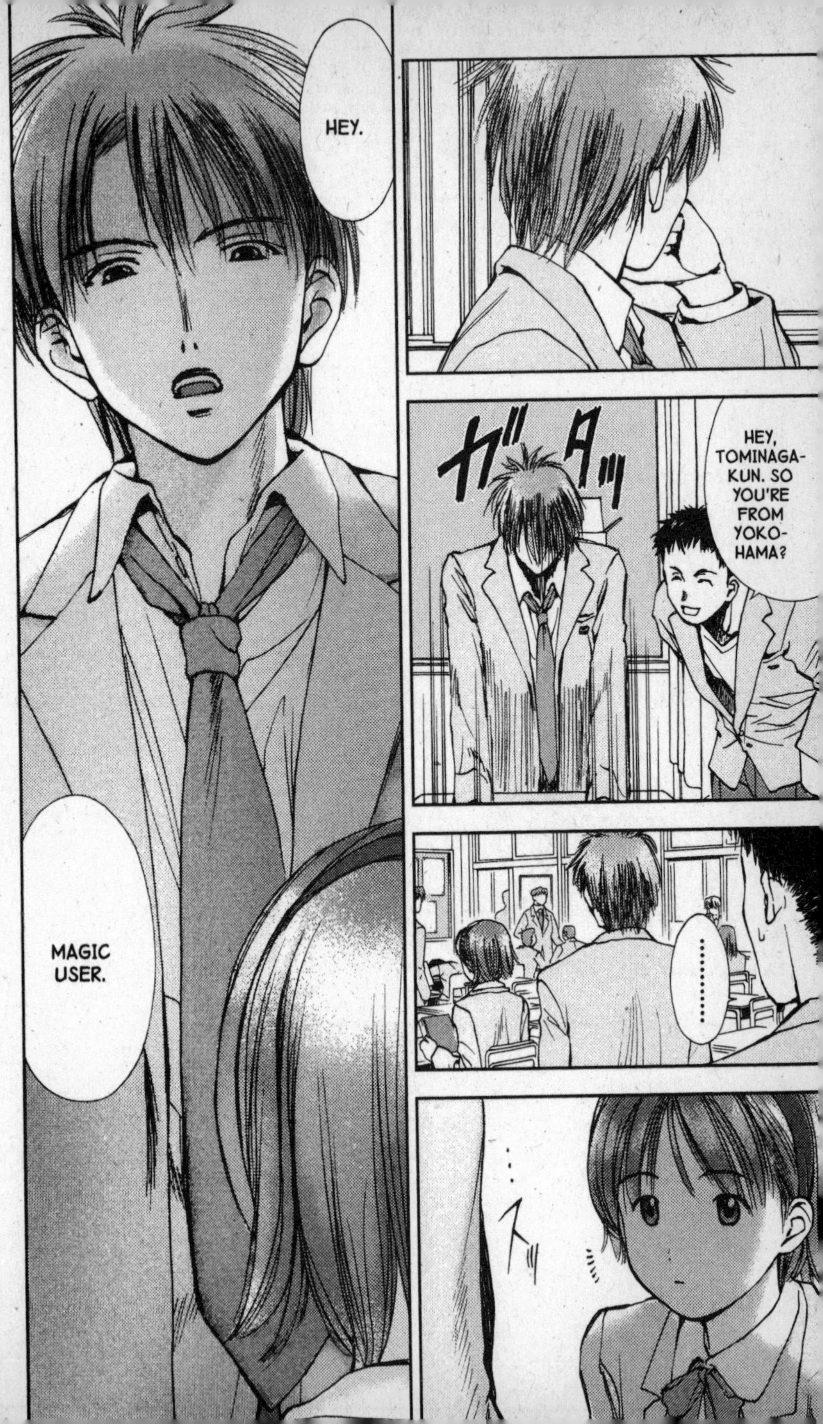
ガタッ
HEY, TOMINAGA-KUN. SO YOU'RE FROM YOKOHAMA?
....
...
スッ
HEY.
MAGIC USER.

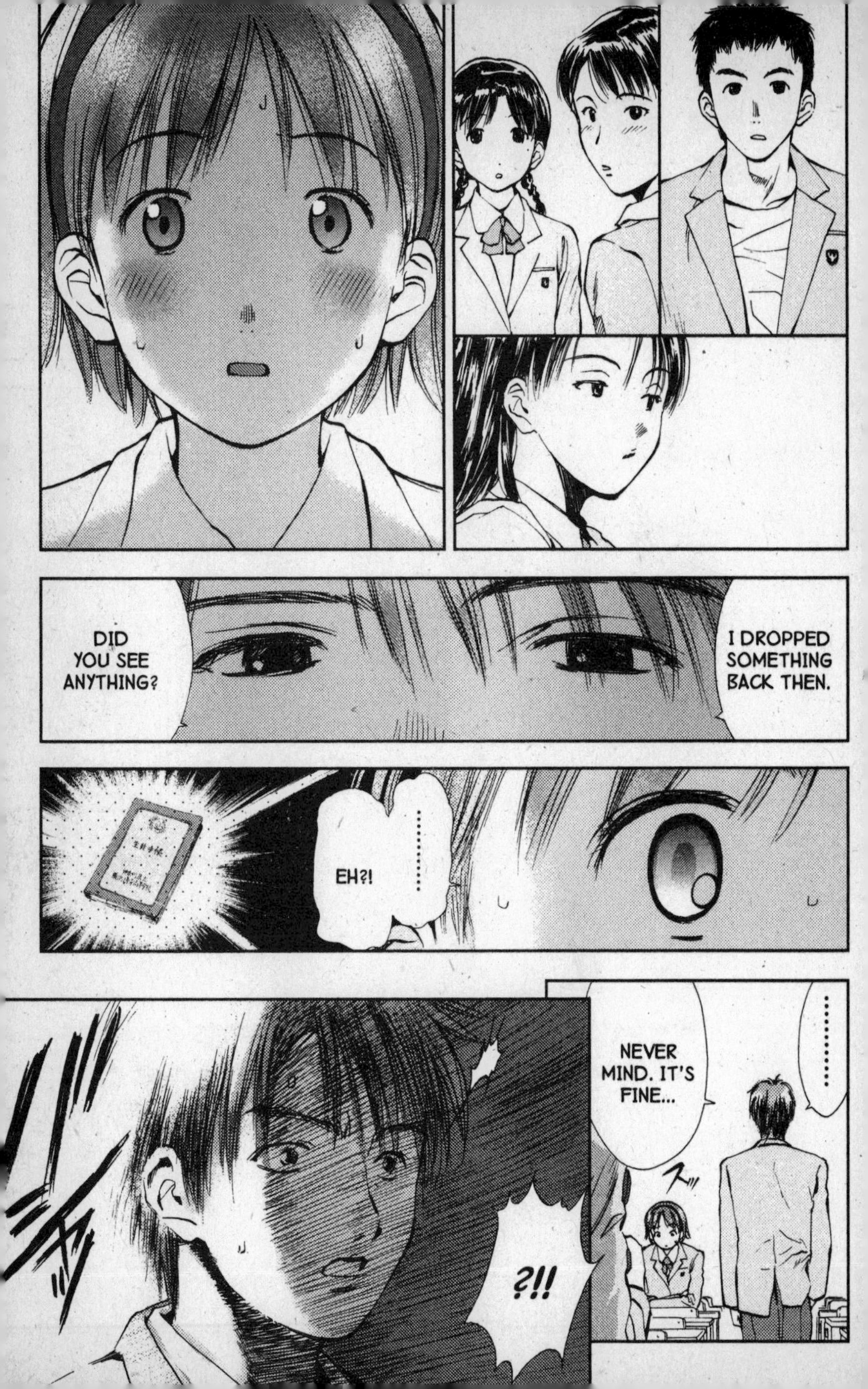

I DROPPED SOMETHING BACK THEN.
DID YOU SEE ANYTHING?
......
EH?!
......
NEVER MIND. IT'S FINE...
?!!

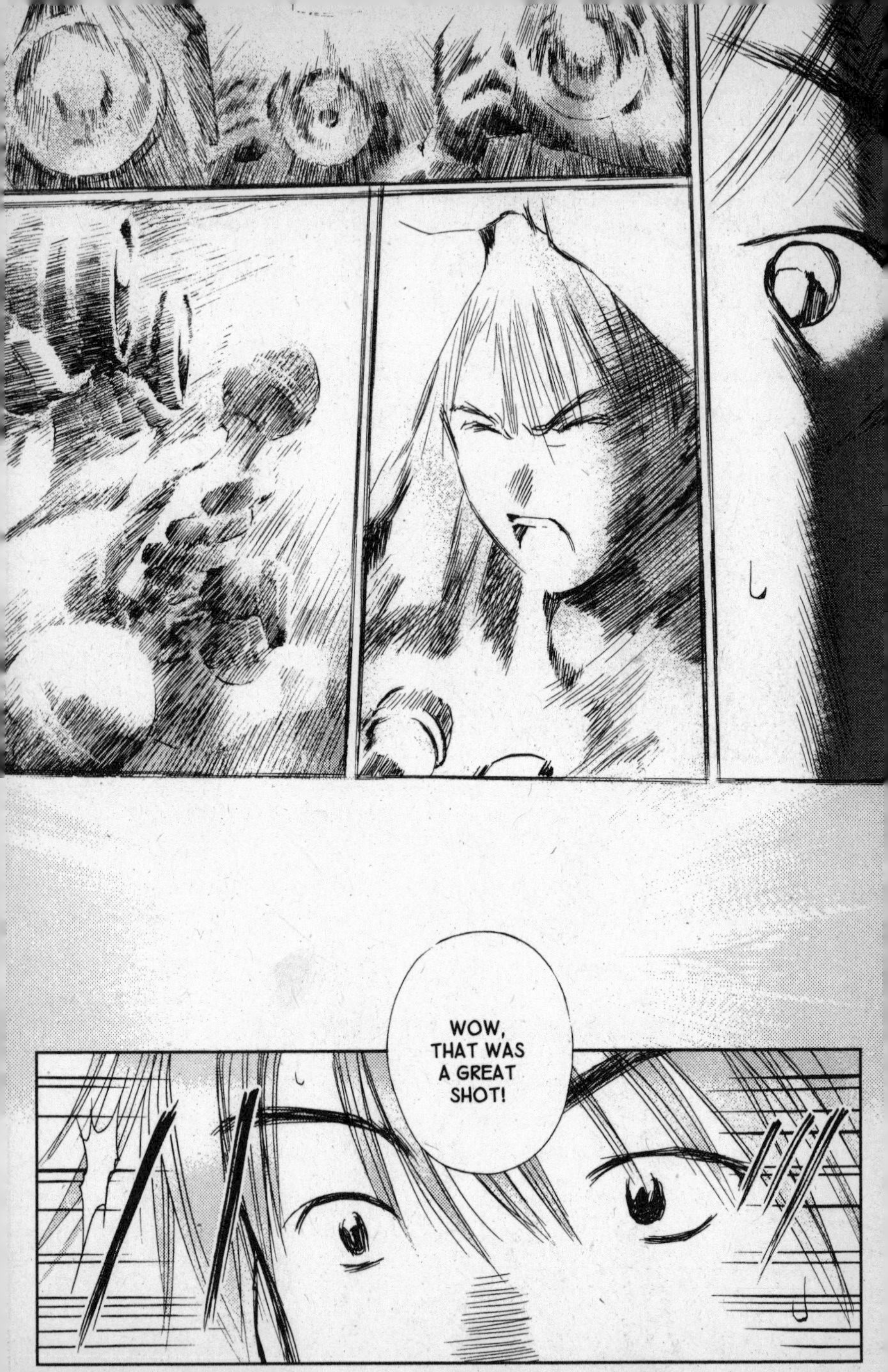
WOW, THAT WAS A GREAT SHOT!

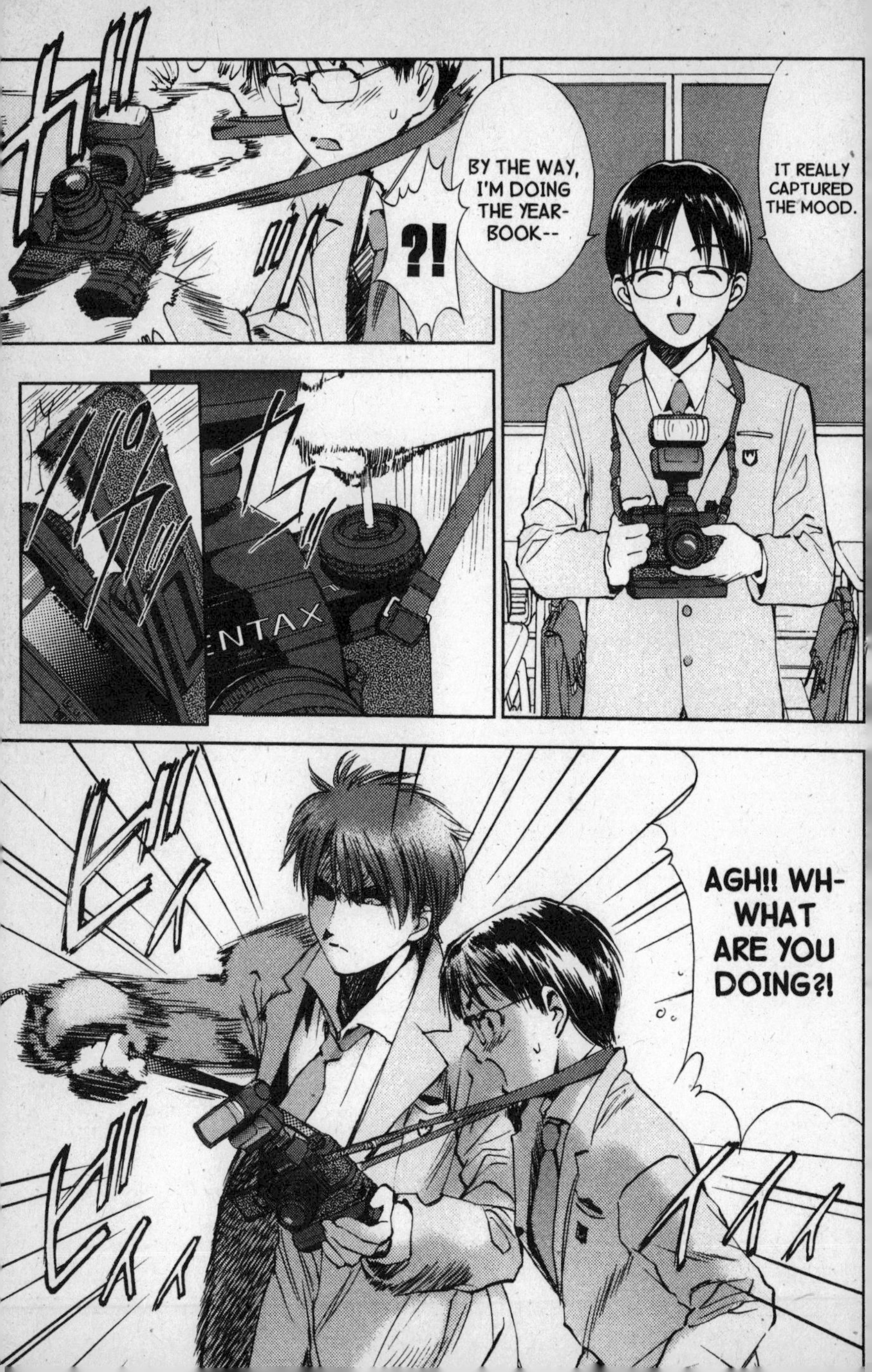
IT REALLY CAPTURED THE MOOD.
BY THE WAY, I'M DOING THE YEAR-BOOK--
?!
ENTAX
AGH!! WH-WHAT ARE YOU DOING?!

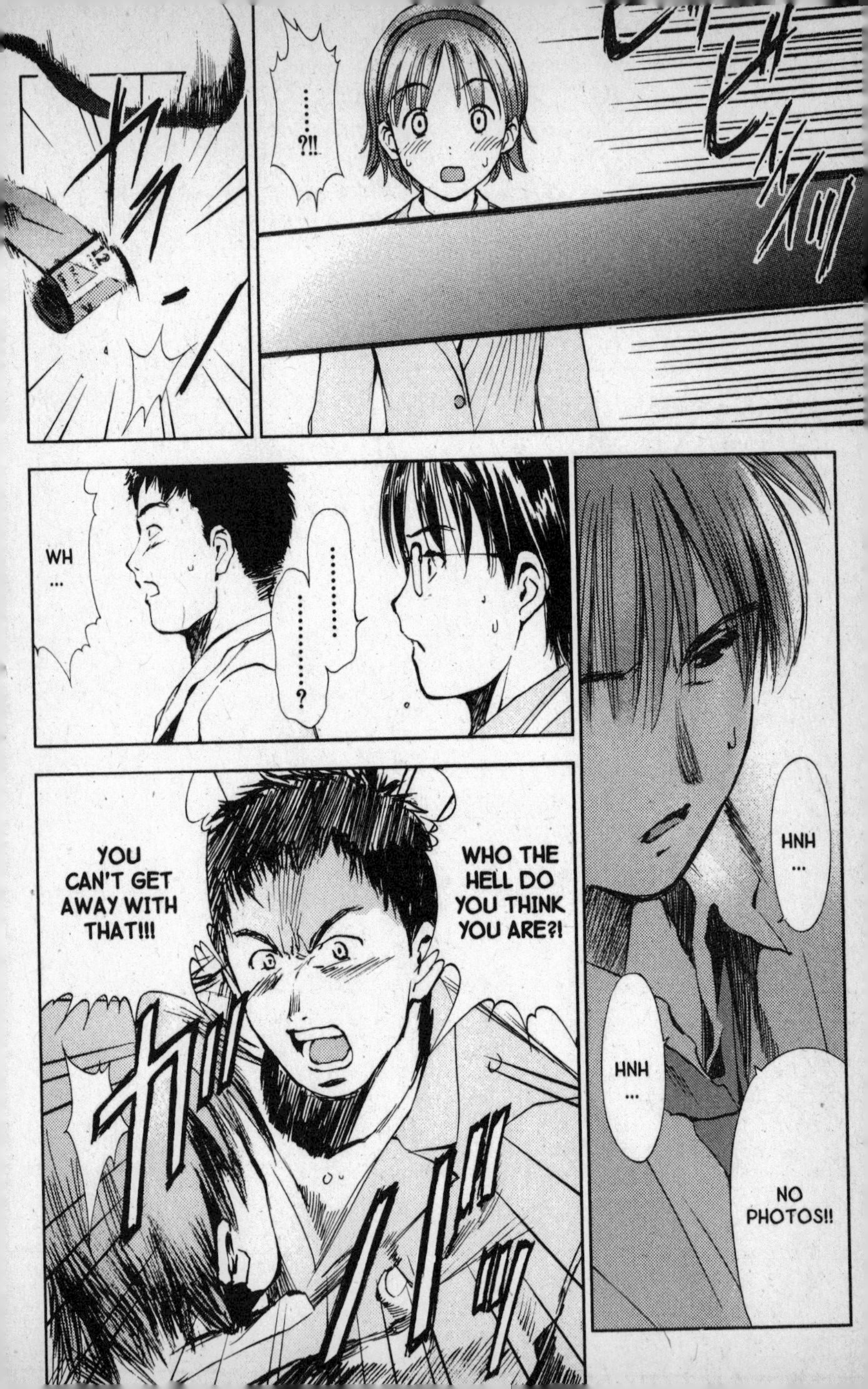
......?!!
HNH ...
HNH ...
NO PHOTOS!!
......
......?
WH ...
WHO THE HELL DO YOU THINK YOU ARE?!
YOU CAN'T GET AWAY WITH THAT!!!

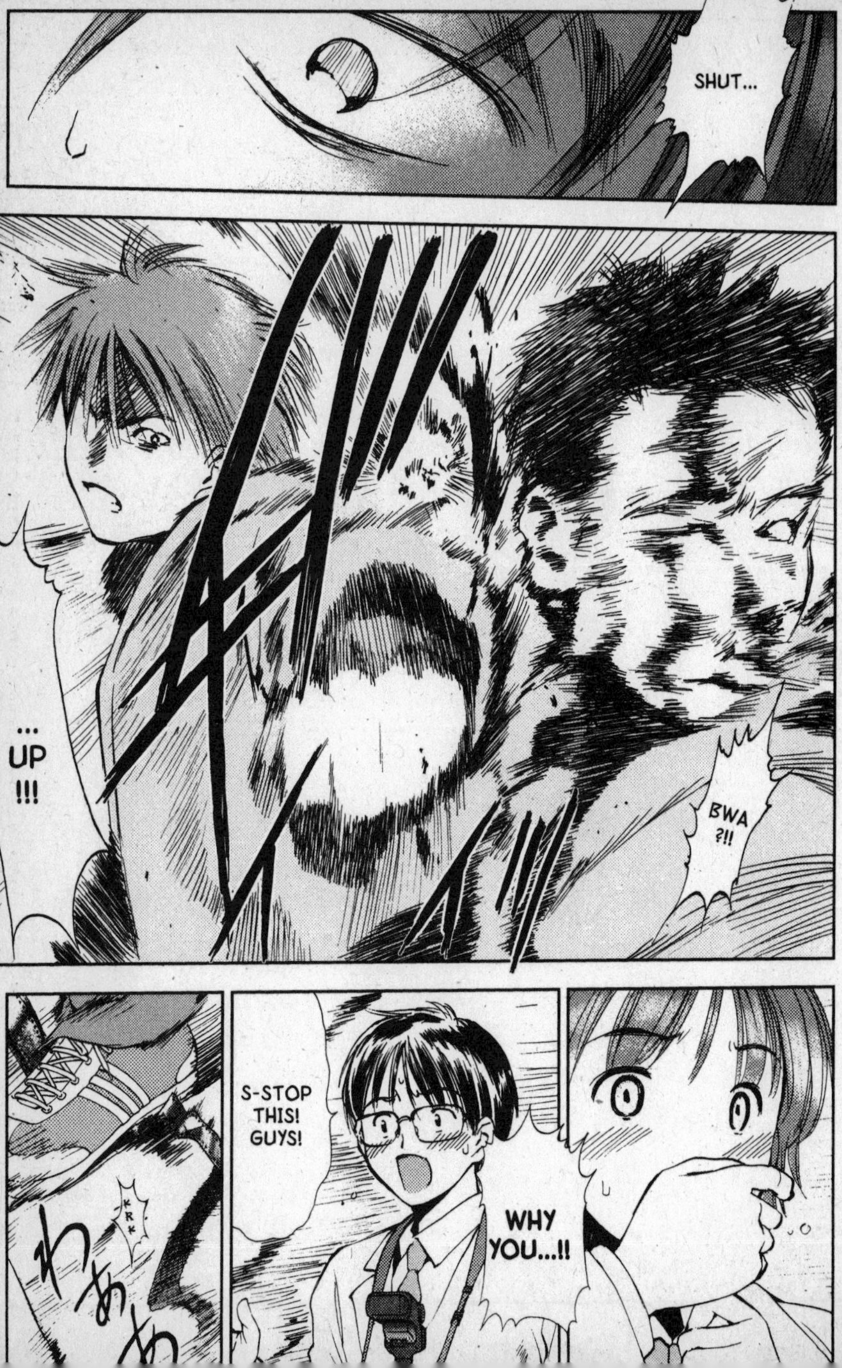
SHUT...
...UP!!!
BWA?!!
S-STOP THIS! GUYS!
WHY YOU...!!
KRK
わあわ

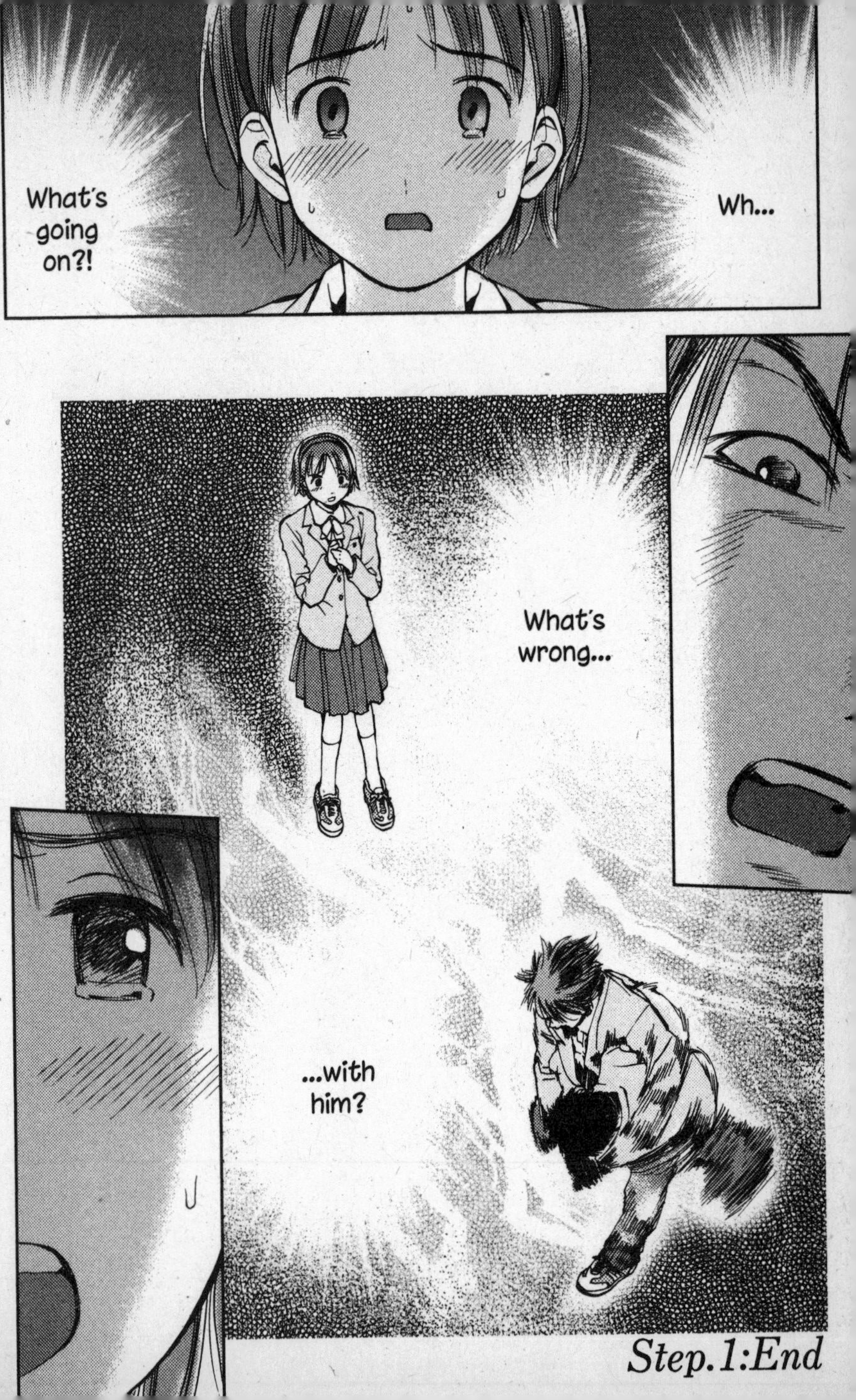
Wh...
What's going on?!
What's wrong...
...with him?
Step.1:End

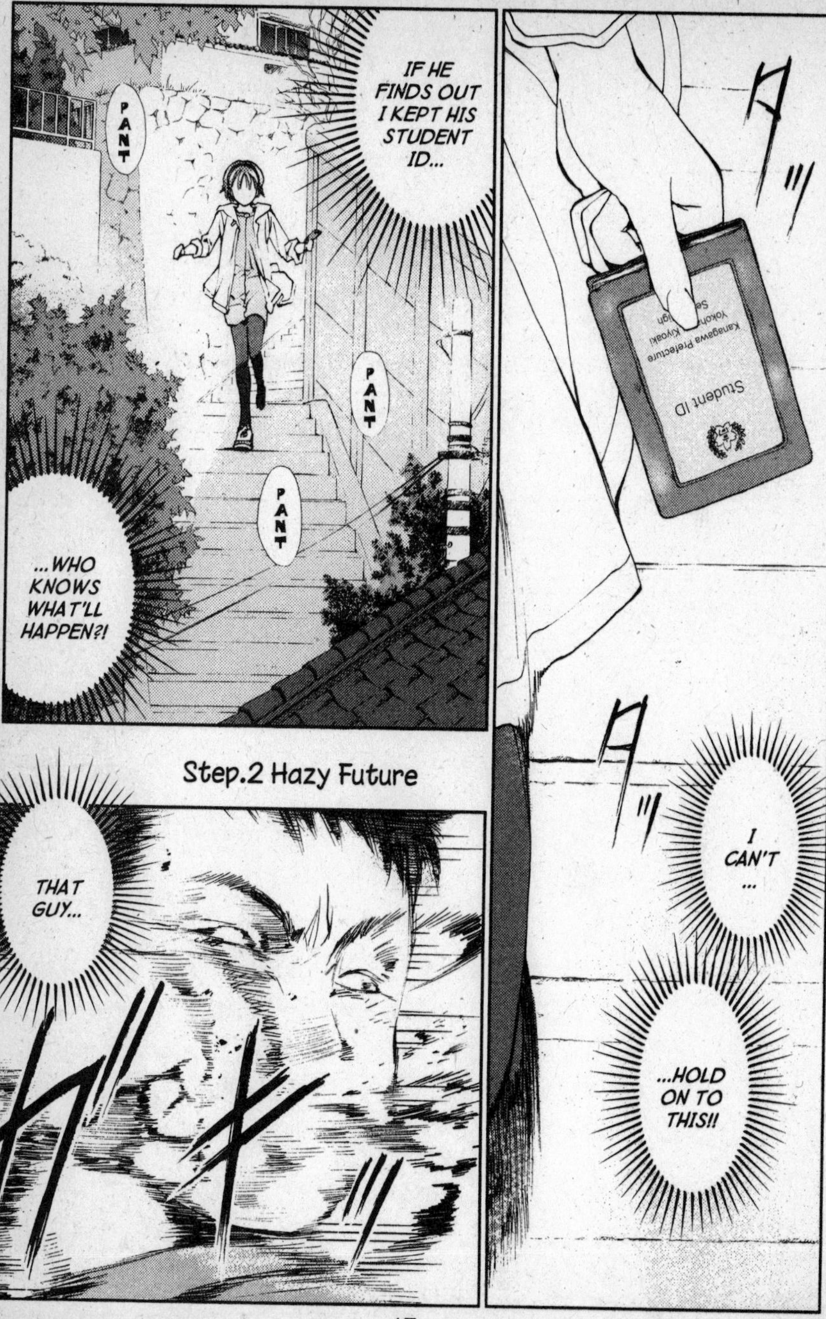
Student ID
Kanagawa Prefecture
I CAN'T ...
...HOLD ON TO THIS!!
IF HE FINDS OUT I KEPT HIS STUDENT ID...
PANT
PANT
PANT
...WHO KNOWS WHAT'LL HAPPEN?!
THAT GUY...

Step.2 Hazy Future

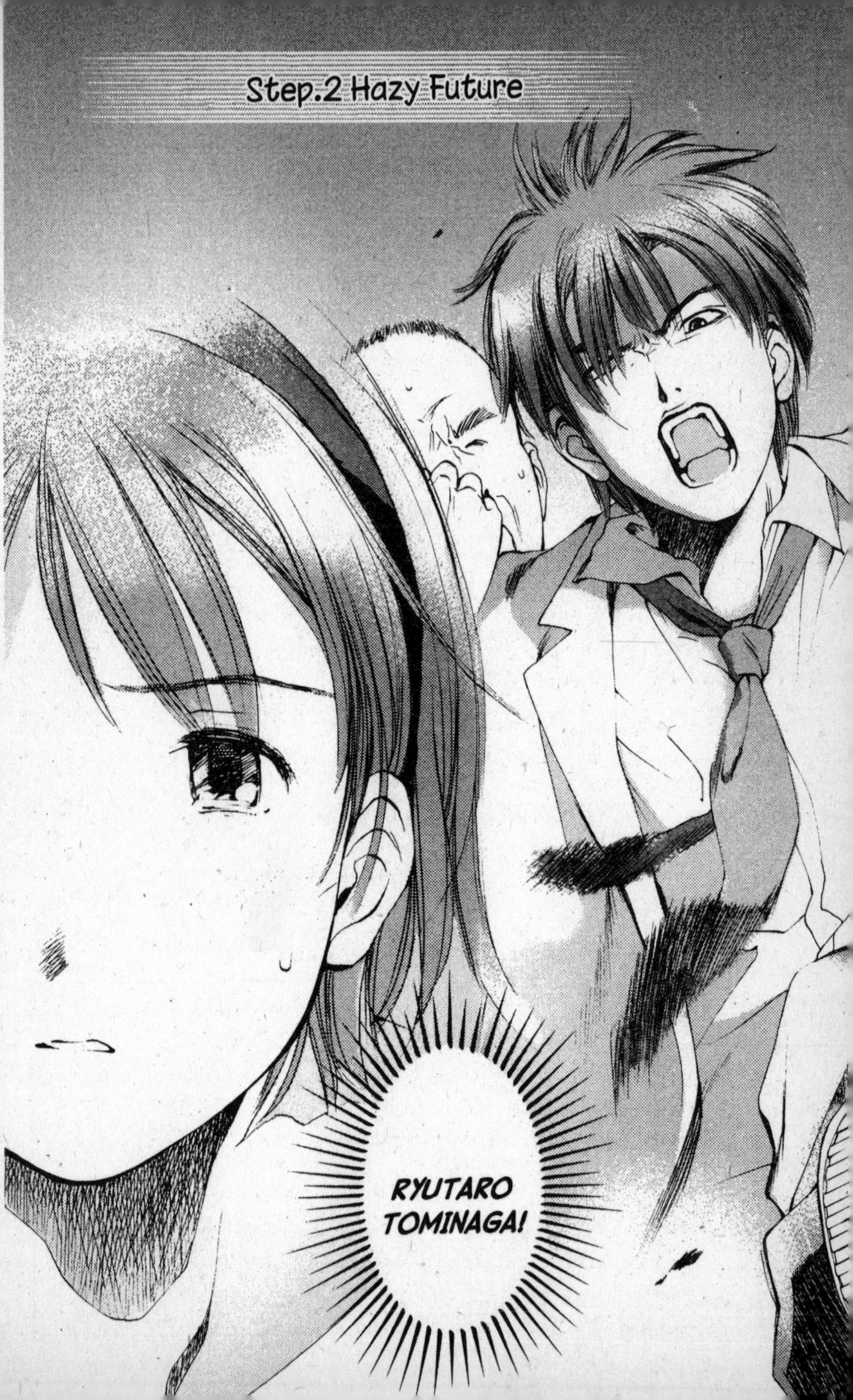

Step.2 Hazy Future
RYUTARO TOMINAGA!

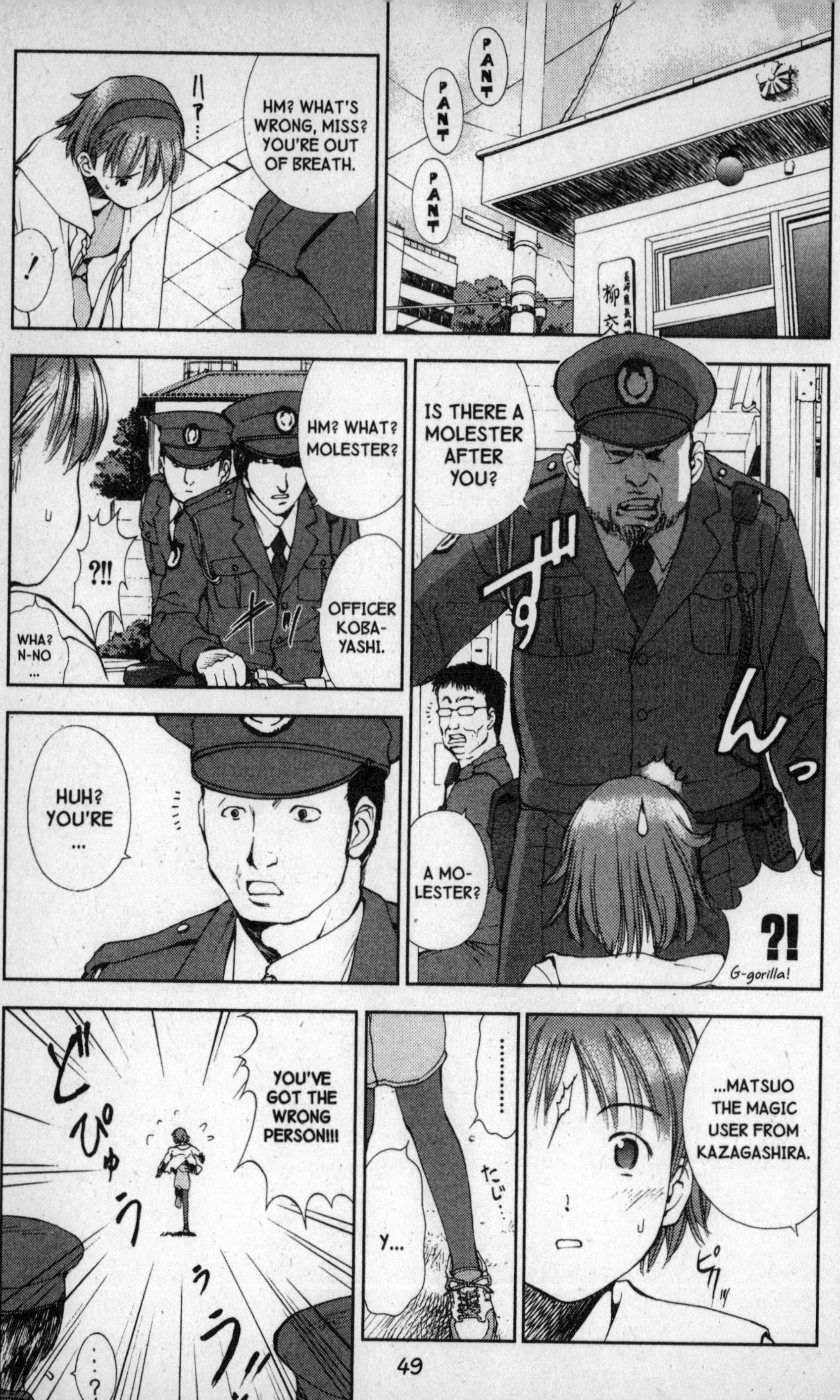
PANT
PANT
PANT
HM? WHAT'S WRONG, MISS? YOU'RE OUT OF BREATH.
ハア…
!
IS THERE A MOLESTER AFTER YOU?
ずん
A MO-LESTER?
?!
G-gorilla!
HM? WHAT? MOLESTER?
OFFICER KOBA-YASHI.
ギリ
?!!
WHA? N-NO ...
HUH? YOU'RE ...
...MATSUO THE MAGIC USER FROM KAZAGASHIRA.
!
ピク
......
たじ…
Y...
YOU'VE GOT THE WRONG PERSON!!!
どぴゅううう!!
...?

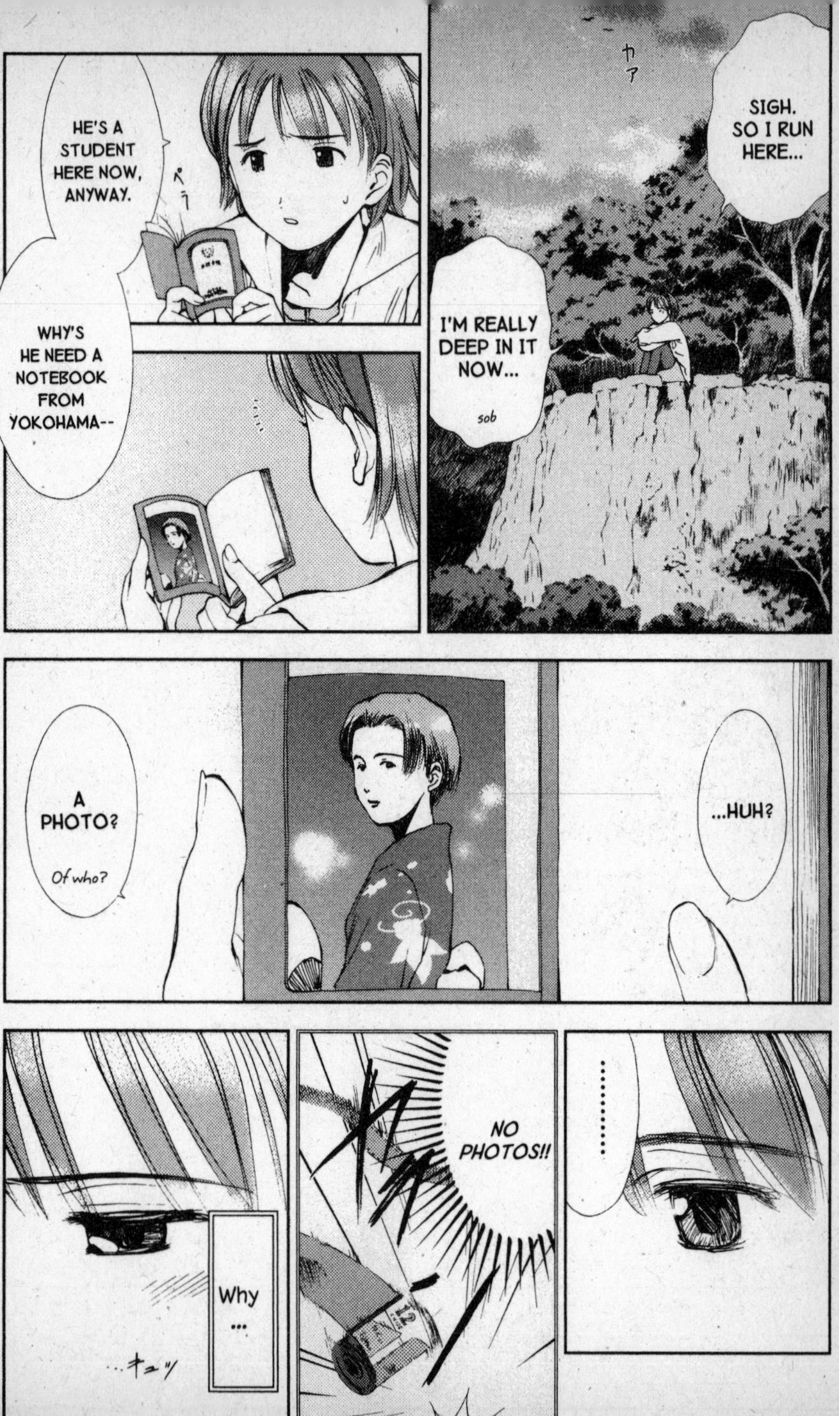
カァ
SIGH. SO I RUN HERE...
I'M REALLY DEEP IN IT NOW...
sob
HE'S A STUDENT HERE NOW, ANYWAY.
ペラ
WHY'S HE NEED A NOTEBOOK FROM YOKOHAMA--
...HUH?
A PHOTO?
Of who?
....
NO PHOTOS!!
Why ...
...キュッ

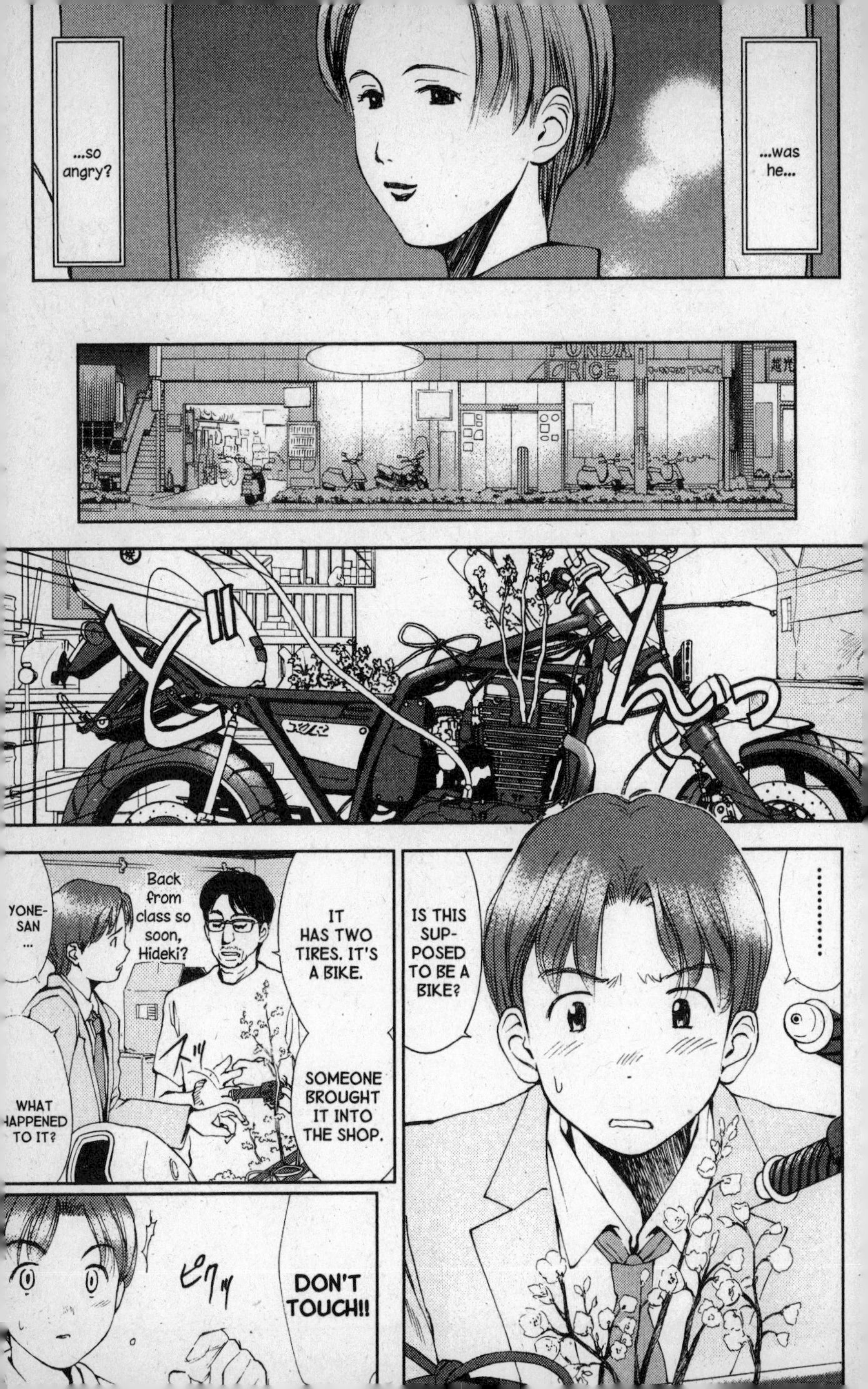
...was he...
...so angry?
......
IS THIS SUP-POSED TO BE A BIKE?
IT HAS TWO TIRES. IT'S A BIKE.
Back from class so soon, Hideki?
YONE-SAN ...
SOMEONE BROUGHT IT INTO THE SHOP.
WHAT HAPPENED TO IT?
DON'T TOUCH!!
ピクッ

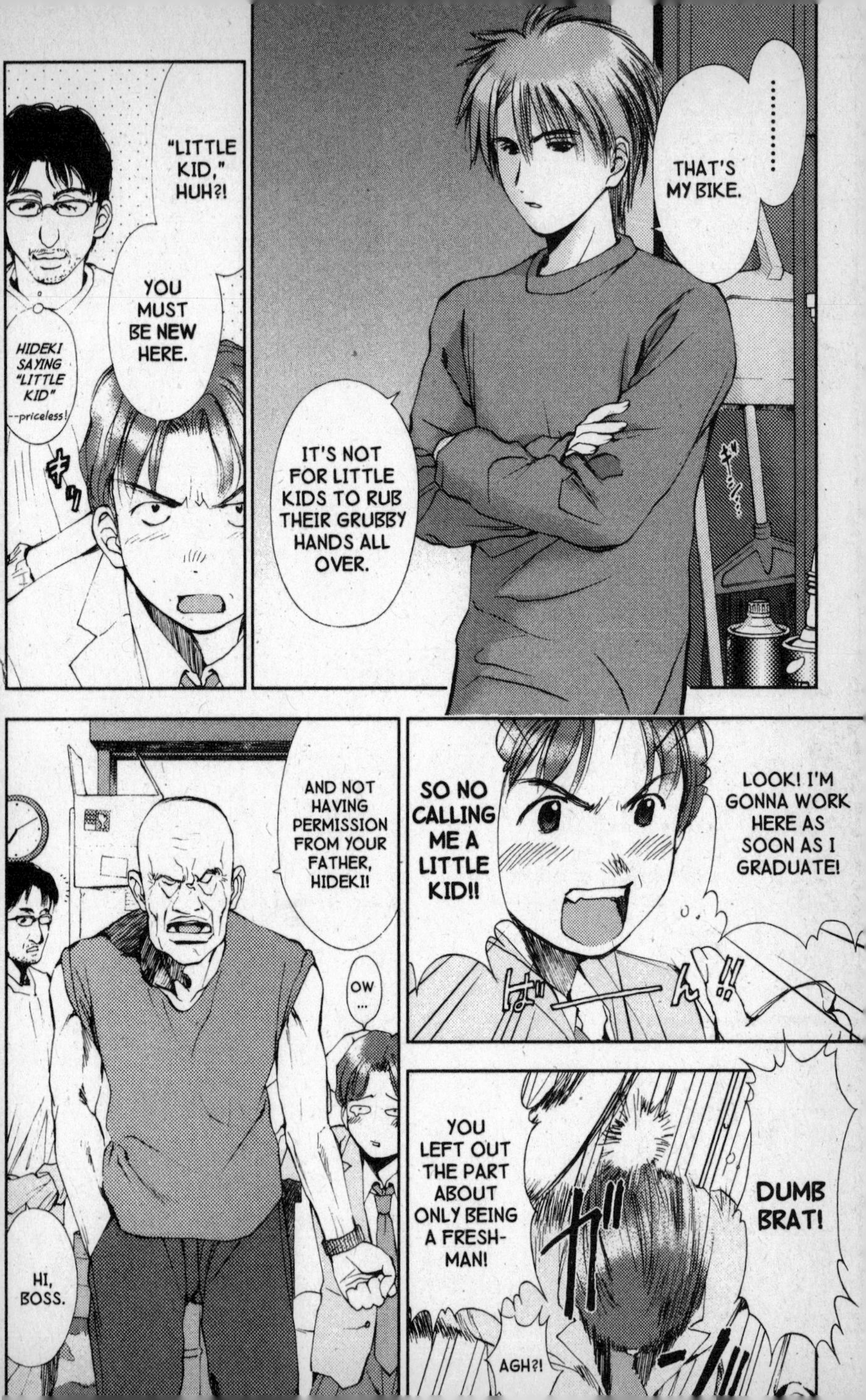
......
THAT'S MY BIKE.
IT'S NOT FOR LITTLE KIDS TO RUB THEIR GRUBBY HANDS ALL OVER.
"LITTLE KID," HUH?!
YOU MUST BE NEW HERE.
HIDEKI SAYING "LITTLE KID" --priceless!
LOOK! I'M GONNA WORK HERE AS SOON AS I GRADUATE!
SO NO CALLING ME A LITTLE KID!!
DUMB BRAT!
YOU LEFT OUT THE PART ABOUT ONLY BEING A FRESH-MAN!
AGH?!
AND NOT HAVING PERMISSION FROM YOUR FATHER, HIDEKI!
OW ...
HI, BOSS.

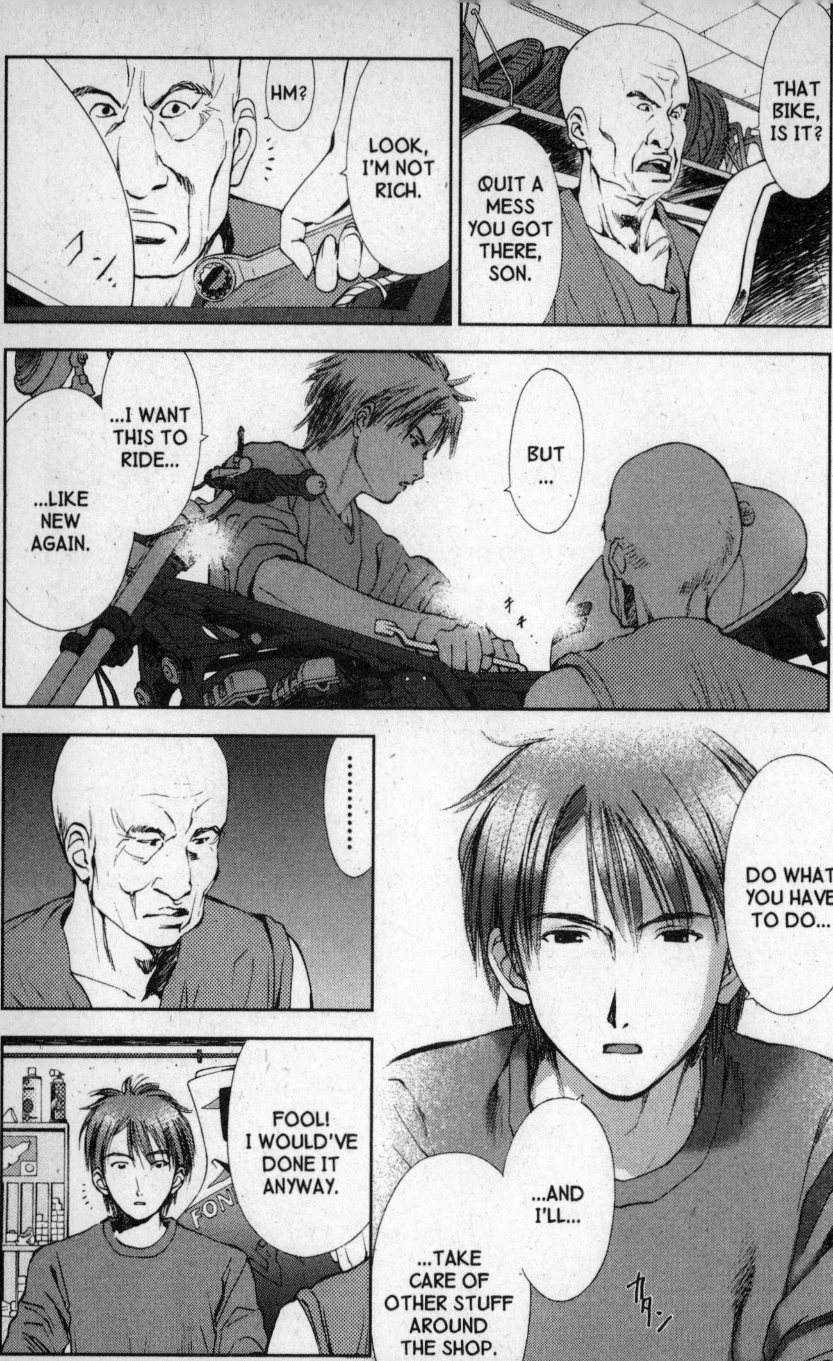
THAT BIKE, IS IT?
QUIT A MESS YOU GOT THERE, SON.
LOOK, I'M NOT RICH.
HM?
BUT ...
...I WANT THIS TO RIDE...
...LIKE NEW AGAIN.
DO WHAT YOU HAVE TO DO...
...AND I'LL...
...TAKE CARE OF OTHER STUFF AROUND THE SHOP.
....
FOOL! I WOULD'VE DONE IT ANYWAY.

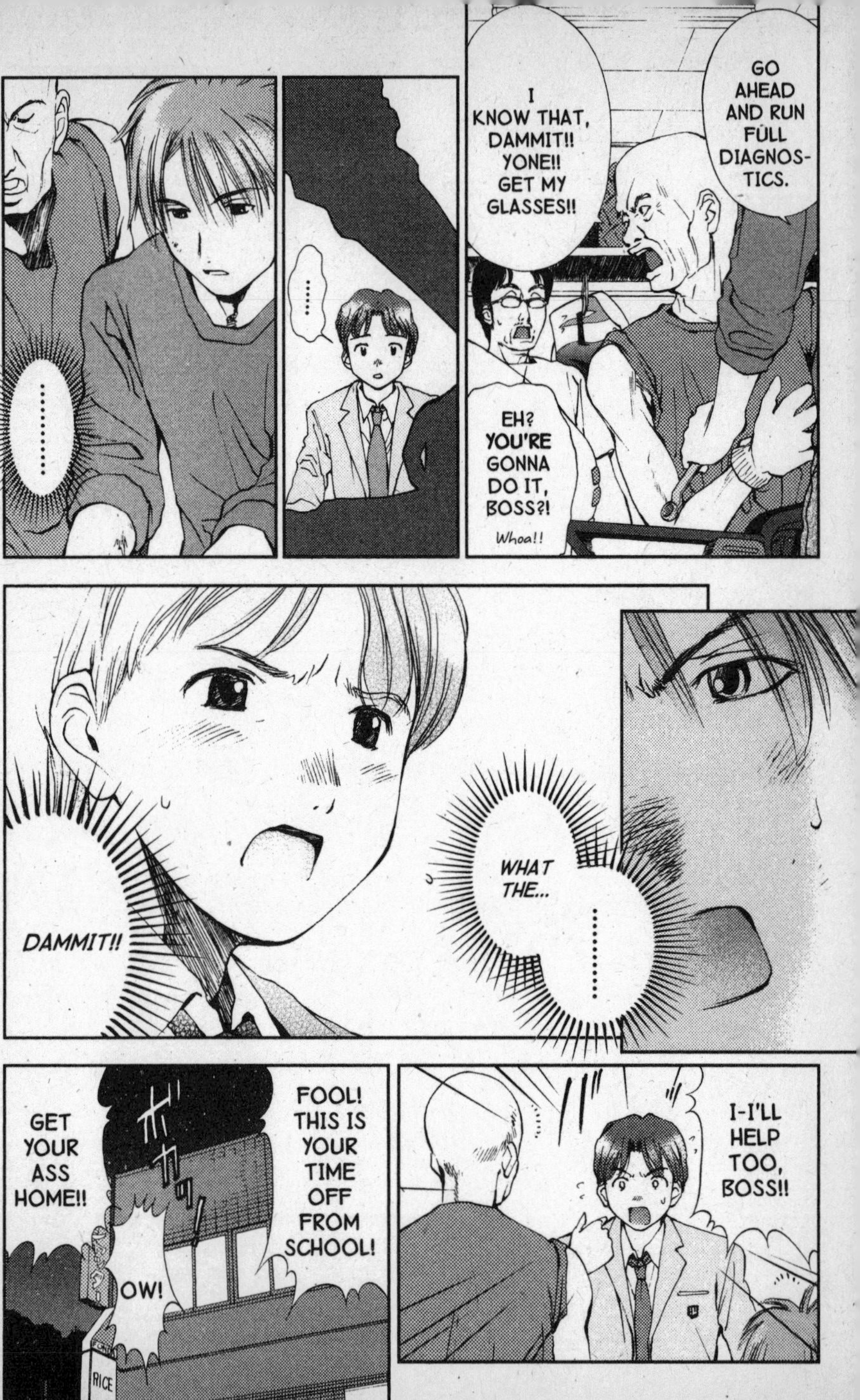
GO AHEAD AND RUN FULL DIAGNOS-TICS.
I KNOW THAT, DAMMIT!! YONE!! GET MY GLASSES!!
EH? YOU'RE GONNA DO IT, BOSS?!
Whoa!!
......
......
WHAT THE... ......
DAMMIT!!
I-I'LL HELP TOO, BOSS!!
FOOL! THIS IS YOUR TIME OFF FROM SCHOOL!
GET YOUR ASS HOME!!
OW!
RICE

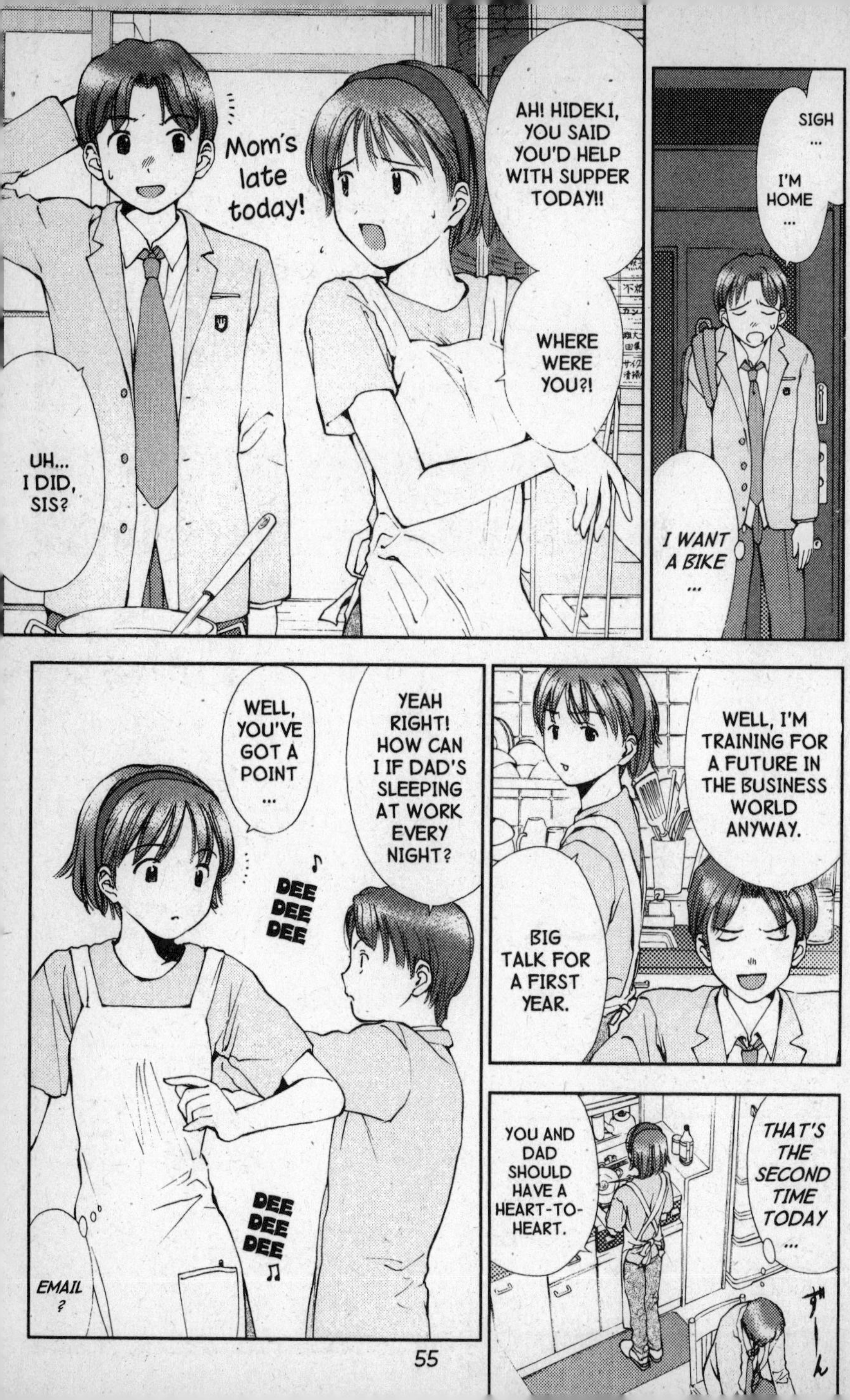
SIGH ... I'M HOME ...
I WANT A BIKE ...
AH! HIDEKI, YOU SAID YOU'D HELP WITH SUPPER TODAY!!
WHERE WERE YOU?!
Mom's late today!
UH... I DID, SIS?
WELL, I'M TRAINING FOR A FUTURE IN THE BUSINESS WORLD ANYWAY.
BIG TALK FOR A FIRST YEAR.
THAT'S THE SECOND TIME TODAY ...
YOU AND DAD SHOULD HAVE A HEART-TO-HEART.
ず〜ん
YEAH RIGHT! HOW CAN I IF DAD'S SLEEPING AT WORK EVERY NIGHT?
WELL, YOU'VE GOT A POINT ...
DEE DEE DEE
DEE DEE DEE
EMAIL ?

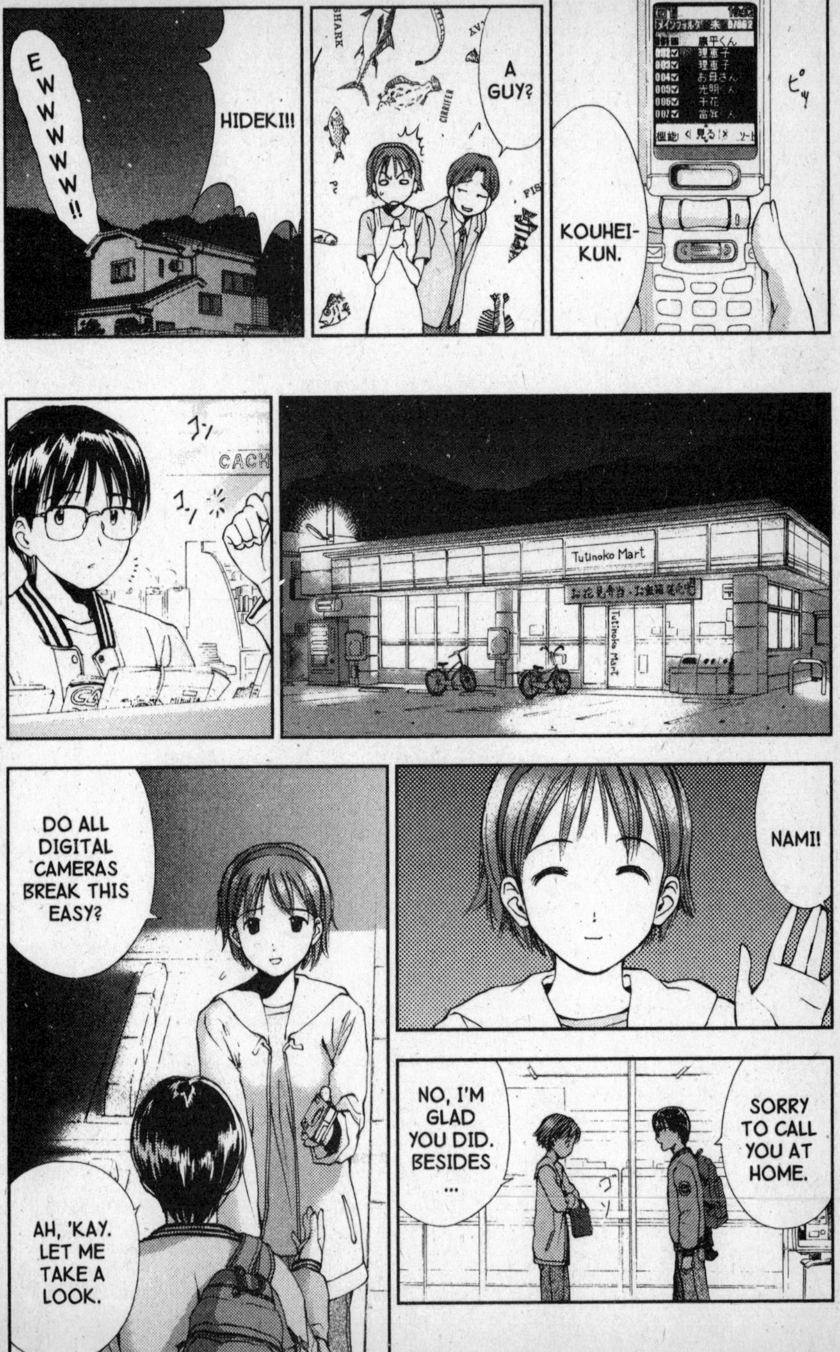
ピッ
KOUHEI-KUN.
SHARK
CIRRIFER
A GUY?
HIDEKI!!
EWWWWWW!!
Tutinoko Mart
Tutinoko Mart
コン
CACH
ゴン
NAMI!
SORRY TO CALL YOU AT HOME.
NO, I'M GLAD YOU DID. BESIDES ...
DO ALL DIGITAL CAMERAS BREAK THIS EASY?
AH, 'KAY. LET ME TAKE A LOOK.

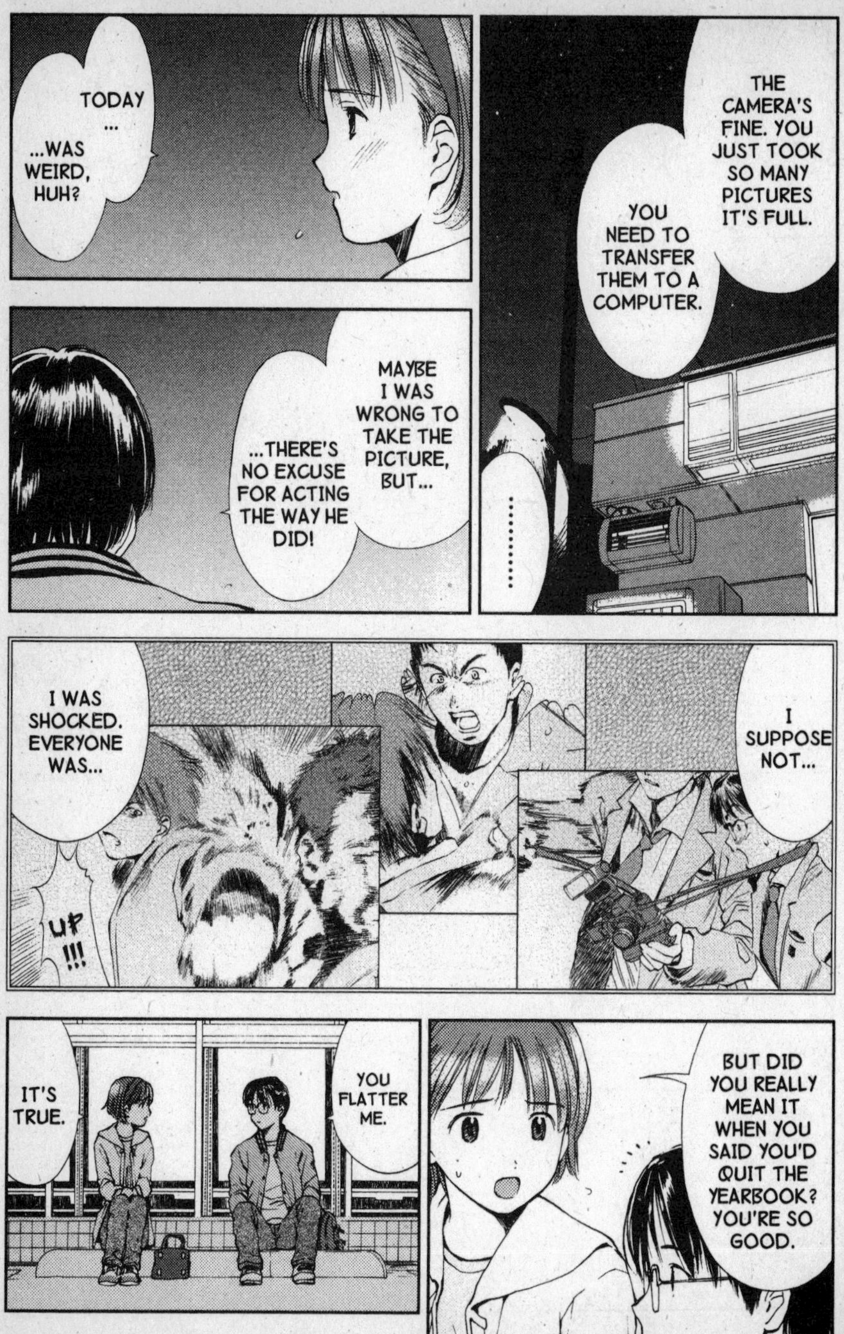
THE CAMERA'S FINE. YOU JUST TOOK SO MANY PICTURES IT'S FULL.
YOU NEED TO TRANSFER THEM TO A COMPUTER.
......
TODAY ... ...WAS WEIRD, HUH?
MAYBE I WAS WRONG TO TAKE THE PICTURE, BUT...
...THERE'S NO EXCUSE FOR ACTING THE WAY HE DID!
I SUPPOSE NOT...
I WAS SHOCKED. EVERYONE WAS...
UP !!!
BUT DID YOU REALLY MEAN IT WHEN YOU SAID YOU'D QUIT THE YEARBOOK? YOU'RE SO GOOD.
YOU FLATTER ME.
IT'S TRUE.

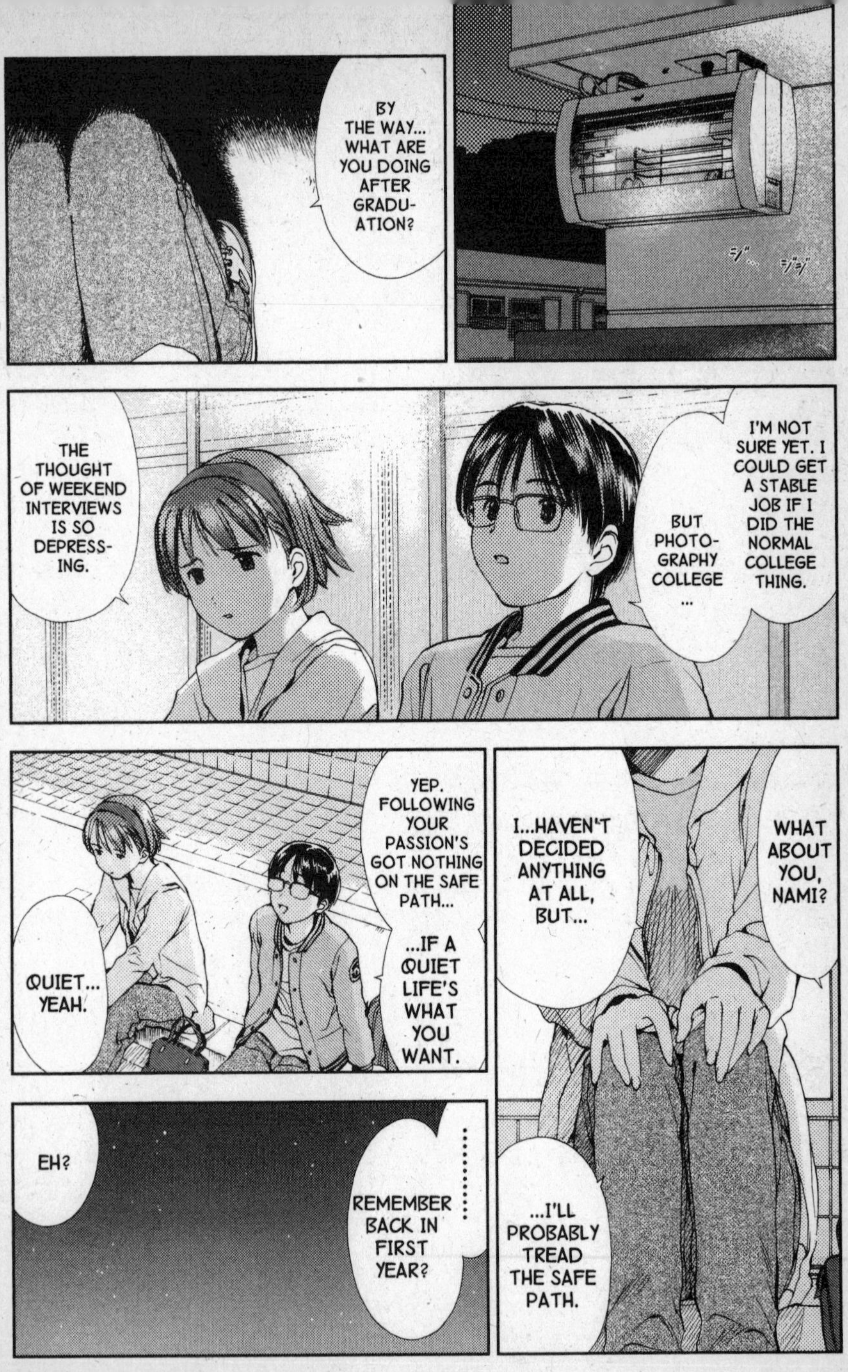
ジ…
ジジ
BY THE WAY... WHAT ARE YOU DOING AFTER GRADUATION?
I'M NOT SURE YET. I COULD GET A STABLE JOB IF I DID THE NORMAL COLLEGE THING.
BUT PHOTOGRAPHY COLLEGE ...
THE THOUGHT OF WEEKEND INTERVIEWS IS SO DEPRESSING.
WHAT ABOUT YOU, NAMI?
I...HAVEN'T DECIDED ANYTHING AT ALL, BUT...
...I'LL PROBABLY TREAD THE SAFE PATH.
YEP. FOLLOWING YOUR PASSION'S GOT NOTHING ON THE SAFE PATH...
...IF A QUIET LIFE'S WHAT YOU WANT.
QUIET... YEAH.
....
REMEMBER BACK IN FIRST YEAR?
EH?

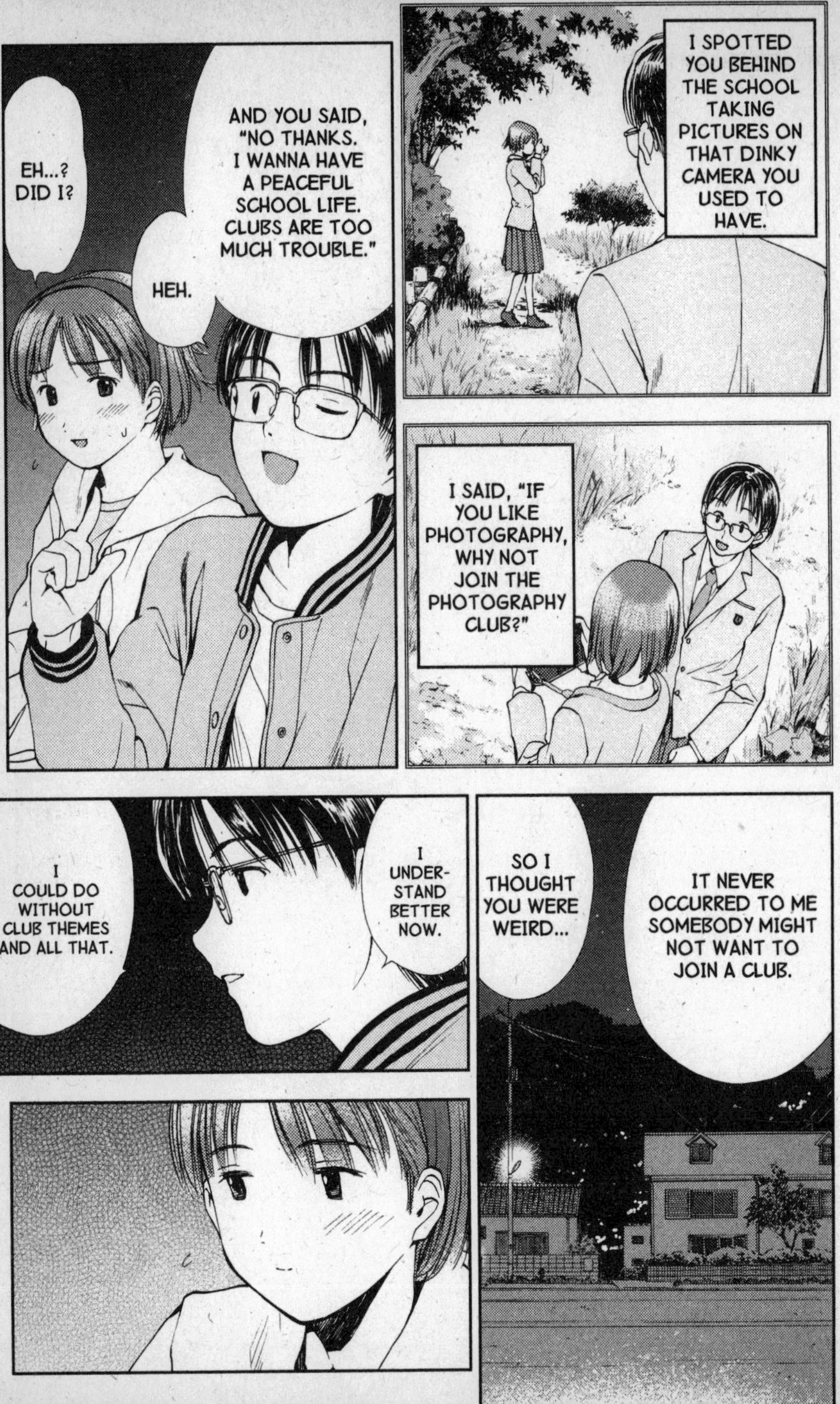
I SPOTTED YOU BEHIND THE SCHOOL TAKING PICTURES ON THAT DINKY CAMERA YOU USED TO HAVE.
I SAID, "IF YOU LIKE PHOTOGRAPHY, WHY NOT JOIN THE PHOTOGRAPHY CLUB?"
AND YOU SAID, "NO THANKS. I WANNA HAVE A PEACEFUL SCHOOL LIFE. CLUBS ARE TOO MUCH TROUBLE."
HEH.
EH...? DID I?
IT NEVER OCCURRED TO ME SOMEBODY MIGHT NOT WANT TO JOIN A CLUB.
SO I THOUGHT YOU WERE WEIRD...
I UNDER-STAND BETTER NOW.
I COULD DO WITHOUT CLUB THEMES AND ALL THAT.

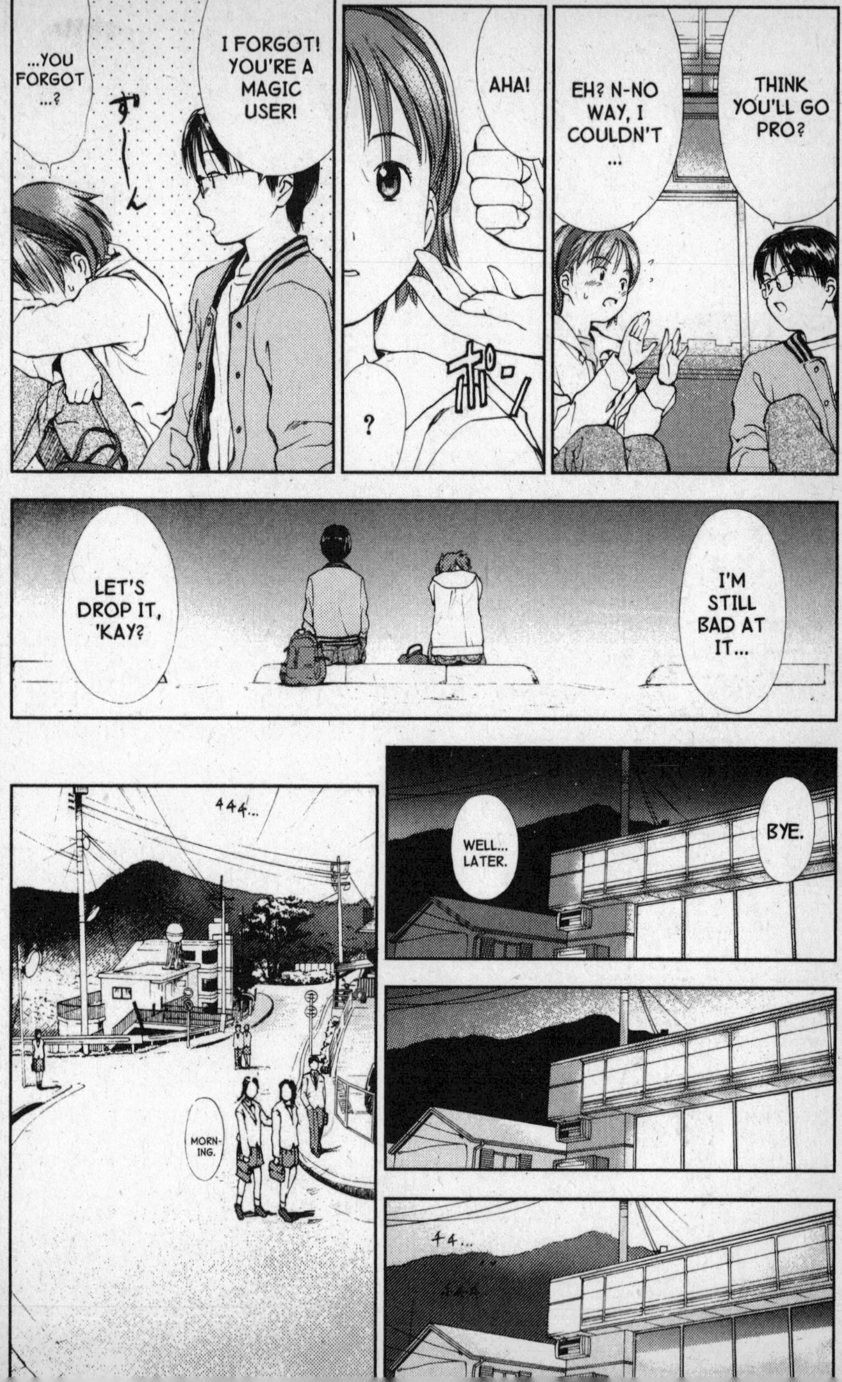

THINK YOU'LL GO PRO?
EH? N-NO WAY, I COULDN'T ...
AHA!
ポーン
?
I FORGOT! YOU'RE A MAGIC USER!
ずーん
...YOU FORGOT ...?
I'M STILL BAD AT IT...
LET'S DROP IT, 'KAY?
BYE.
WELL... LATER.
44...
444...
MORN-ING.

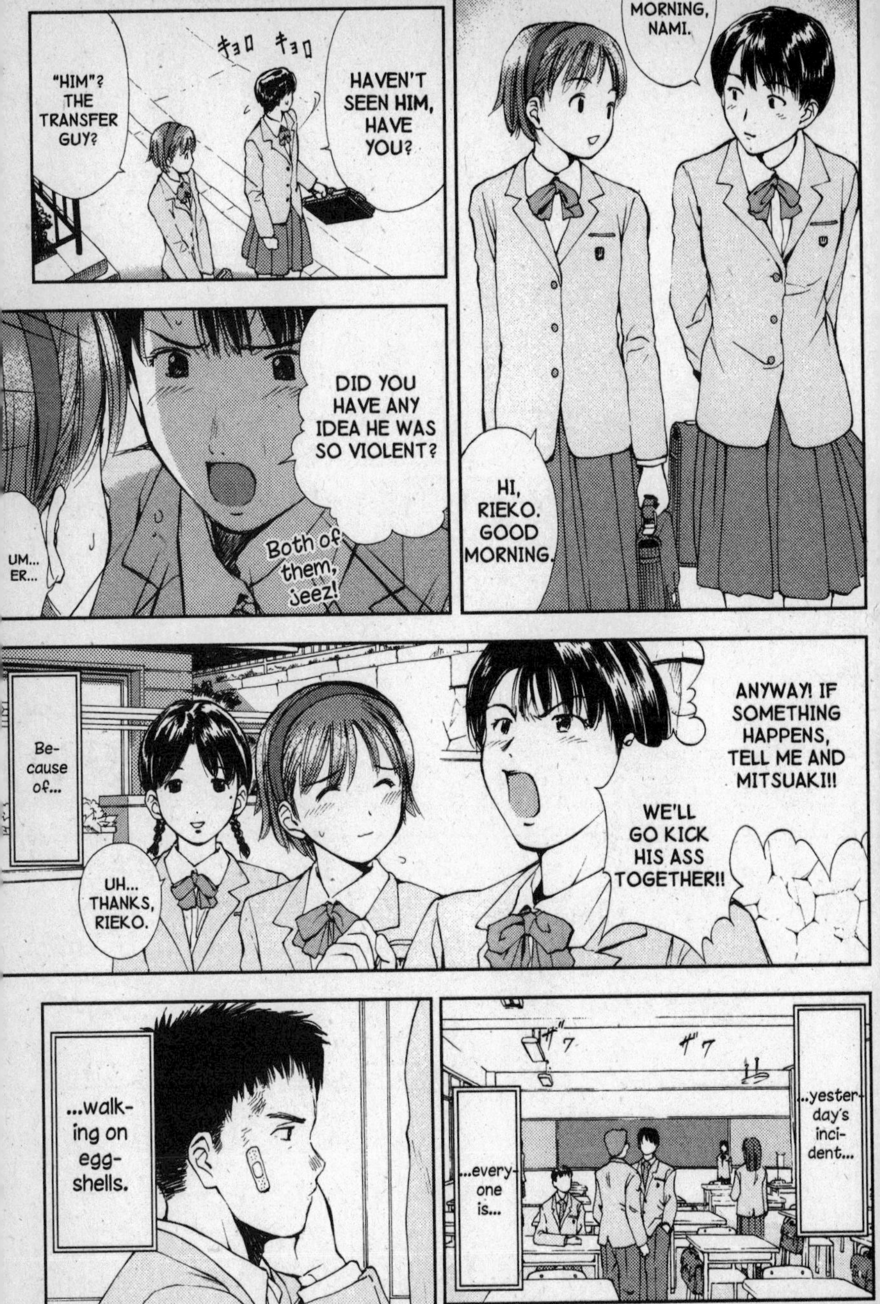
MORNING, NAMI.
HI, RIEKO. GOOD MORNING.
キョロ キョロ
HAVEN'T SEEN HIM, HAVE YOU?
"HIM"? THE TRANSFER GUY?
DID YOU HAVE ANY IDEA HE WAS SO VIOLENT?
Both of them, jeez!
UM... ER...
ANYWAY! IF SOMETHING HAPPENS, TELL ME AND MITSUAKI!!
WE'LL GO KICK HIS ASS TOGETHER!!
UH... THANKS, RIEKO.
Be-cause of...
ザワ ザワ
...yester-day's inci-dent...
...every-one is...
...walk-ing on egg-shells.

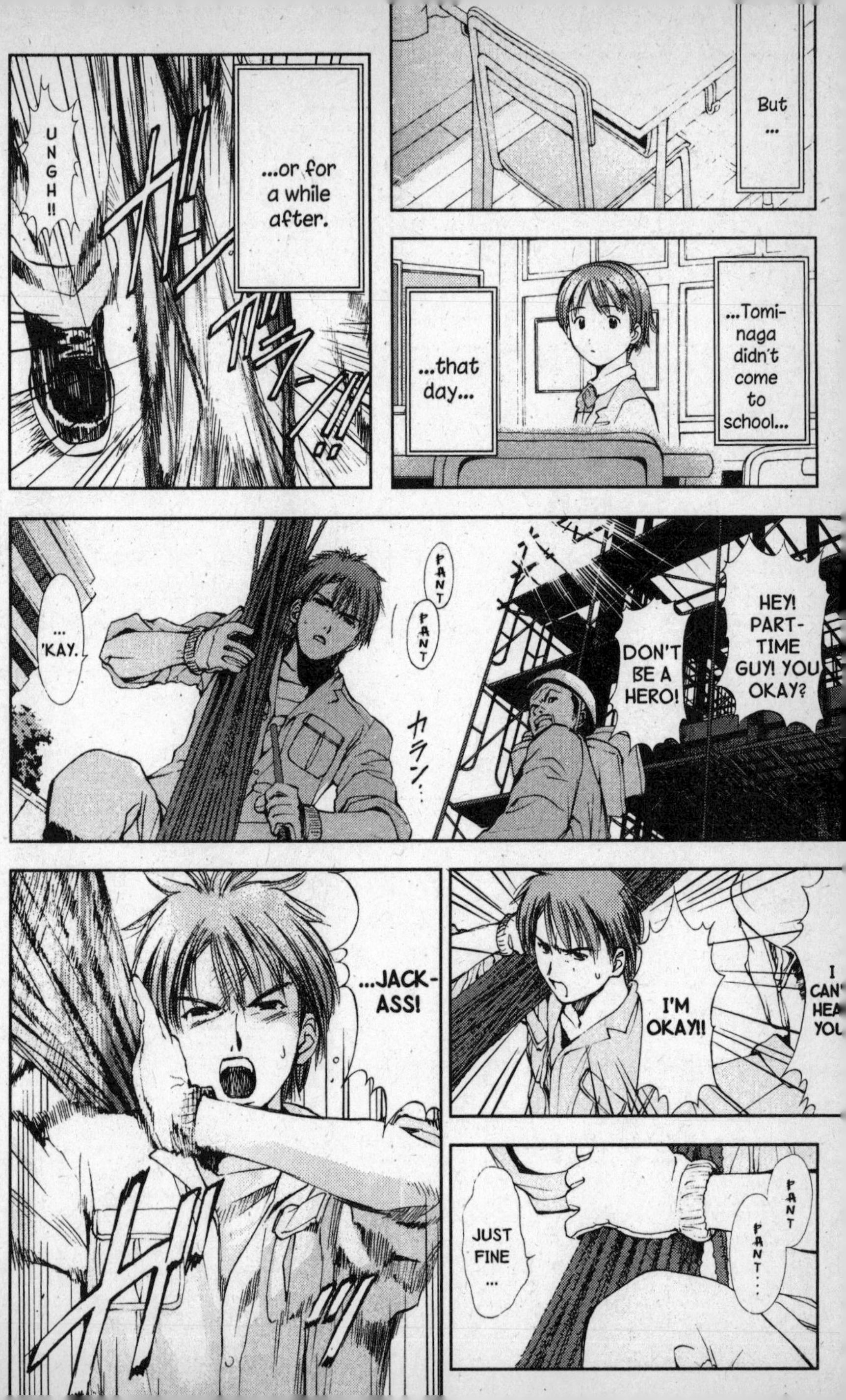
But ...
...Tomi-naga didn't come to school...
...that day...
...or for a while after.
UNGH!!
HEY! PART-TIME GUY! YOU OKAY?
DON'T BE A HERO!
カラン…
PANT PANT
... 'KAY.
I CAN' HEA YOU
I'M OKAY!!
PANT PANT...
JUST FINE ...
...JACK-ASS!

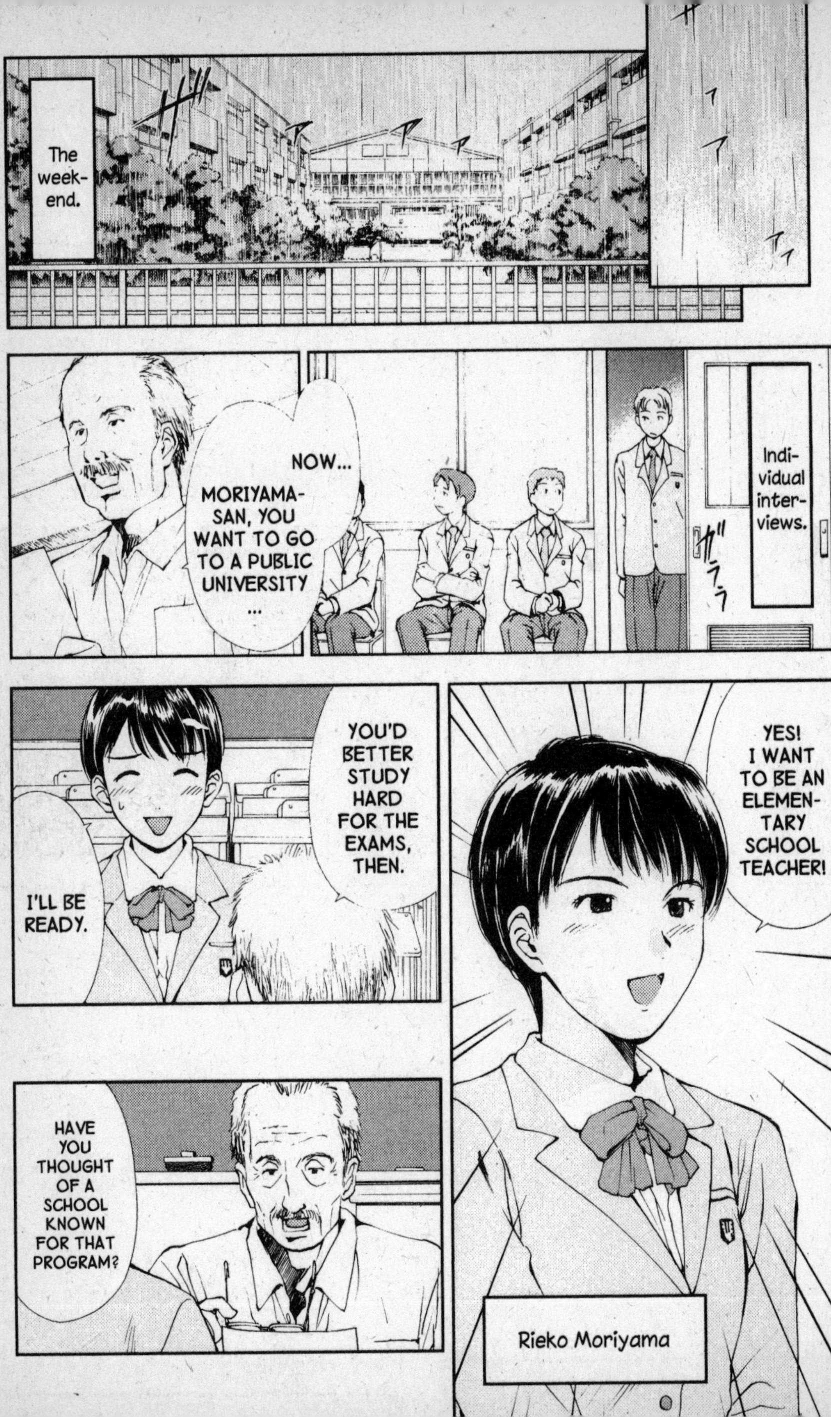
The weekend.
Individual interviews.
NOW...
MORIYAMA-SAN, YOU WANT TO GO TO A PUBLIC UNIVERSITY ...
YES! I WANT TO BE AN ELEMENTARY SCHOOL TEACHER!
Rieko Moriyama
YOU'D BETTER STUDY HARD FOR THE EXAMS, THEN.
I'LL BE READY.
HAVE YOU THOUGHT OF A SCHOOL KNOWN FOR THAT PROGRAM?

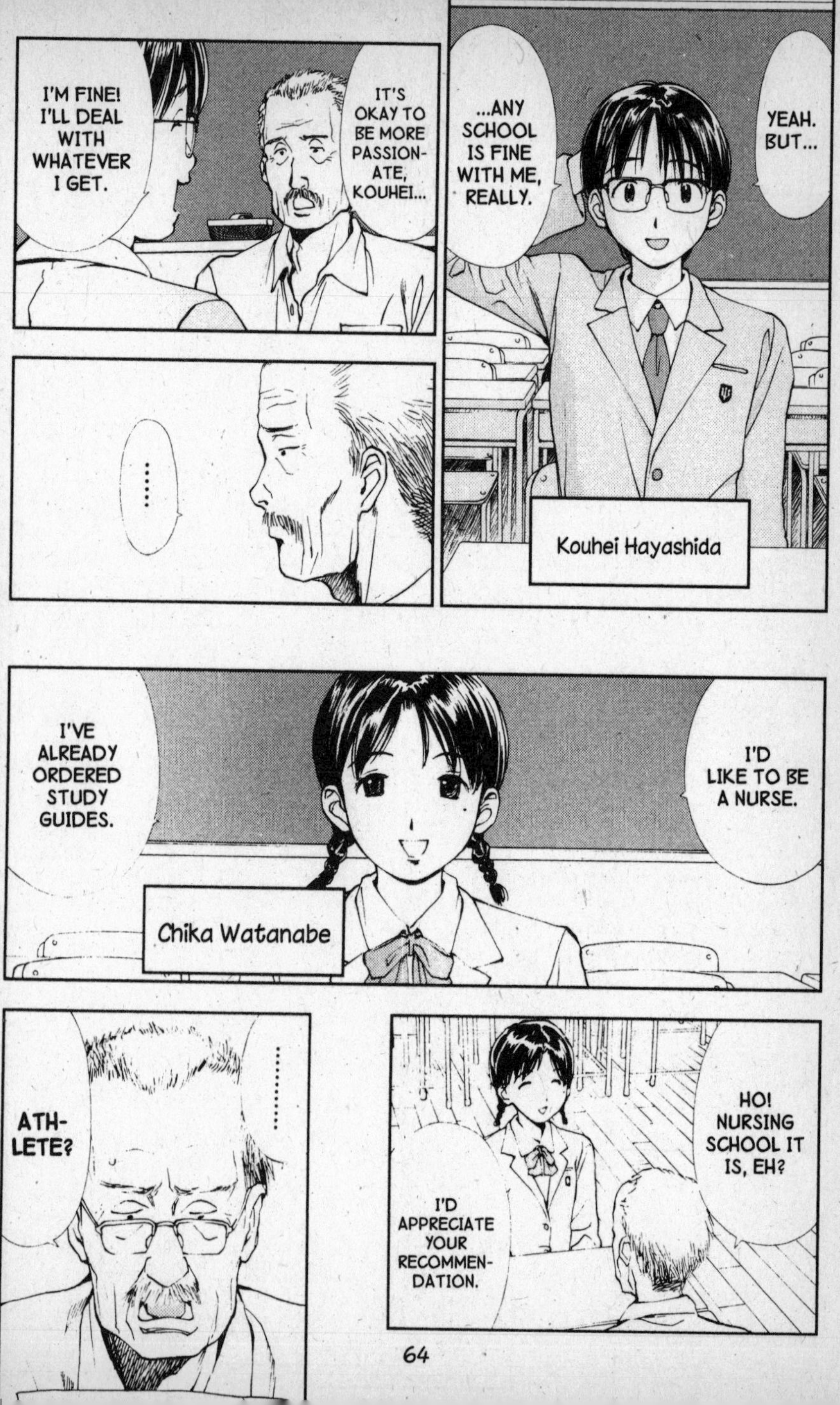
YEAH. BUT...
...ANY SCHOOL IS FINE WITH ME, REALLY.
Kouhei Hayashida
IT'S OKAY TO BE MORE PASSION-ATE, KOUHEI...
I'M FINE! I'LL DEAL WITH WHATEVER I GET.
......
I'D LIKE TO BE A NURSE.
I'VE ALREADY ORDERED STUDY GUIDES.
Chika Watanabe
HO! NURSING SCHOOL IT IS, EH?
I'D APPRECIATE YOUR RECOMMEN-DATION.
......
ATH-LETE?

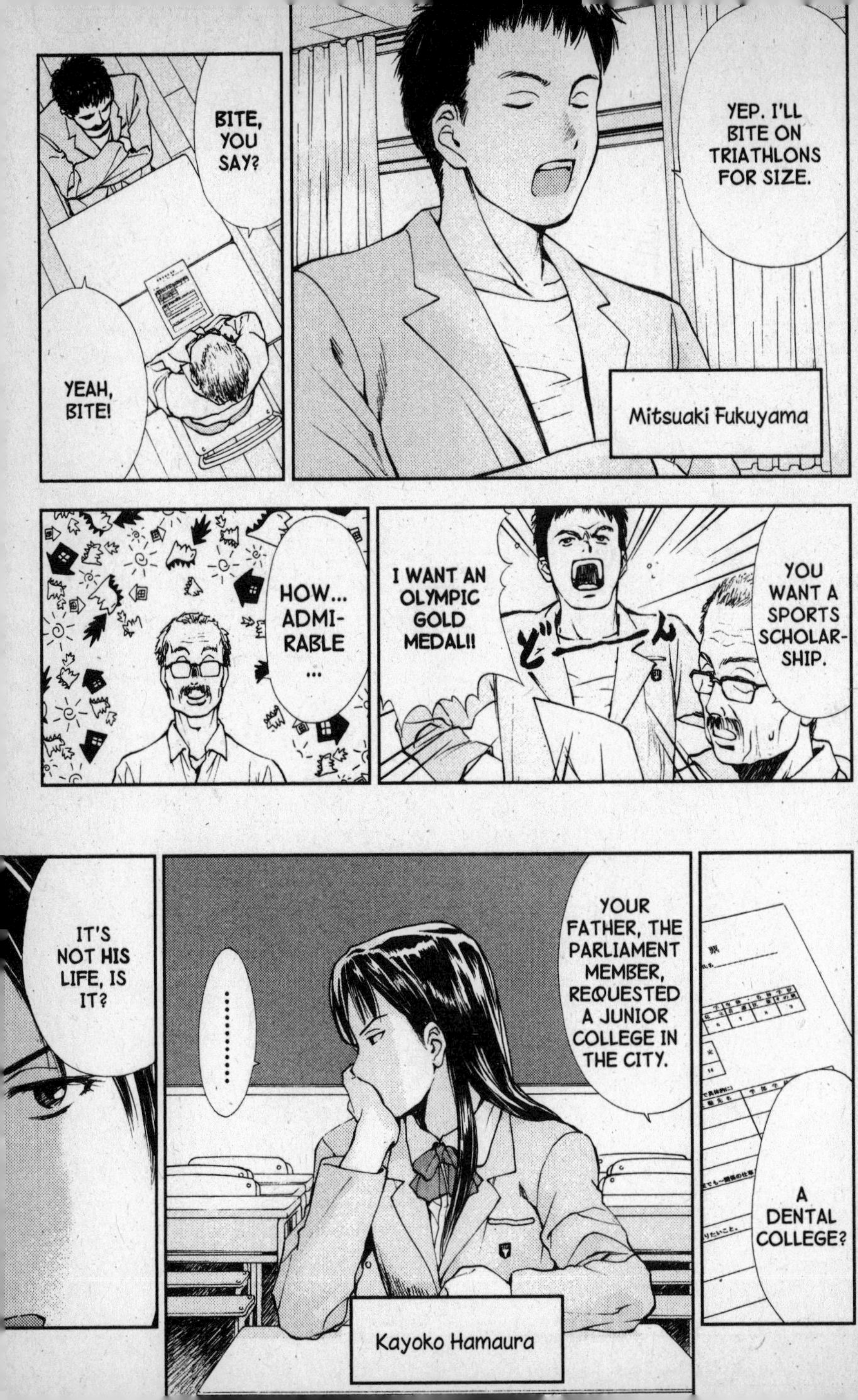
YEP. I'LL BITE ON TRIATHLONS FOR SIZE.
Mitsuaki Fukuyama
BITE, YOU SAY?
YEAH, BITE!
YOU WANT A SPORTS SCHOLARSHIP.
I WANT AN OLYMPIC GOLD MEDAL!!
どーーん
HOW... ADMIRABLE...
A DENTAL COLLEGE?
YOUR FATHER, THE PARLIAMENT MEMBER, REQUESTED A JUNIOR COLLEGE IN THE CITY.
....
Kayoko Hamaura
IT'S NOT HIS LIFE, IS IT?

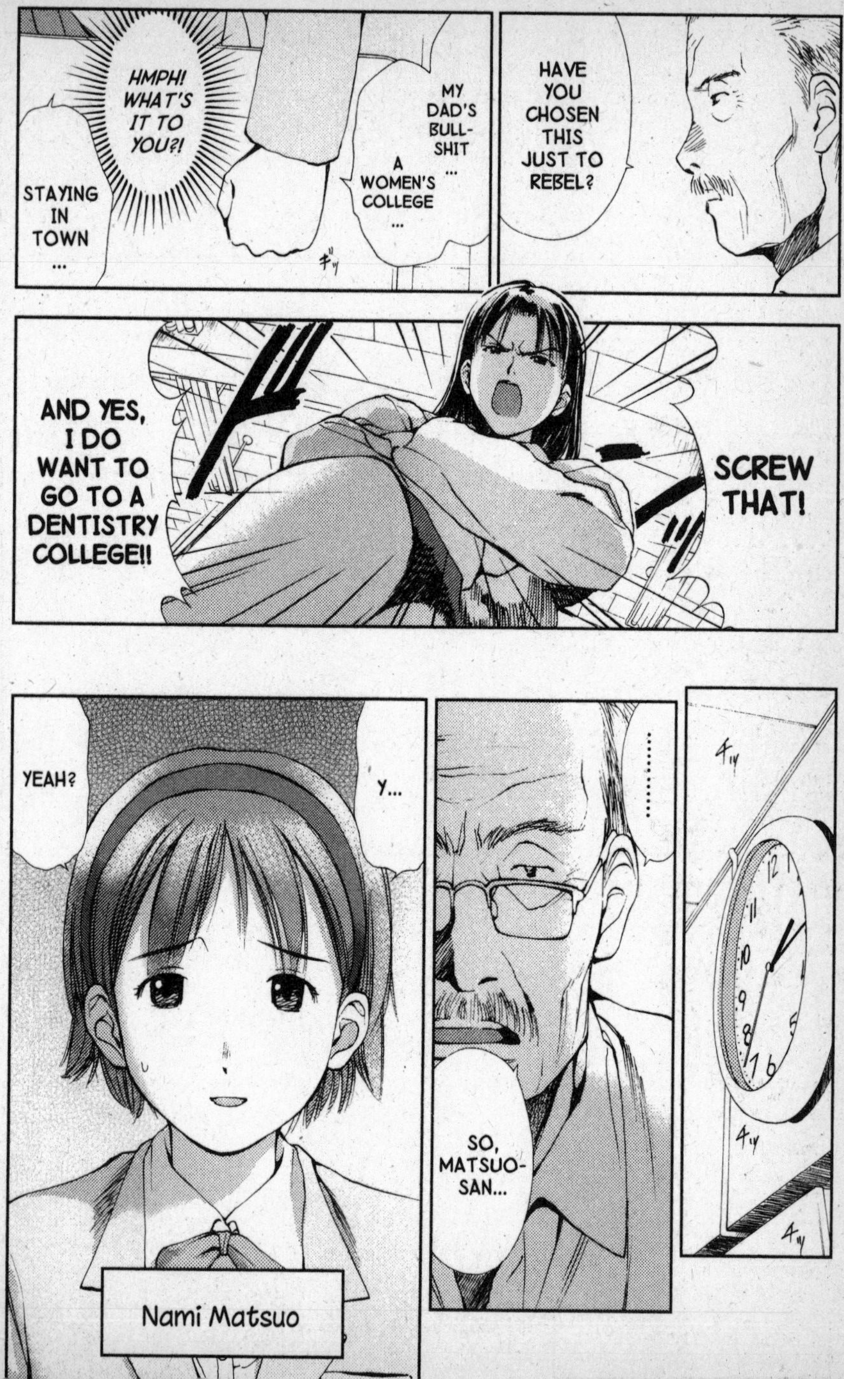
HAVE YOU CHOSEN THIS JUST TO REBEL?
MY DAD'S BULL-SHIT ...
A WOMEN'S COLLEGE ...
HMPH! WHAT'S IT TO YOU?!
STAYING IN TOWN ...
ギッ
SCREW THAT!
AND YES, I DO WANT TO GO TO A DENTISTRY COLLEGE!!
チッ
チッ
チッ
......
SO, MATSUO-SAN...
Y...
YEAH?
Nami Matsuo

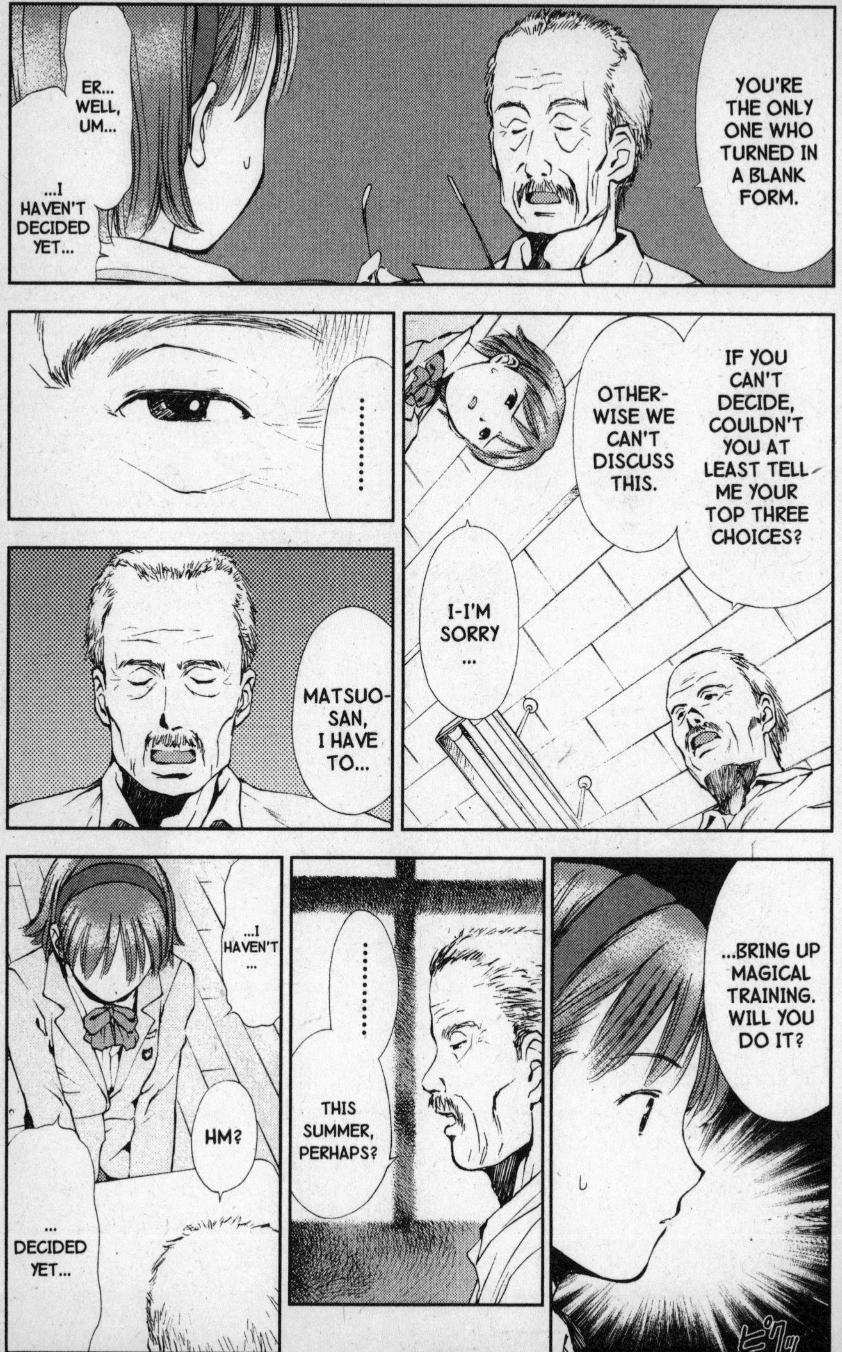
YOU'RE THE ONLY ONE WHO TURNED IN A BLANK FORM.
ER... WELL, UM...
...I HAVEN'T DECIDED YET...
IF YOU CAN'T DECIDE, COULDN'T YOU AT LEAST TELL ME YOUR TOP THREE CHOICES?
OTHER-WISE WE CAN'T DISCUSS THIS.
I-I'M SORRY ...
....
MATSUO-SAN, I HAVE TO...
...BRING UP MAGICAL TRAINING. WILL YOU DO IT?
....
THIS SUMMER, PERHAPS?
...I HAVEN'T ...
HM?
... DECIDED YET...

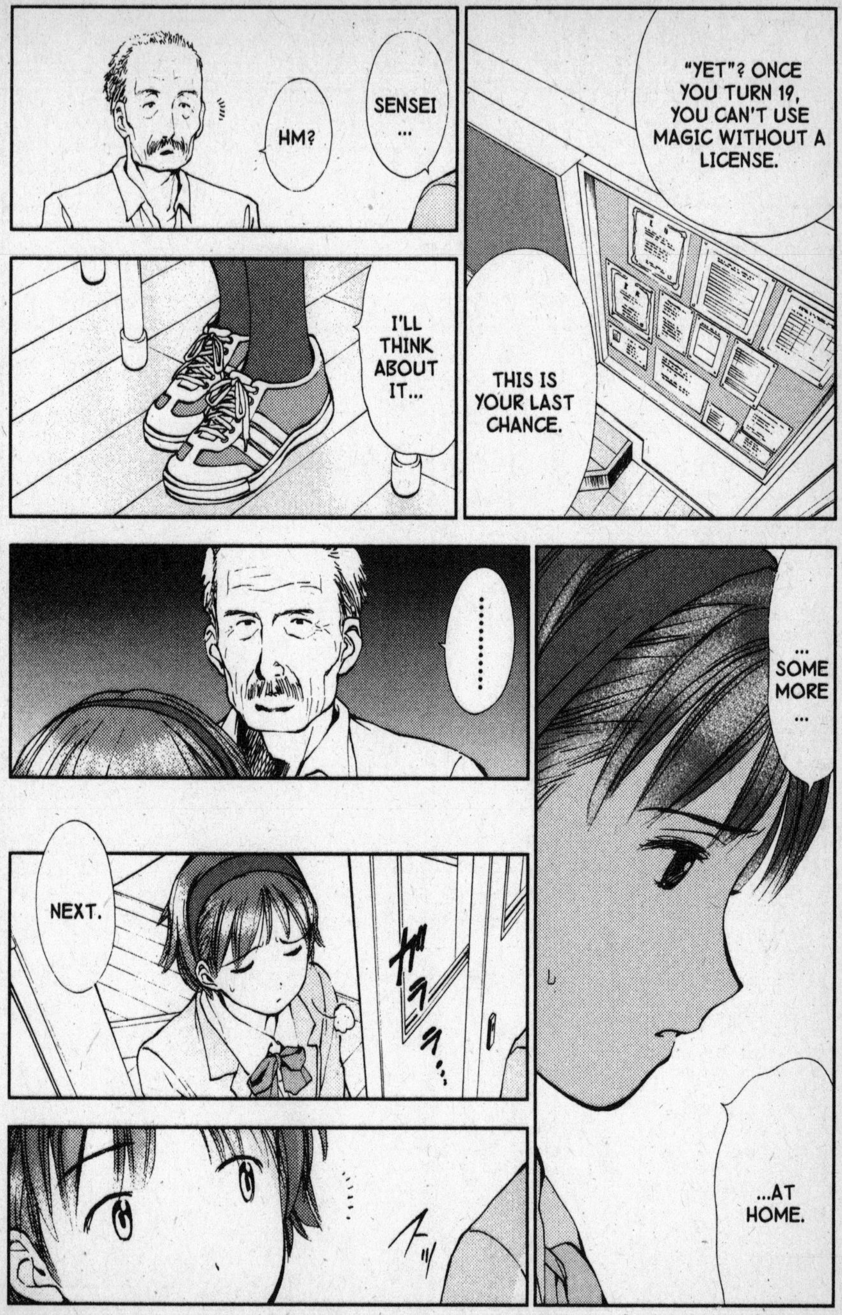
"YET"? ONCE YOU TURN 19, YOU CAN'T USE MAGIC WITHOUT A LICENSE.
THIS IS YOUR LAST CHANCE.
SENSEI ...
HM?
I'LL THINK ABOUT IT...
... SOME MORE ...
...AT HOME.
....
NEXT.
ガラララ…
スッ

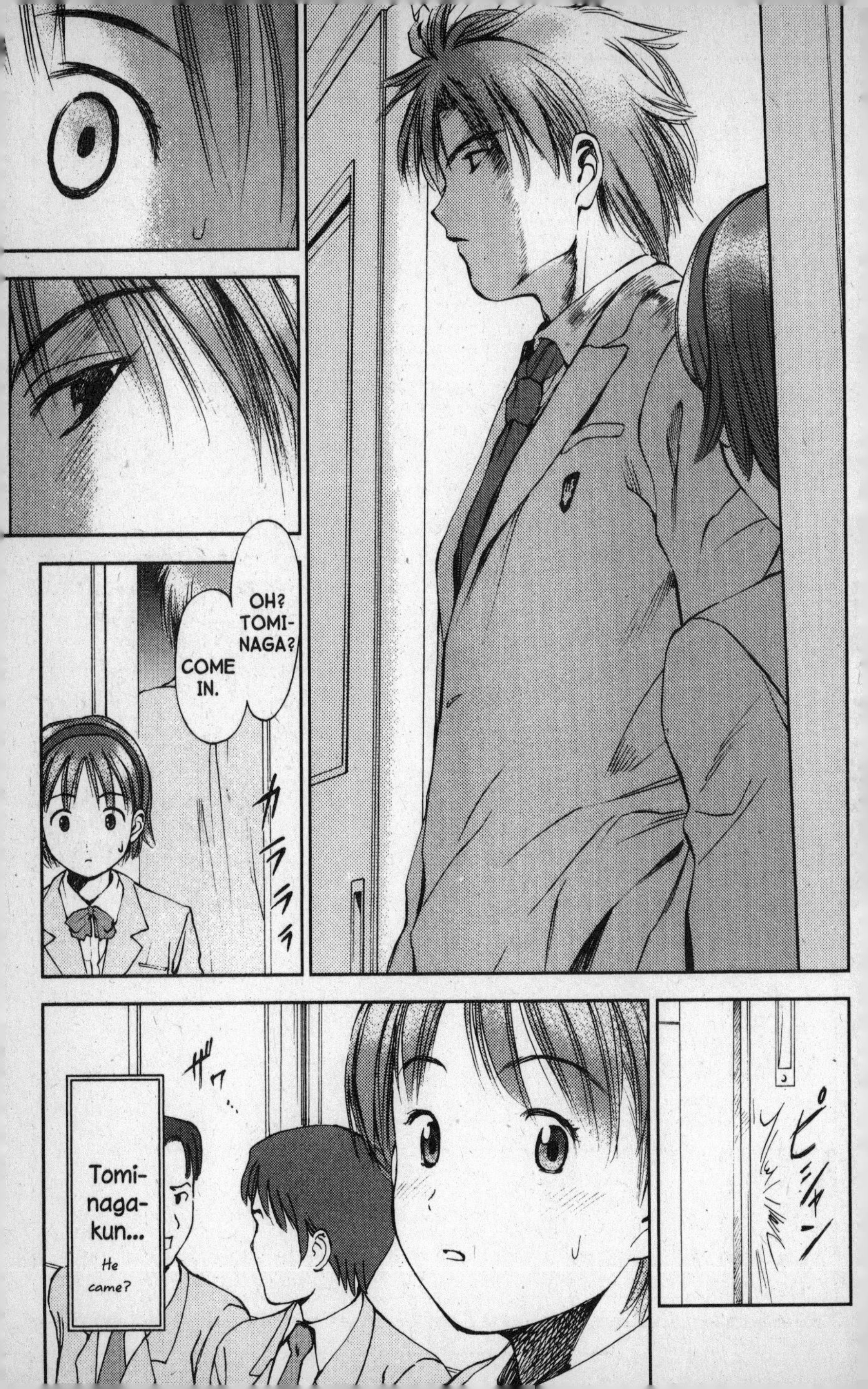
OH? TOMI-NAGA?
COME IN.
カラララ
ピシャン
ザワ...
Tomi-naga-kun...
He came?

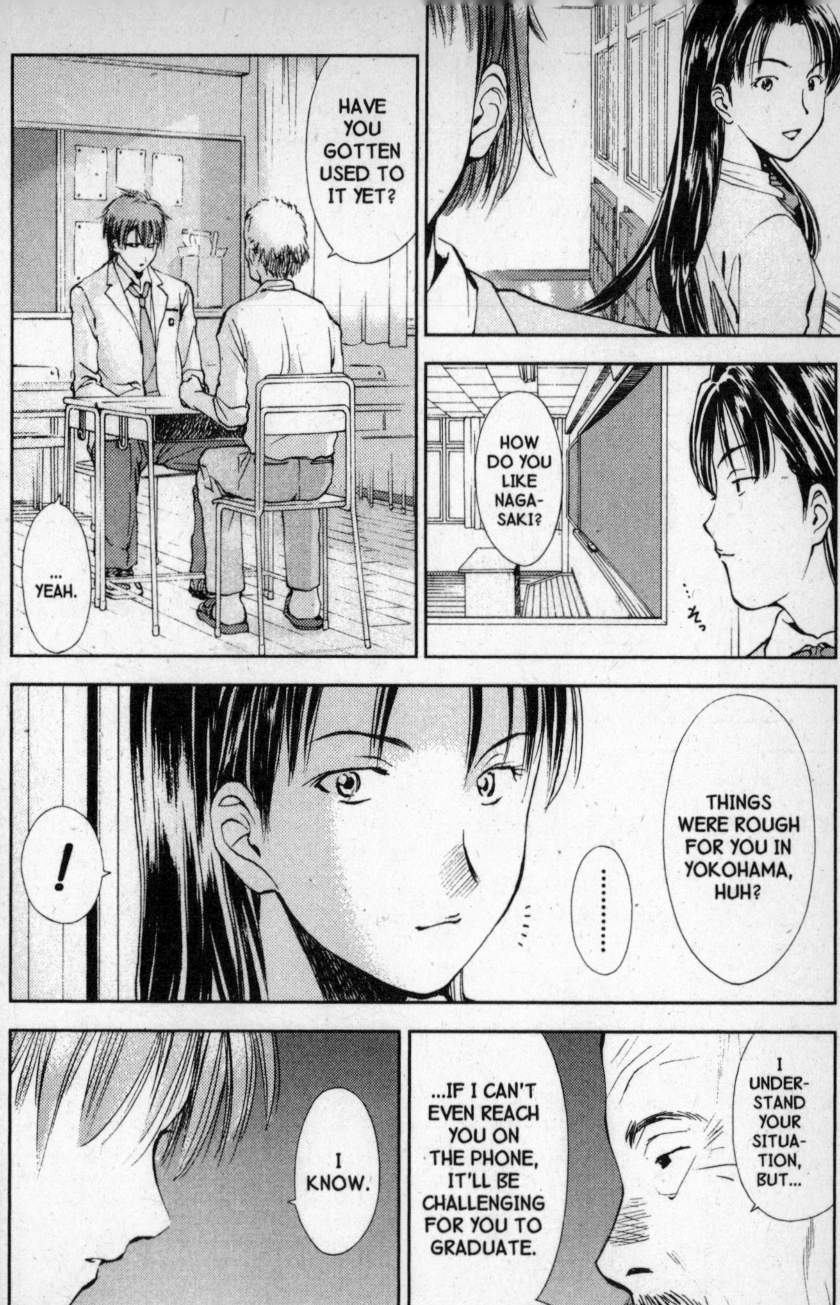
HOW DO YOU LIKE NAGA-SAKI?
HAVE YOU GOTTEN USED TO IT YET?
... YEAH.
THINGS WERE ROUGH FOR YOU IN YOKOHAMA, HUH?
......
!
I UNDER-STAND YOUR SITUA-TION, BUT...
...IF I CAN'T EVEN REACH YOU ON THE PHONE, IT'LL BE CHALLENGING FOR YOU TO GRADUATE.
I KNOW.

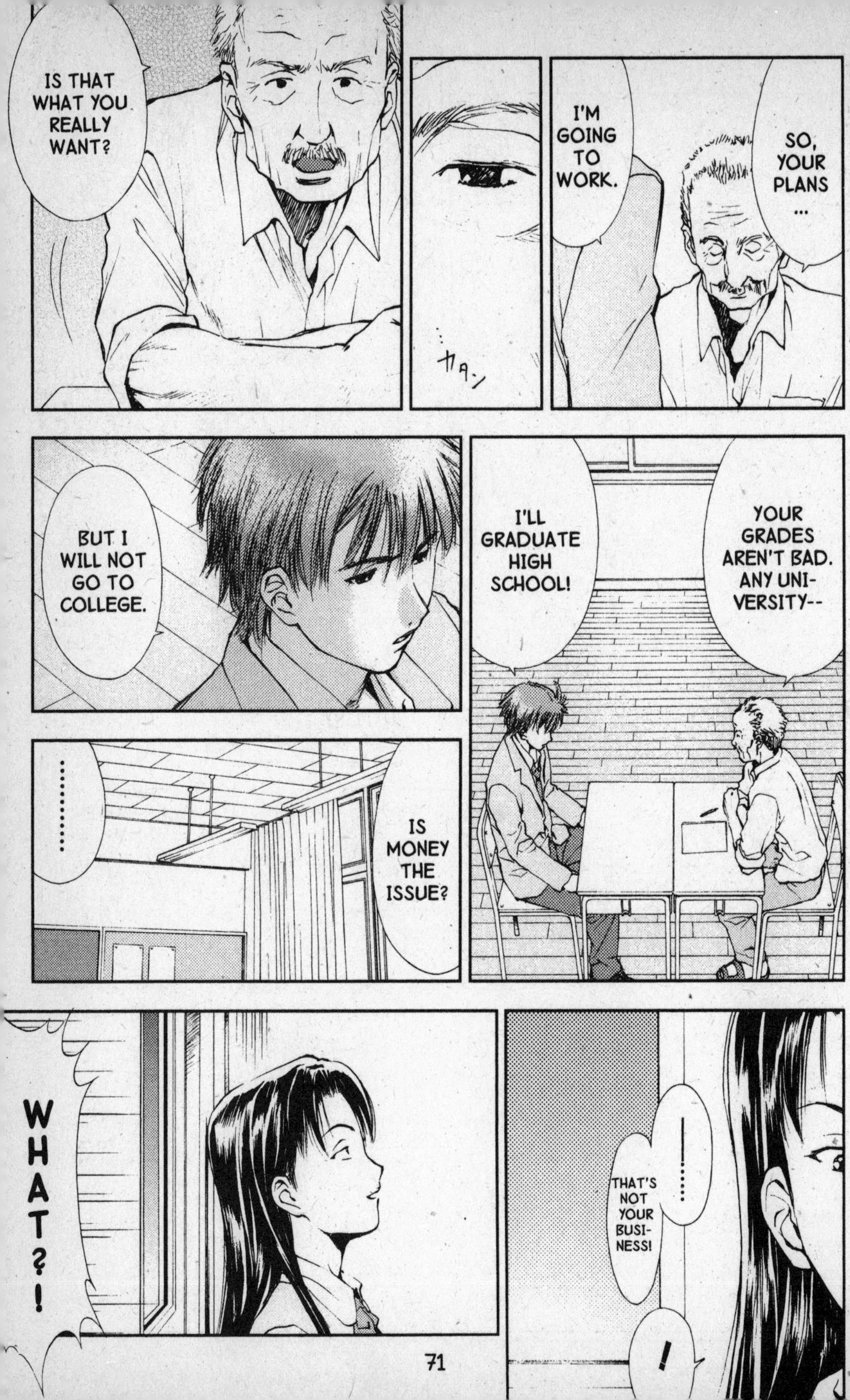

SO, YOUR PLANS ...
I'M GOING TO WORK.
IS THAT WHAT YOU REALLY WANT?
YOUR GRADES AREN'T BAD. ANY UNI-VERSITY--
I'LL GRADUATE HIGH SCHOOL!
BUT I WILL NOT GO TO COLLEGE.
IS MONEY THE ISSUE?
....
......
THAT'S NOT YOUR BUSI-NESS!
!
WHAT?!

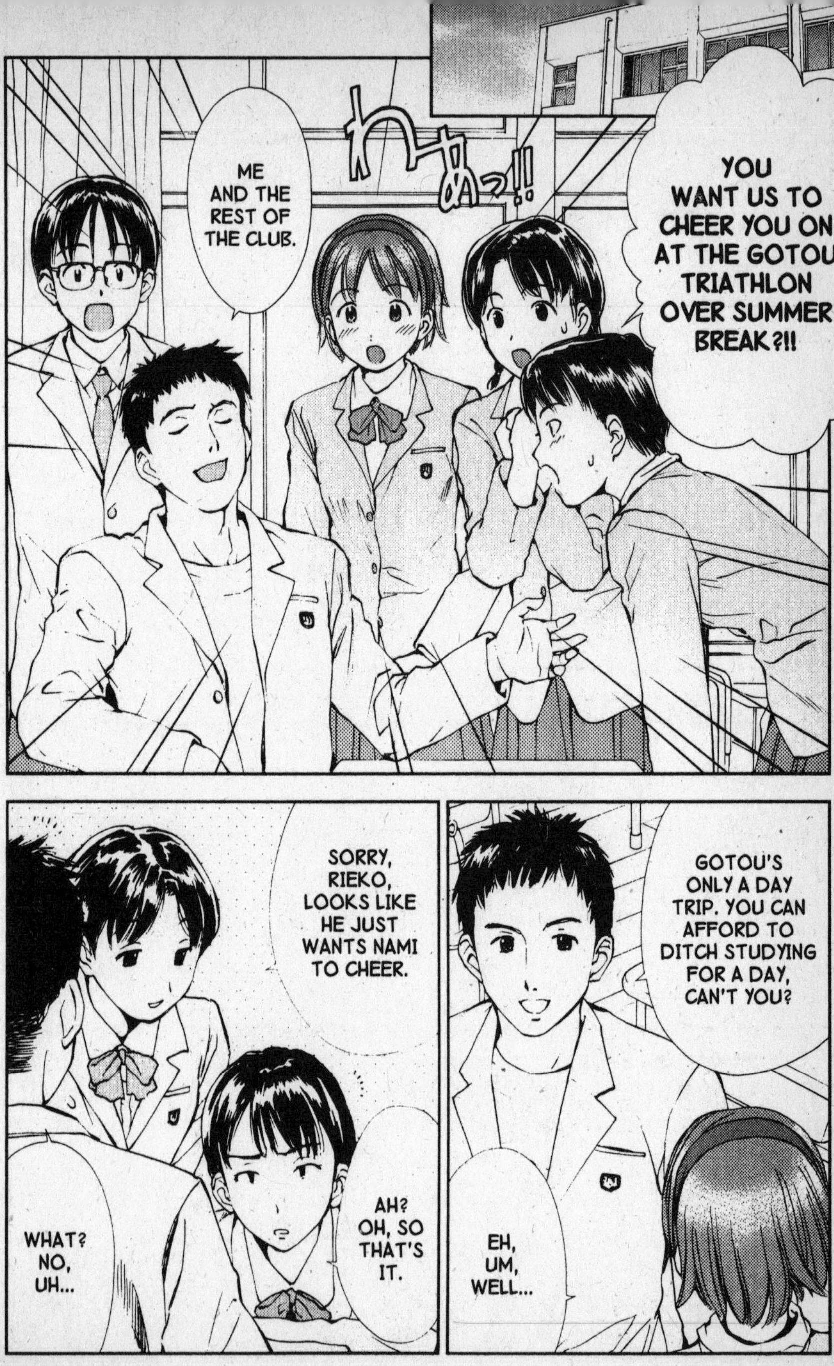
YOU WANT US TO CHEER YOU ON AT THE GOTOU TRIATHLON OVER SUMMER BREAK?!!
わぁっ!!
ME AND THE REST OF THE CLUB.
GOTOU'S ONLY A DAY TRIP. YOU CAN AFFORD TO DITCH STUDYING FOR A DAY, CAN'T YOU?
EH, UM, WELL...
SORRY, RIEKO, LOOKS LIKE HE JUST WANTS NAMI TO CHEER.
AH? OH, SO THAT'S IT.
WHAT? NO, UH...

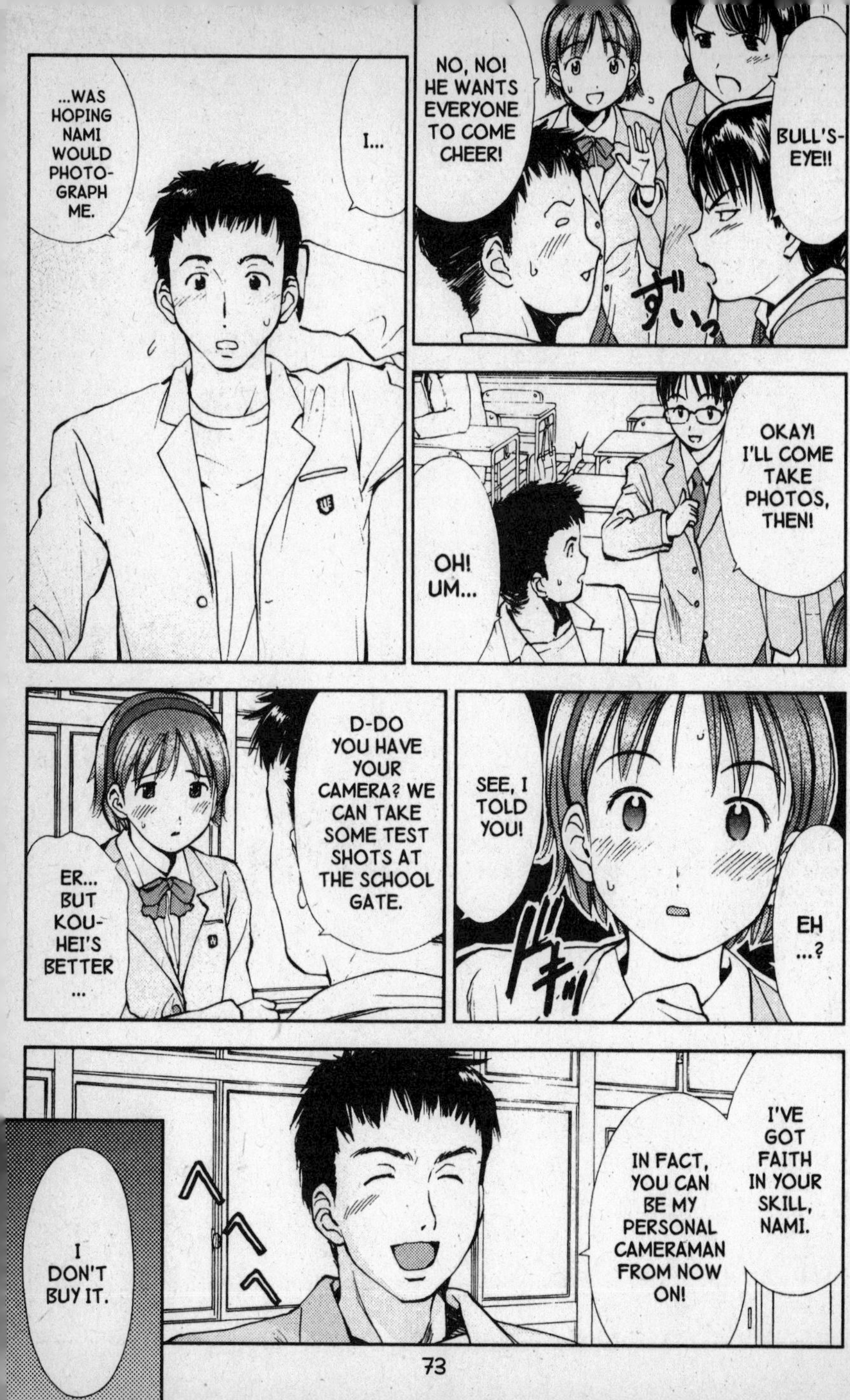
BULL'S-EYE!!
NO, NO! HE WANTS EVERYONE TO COME CHEER!
ずいっ
OKAY! I'LL COME TAKE PHOTOS, THEN!
OH! UM...
I...
...WAS HOPING NAMI WOULD PHOTOGRAPH ME.
EH ...?
SEE, I TOLD YOU!
D-DO YOU HAVE YOUR CAMERA? WE CAN TAKE SOME TEST SHOTS AT THE SCHOOL GATE.
ER... BUT KOU-HEI'S BETTER ...
I'VE GOT FAITH IN YOUR SKILL, NAMI.
IN FACT, YOU CAN BE MY PERSONAL CAMERAMAN FROM NOW ON!
I DON'T BUY IT.

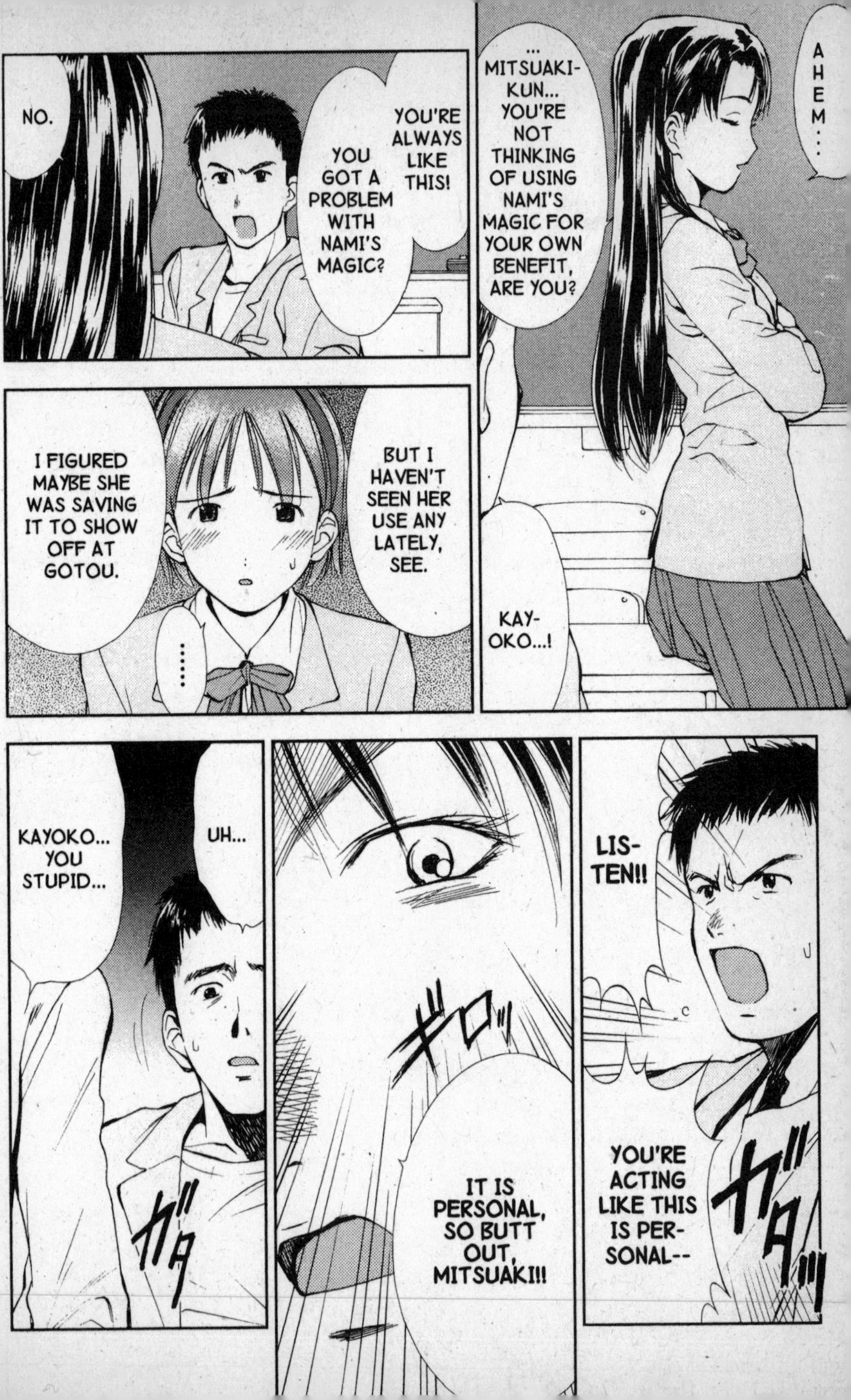
AHEM...
... MITSUAKI-KUN... YOU'RE NOT THINKING OF USING NAMI'S MAGIC FOR YOUR OWN BENEFIT, ARE YOU?
KAY-OKO...!
YOU'RE ALWAYS LIKE THIS!
YOU GOT A PROBLEM WITH NAMI'S MAGIC?
NO.
BUT I HAVEN'T SEEN HER USE ANY LATELY, SEE.
I FIGURED MAYBE SHE WAS SAVING IT TO SHOW OFF AT GOTOU.
......
LIS-TEN!!
YOU'RE ACTING LIKE THIS IS PER-SONAL--
ガタッ
ギロッ
IT IS PERSONAL, SO BUTT OUT, MITSUAKI!!
UH...
KAYOKO... YOU STUPID...
ガタ

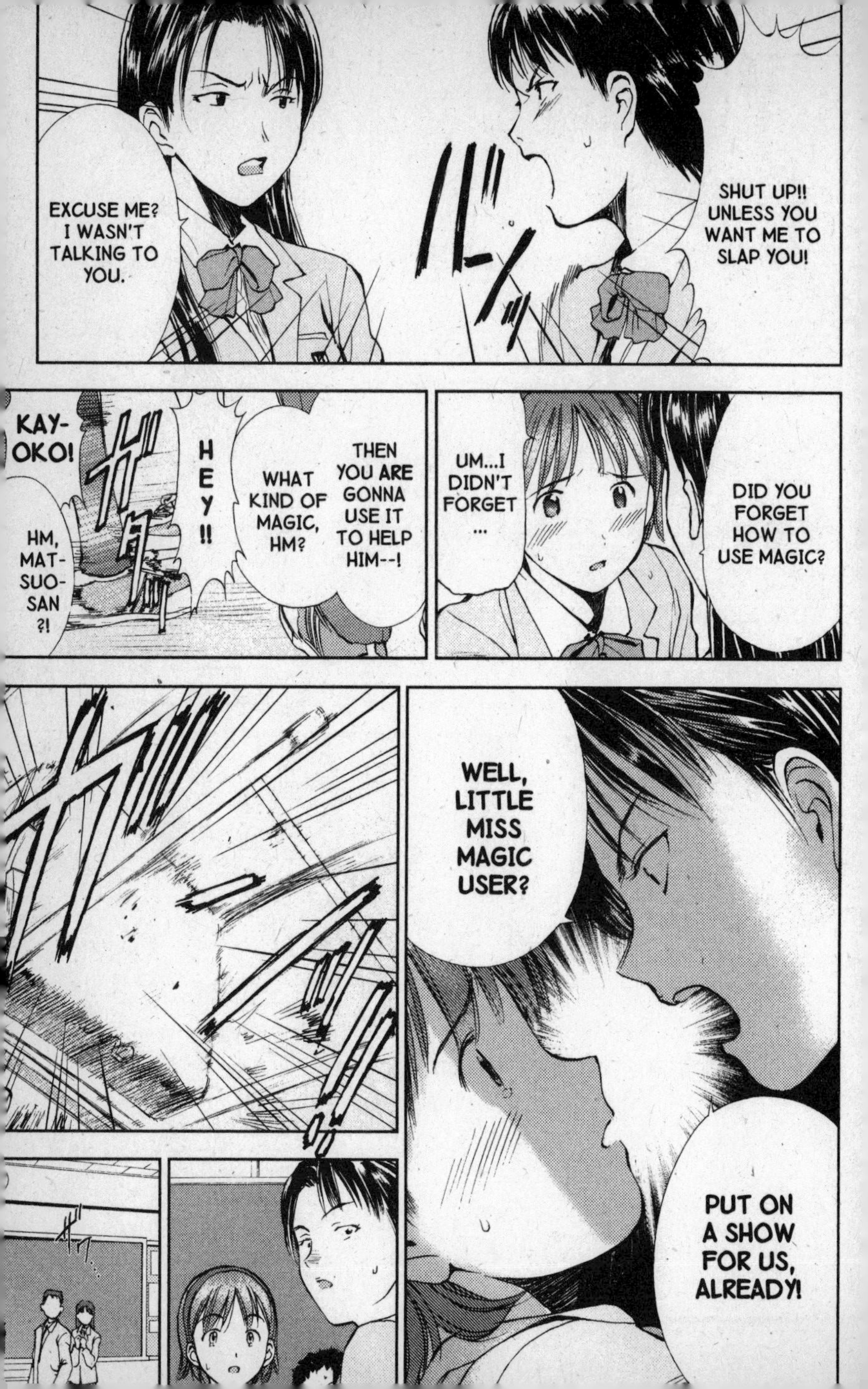
SHUT UP!! UNLESS YOU WANT ME TO SLAP YOU!
EXCUSE ME? I WASN'T TALKING TO YOU.
DID YOU FORGET HOW TO USE MAGIC?
UM...I DIDN'T FORGET ...
THEN YOU ARE GONNA USE IT TO HELP HIM--!
WHAT KIND OF MAGIC, HM?
HEY!!
KAY-OKO!
HM, MAT-SUO-SAN ?!
WELL, LITTLE MISS MAGIC USER?
PUT ON A SHOW FOR US, ALREADY!

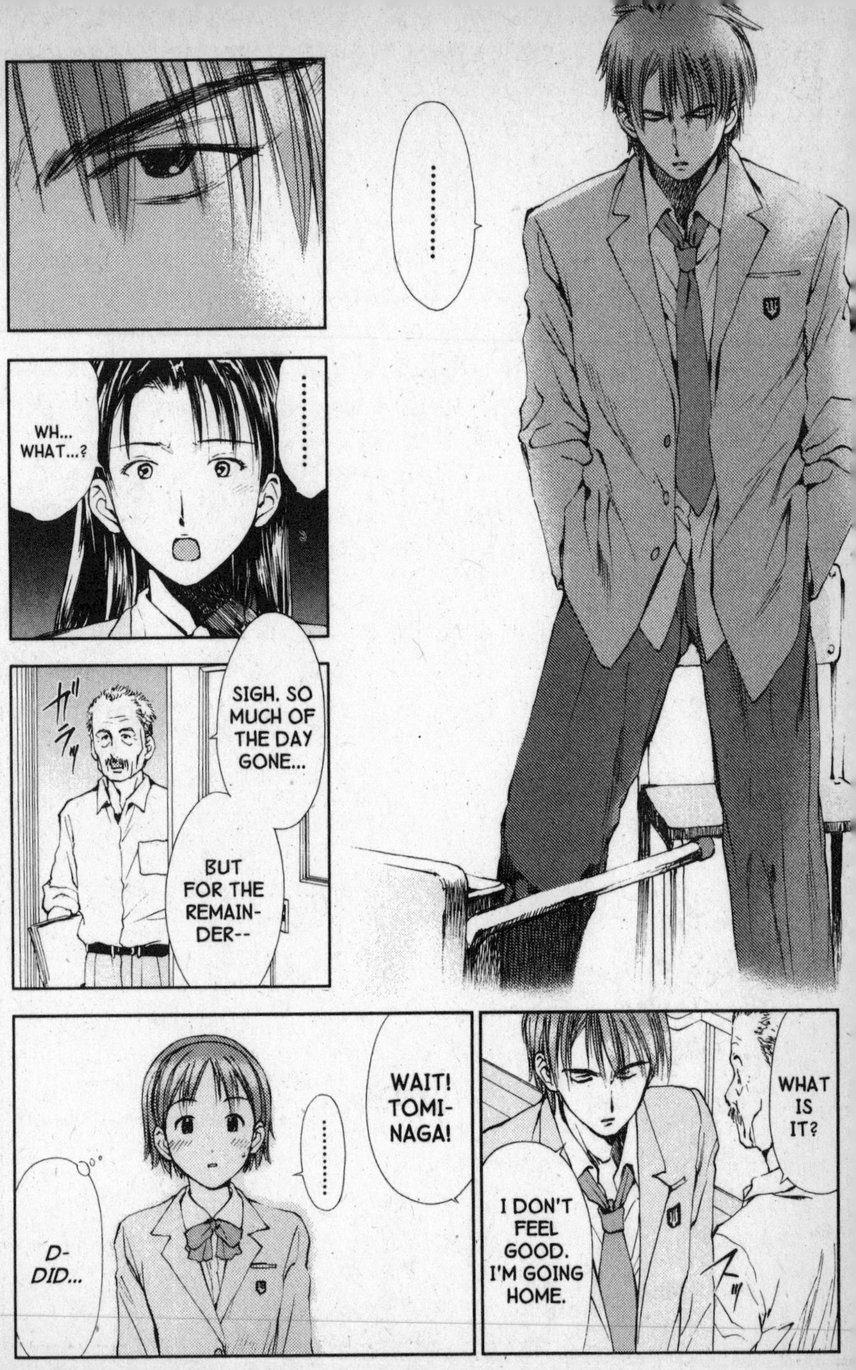
......
......
WH... WHAT...?
ガラッ
SIGH. SO MUCH OF THE DAY GONE...
BUT FOR THE REMAIN-DER--
WHAT IS IT?
I DON'T FEEL GOOD. I'M GOING HOME.
スッ
WAIT! TOMI-NAGA!
......
D-DID...

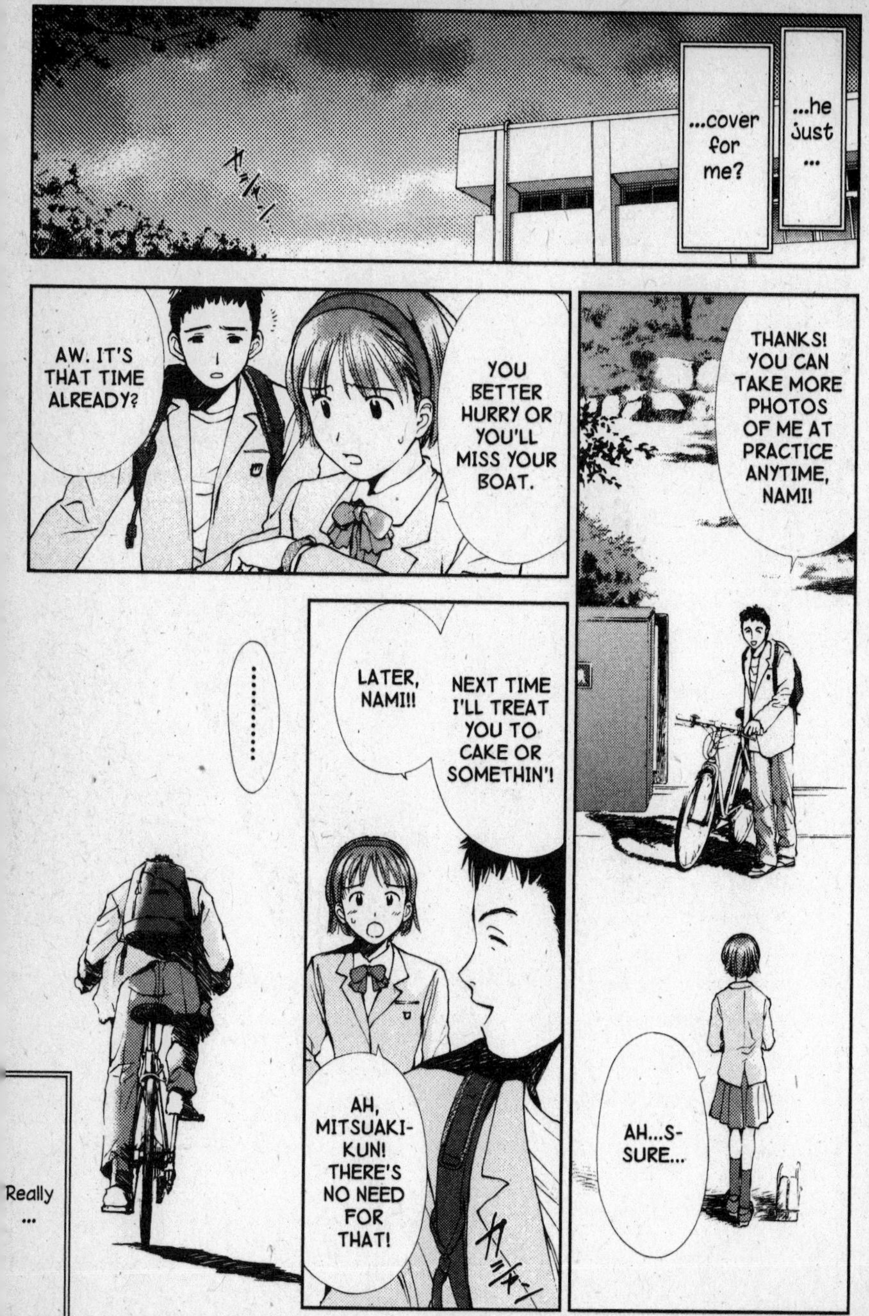
...he just ...
...cover for me?
THANKS! YOU CAN TAKE MORE PHOTOS OF ME AT PRACTICE ANYTIME, NAMI!
AH...S-SURE...
YOU BETTER HURRY OR YOU'LL MISS YOUR BOAT.
AW. IT'S THAT TIME ALREADY?
NEXT TIME I'LL TREAT YOU TO CAKE OR SOMETHIN'!
LATER, NAMI!!
AH, MITSUAKI-KUN! THERE'S NO NEED FOR THAT!
......
Really ...

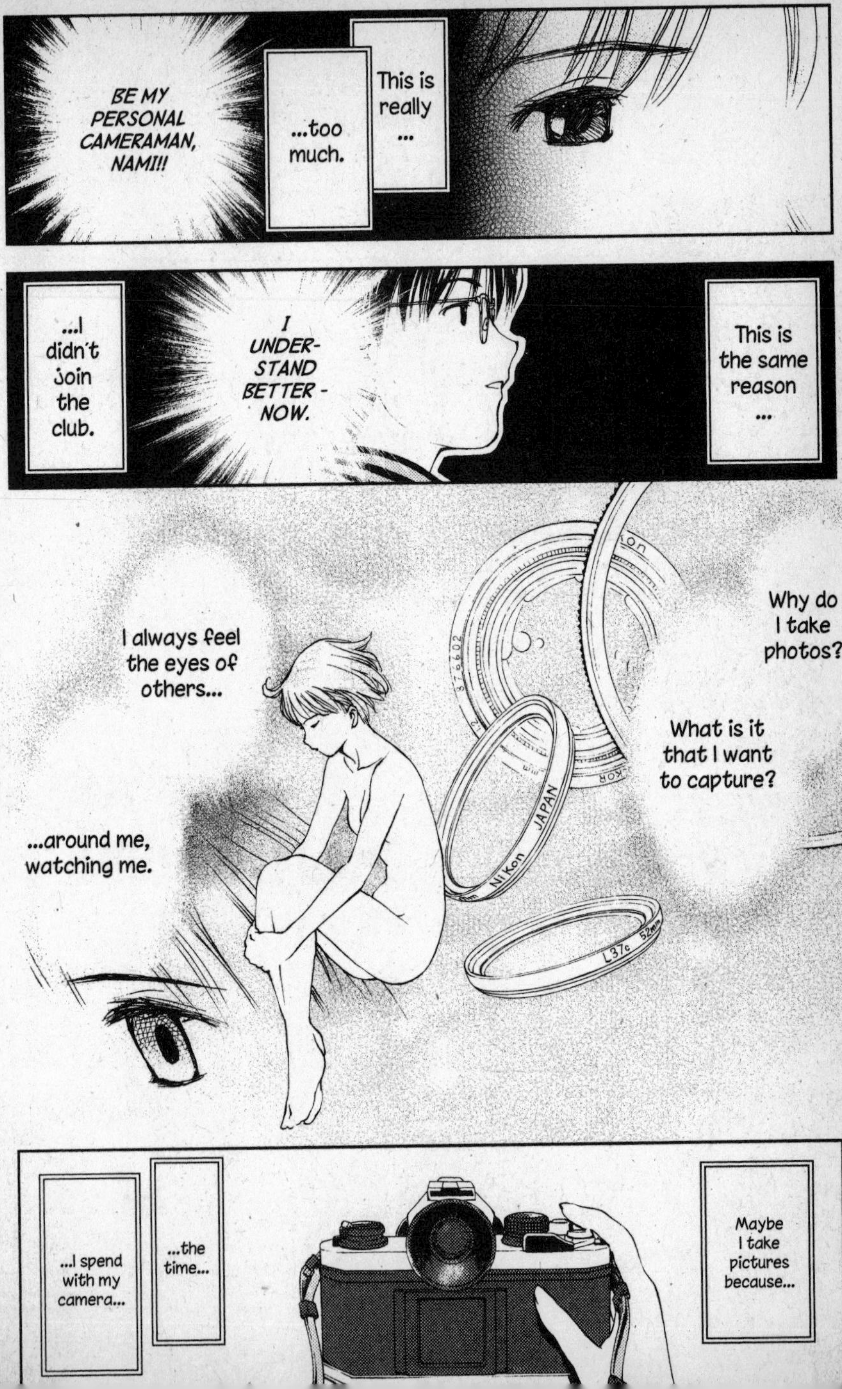
This is really ...
...too much.
BE MY PERSONAL CAMERAMAN, NAMI!!
This is the same reason ...
I UNDER-STAND BETTER - NOW.
...I didn't join the club.
Why do I take photos?
What is it that I want to capture?
I always feel the eyes of others...
...around me, watching me.
Nikon JAPAN
L37c 52mm
Maybe I take pictures because...
...the time...
...I spend with my camera...

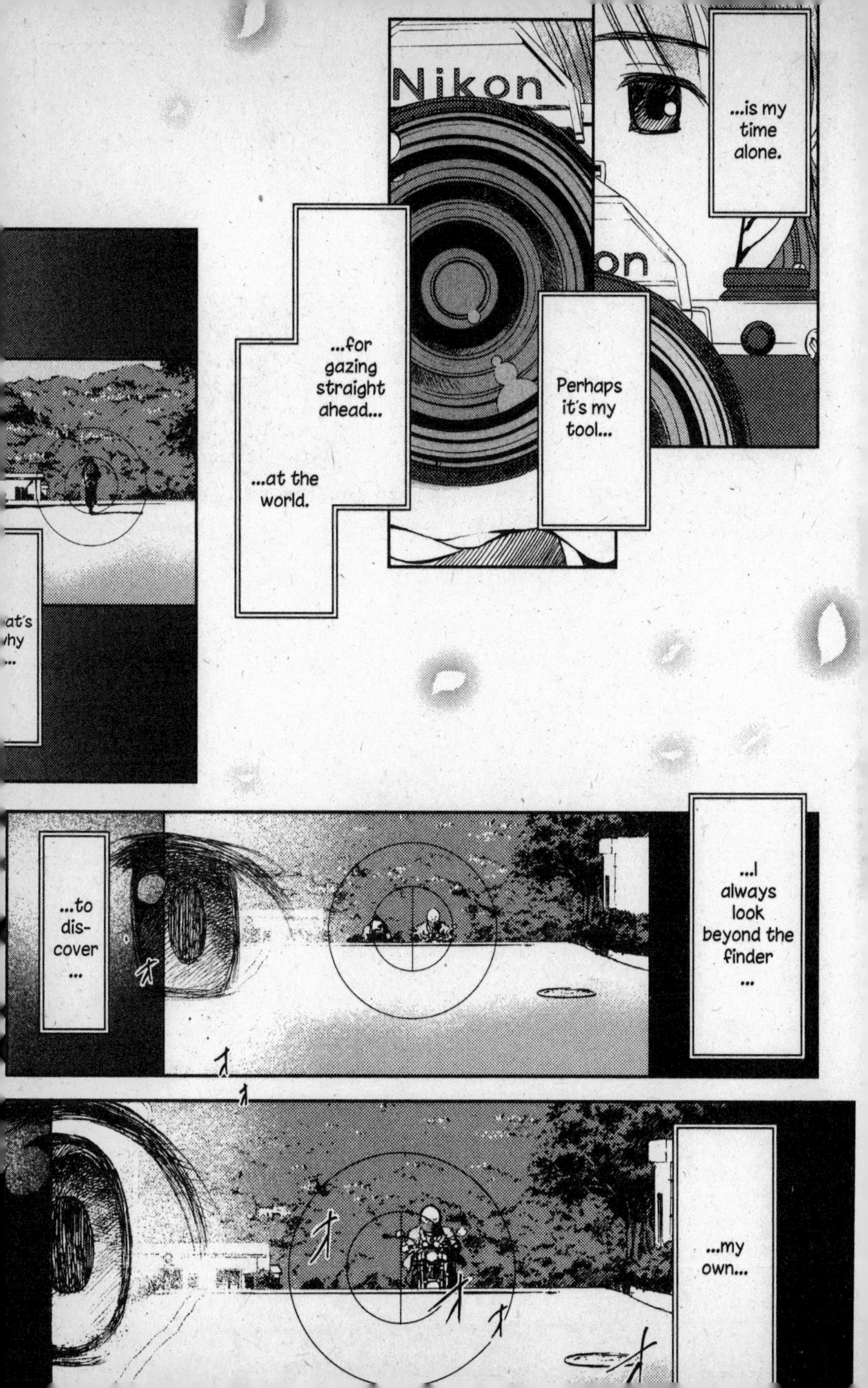
Nikon
...is my time alone.
Perhaps it's my tool...
...for gazing straight ahead...
...at the world.
at's why ...
...I always look beyond the finder ...
...to dis-cover ...
...my own...

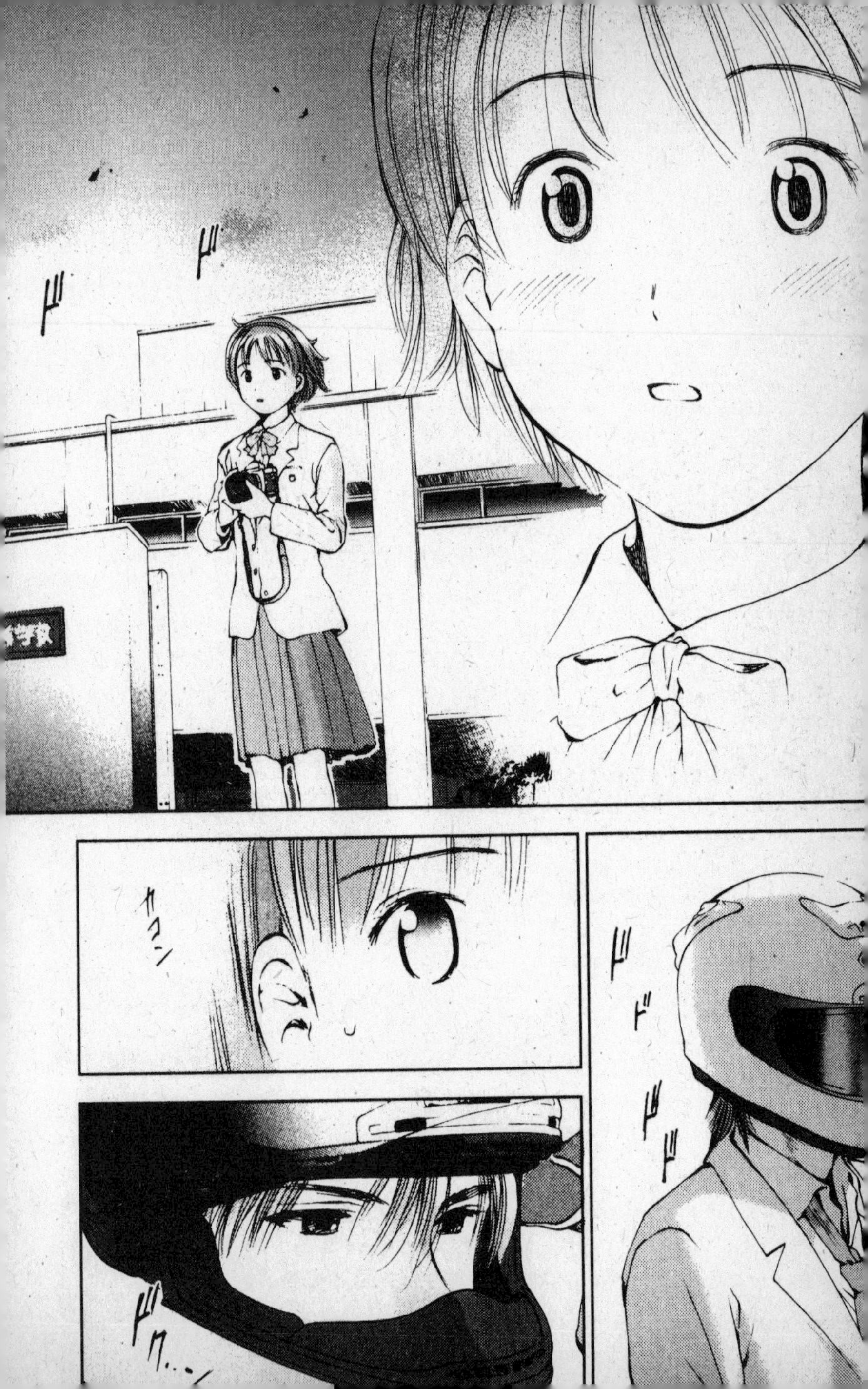
ドド
ドドドド
カコン
ドゥ…ン

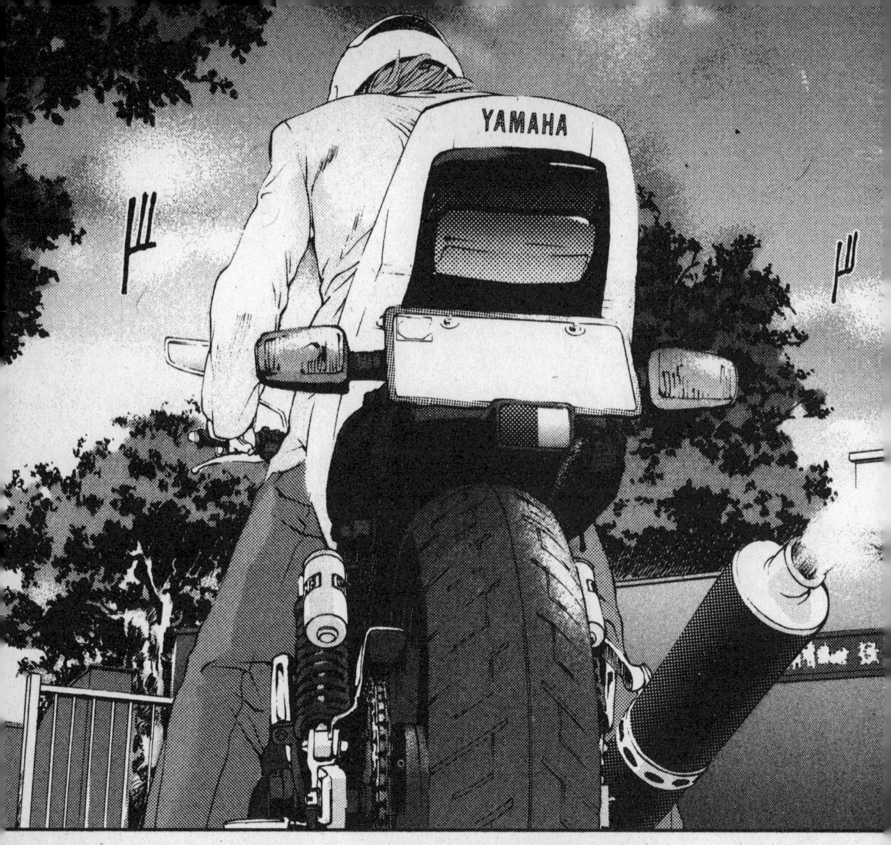
YAMAHA
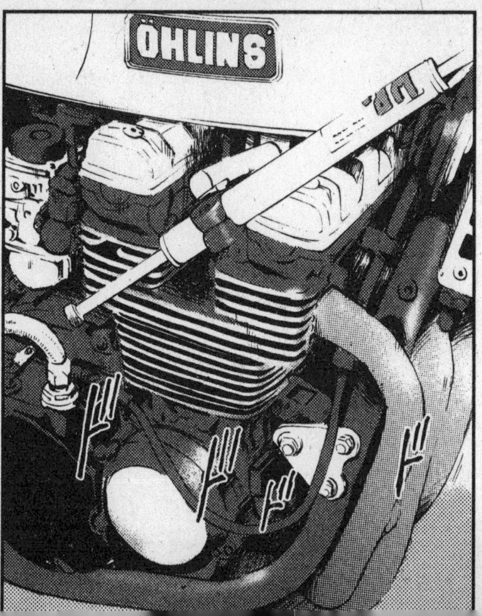
ÖHLINS
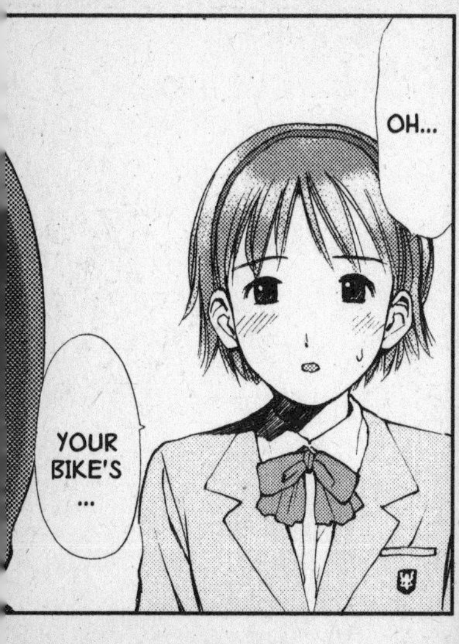
OH...
YOUR BIKE'S ...

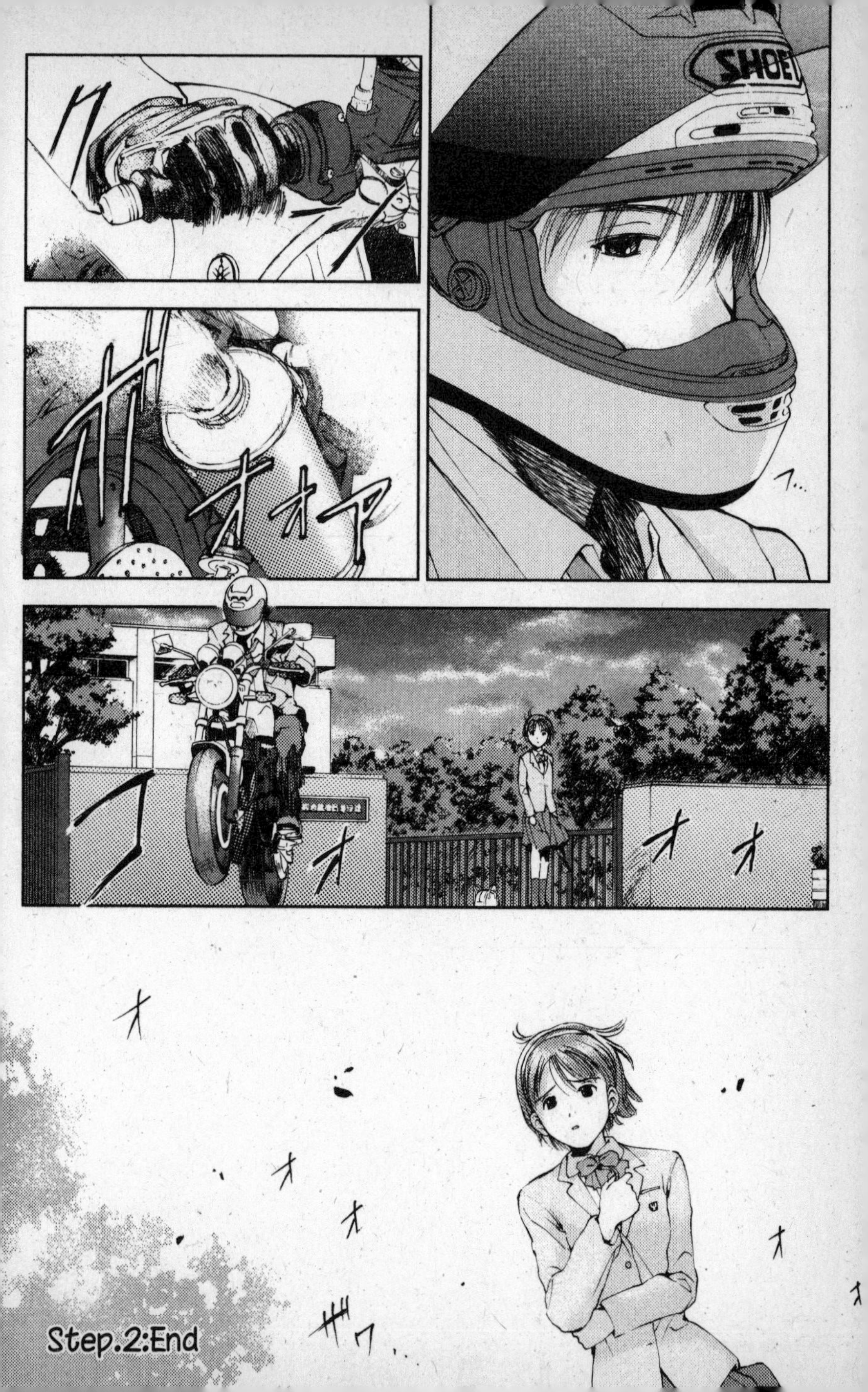
SHOEI
フ…
ク
ガオオア
ゴオオオオ
オ
オ
オ
オ
ザワ..
Step.2:End

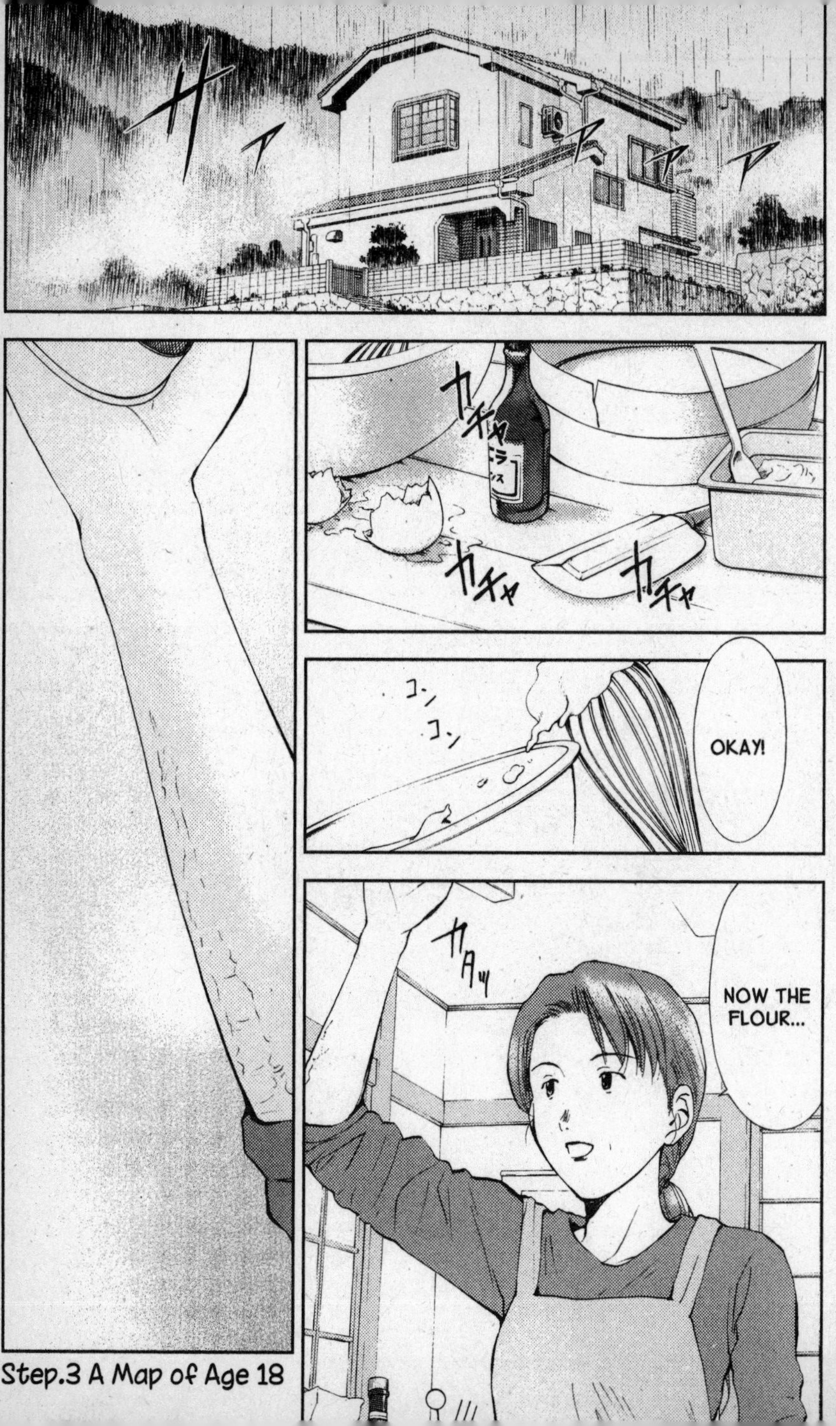
ザァァァァ
カチャ
カチャ
カチャ
コン
コン
OKAY!
ガタッ
NOW THE FLOUR...

Step.3 A Map of Age 18

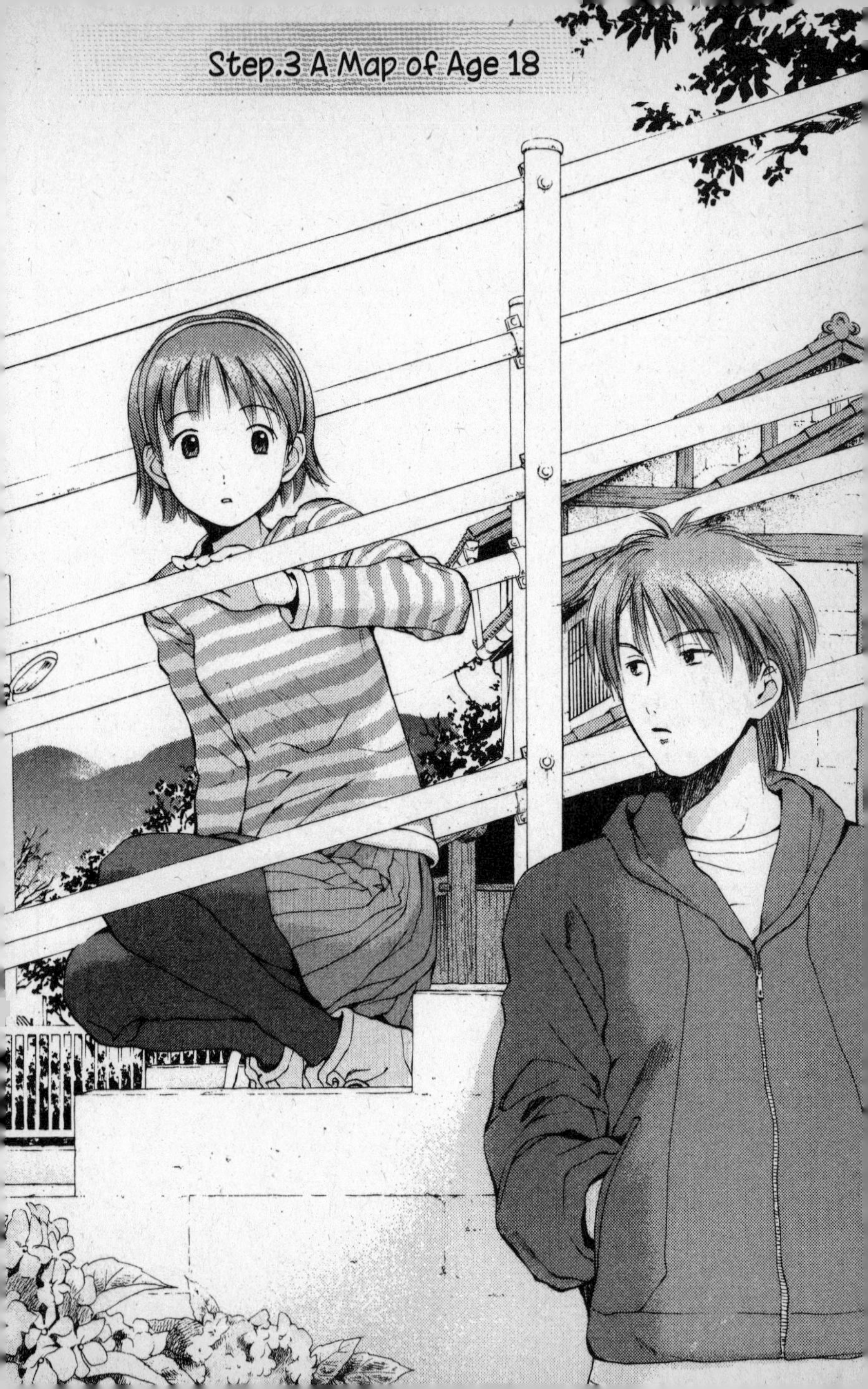
Step.3 A Map of Age 18

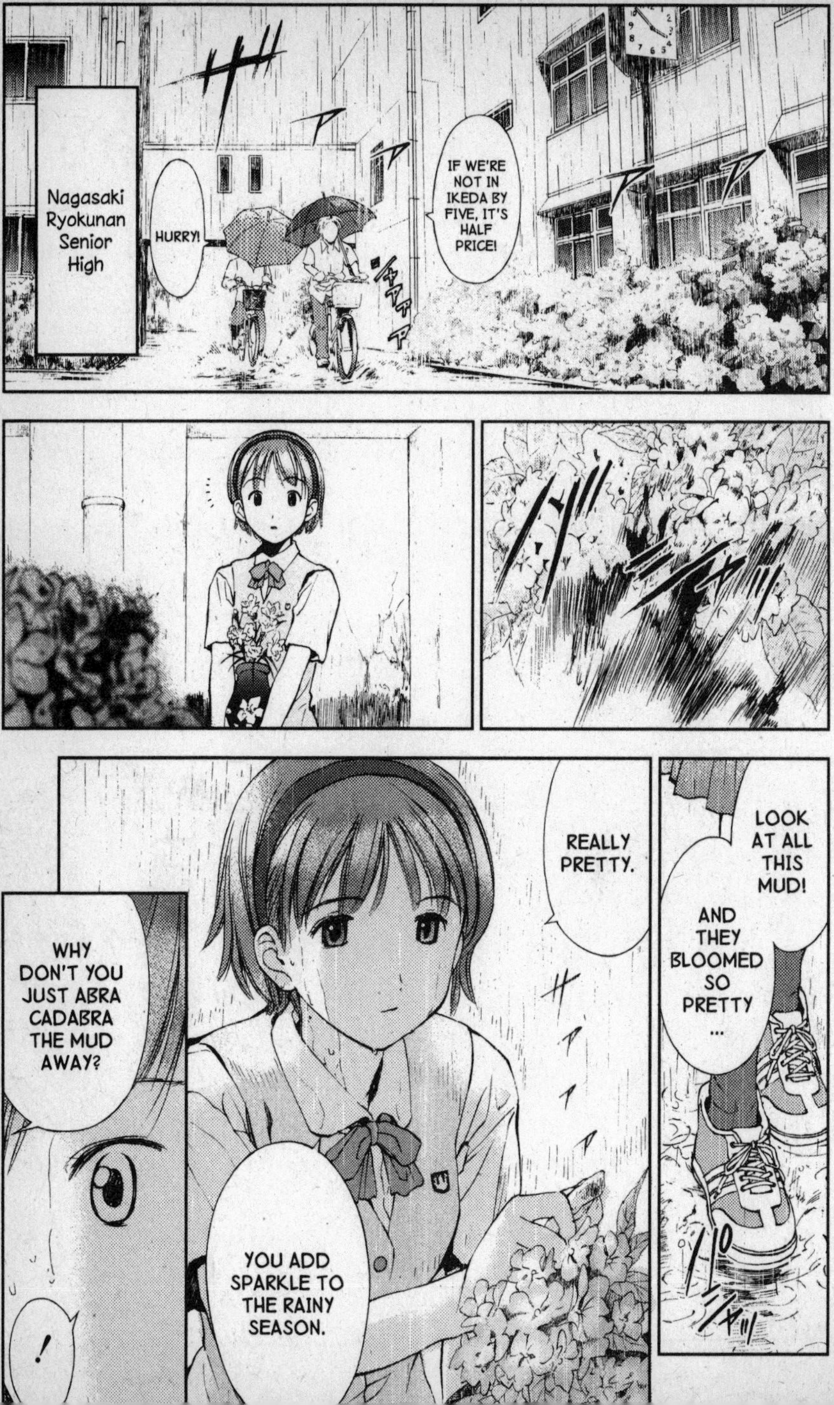
IF WE'RE NOT IN IKEDA BY FIVE, IT'S HALF PRICE!
HURRY!
Nagasaki Ryokunan Senior High
LOOK AT ALL THIS MUD!
AND THEY BLOOMED SO PRETTY ...
REALLY PRETTY.
YOU ADD SPARKLE TO THE RAINY SEASON.
WHY DON'T YOU JUST ABRA CADABRA THE MUD AWAY?
!

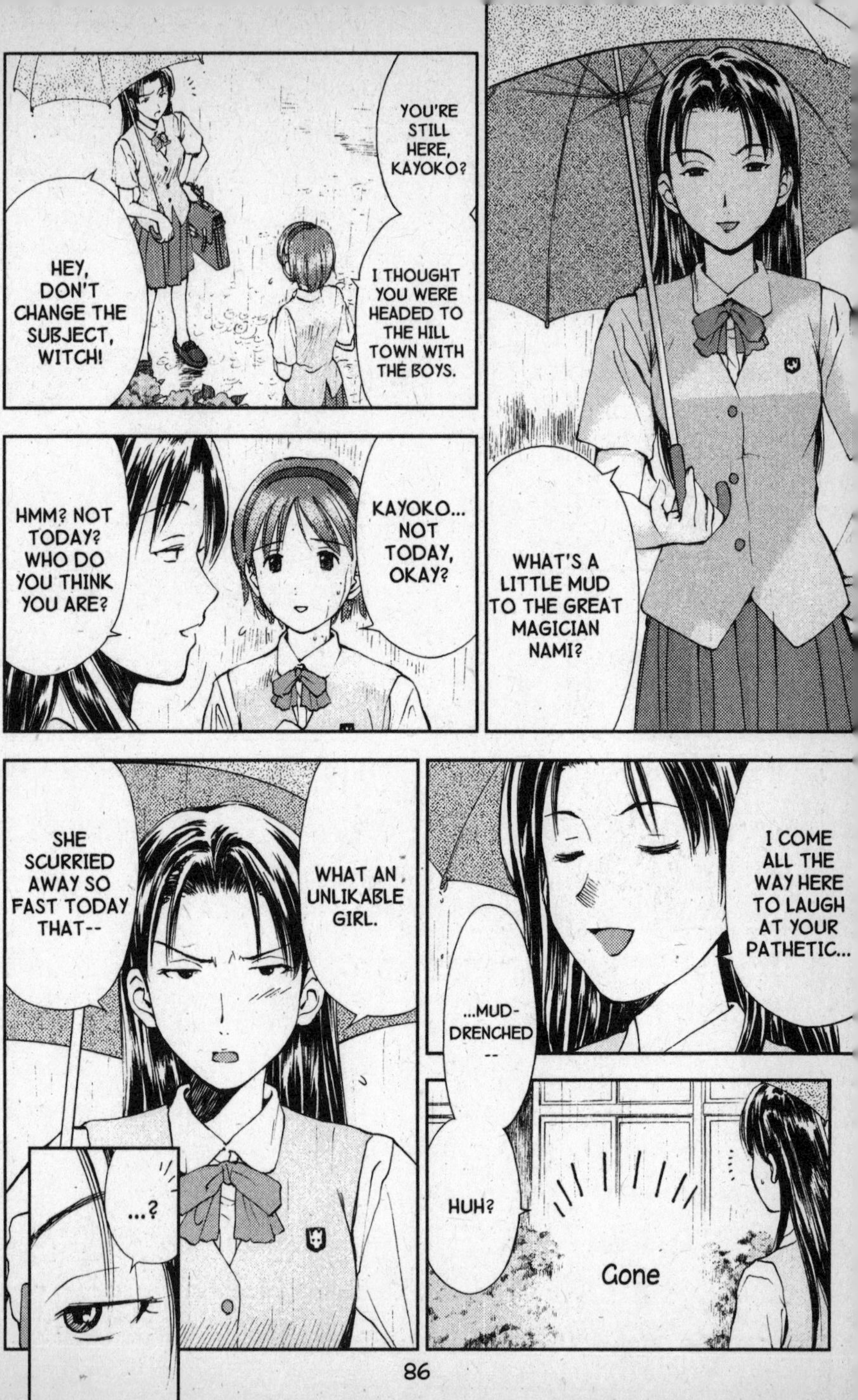
WHAT'S A LITTLE MUD TO THE GREAT MAGICIAN NAMI?
YOU'RE STILL HERE, KAYOKO?
I THOUGHT YOU WERE HEADED TO THE HILL TOWN WITH THE BOYS.
HEY, DON'T CHANGE THE SUBJECT, WITCH!
KAYOKO... NOT TODAY, OKAY?
HMM? NOT TODAY? WHO DO YOU THINK YOU ARE?
I COME ALL THE WAY HERE TO LAUGH AT YOUR PATHETIC...
...MUD-DRENCHED--
HUH?
Gone
WHAT AN UNLIKABLE GIRL.
SHE SCURRIED AWAY SO FAST TODAY THAT--
...?

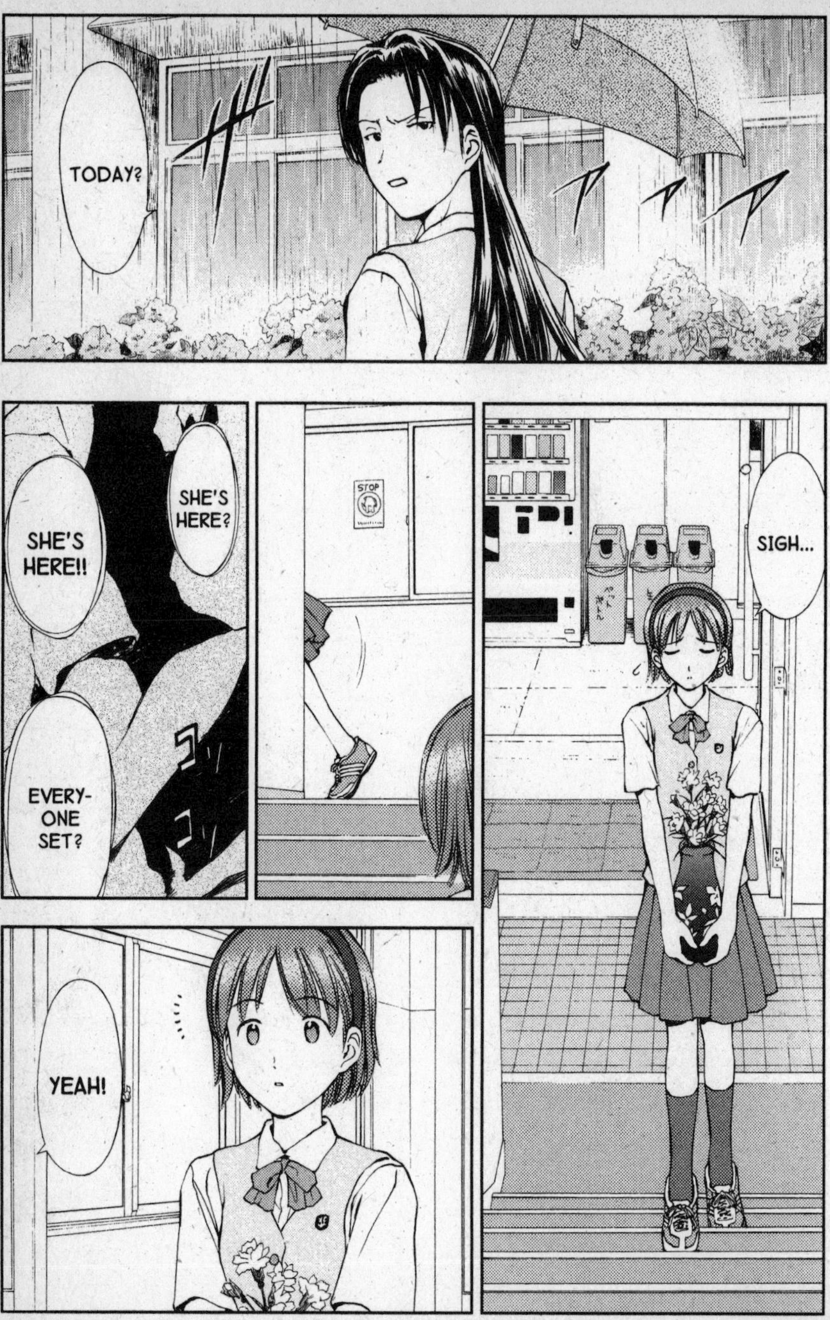
TODAY?
SIGH...
SHE'S HERE?
SHE'S HERE!!
EVERY-ONE SET?
YEAH!

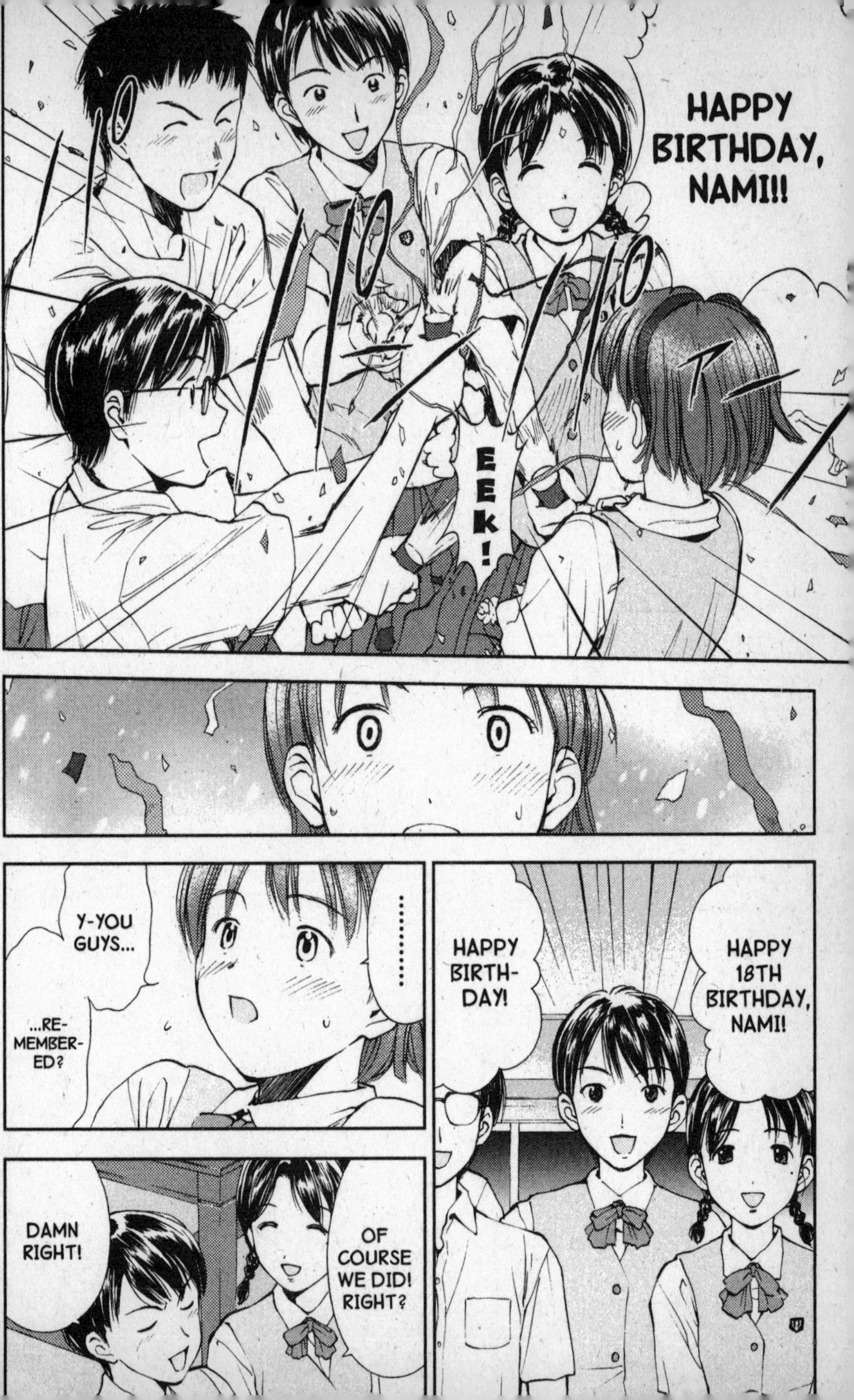
HAPPY BIRTHDAY, NAMI!!
EEK!
HAPPY 18TH BIRTHDAY, NAMI!
HAPPY BIRTH-DAY!
......
Y-YOU GUYS...
...RE-MEMBER-ED?
OF COURSE WE DID! RIGHT?
DAMN RIGHT!

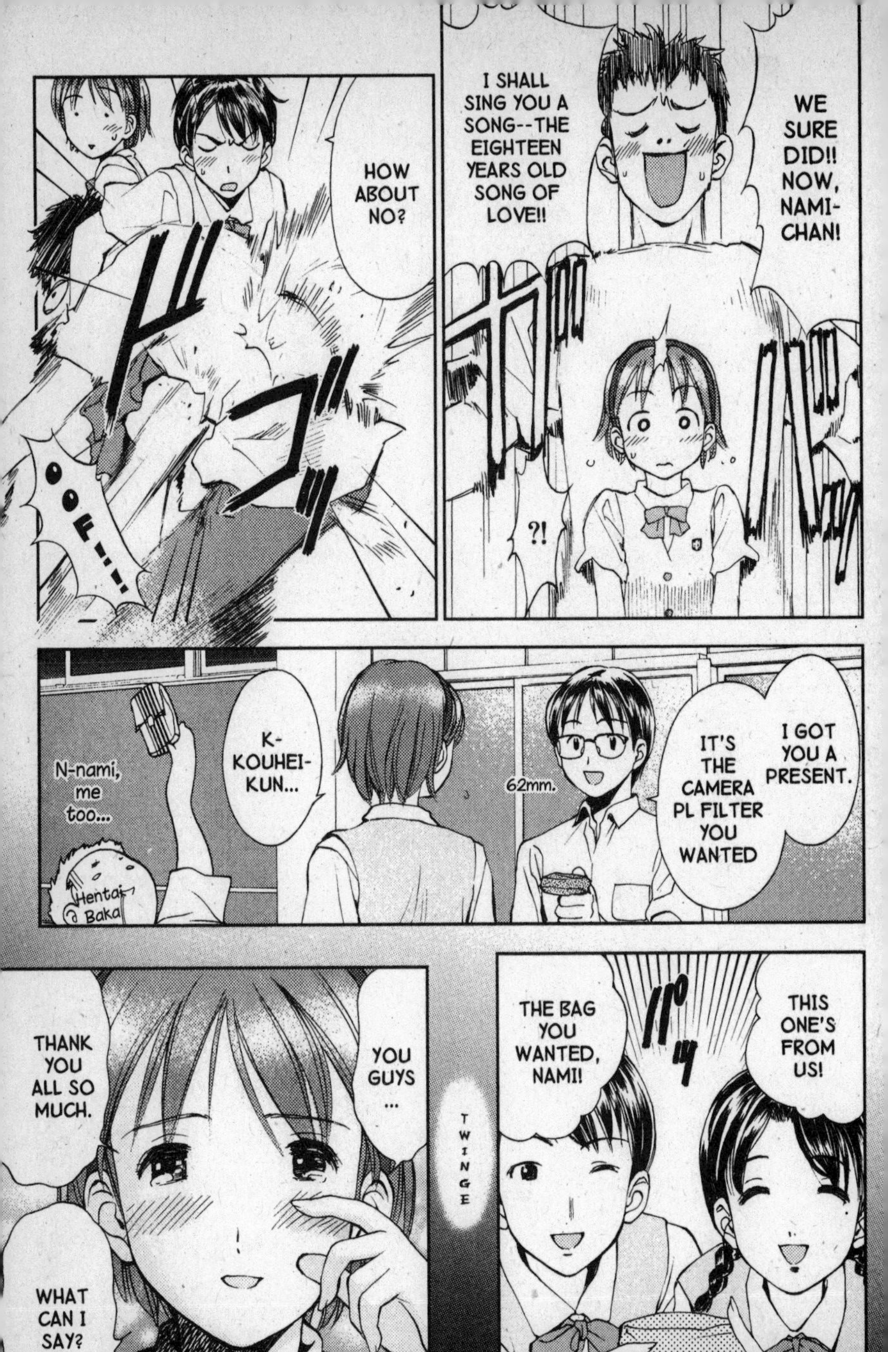
WE SURE DID!! NOW, NAMI-CHAN!
I SHALL SING YOU A SONG--THE EIGHTEEN YEARS OLD SONG OF LOVE!!
?!
HOW ABOUT NO?
OOF!!!!
I GOT YOU A PRESENT.
IT'S THE CAMERA PL FILTER YOU WANTED
62mm.
K-KOUHEI-KUN...
N-nami, me too...
Hentai Baka
THIS ONE'S FROM US!
THE BAG YOU WANTED, NAMI!
TWINGE
YOU GUYS ...
THANK YOU ALL SO MUCH.
WHAT CAN I SAY?

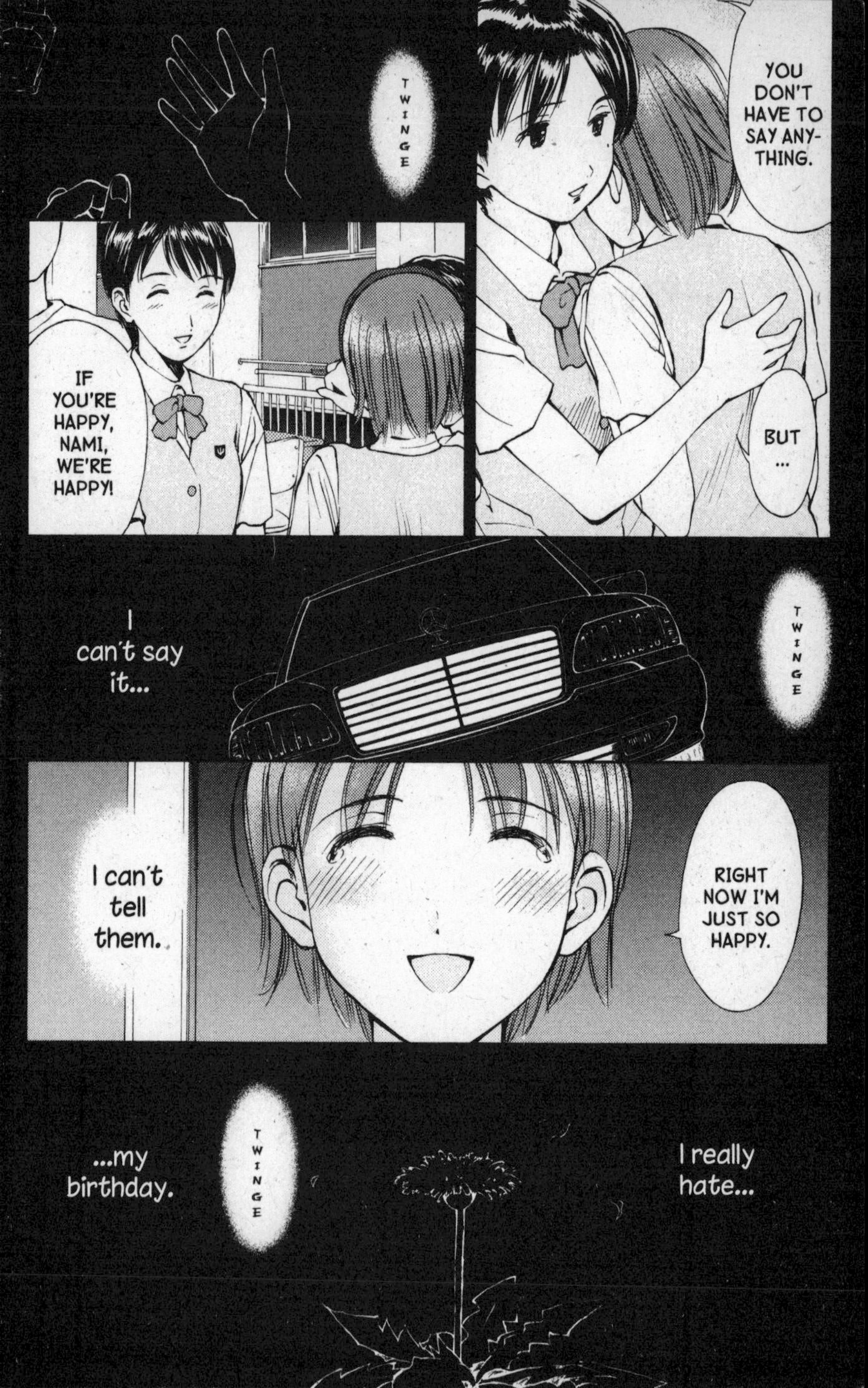
YOU DON'T HAVE TO SAY ANY-THING.
BUT ...
TWINGE
IF YOU'RE HAPPY, NAMI, WE'RE HAPPY!
TWINGE
I can't say it...
RIGHT NOW I'M JUST SO HAPPY.
I can't tell them.
I really hate...
TWINGE
...my birthday.

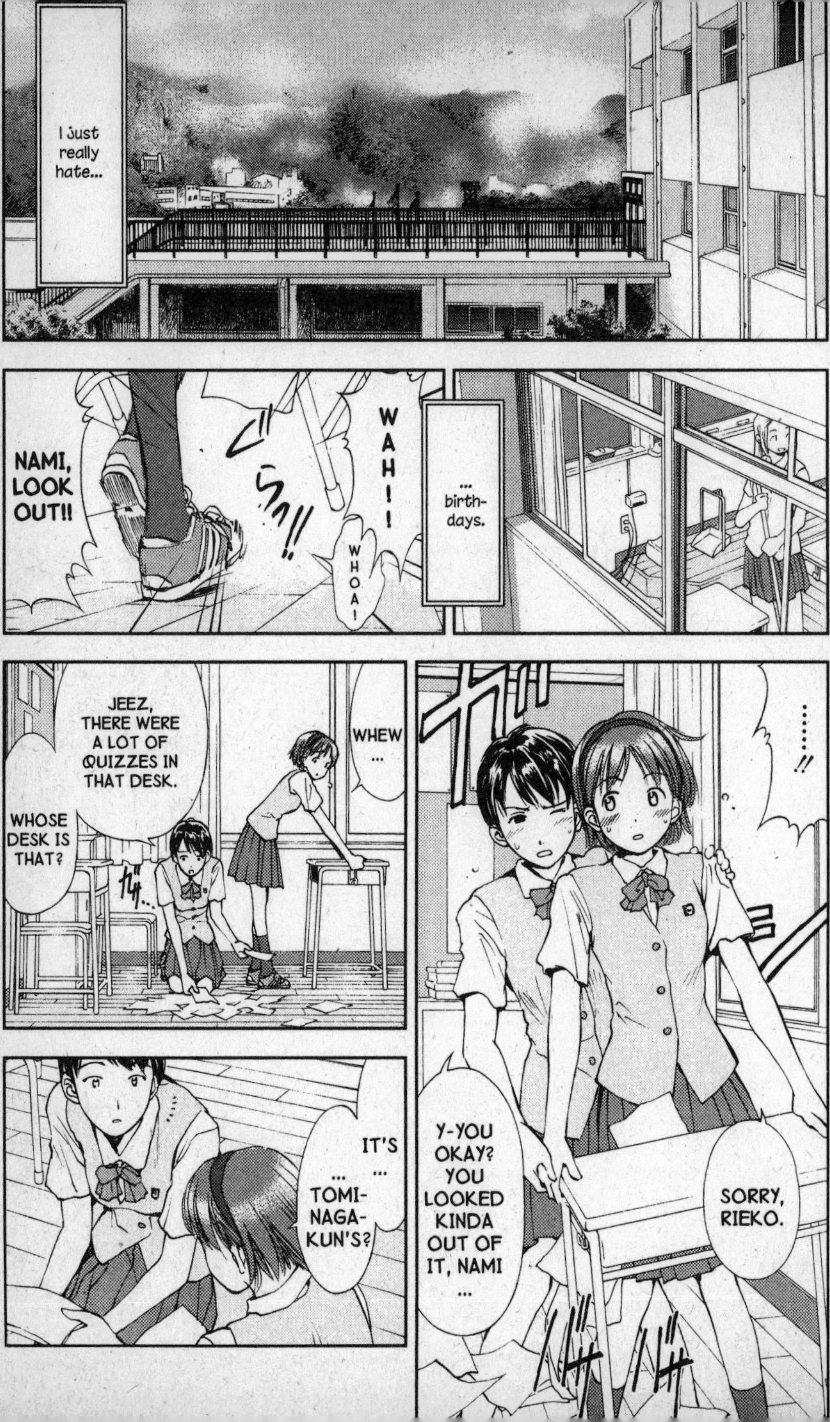
I just really hate...
... birth-days.
WAH!!
WHOA!
NAMI, LOOK OUT!!
......!!
SORRY, RIEKO.
Y-YOU OKAY? YOU LOOKED KINDA OUT OF IT, NAMI ...
WHEW ...
JEEZ, THERE WERE A LOT OF QUIZZES IN THAT DESK.
WHOSE DESK IS THAT?
IT'S ... TOMI-NAGA-KUN'S?

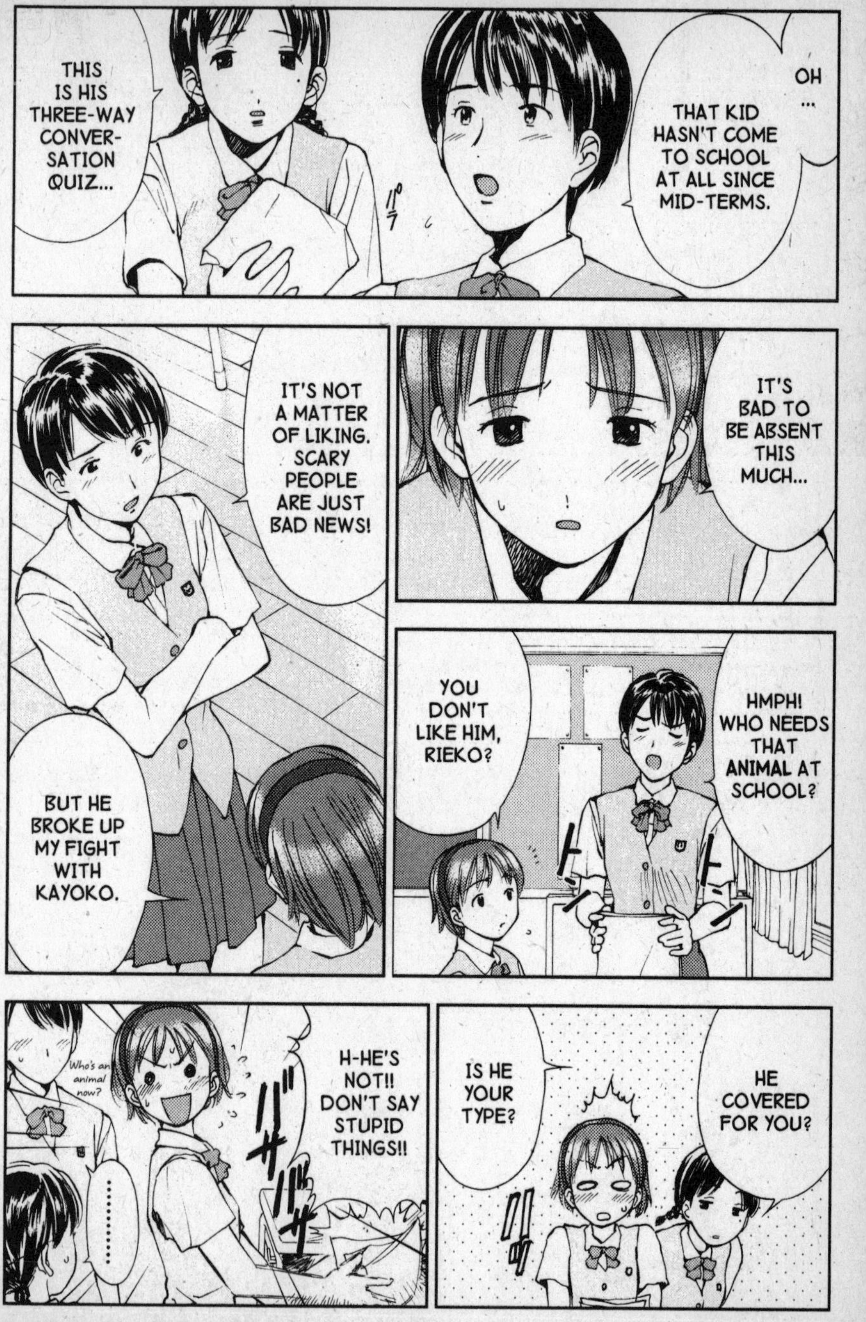
OH ...
THAT KID HASN'T COME TO SCHOOL AT ALL SINCE MID-TERMS.
THIS IS HIS THREE-WAY CONVERSATION QUIZ...
IT'S BAD TO BE ABSENT THIS MUCH...
HMPH! WHO NEEDS THAT ANIMAL AT SCHOOL?
YOU DON'T LIKE HIM, RIEKO?
IT'S NOT A MATTER OF LIKING. SCARY PEOPLE ARE JUST BAD NEWS!
BUT HE BROKE UP MY FIGHT WITH KAYOKO.
HE COVERED FOR YOU?
IS HE YOUR TYPE?
H-HE'S NOT!! DON'T SAY STUPID THINGS!!
Who's an animal now?
....

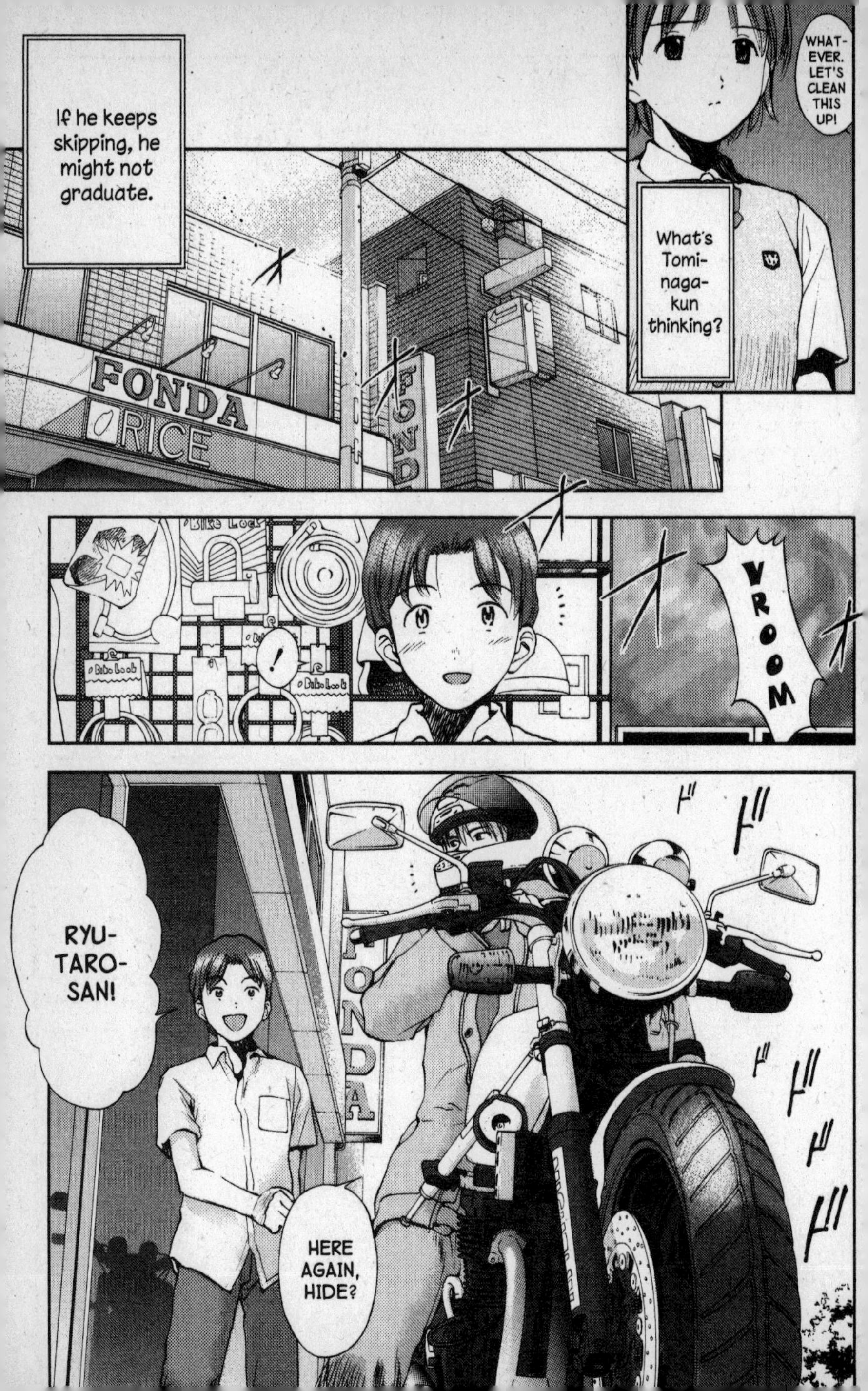
WHAT-EVER. LET'S CLEAN THIS UP!
What's Tomi-naga-kun thinking?
If he keeps skipping, he might not graduate.
FONDA RICE
FONDA
VROOM
!
RYU-TARO-SAN!
HERE AGAIN, HIDE?
FONDA

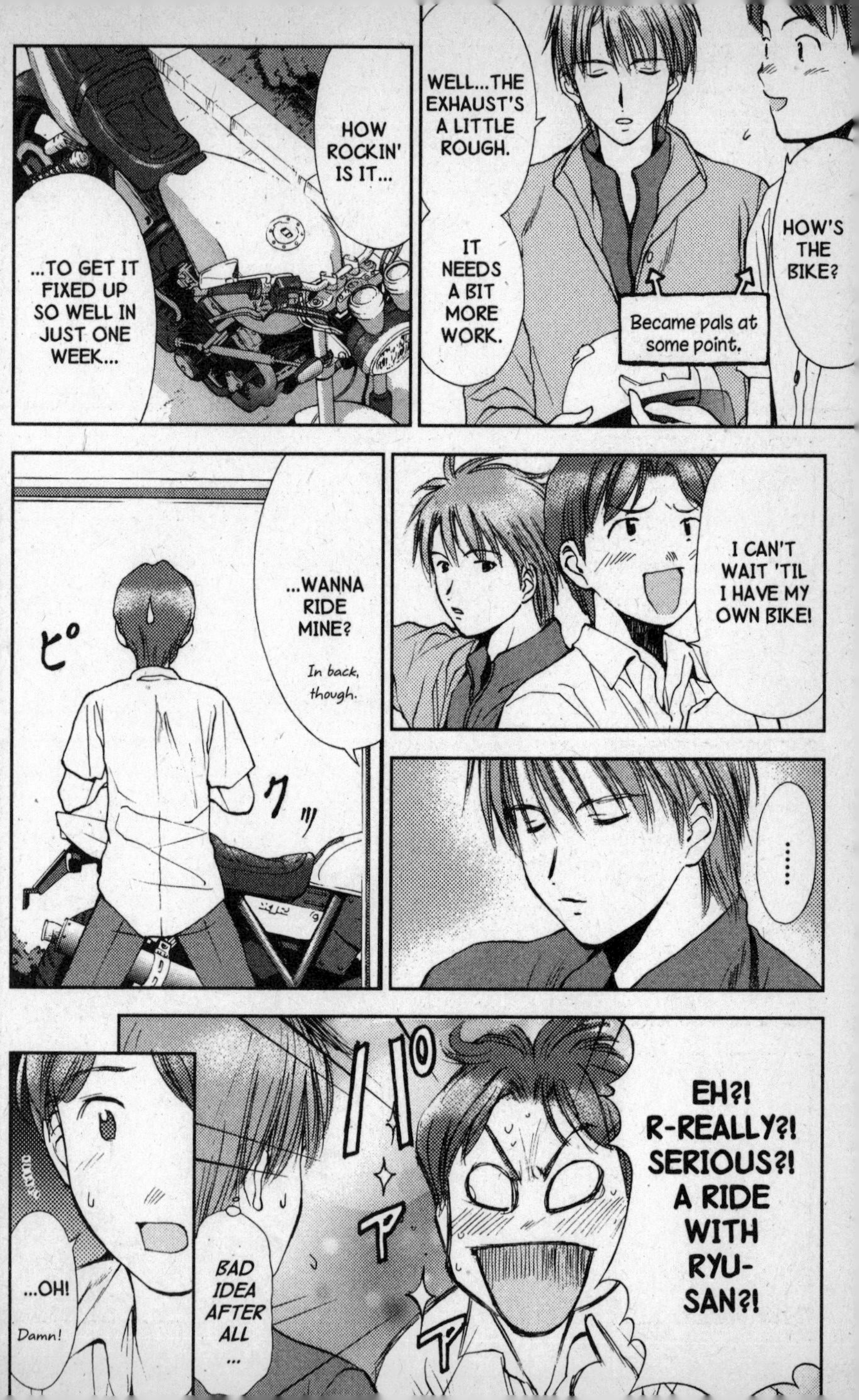
HOW'S THE BIKE?
WELL...THE EXHAUST'S A LITTLE ROUGH.
IT NEEDS A BIT MORE WORK.
Became pals at some point.
HOW ROCKIN' IS IT...
...TO GET IT FIXED UP SO WELL IN JUST ONE WEEK...
I CAN'T WAIT 'TIL I HAVE MY OWN BIKE!
......
...WANNA RIDE MINE?
In back, though.
ピ
クッ
EH?! R-REALLY?! SERIOUS?! A RIDE WITH RYU-SAN?!
パア
BAD IDEA AFTER ALL ...
...OH!
Damn!

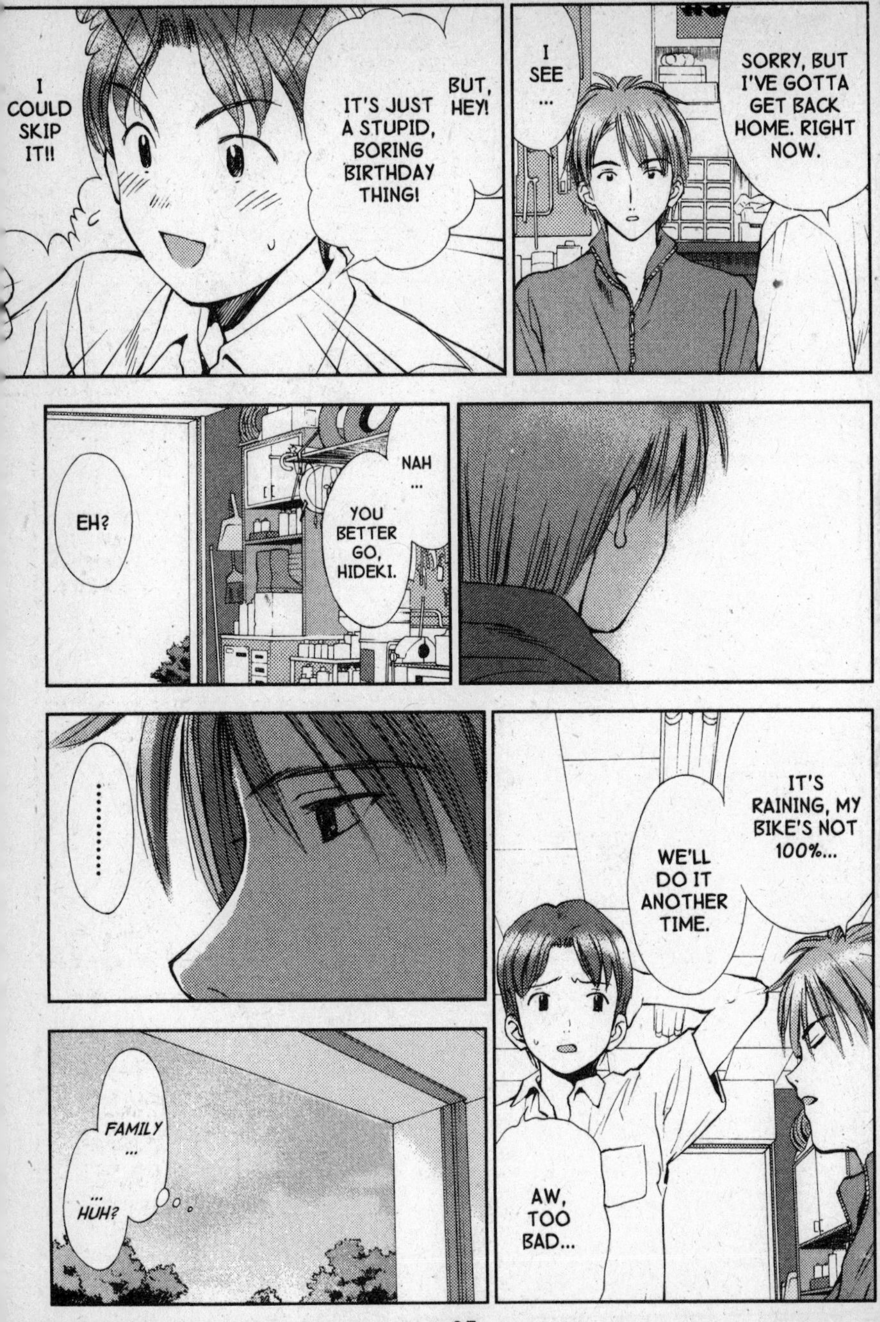
SORRY, BUT I'VE GOTTA GET BACK HOME. RIGHT NOW.
I SEE ...
BUT, HEY!
IT'S JUST A STUPID, BORING BIRTHDAY THING!
I COULD SKIP IT!!
NAH ...
YOU BETTER GO, HIDEKI.
EH?
IT'S RAINING, MY BIKE'S NOT 100%...
WE'LL DO IT ANOTHER TIME.
AW, TOO BAD...
....
FAMILY ...
... HUH?

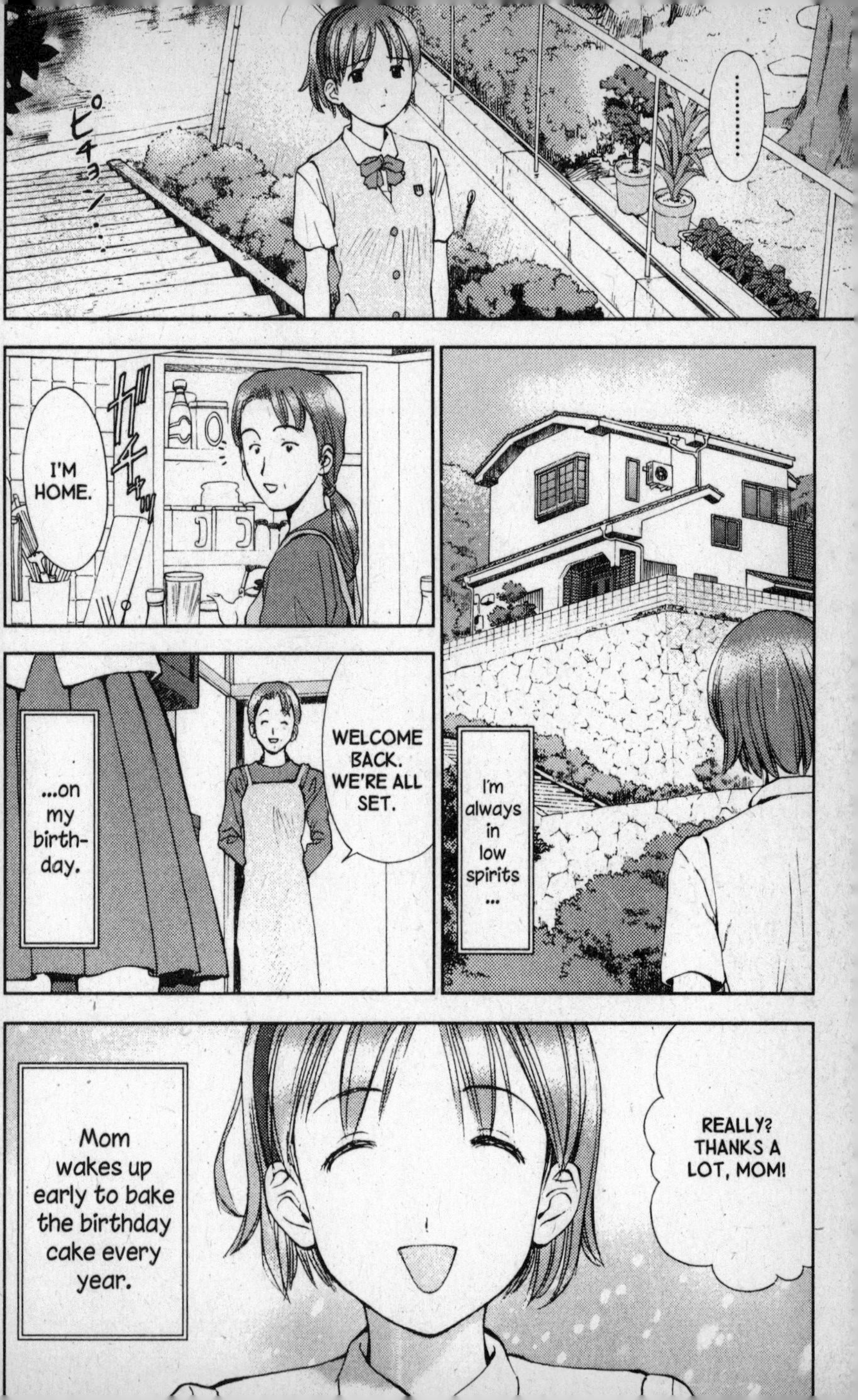
……
I'm always in low spirits ...
I'M HOME.
WELCOME BACK. WE'RE ALL SET.
...on my birth-day.
REALLY? THANKS A LOT, MOM!
Mom wakes up early to bake the birthday cake every year.

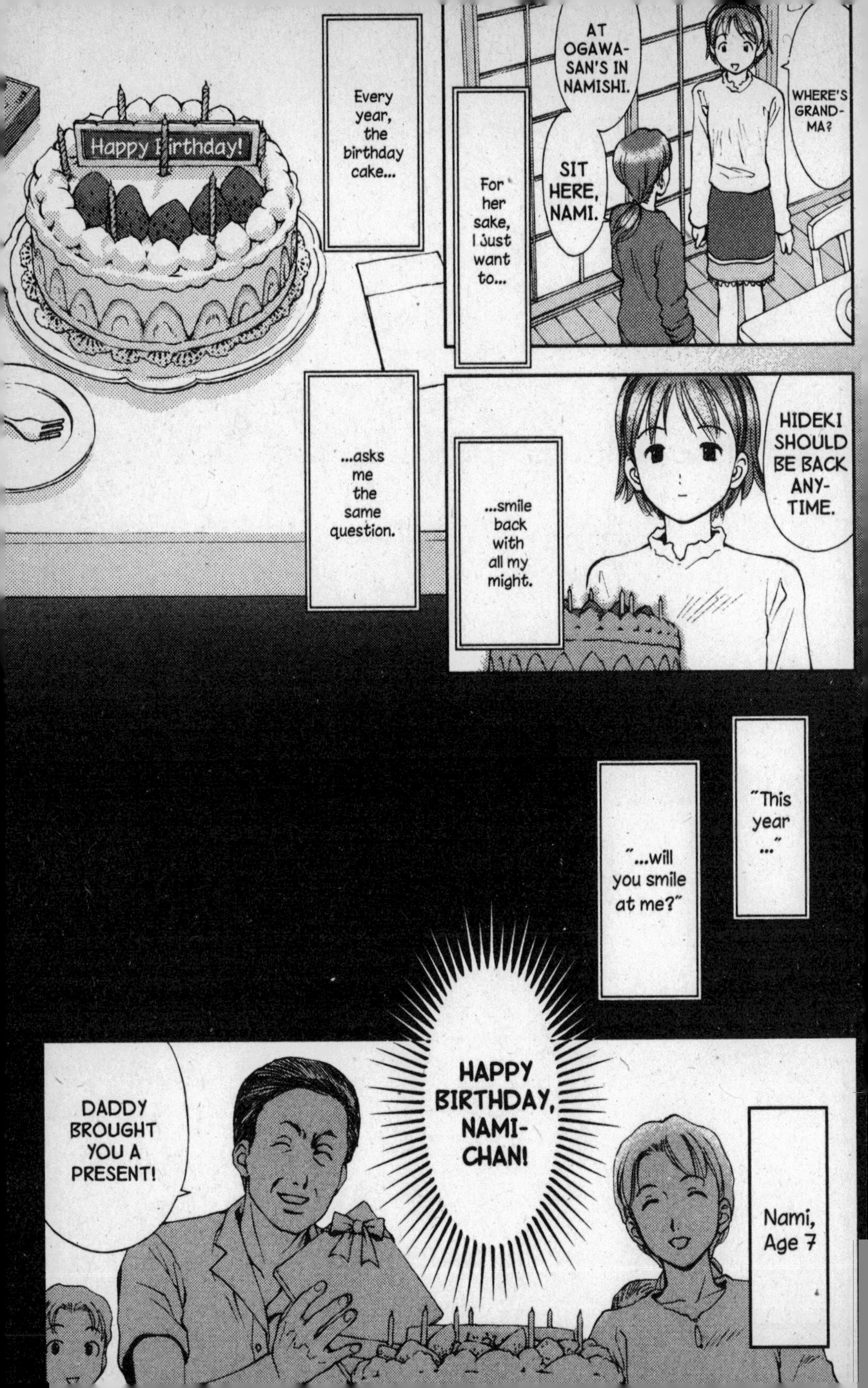
WHERE'S GRANDMA?
AT OGAWA-SAN'S IN NAMISHI.
SIT HERE, NAMI.
For her sake, I just want to...
HIDEKI SHOULD BE BACK ANYTIME.
...smile back with all my might.
Happy Birthday!
Every year, the birthday cake...
...asks me the same question.
"This year..."
"...will you smile at me?"
Nami, Age 7
HAPPY BIRTHDAY, NAMI-CHAN!
DADDY BROUGHT YOU A PRESENT!

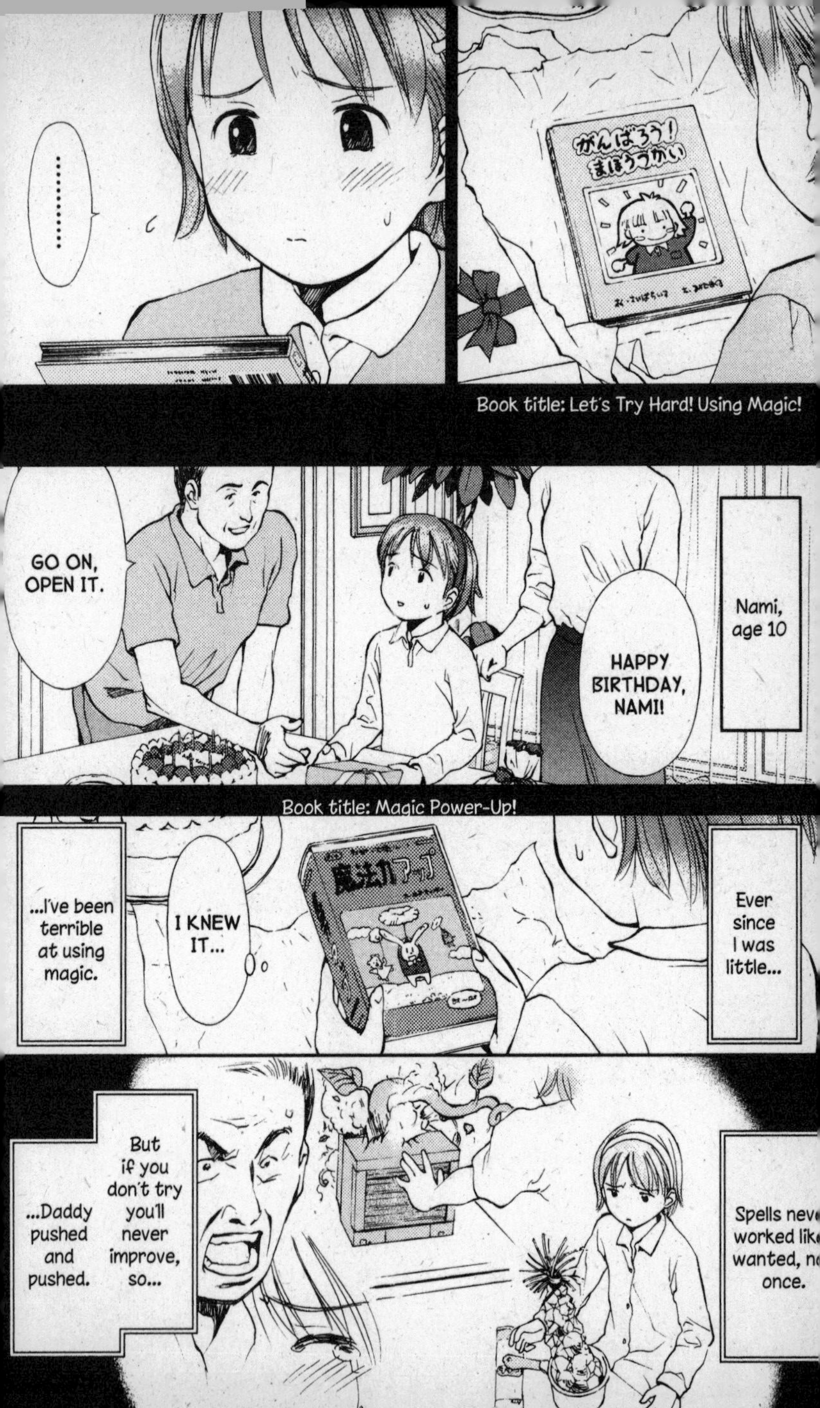
がんばろう！
まほうつかい
......
Book title: Let's Try Hard! Using Magic!
Nami, age 10
HAPPY BIRTHDAY, NAMI!
GO ON, OPEN IT.
Book title: Magic Power-Up!
Ever since I was little...
魔法力アップ
I KNEW IT...
...I've been terrible at using magic.
Spells neve worked lik wanted, n once.
But if you don't try you'll never improve, so...
...Daddy pushed and pushed.

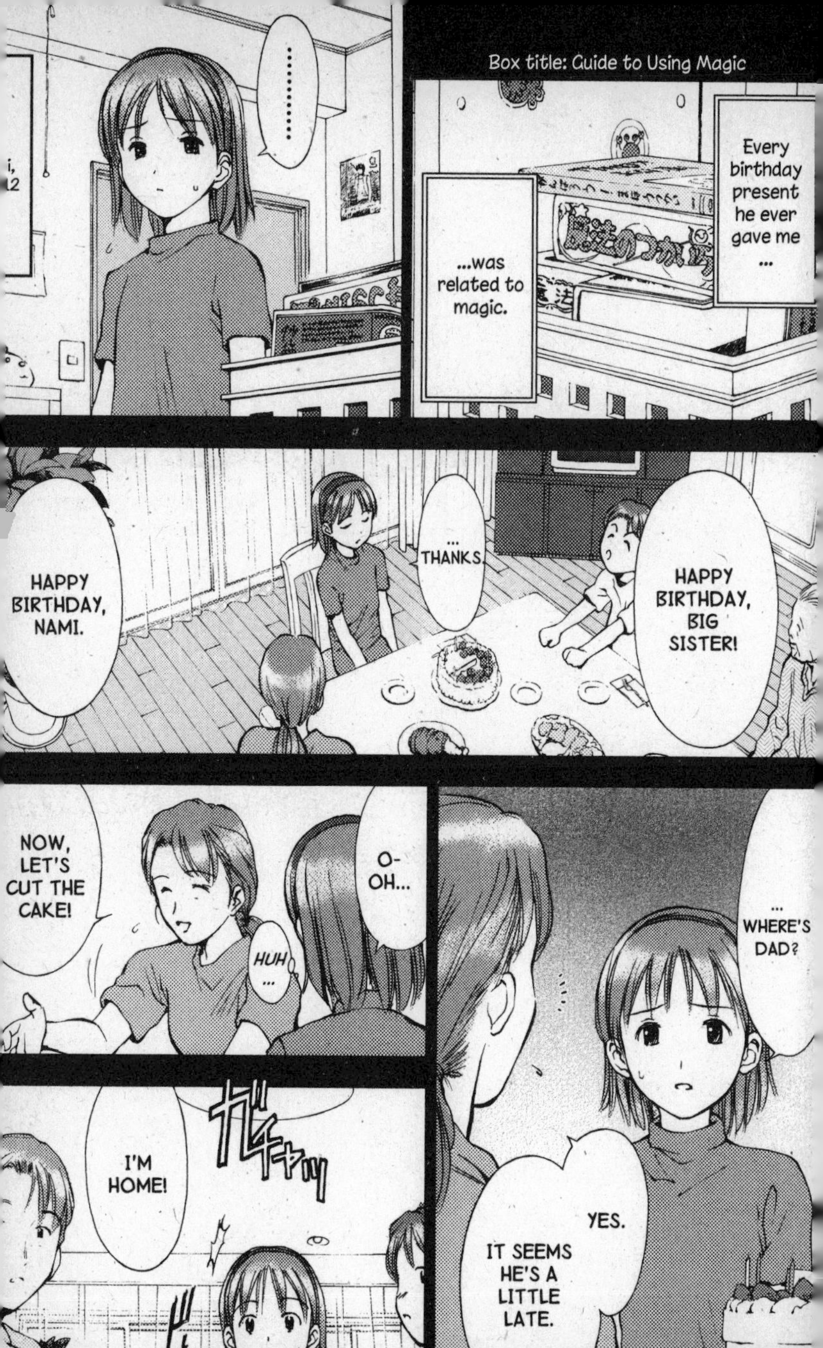
Box title: Guide to Using Magic
Every birthday present he ever gave me ...
...was related to magic.
....
HAPPY BIRTHDAY, BIG SISTER!
... THANKS.
HAPPY BIRTHDAY, NAMI.
... WHERE'S DAD?
YES.
IT SEEMS HE'S A LITTLE LATE.
O-OH...
HUH ...
NOW, LET'S CUT THE CAKE!
I'M HOME!

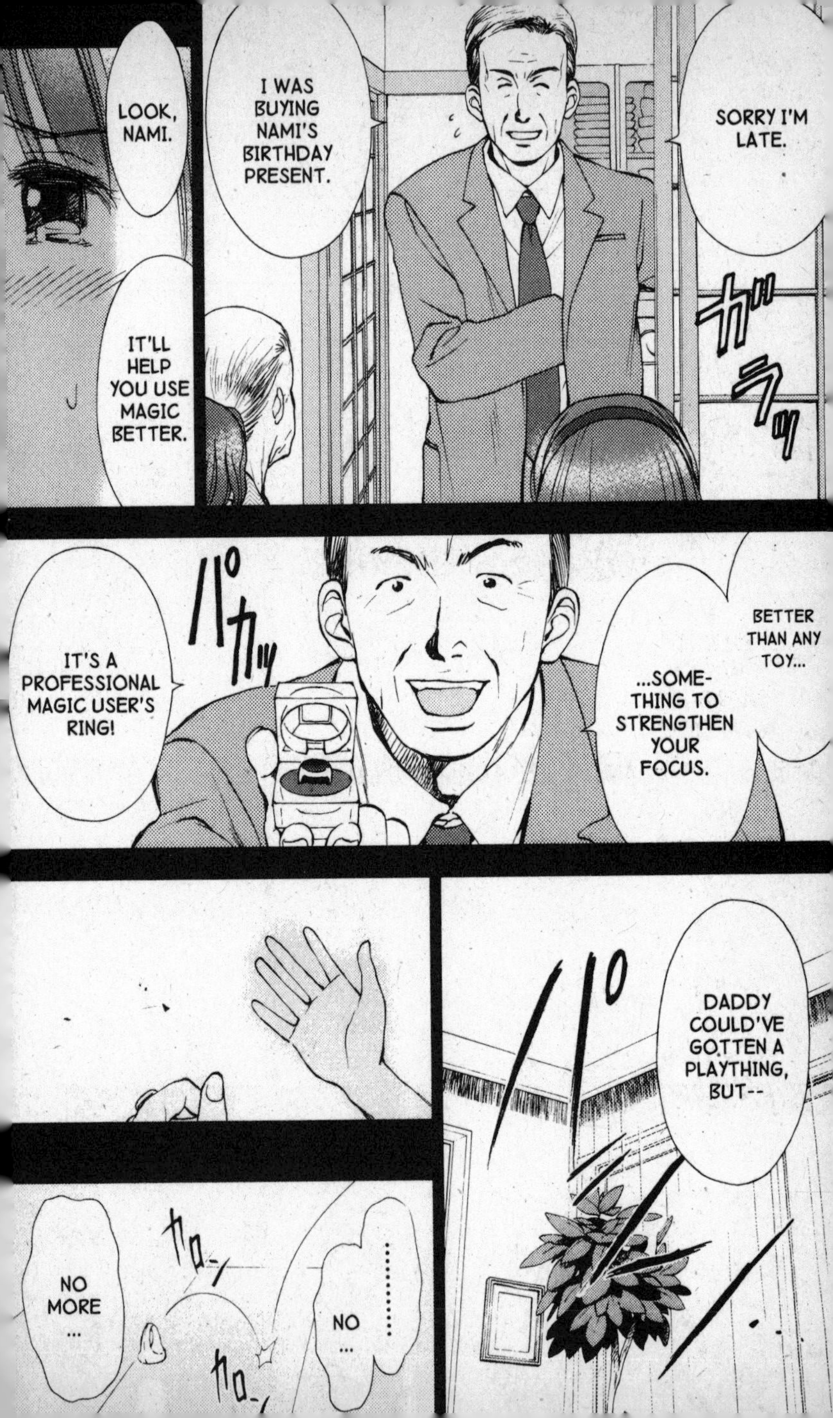
SORRY I'M LATE.
ガラッ
I WAS BUYING NAMI'S BIRTHDAY PRESENT.
LOOK, NAMI.
IT'LL HELP YOU USE MAGIC BETTER.
BETTER THAN ANY TOY...
...SOME-THING TO STRENGTHEN YOUR FOCUS.
パカッ
IT'S A PROFESSIONAL MAGIC USER'S RING!
パ
DADDY COULD'VE GOTTEN A PLAYTHING, BUT--
......
NO ...
NO MORE ...

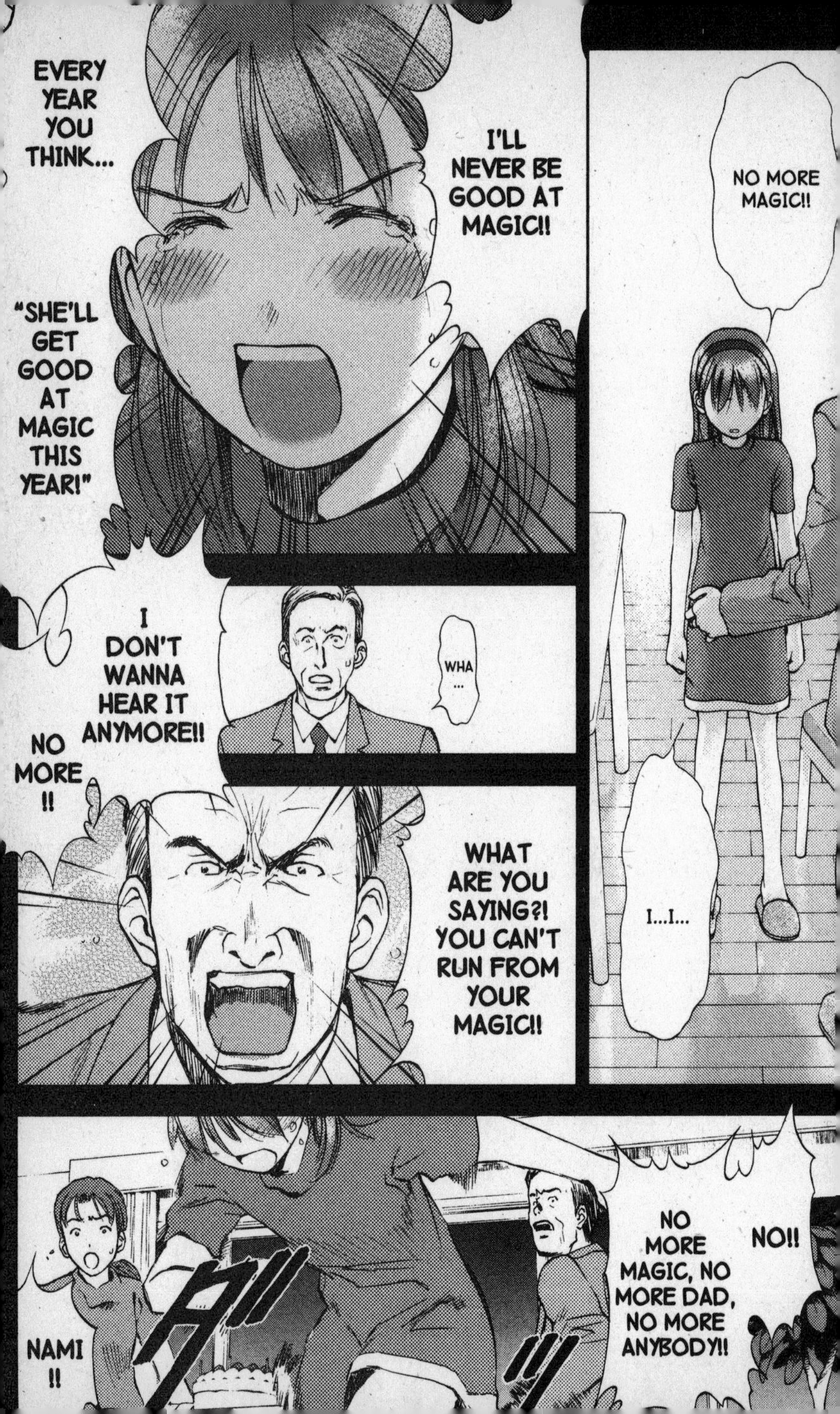
NO MORE MAGIC!!
I...I...
I'LL NEVER BE GOOD AT MAGIC!!
EVERY YEAR YOU THINK...
"SHE'LL GET GOOD AT MAGIC THIS YEAR!"
WHA ...
I DON'T WANNA HEAR IT ANYMORE!!
NO MORE !!
WHAT ARE YOU SAYING?! YOU CAN'T RUN FROM YOUR MAGIC!!
NO!!
NO MORE MAGIC, NO MORE DAD, NO MORE ANYBODY!!
NAMI !!

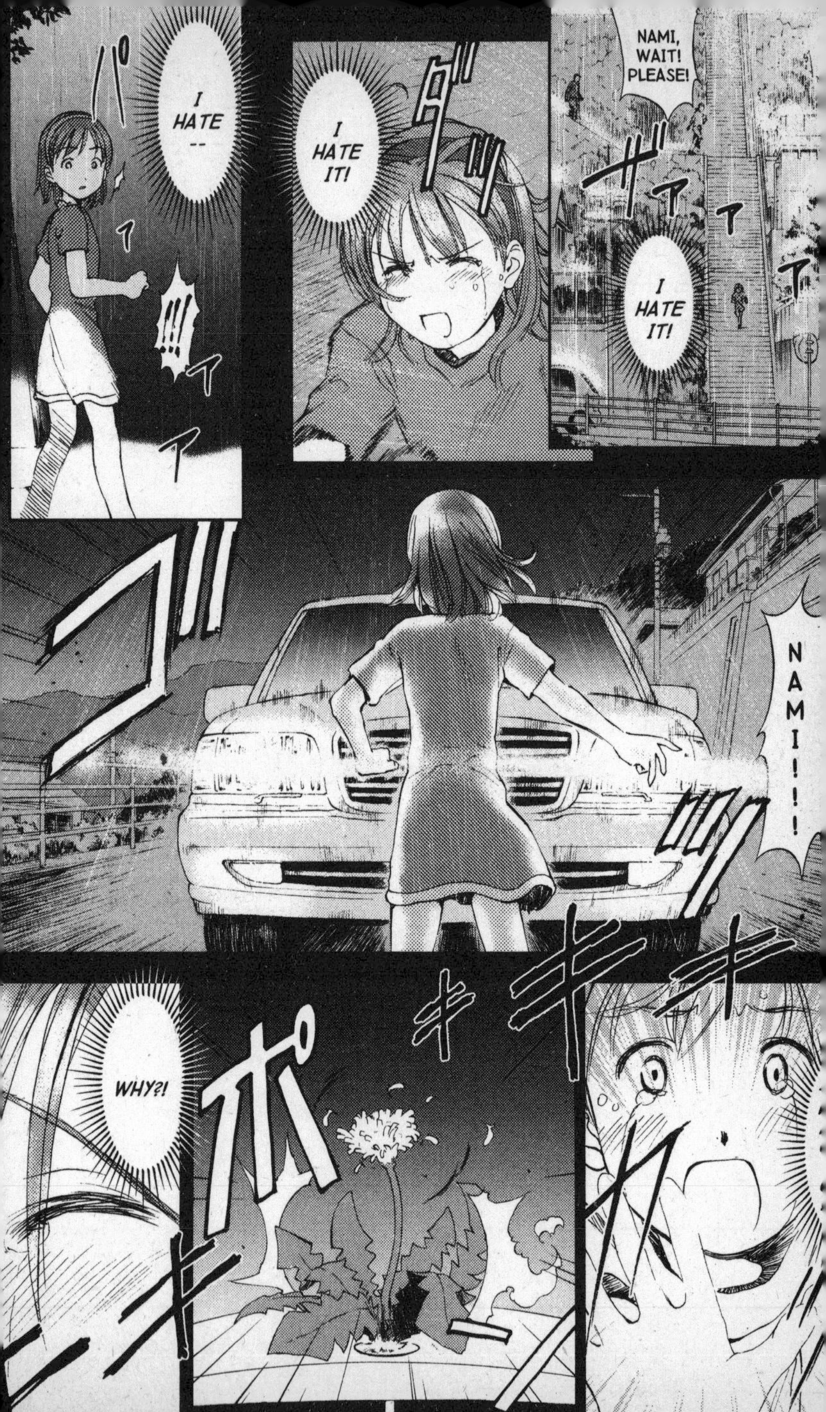
NAMI, WAIT! PLEASE!
I HATE IT!
I HATE IT!
I HATE --
NAMI!!!!
WHY?!

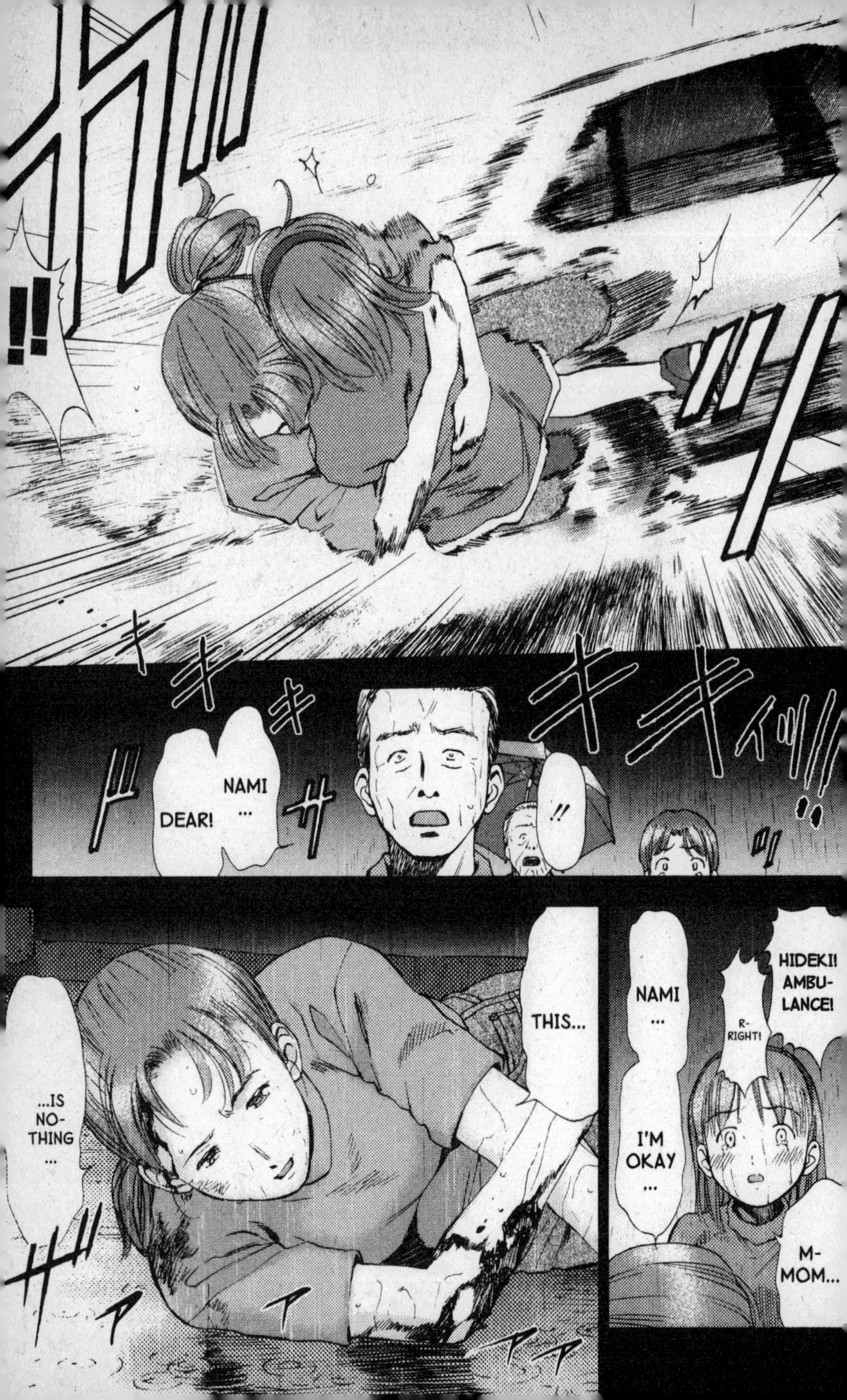
!!
!!
NAMI ... DEAR!
HIDEKI! AMBU-LANCE!
R-RIGHT!
NAMI ... I'M OKAY ...
M-MOM...
THIS...
...IS NO-THING ...

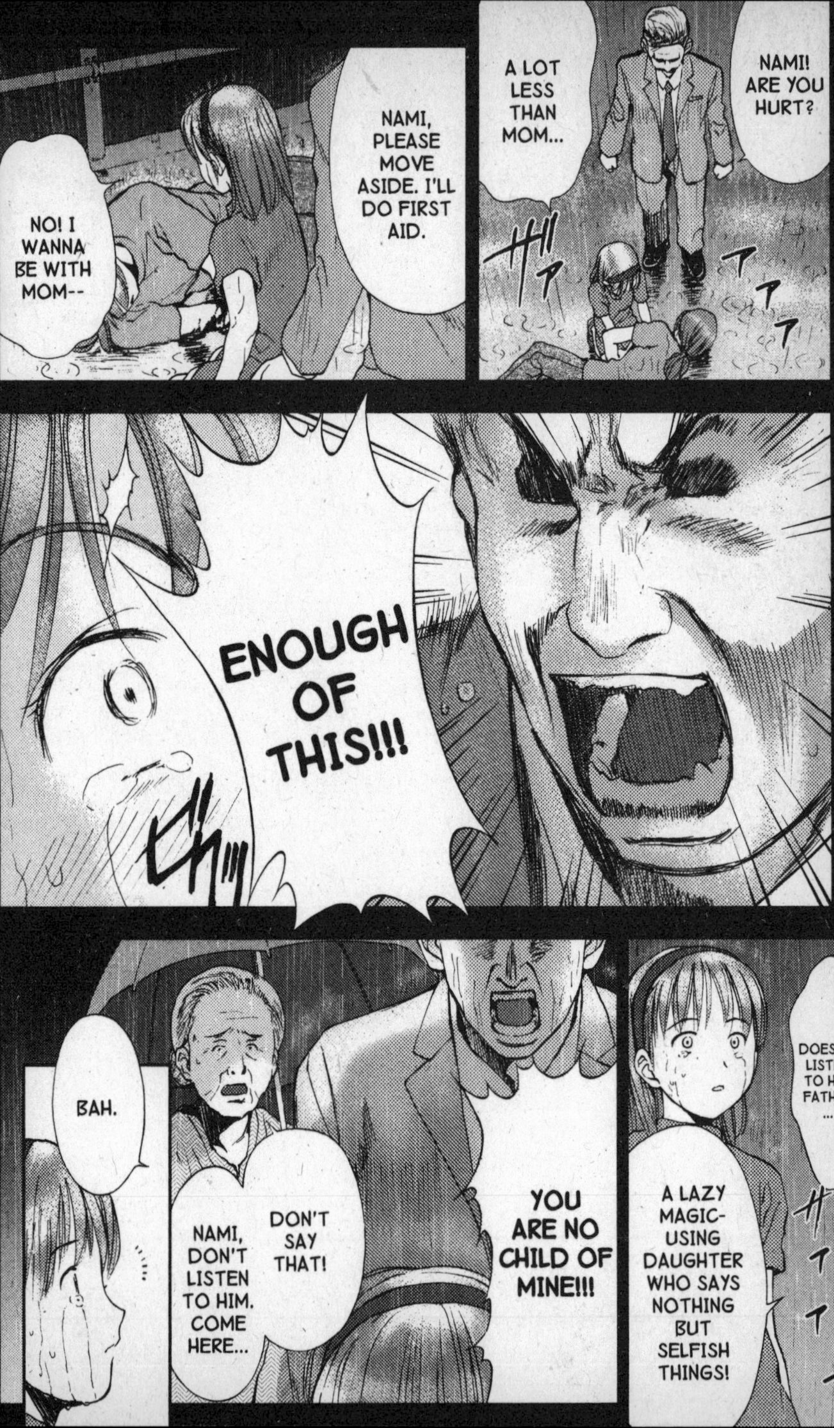
NAMI! ARE YOU HURT?
A LOT LESS THAN MOM...
NAMI, PLEASE MOVE ASIDE. I'LL DO FIRST AID.
NO! I WANNA BE WITH MOM--
ENOUGH OF THIS!!!
DOESN'T LISTEN TO HER FATHER ...
A LAZY MAGIC-USING DAUGHTER WHO SAYS NOTHING BUT SELFISH THINGS!
YOU ARE NO CHILD OF MINE!!!
DON'T SAY THAT!
NAMI, DON'T LISTEN TO HIM. COME HERE...
BAH.
......

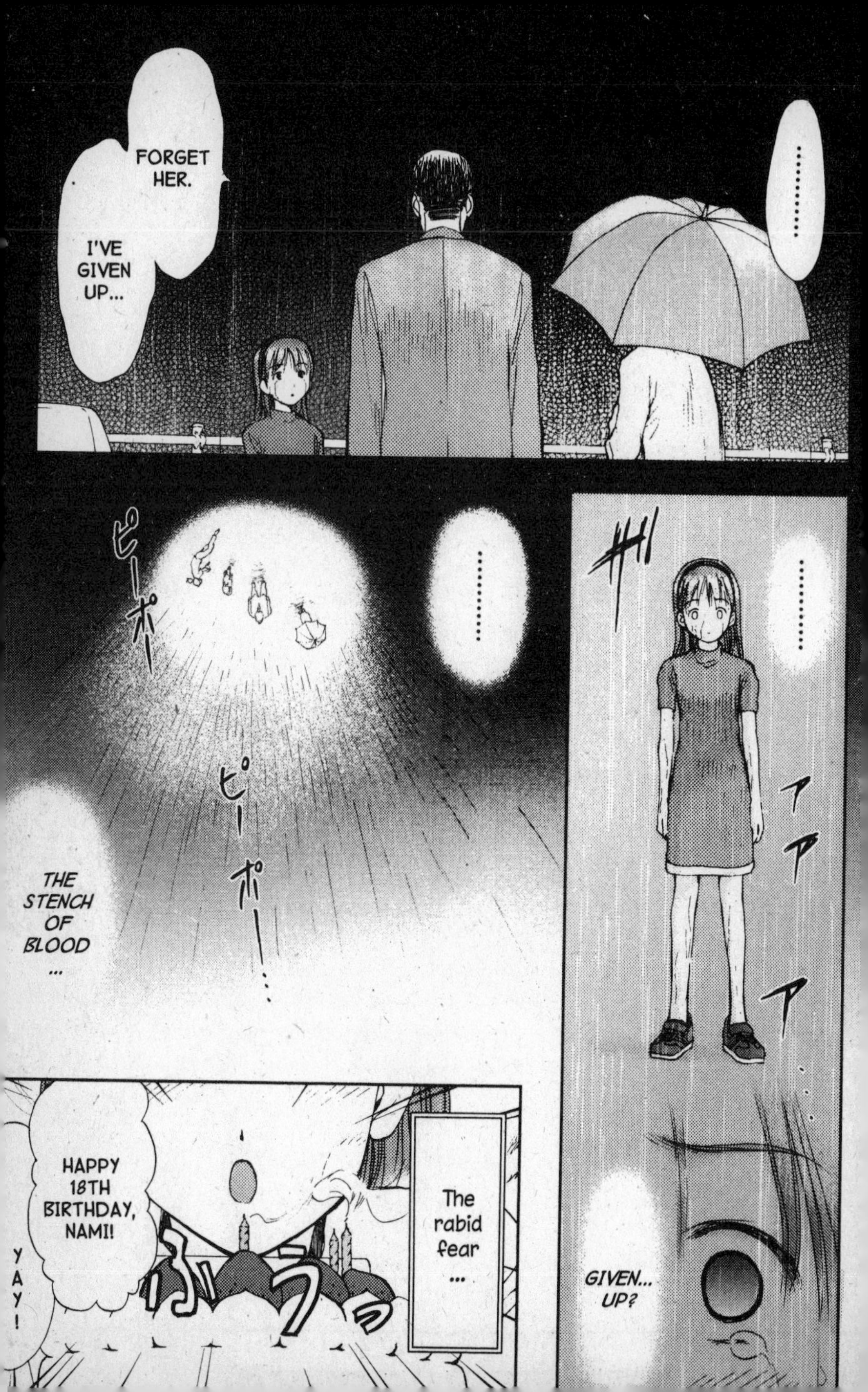
......
FORGET HER.
I'VE GIVEN UP...
......
ザァァァ
GIVEN... UP?
......
ピーポー
ピーポー…
THE STENCH OF BLOOD ...
The rabid fear ...
HAPPY 18TH BIRTHDAY, NAMI!
ふうっ
YAY!

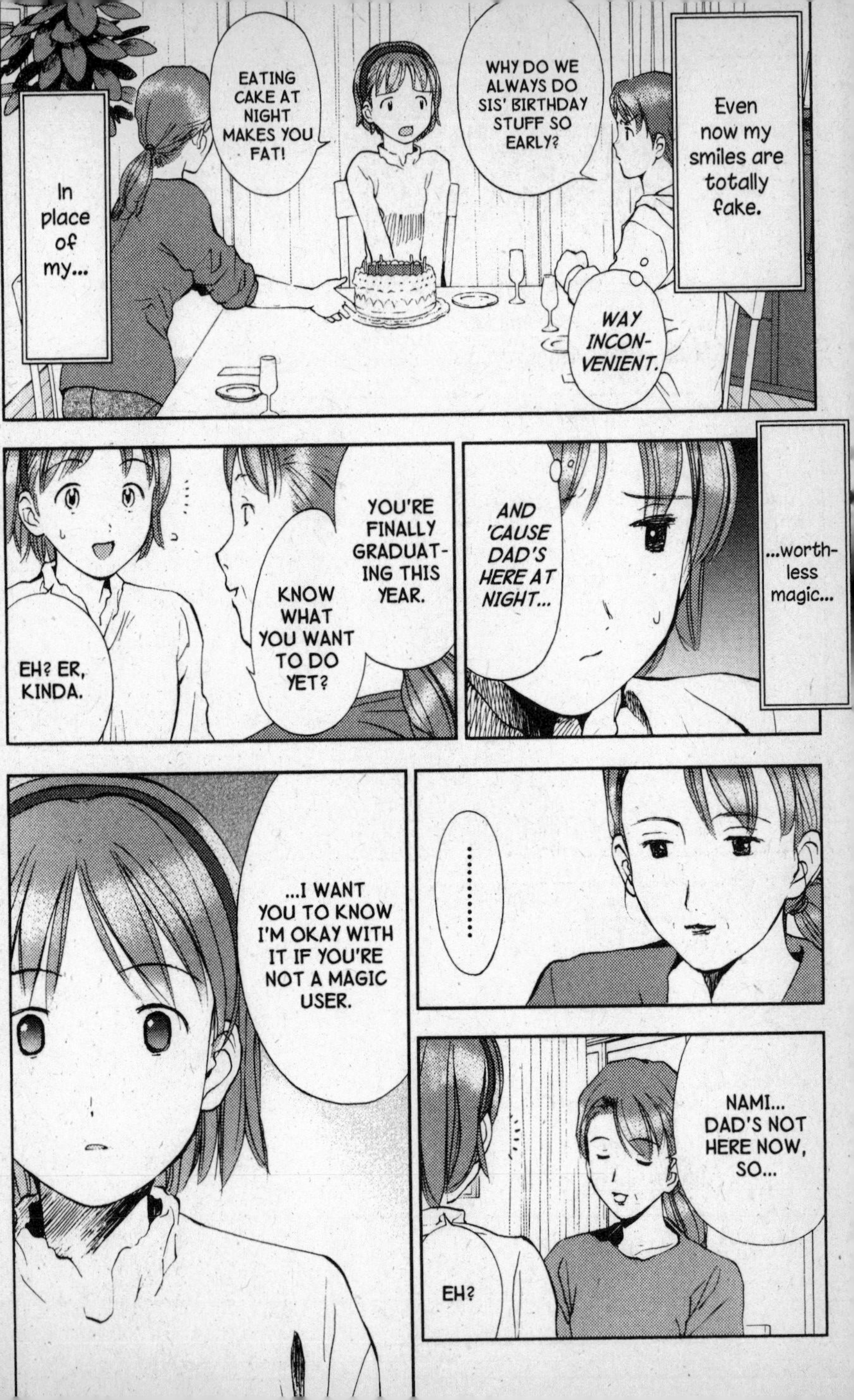
Even now my smiles are totally fake.
WHY DO WE ALWAYS DO SIS' BIRTHDAY STUFF SO EARLY?
WAY INCON-VENIENT.
EATING CAKE AT NIGHT MAKES YOU FAT!
In place of my...
...worth-less magic...
AND 'CAUSE DAD'S HERE AT NIGHT...
YOU'RE FINALLY GRADUAT-ING THIS YEAR.
KNOW WHAT YOU WANT TO DO YET?
EH? ER, KINDA.
....
NAMI... DAD'S NOT HERE NOW, SO...
EH?
...I WANT YOU TO KNOW I'M OKAY WITH IT IF YOU'RE NOT A MAGIC USER.

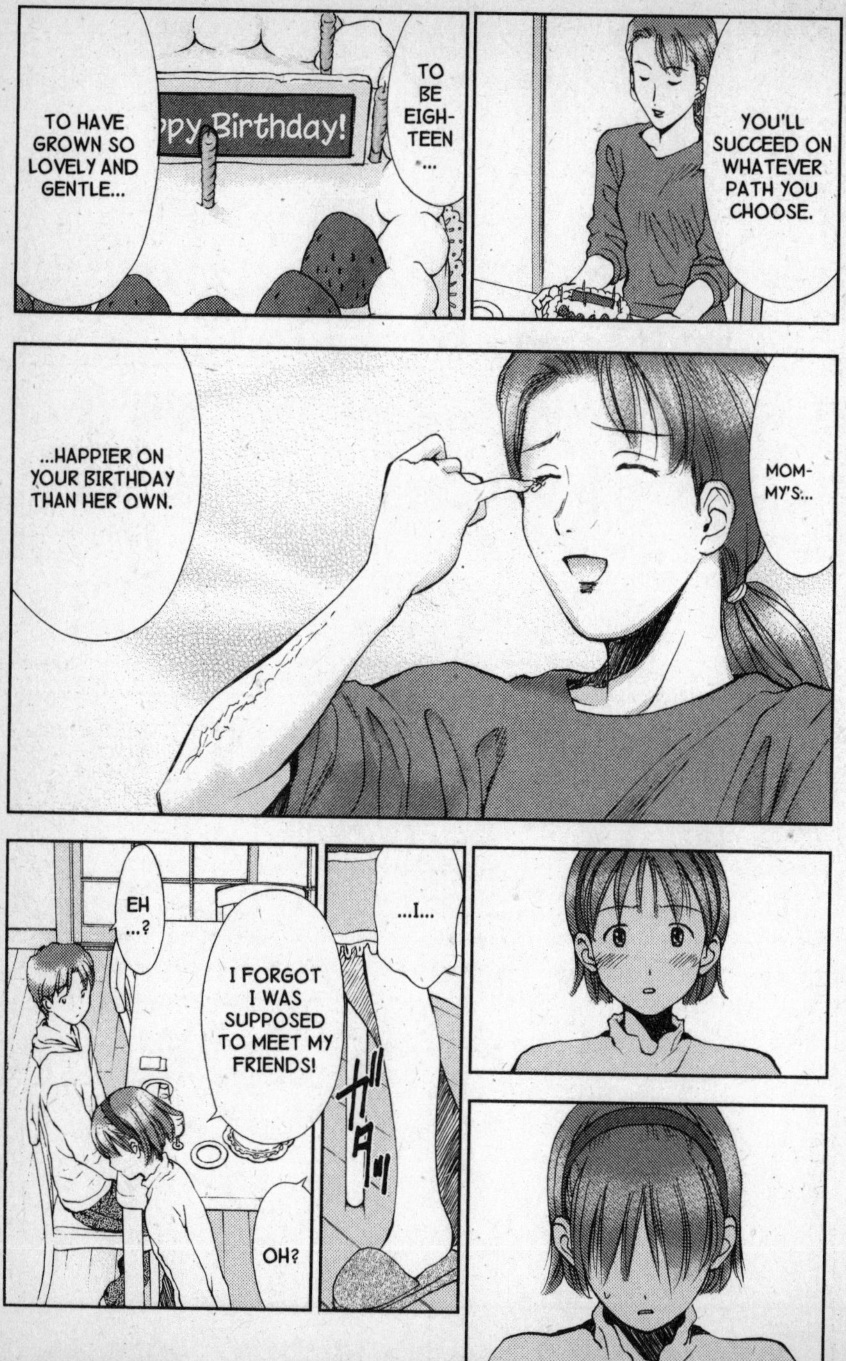
YOU'LL SUCCEED ON WHATEVER PATH YOU CHOOSE.
TO BE EIGHTEEN...
ppy Birthday!
TO HAVE GROWN SO LOVELY AND GENTLE...
MOMMY'S...
...HAPPIER ON YOUR BIRTHDAY THAN HER OWN.
...I...
I FORGOT I WAS SUPPOSED TO MEET MY FRIENDS!
ガタッ
OH?
EH ...?

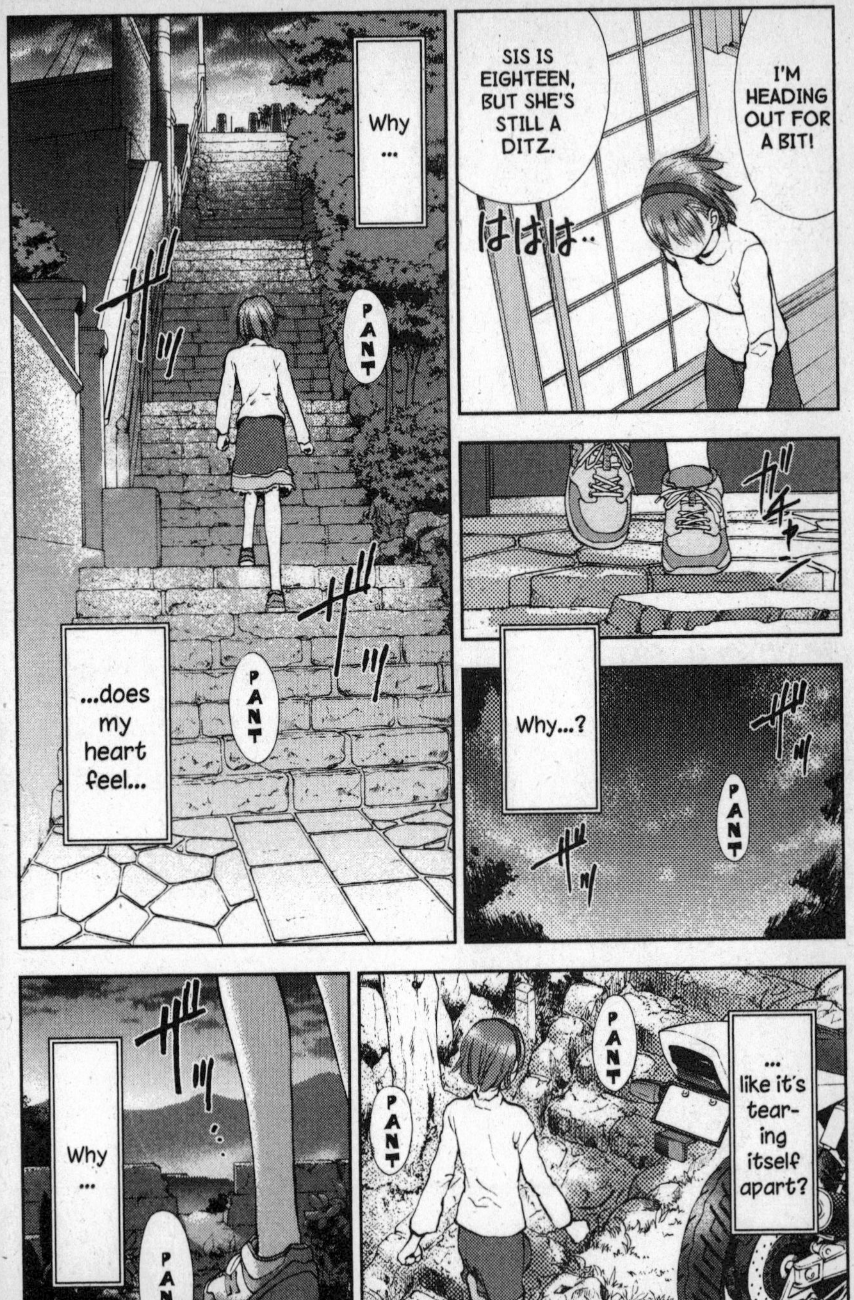

I'M HEADING OUT FOR A BIT!
SIS IS EIGHTEEN, BUT SHE'S STILL A DITZ.
ははは..
ガチャン
ザッ
Why...?
PANT
ザッ
Why ...
ザッ
PANT
ザッ
PANT
...does my heart feel...
... like it's tearing itself apart?
PANT
PANT
ザッ
Why ...
PANT

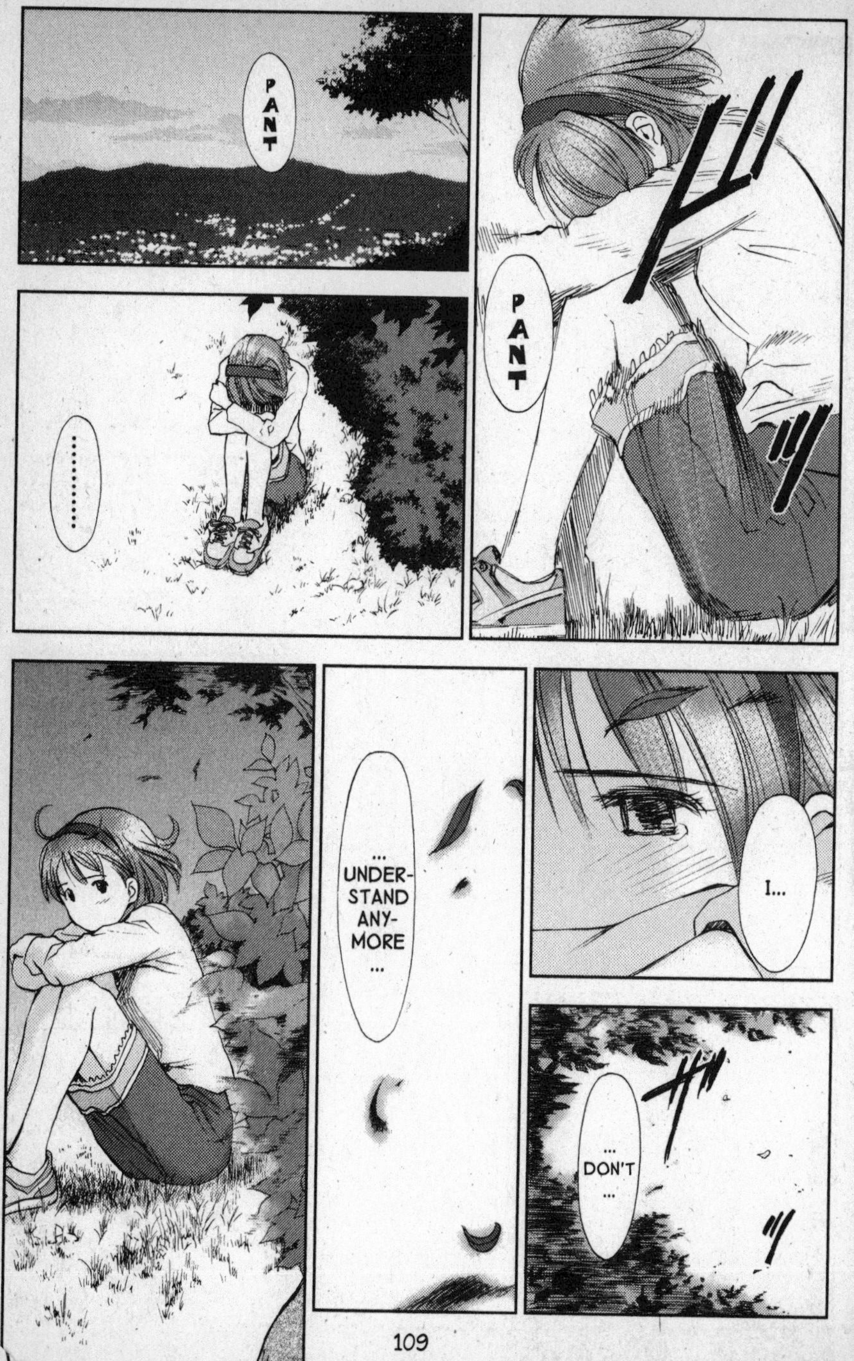
PANT
PANT
....
I...
...DON'T...
...UNDERSTAND ANYMORE...

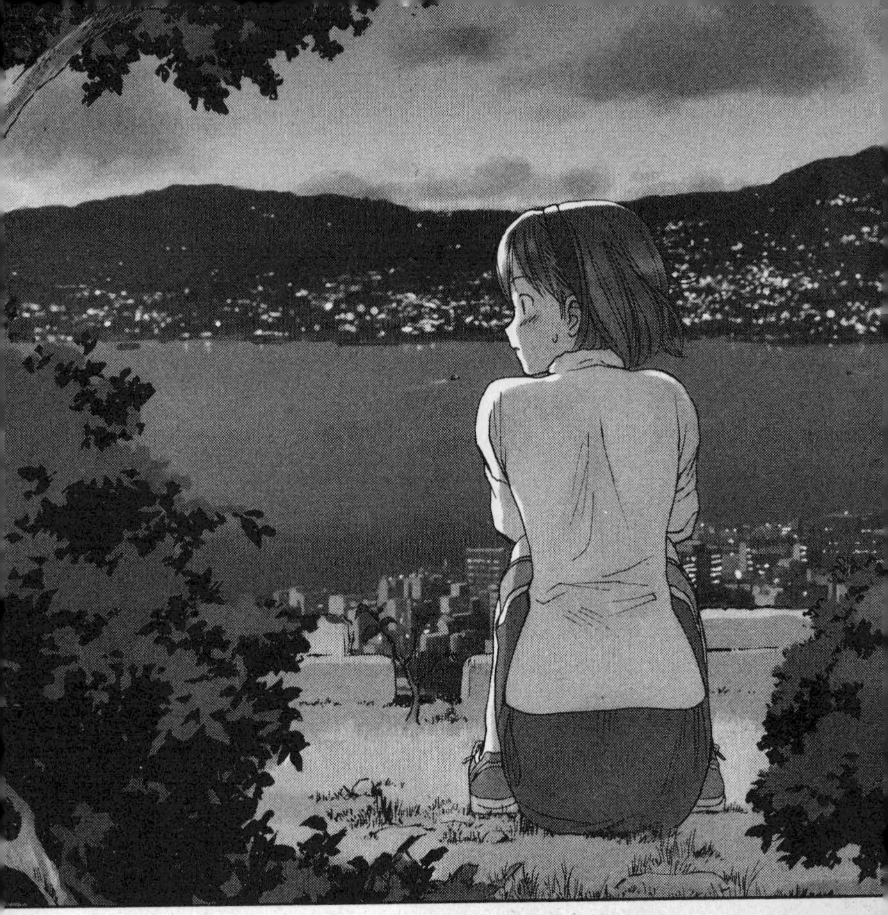

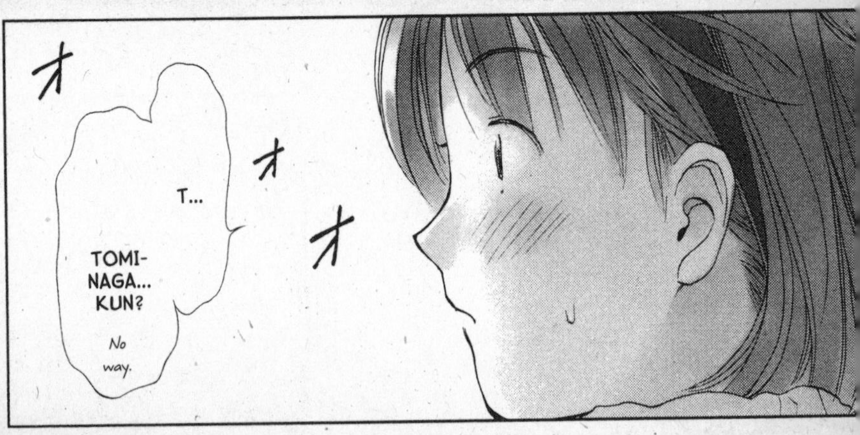
オ
オ
オ
T...
TOMI-
NAGA...
KUN?
No
way.

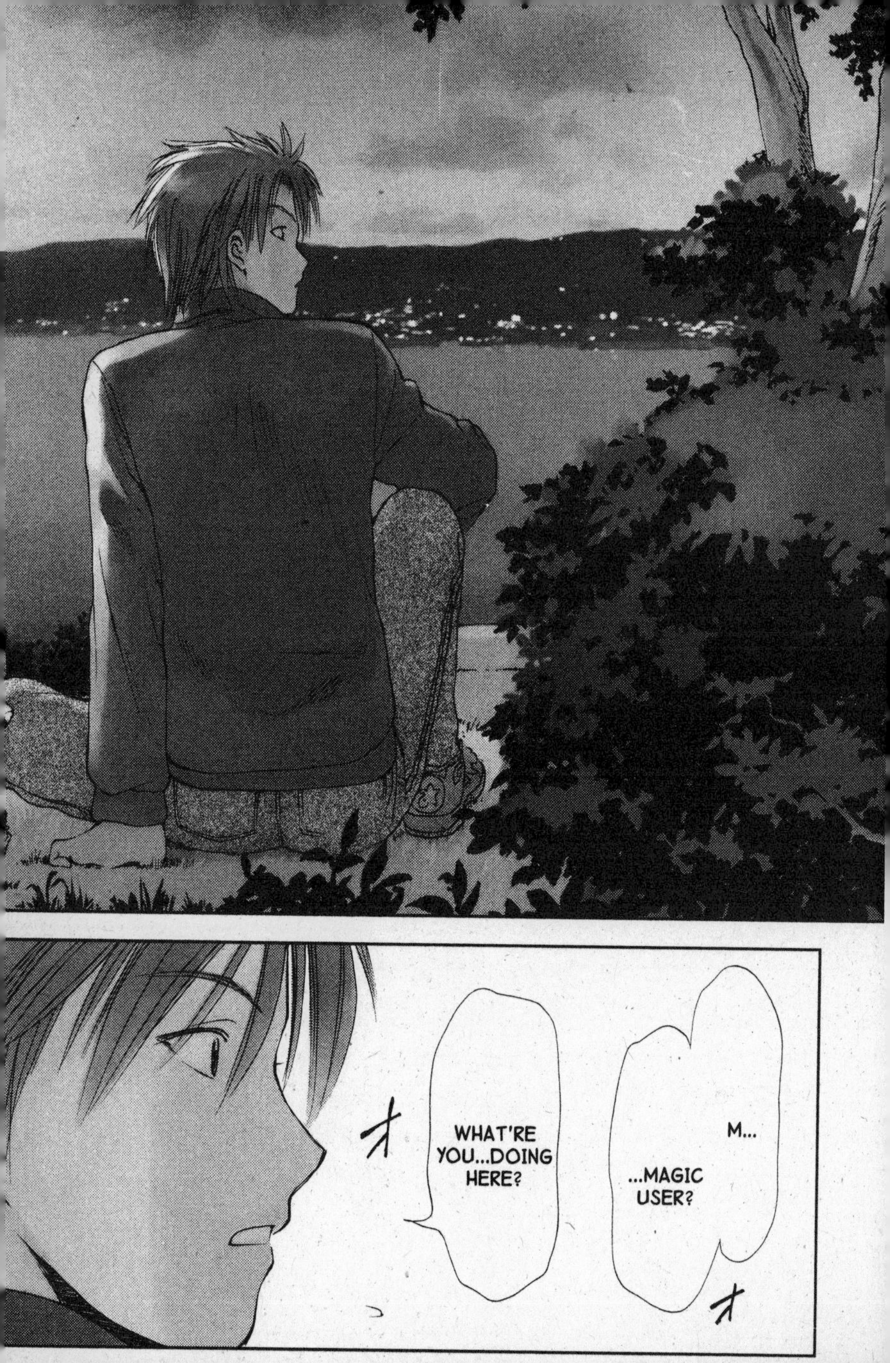
M... ...MAGIC USER?
WHAT'RE YOU...DOING HERE?

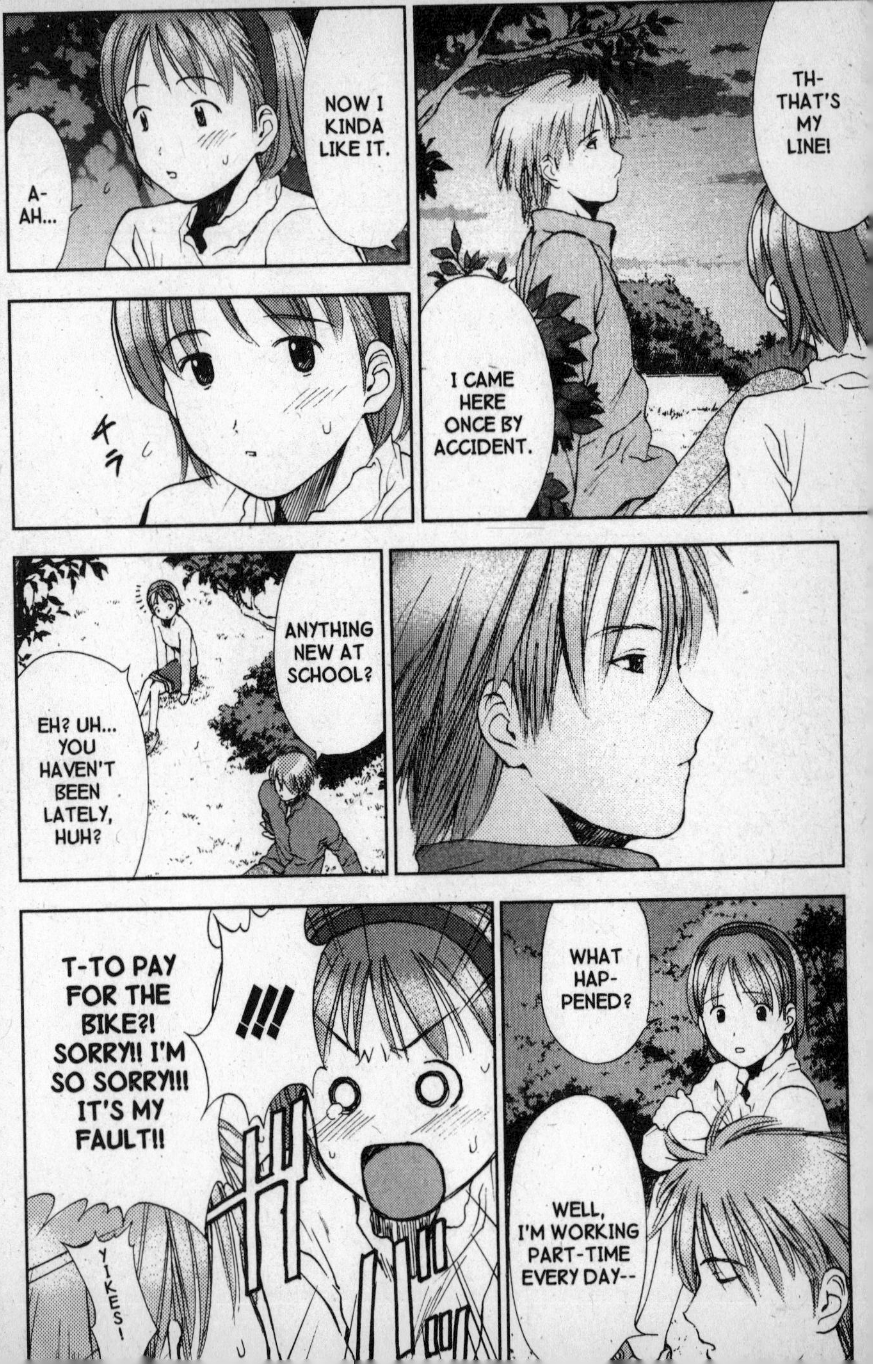
TH- THAT'S MY LINE!
I CAME HERE ONCE BY ACCIDENT.
NOW I KINDA LIKE IT.
A- AH...
キラ
ANYTHING NEW AT SCHOOL?
EH? UH... YOU HAVEN'T BEEN LATELY, HUH?
WHAT HAP- PENED?
WELL, I'M WORKING PART-TIME EVERY DAY--
!!!
T-TO PAY FOR THE BIKE?! SORRY!! I'M SO SORRY!!! IT'S MY FAULT!!
YIKES!

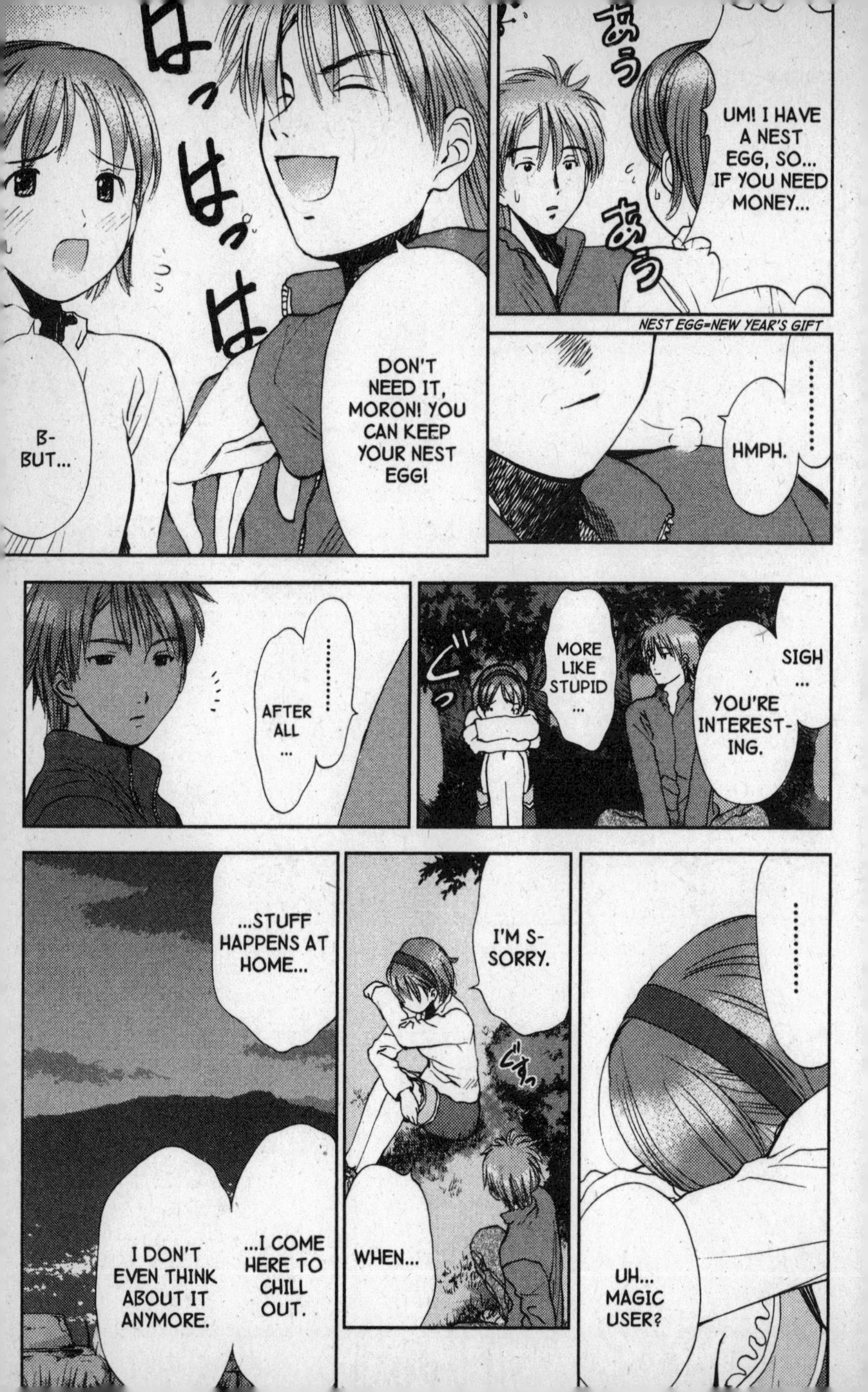
あう
あう
UM! I HAVE A NEST EGG, SO... IF YOU NEED MONEY...
NEST EGG=NEW YEAR'S GIFT
......
HMPH.
はっはっは
DON'T NEED IT, MORON! YOU CAN KEEP YOUR NEST EGG!
B-BUT...
SIGH... YOU'RE INTERESTING.
MORE LIKE STUPID...
ぐっ
......
AFTER ALL...
......
UH... MAGIC USER?
I'M S-SORRY.
ぐすっ
WHEN...
...STUFF HAPPENS AT HOME...
...I COME HERE TO CHILL OUT.
I DON'T EVEN THINK ABOUT IT ANYMORE.

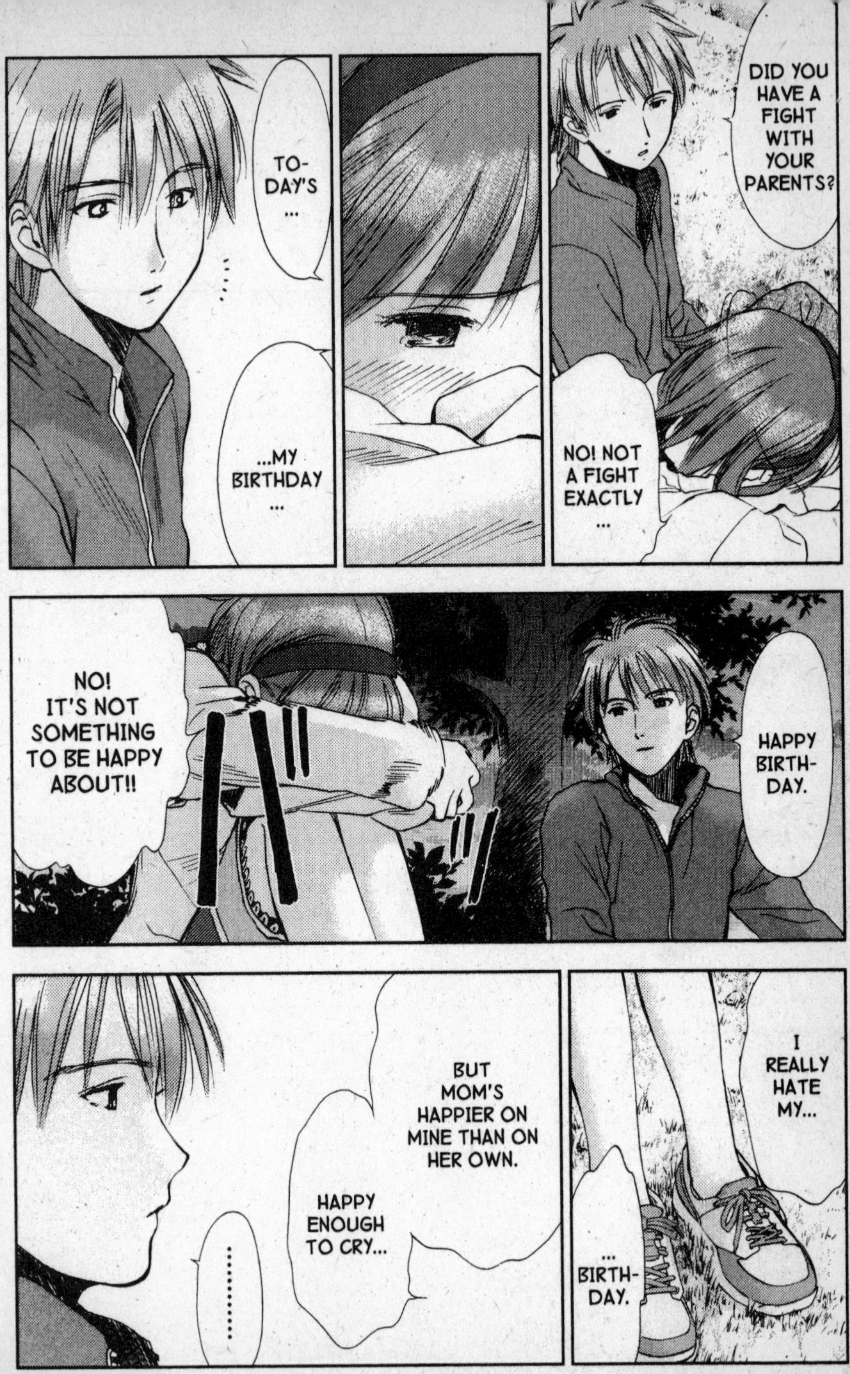
DID YOU HAVE A FIGHT WITH YOUR PARENTS?
NO! NOT A FIGHT EXACTLY ...
TO-DAY'S ...
....
...MY BIRTHDAY ...
HAPPY BIRTH-DAY.
NO! IT'S NOT SOMETHING TO BE HAPPY ABOUT!!
I REALLY HATE MY...
... BIRTH-DAY.
BUT MOM'S HAPPIER ON MINE THAN ON HER OWN.
HAPPY ENOUGH TO CRY...
....

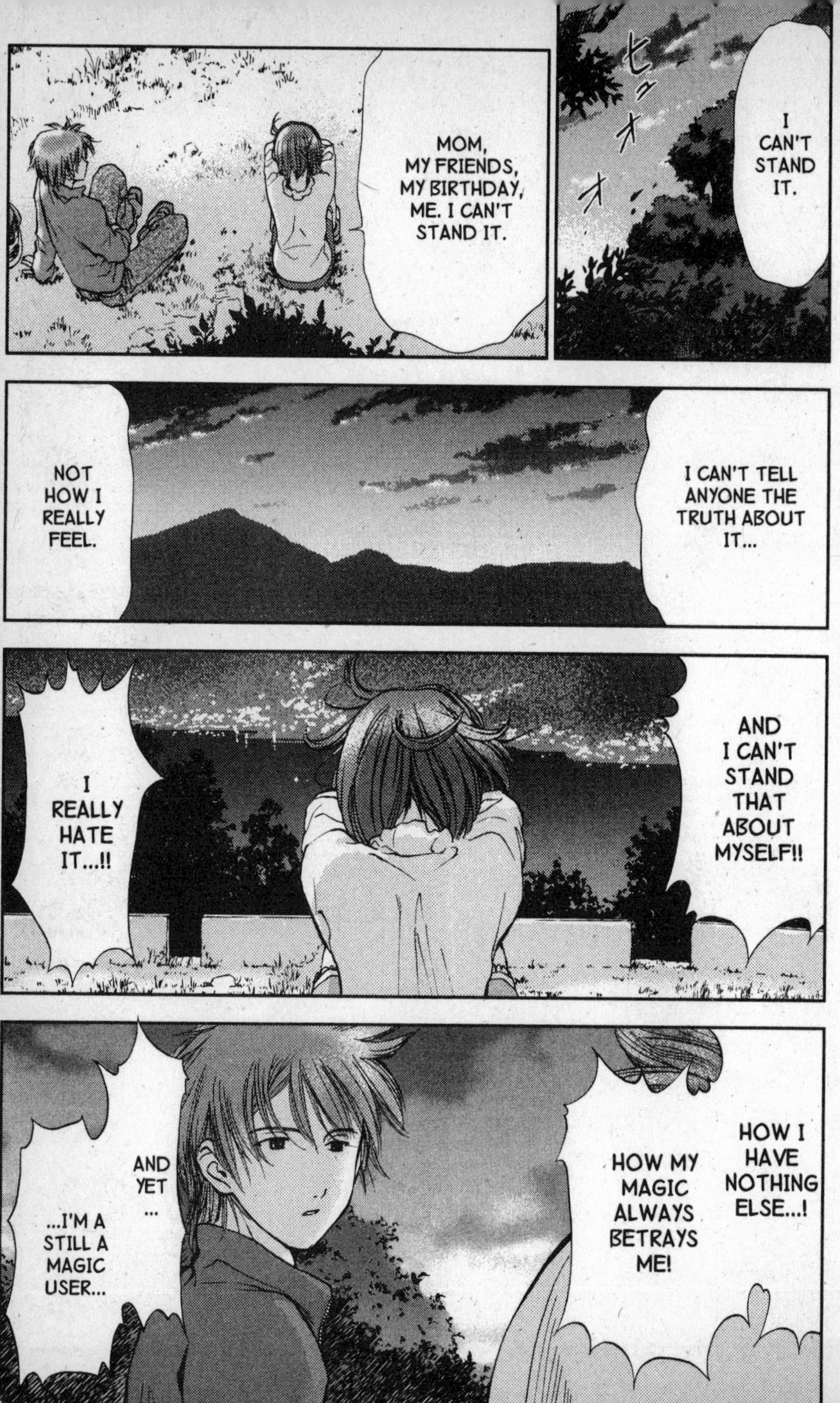
ヒュオオォ
I CAN'T STAND IT.
MOM, MY FRIENDS, MY BIRTHDAY, ME. I CAN'T STAND IT.
I CAN'T TELL ANYONE THE TRUTH ABOUT IT...
NOT HOW I REALLY FEEL.
AND I CAN'T STAND THAT ABOUT MYSELF!!
I REALLY HATE IT...!!
HOW I HAVE NOTHING ELSE...!
HOW MY MAGIC ALWAYS BETRAYS ME!
AND YET ...
...I'M A STILL A MAGIC USER...

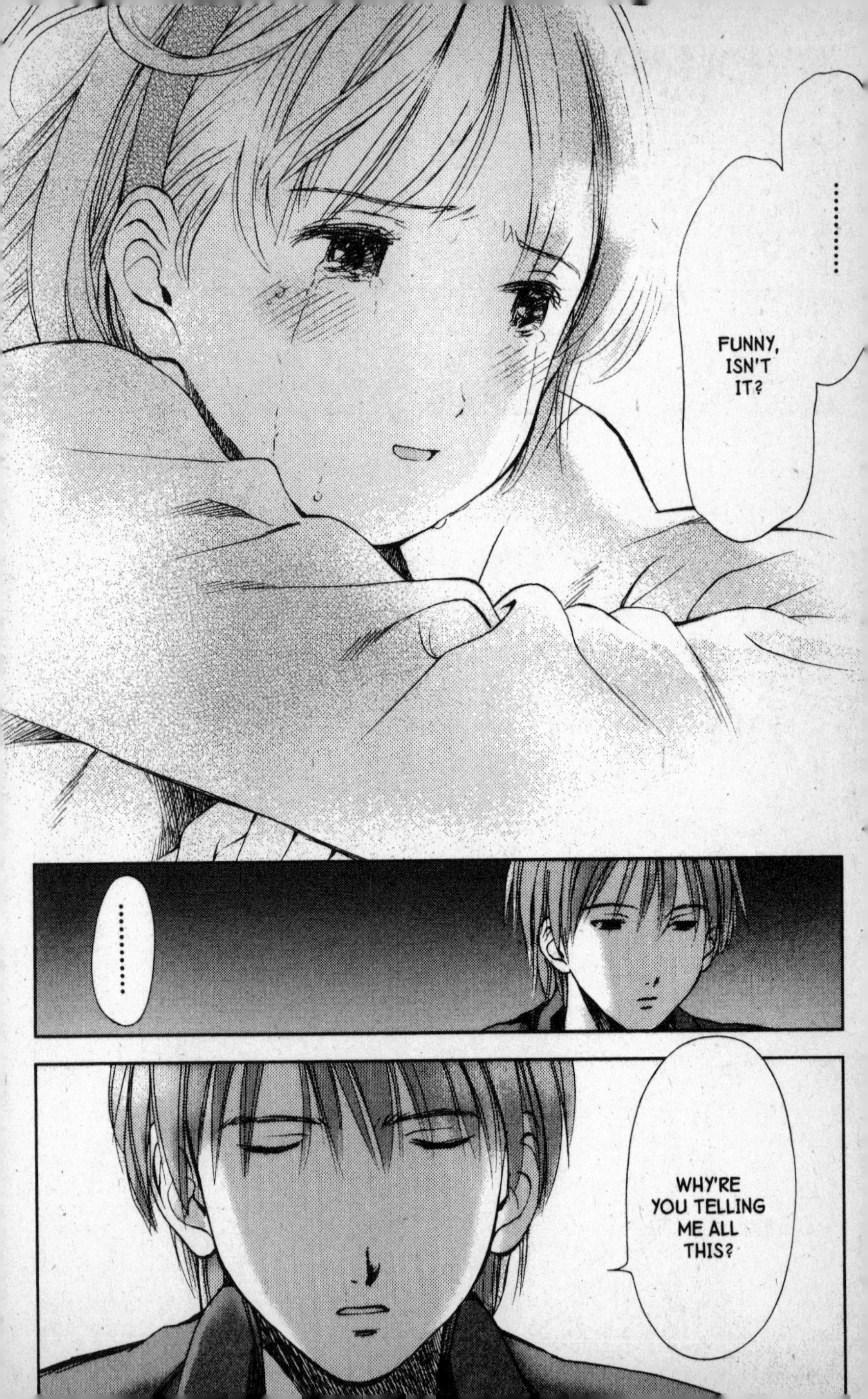
....
FUNNY, ISN'T IT?
....
WHY'RE YOU TELLING ME ALL THIS?

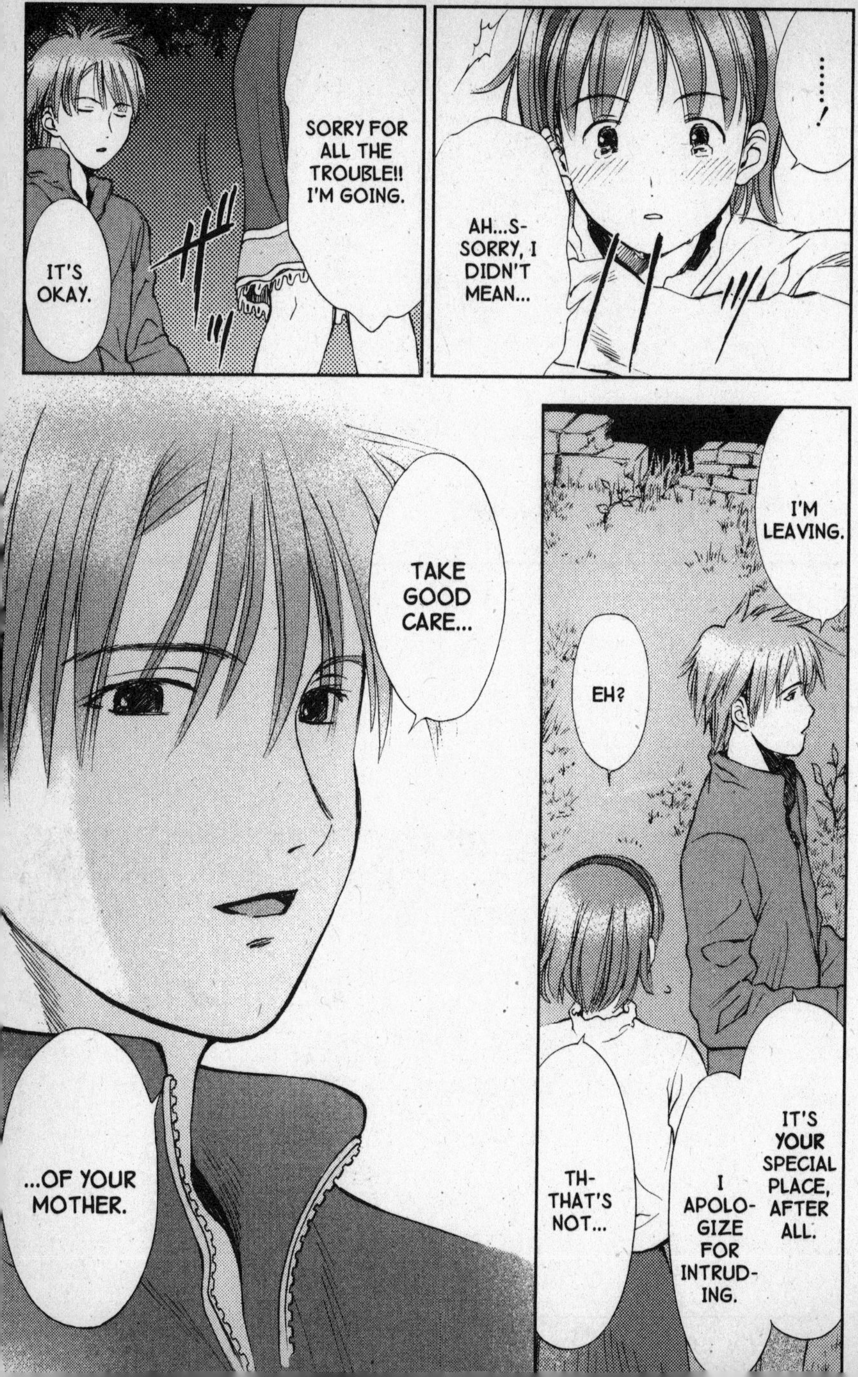
......!
AH...S-SORRY, I DIDN'T MEAN...
SORRY FOR ALL THE TROUBLE!! I'M GOING.
IT'S OKAY.
I'M LEAVING.
EH?
IT'S YOUR SPECIAL PLACE, AFTER ALL.
I APOLOGIZE FOR INTRUDING.
TH-THAT'S NOT...
TAKE GOOD CARE...
...OF YOUR MOTHER.

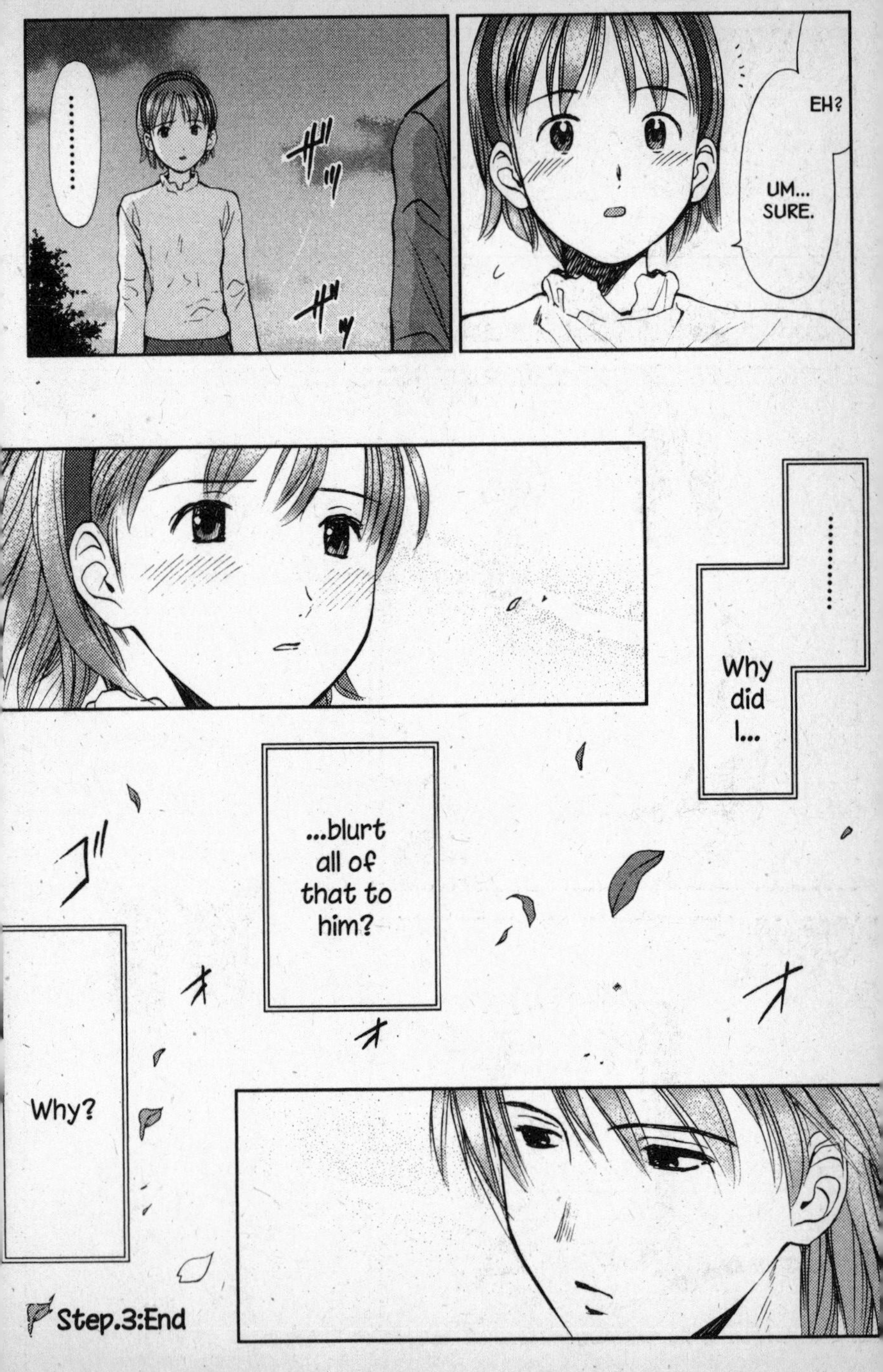
EH?
UM... SURE.
......
ザッ
ザッ
......
Why did I...
...blurt all of that to him?
ゴッ
オ
オ
オ
Why?
Step.3:End

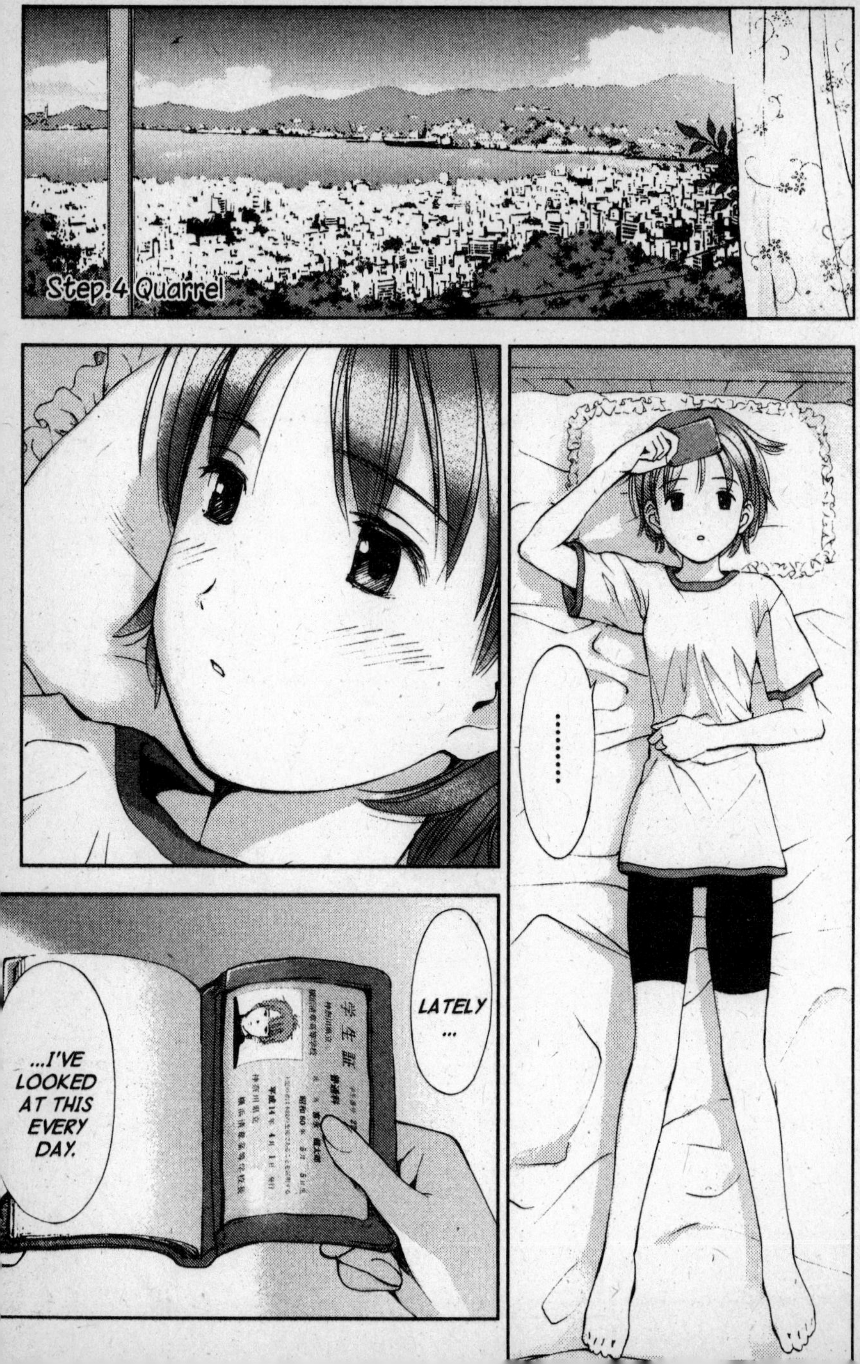
Step.4 Quarrel
....
LATELY ...
学生証
...I'VE LOOKED AT THIS EVERY DAY.

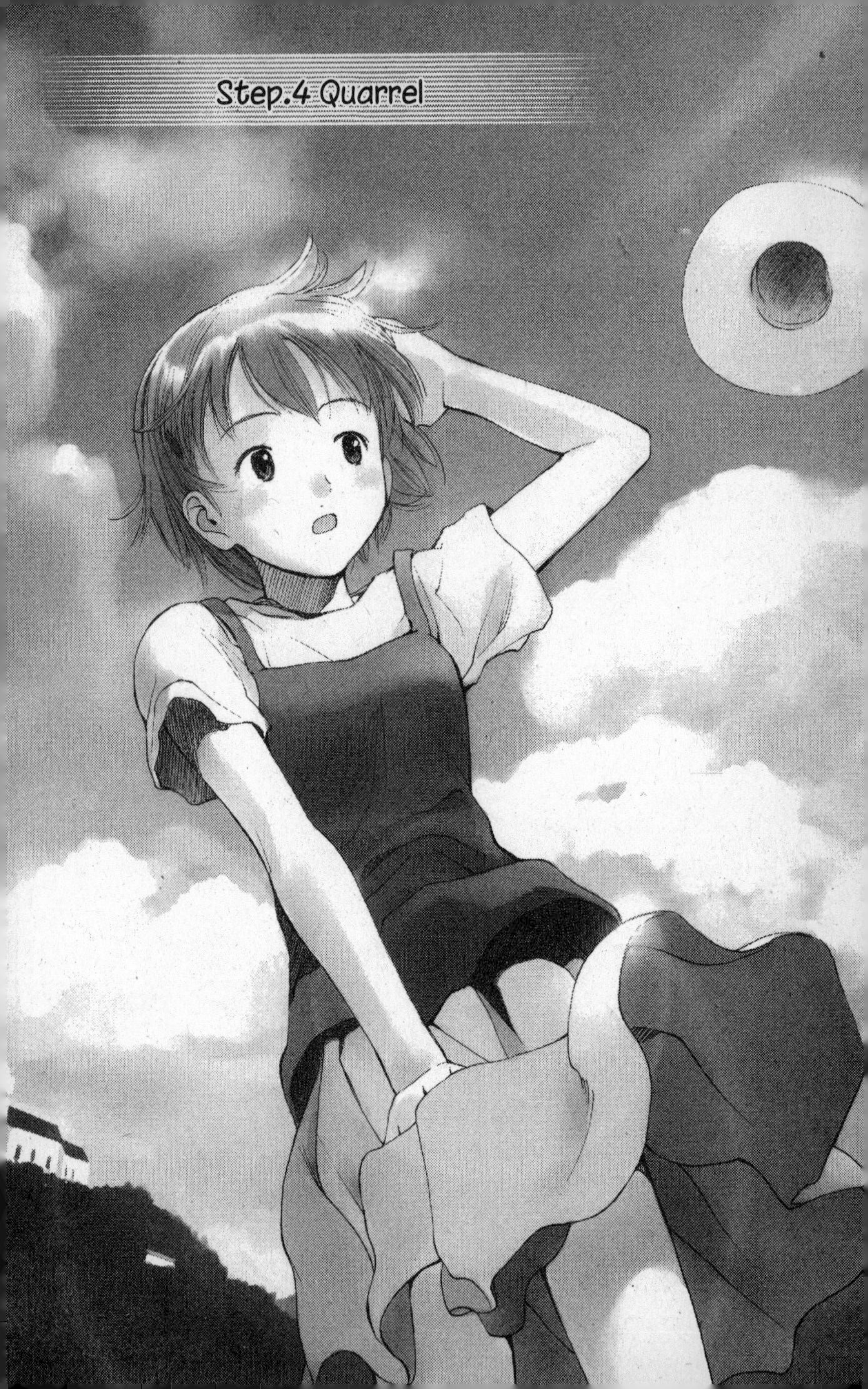
Step.4 Quarrel

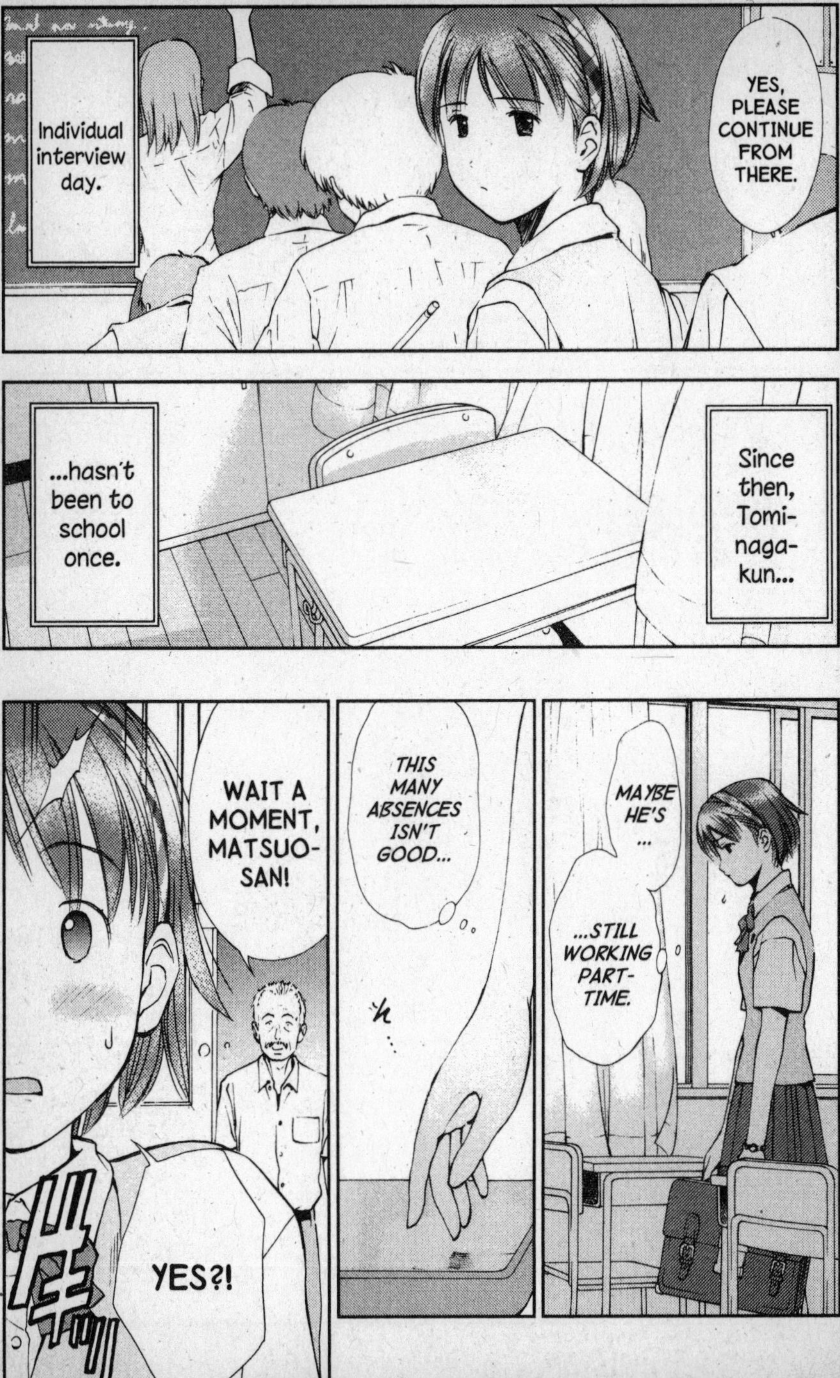
YES, PLEASE CONTINUE FROM THERE.
Individual interview day.
Since then, Tomi-naga-kun...
...hasn't been to school once.
MAYBE HE'S ...
...STILL WORKING PART-TIME.
THIS MANY ABSENCES ISN'T GOOD...
h...
WAIT A MOMENT, MATSUO-SAN!
YES?!

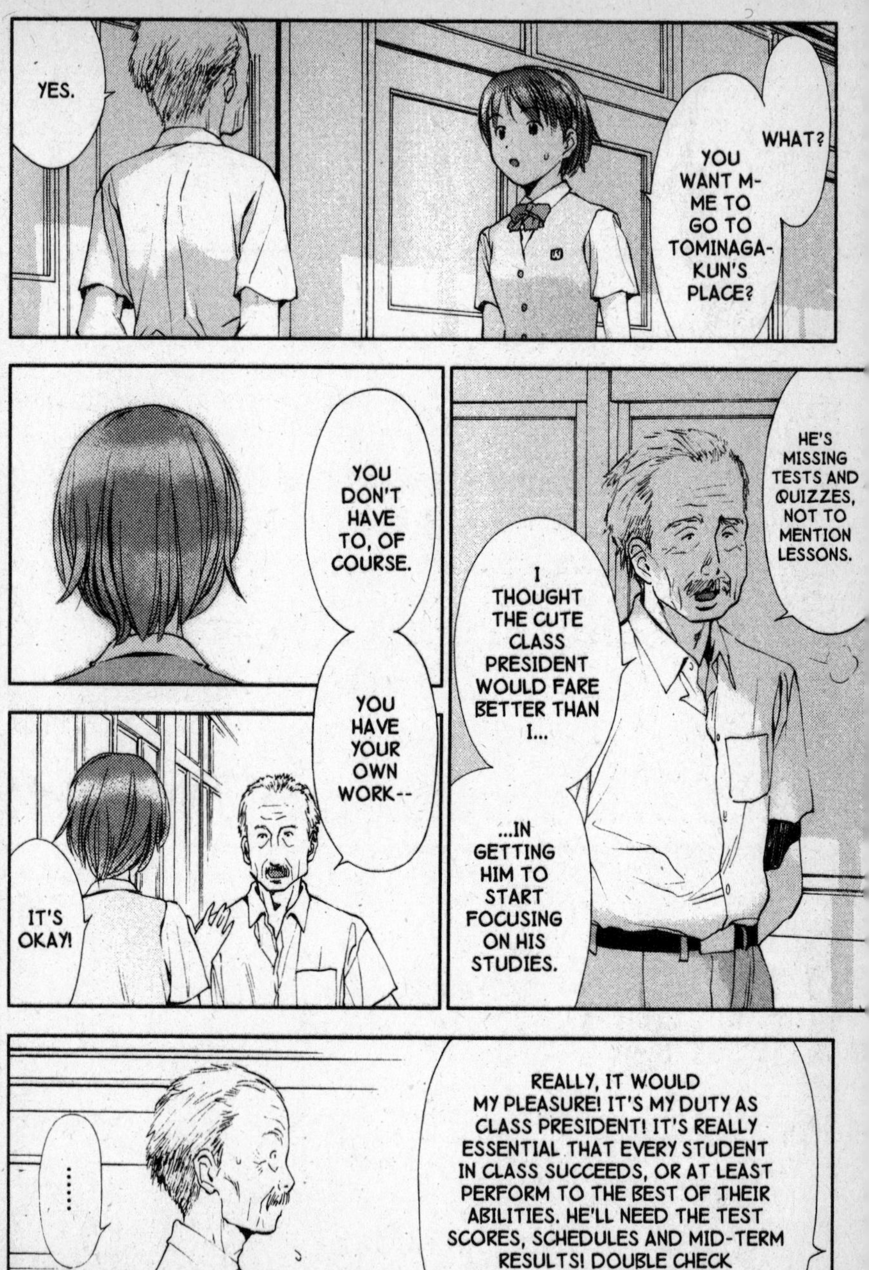
WHAT? YOU WANT M-ME TO GO TO TOMINAGA-KUN'S PLACE?
YES.
HE'S MISSING TESTS AND QUIZZES, NOT TO MENTION LESSONS.
...I THOUGHT THE CUTE CLASS PRESIDENT WOULD FARE BETTER THAN I...
...IN GETTING HIM TO START FOCUSING ON HIS STUDIES.
YOU DON'T HAVE TO, OF COURSE.
YOU HAVE YOUR OWN WORK--
IT'S OKAY!
REALLY, IT WOULD MY PLEASURE! IT'S MY DUTY AS CLASS PRESIDENT! IT'S REALLY ESSENTIAL THAT EVERY STUDENT IN CLASS SUCCEEDS, OR AT LEAST PERFORM TO THE BEST OF THEIR ABILITIES. HE'LL NEED THE TEST SCORES, SCHEDULES AND MID-TERM RESULTS! DOUBLE CHECK HIS ADDRESS!
......

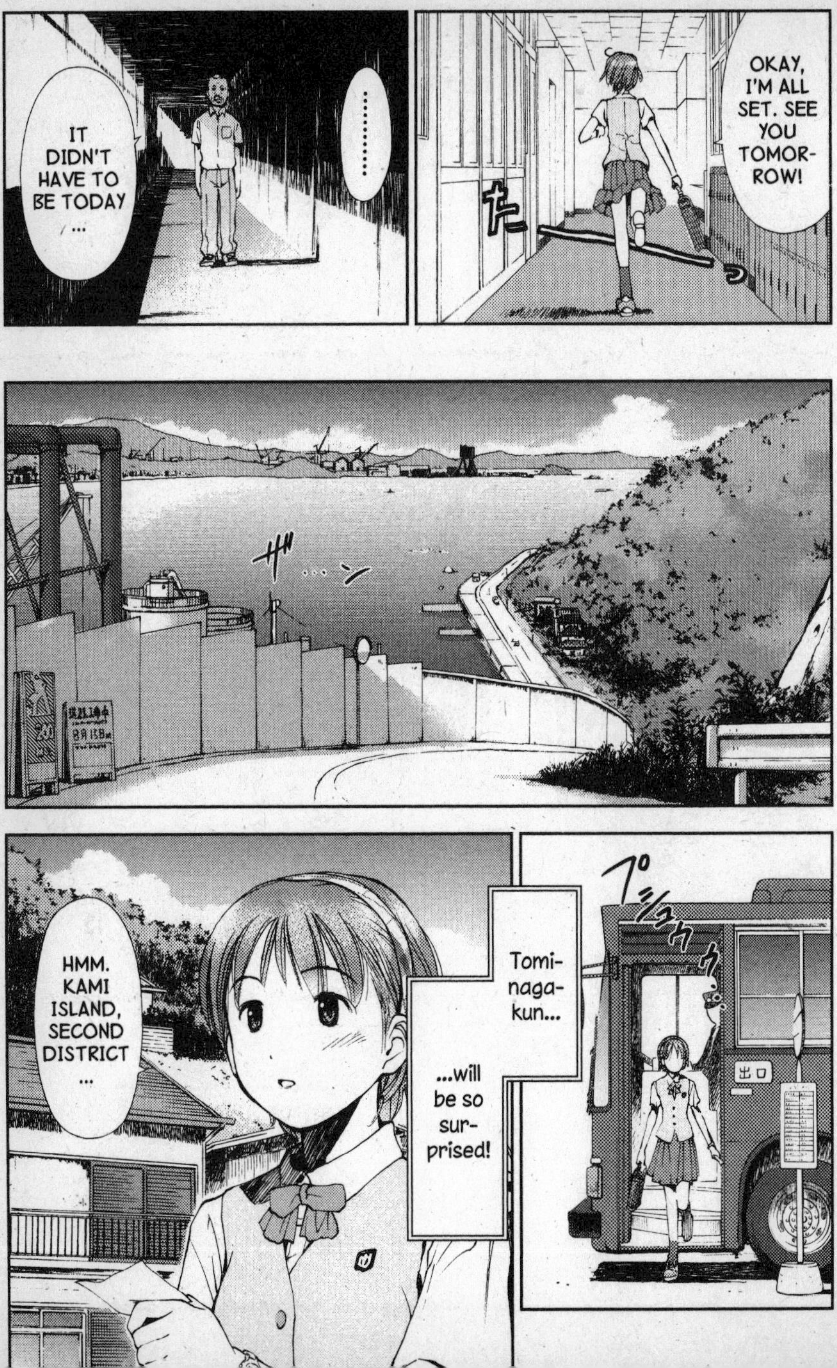

OKAY, I'M ALL SET. SEE YOU TOMORROW!
......
IT DIDN'T HAVE TO BE TODAY...
出口
Tomi-naga-kun...
...will be so sur-prised!
HMM. KAMI ISLAND, SECOND DISTRICT...

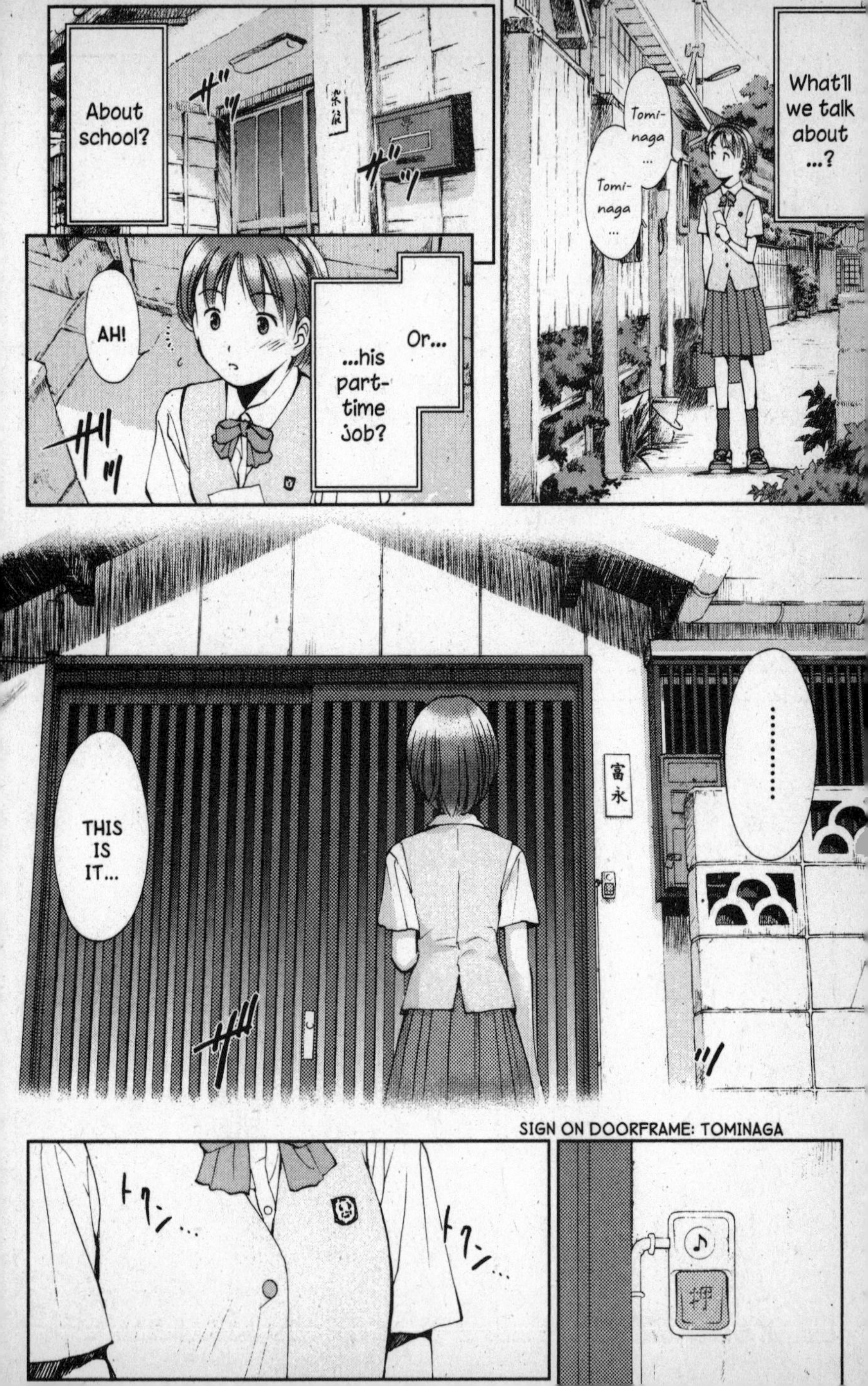
What'll we talk about ...?
Tomi-naga ...
Tomi-naga ...
About school?
Or...
...his part-time job?
AH!
....
THIS IS IT...
富永
トクン...
トクン...
SIGN ON DOORFRAME: TOMINAGA

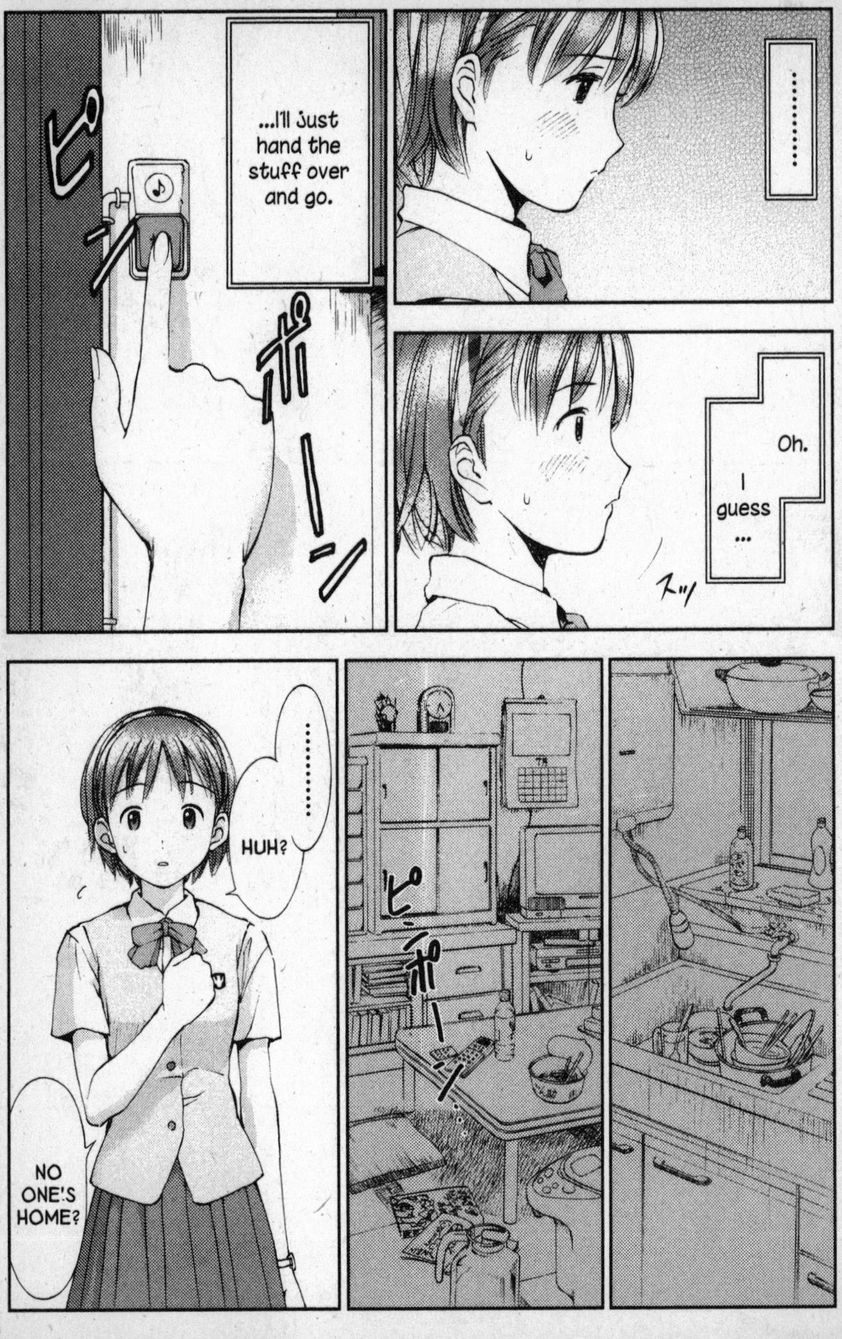
……
Oh. I guess…
スッ
...I'll just hand the stuff over and go.
ピンポーン
ピンポーン…
……
HUH?
NO ONE'S HOME?

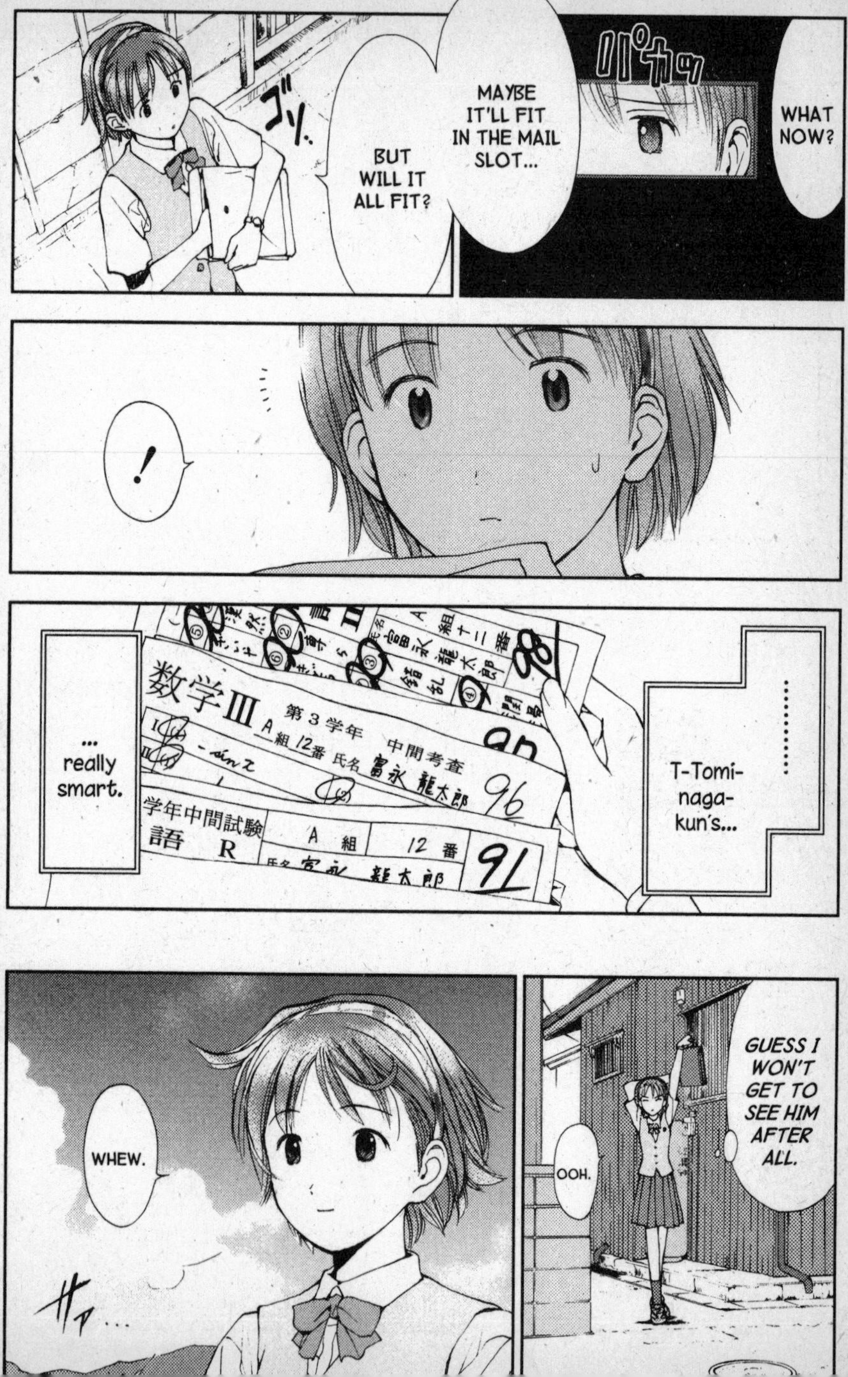
WHAT NOW?
MAYBE IT'LL FIT IN THE MAIL SLOT...
BUT WILL IT ALL FIT?
!
T-Tomi-naga-kun's...
......
... really smart.
GUESS I WON'T GET TO SEE HIM AFTER ALL.
OOH.
WHEW.

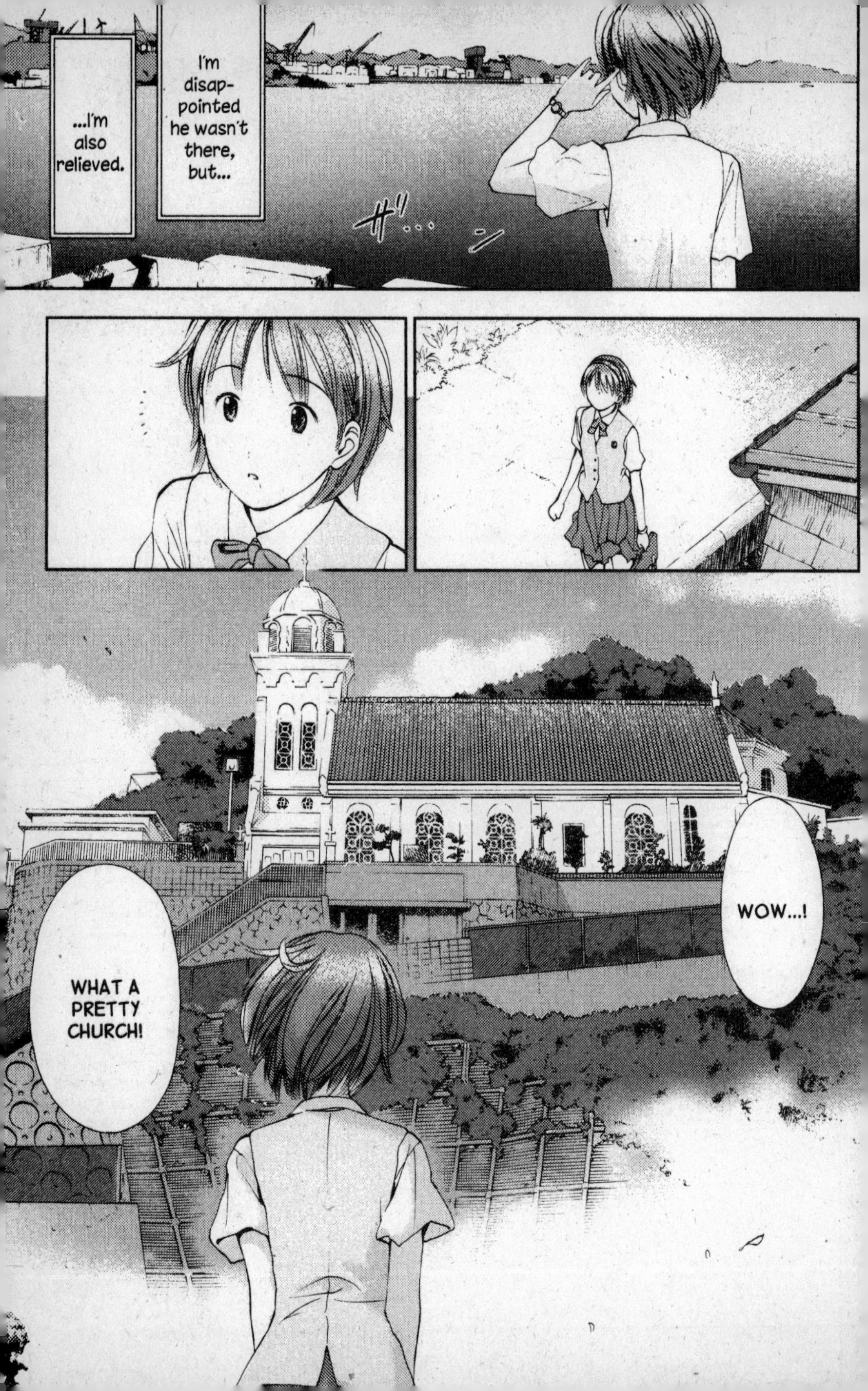
I'm disappointed he wasn't there, but...
...I'm also relieved.
ザ…ン
WOW...!
WHAT A PRETTY CHURCH!

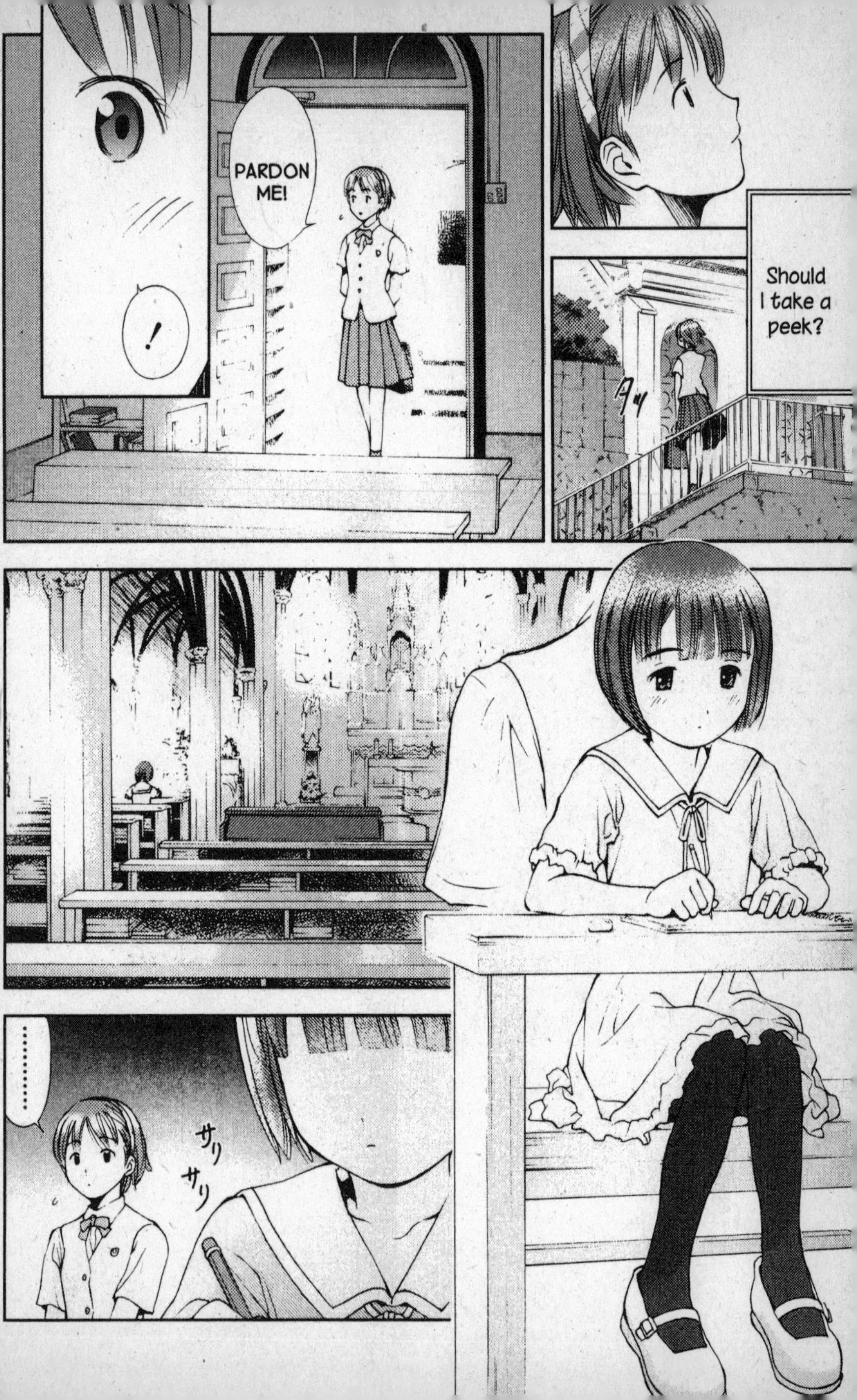
Should I take a peek?
タッ
PARDON ME!
!
......
サリ
サリ

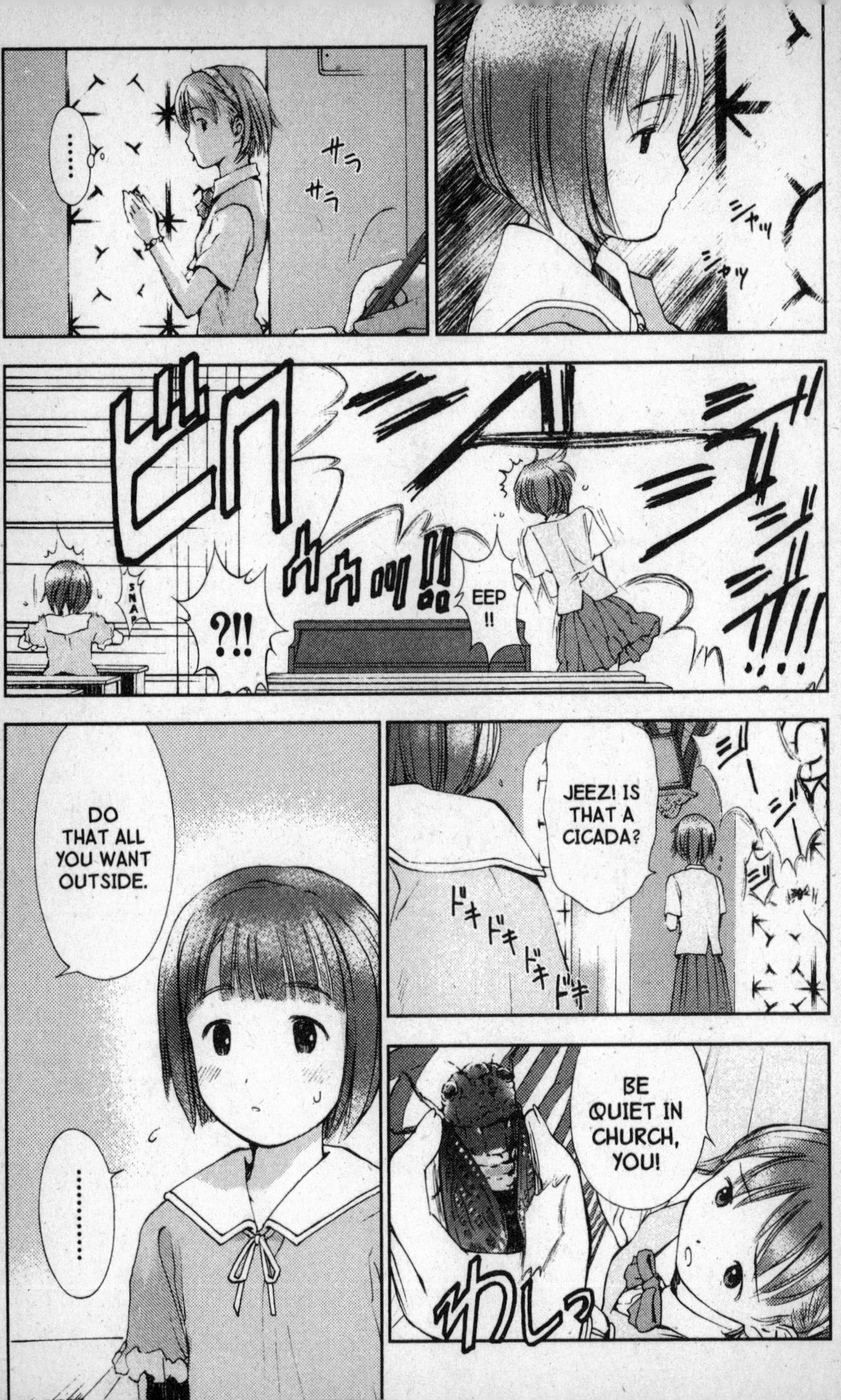

シャッ
シャッ
……
サラ
サラ
ジジジ!!!
ビクンッ!!
EEP !!
?!!
SNAP
JEEZ! IS THAT A CICADA?
ドキ ドキ ドキ ドキ
BE QUIET IN CHURCH, YOU!
わしっ
DO THAT ALL YOU WANT OUTSIDE.
……

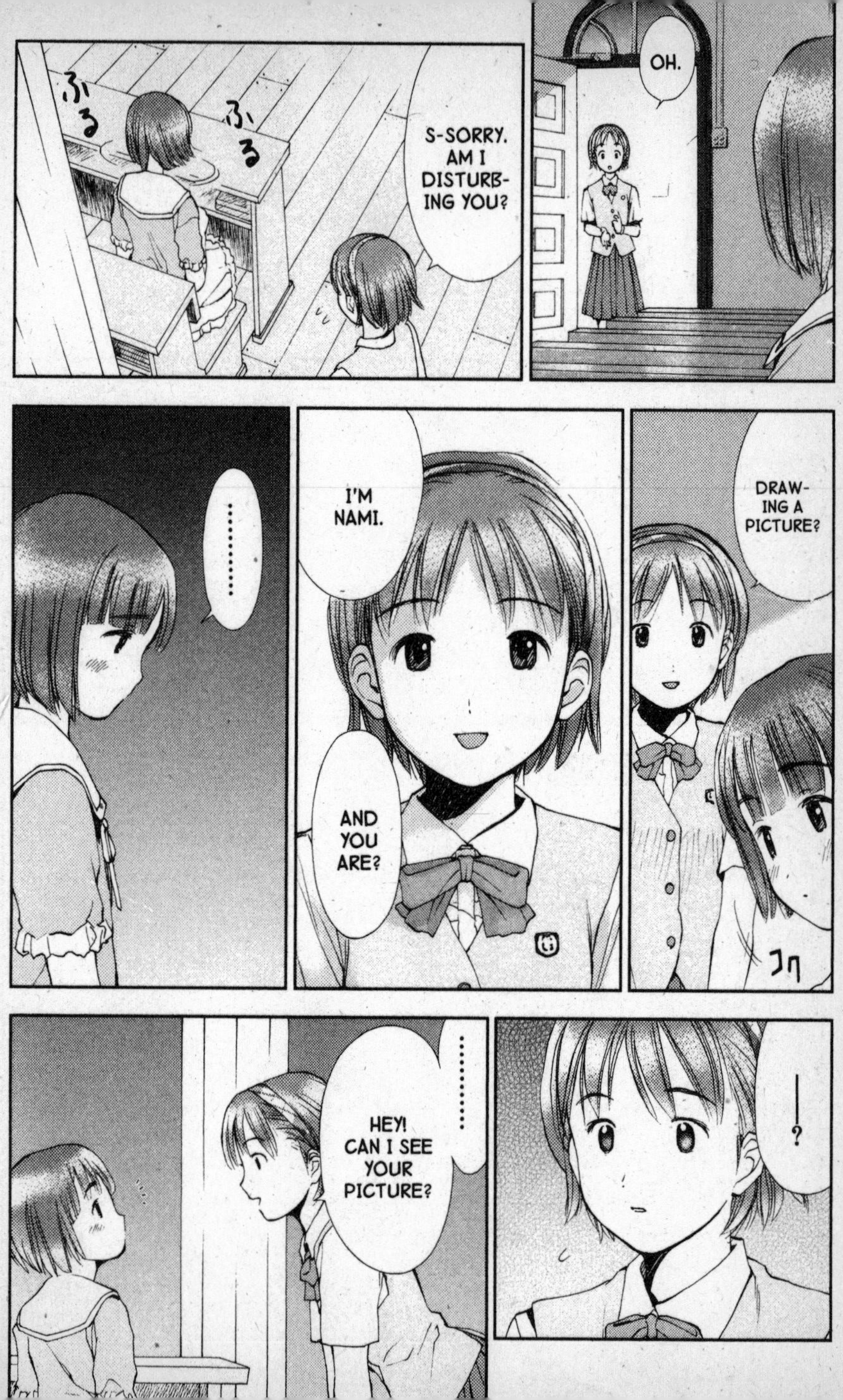
OH.
S-SORRY. AM I DISTURB-ING YOU?
ふる
ふる
DRAW-ING A PICTURE?
コク
I'M NAMI.
AND YOU ARE?
....
—?
....
HEY! CAN I SEE YOUR PICTURE?

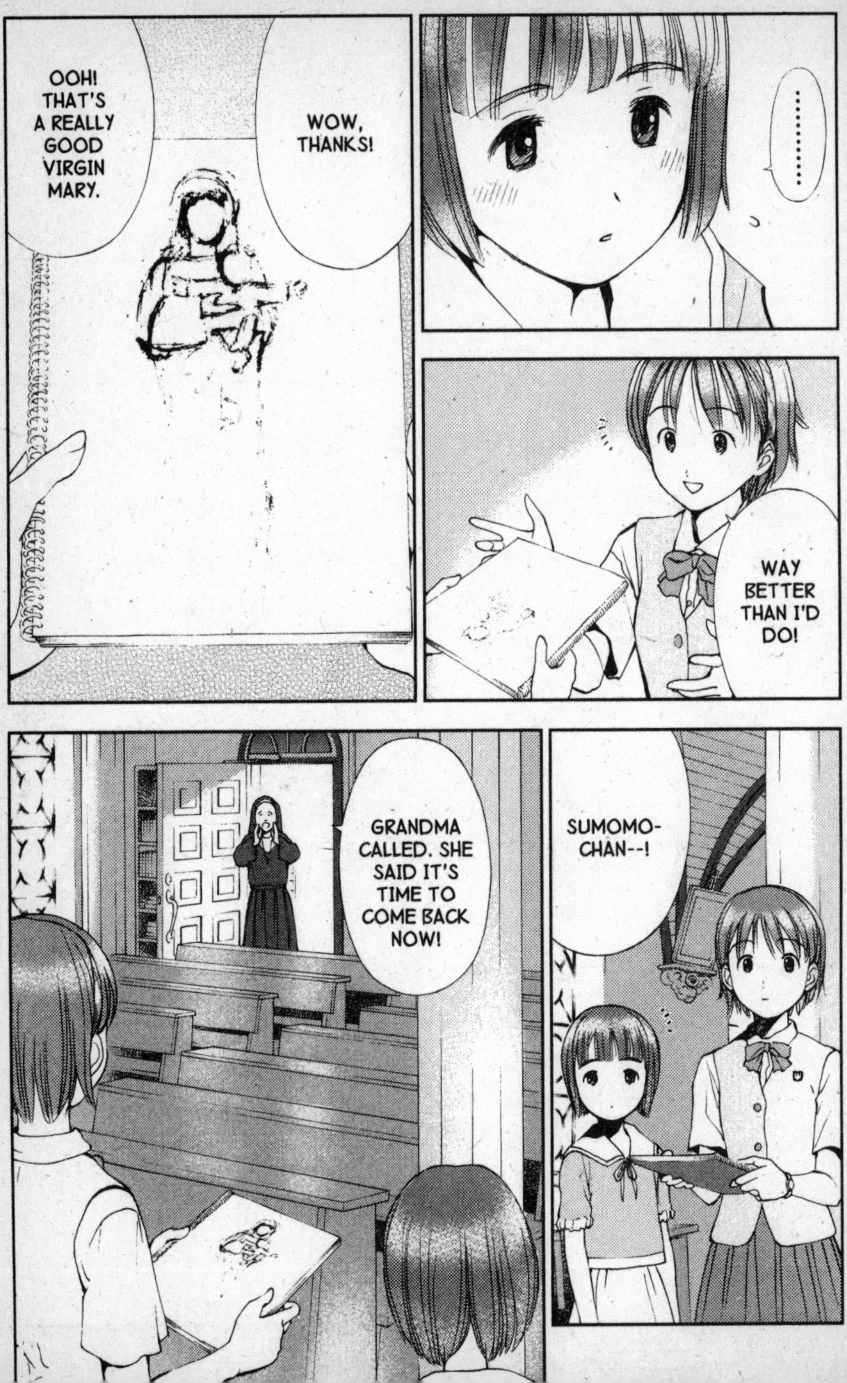
......
WAY BETTER THAN I'D DO!
WOW, THANKS!
OOH! THAT'S A REALLY GOOD VIRGIN MARY.
SUMOMO-CHAN--!
GRANDMA CALLED. SHE SAID IT'S TIME TO COME BACK NOW!

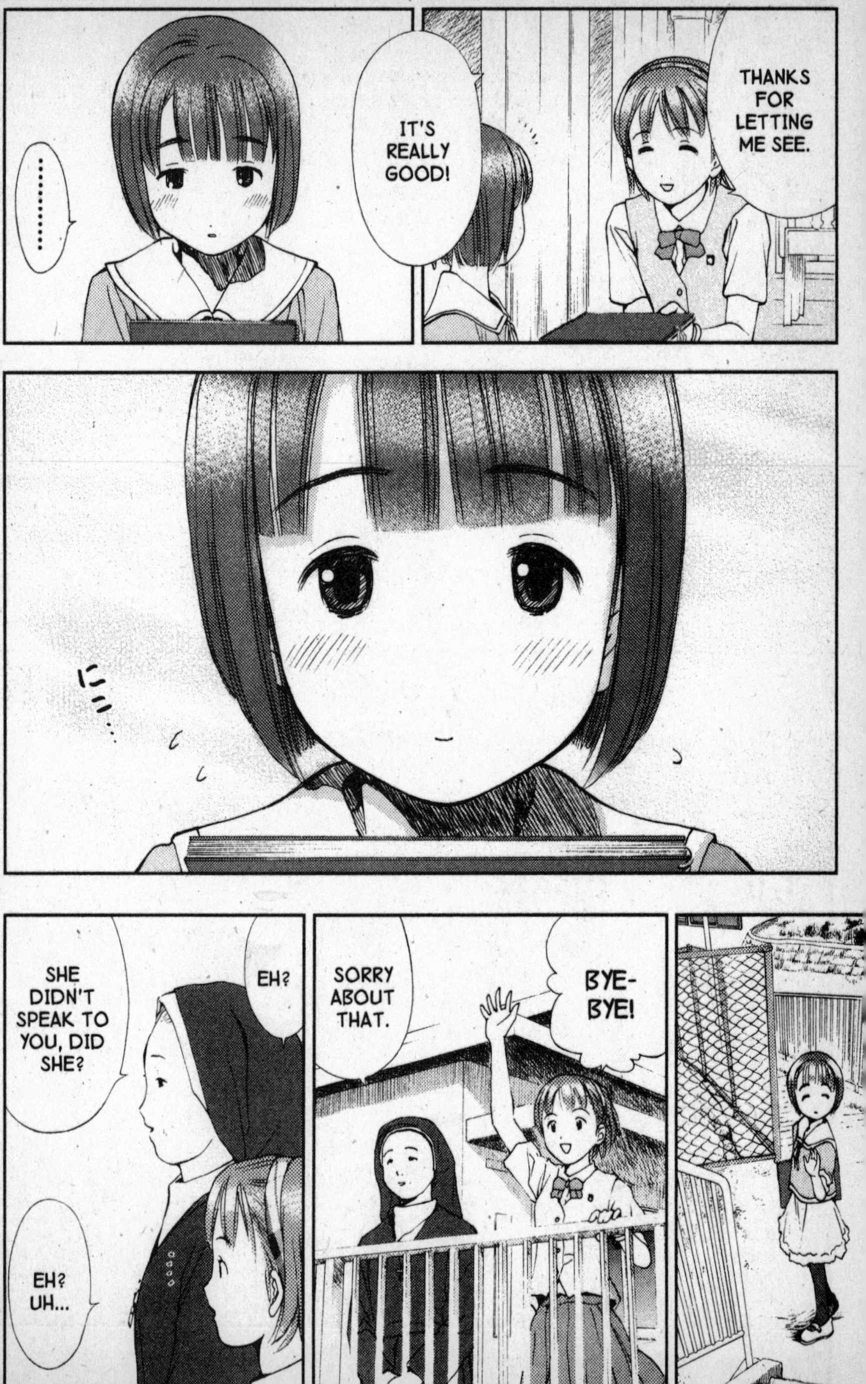
THANKS FOR LETTING ME SEE.
IT'S REALLY GOOD!
……
にこ…
BYE-BYE!
SORRY ABOUT THAT.
EH?
SHE DIDN'T SPEAK TO YOU, DID SHE?
EH? UH...

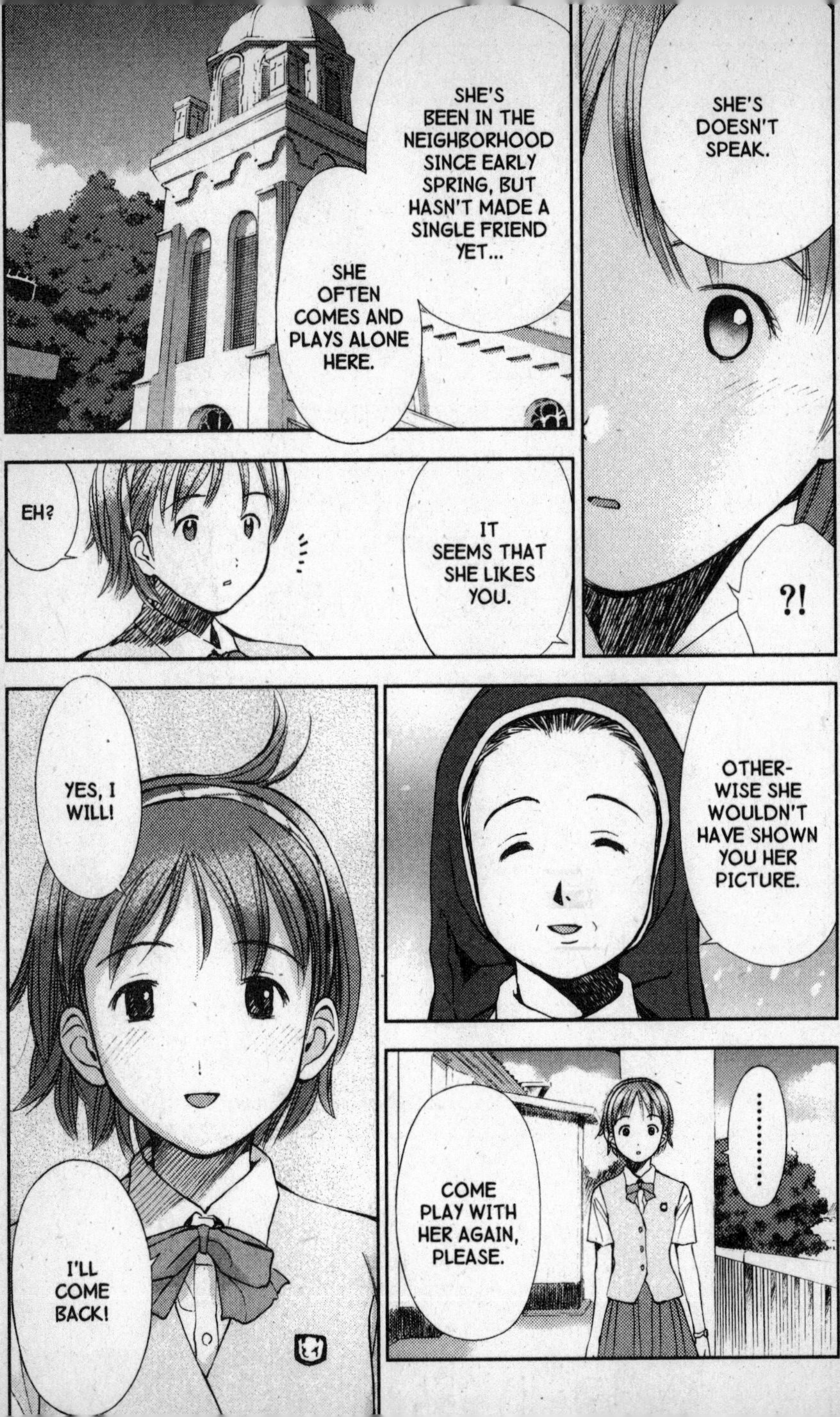
SHE'S DOESN'T SPEAK.
?!
SHE'S BEEN IN THE NEIGHBORHOOD SINCE EARLY SPRING, BUT HASN'T MADE A SINGLE FRIEND YET...
SHE OFTEN COMES AND PLAYS ALONE HERE.
IT SEEMS THAT SHE LIKES YOU.
EH?
OTHER-WISE SHE WOULDN'T HAVE SHOWN YOU HER PICTURE.
....
COME PLAY WITH HER AGAIN, PLEASE.
YES, I WILL!
I'LL COME BACK!

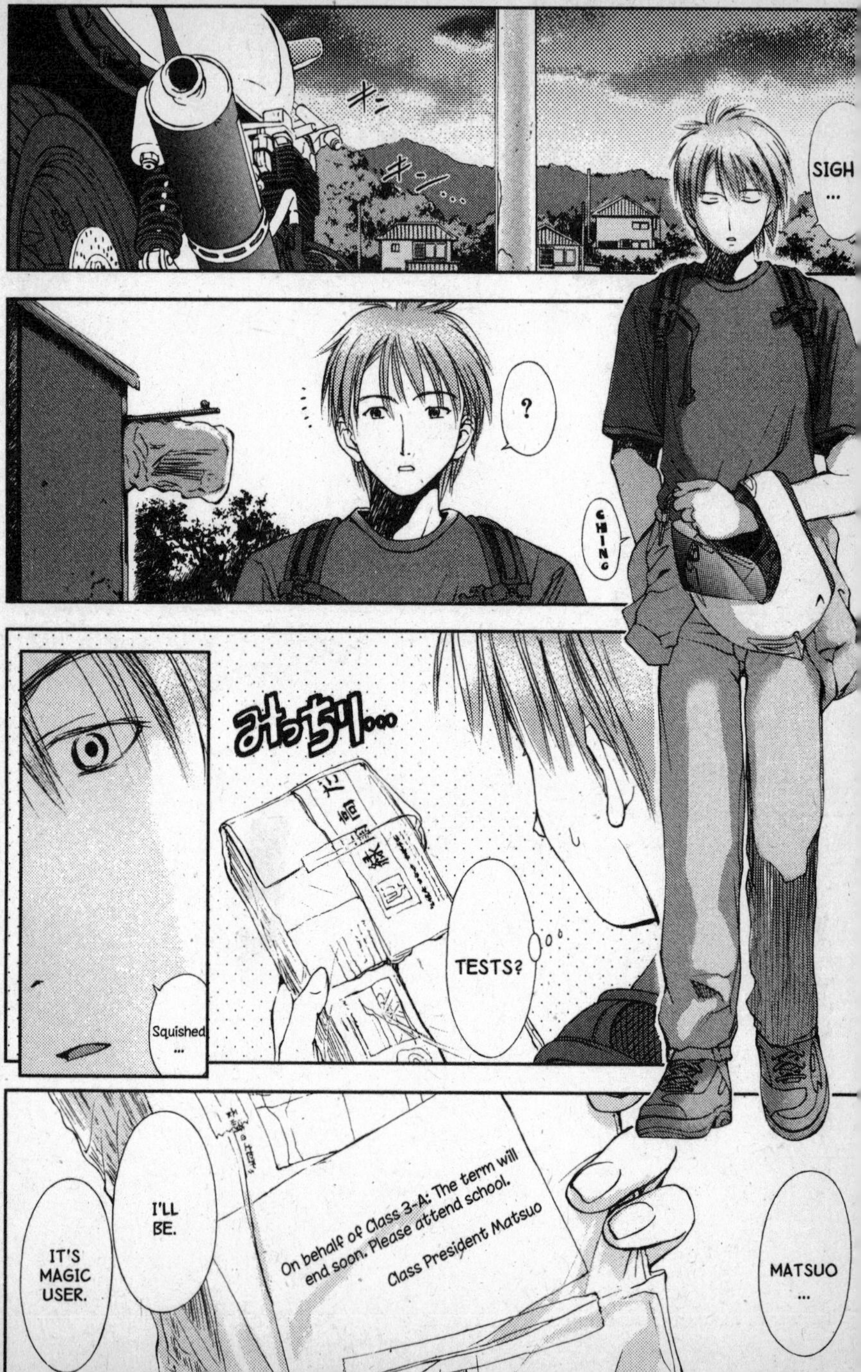
SIGH ...
キン
キン…
?
CHING
みっちり…
TESTS?
Squished ...
MATSUO ...
On behalf of Class 3-A: The term will end soon. Please attend school.
Class President Matsuo
I'LL BE.
IT'S MAGIC USER.

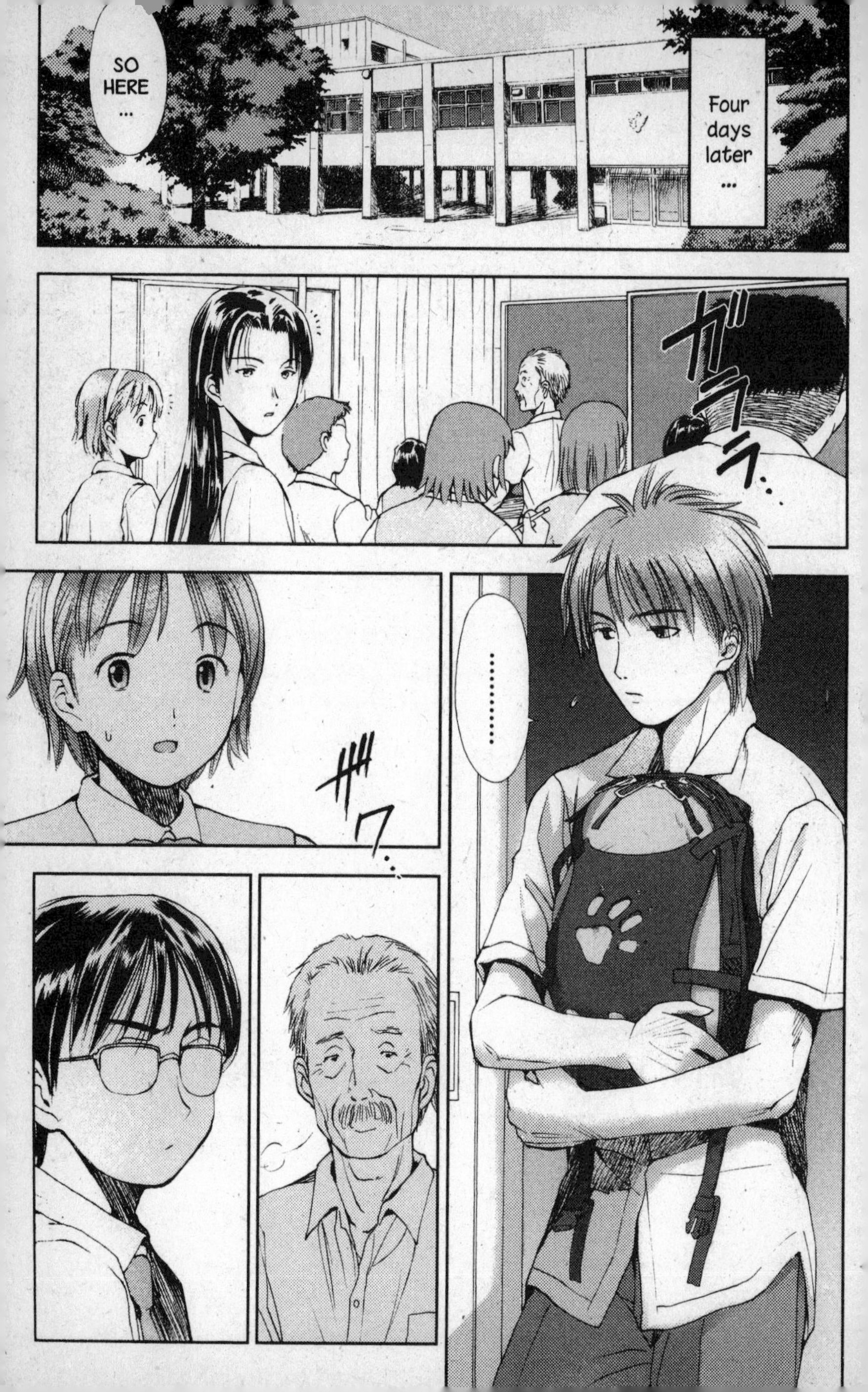
Four days later ...
SO HERE ...
ガラ ...
......
ザワ ...

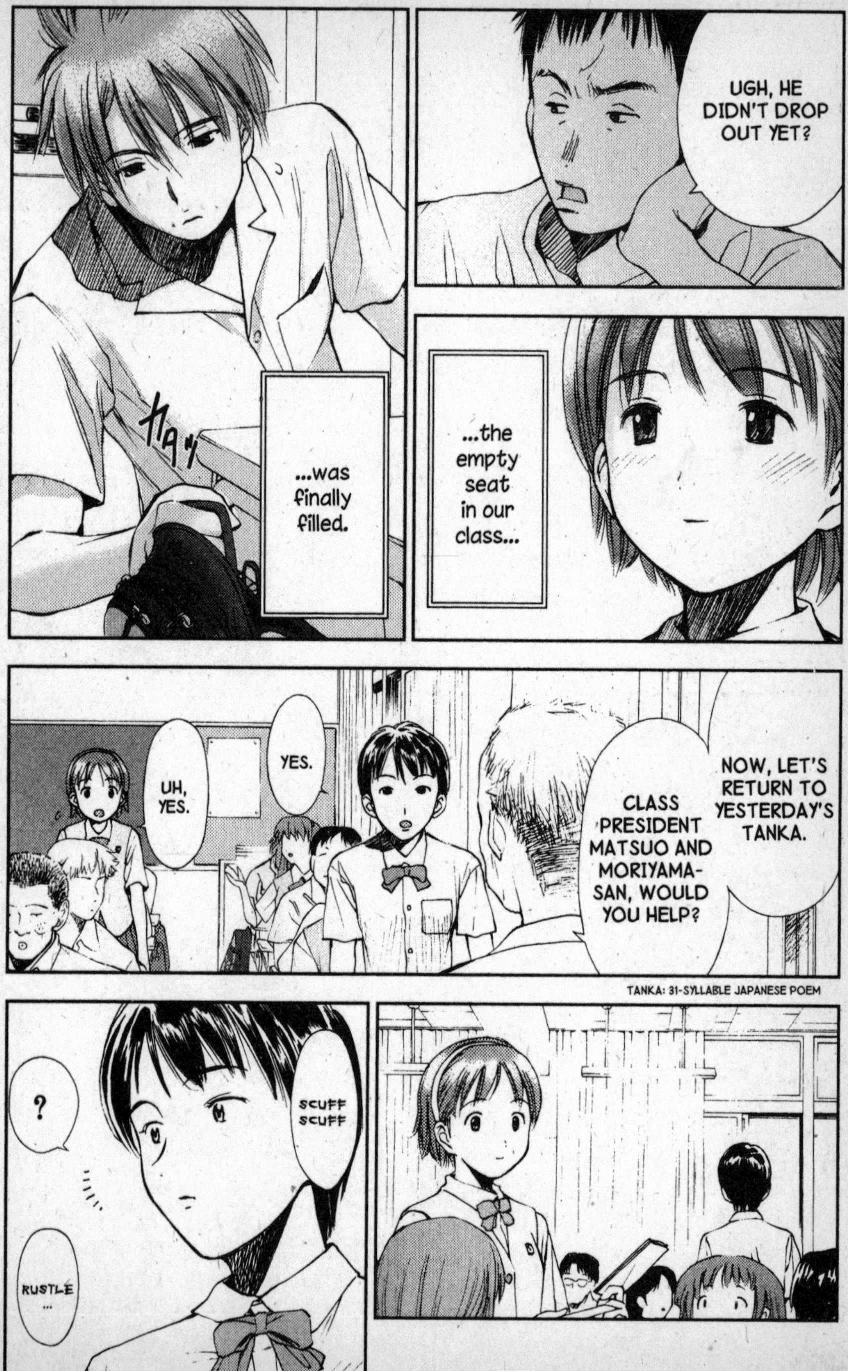
UGH, HE DIDN'T DROP OUT YET?
...the empty seat in our class...
...was finally filled.
ガタッ
NOW, LET'S RETURN TO YESTERDAY'S TANKA.
CLASS PRESIDENT MATSUO AND MORIYAMA-SAN, WOULD YOU HELP?
YES.
UH, YES.
SCUFF SCUFF
?
RUSTLE ...

TANKA: 31-SYLLABLE JAPANESE POEM

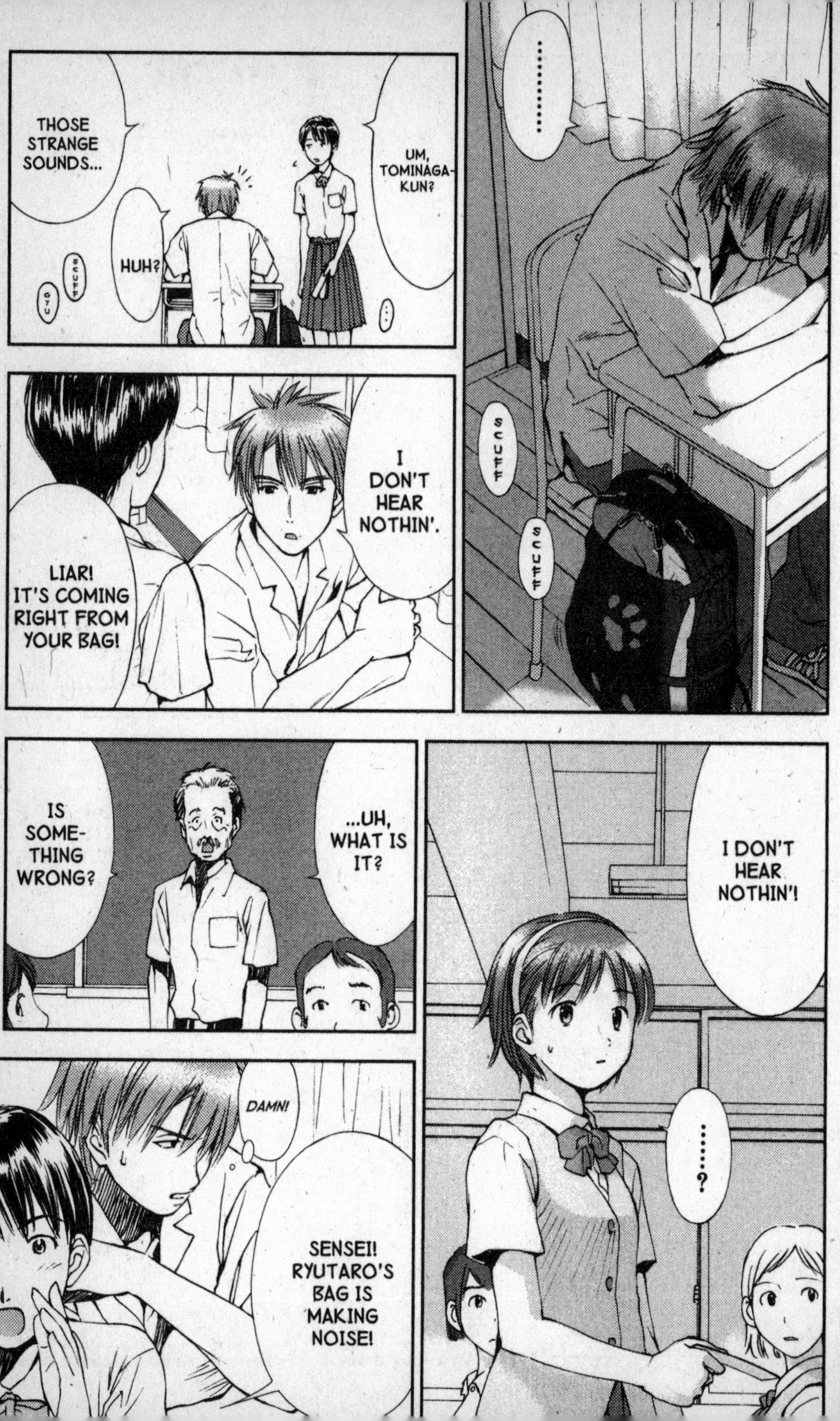
......
SCUFF
SCUFF
UM, TOMINAGA-KUN?
THOSE STRANGE SOUNDS...
...
HUH?
SCUFF
GYU
I DON'T HEAR NOTHIN'.
LIAR! IT'S COMING RIGHT FROM YOUR BAG!
I DON'T HEAR NOTHIN'!
......?
...UH, WHAT IS IT?
IS SOMETHING WRONG?
DAMN!
SENSEI! RYUTARO'S BAG IS MAKING NOISE!

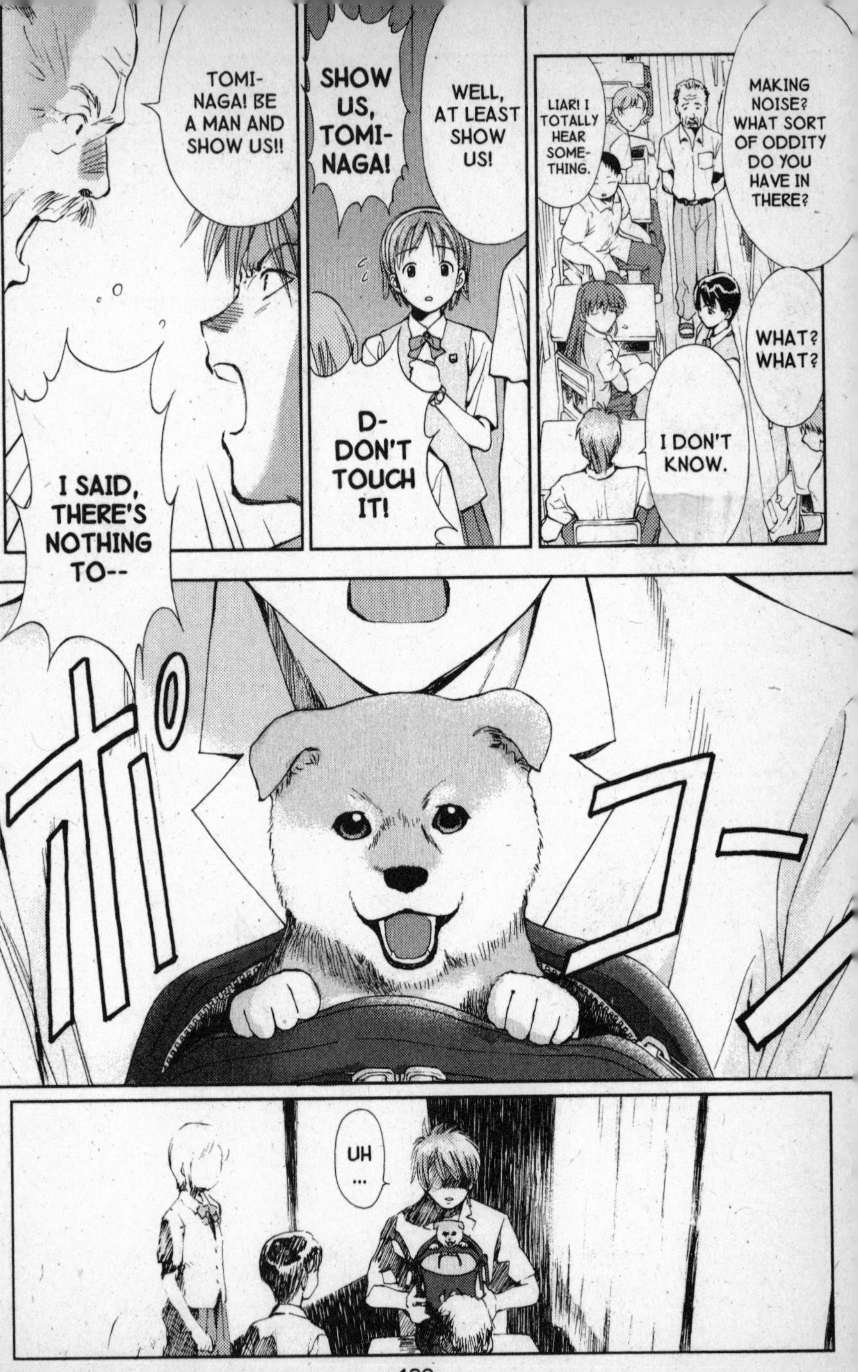

MAKING NOISE? WHAT SORT OF ODDITY DO YOU HAVE IN THERE?
LIAR! I TOTALLY HEAR SOME-THING.
WHAT? WHAT?
I DON'T KNOW.
WELL, AT LEAST SHOW US!
SHOW US, TOMI-NAGA!
D-DON'T TOUCH IT!
TOMI-NAGA! BE A MAN AND SHOW US!!
I SAID, THERE'S NOTHING TO--
ポコーン
UH ...

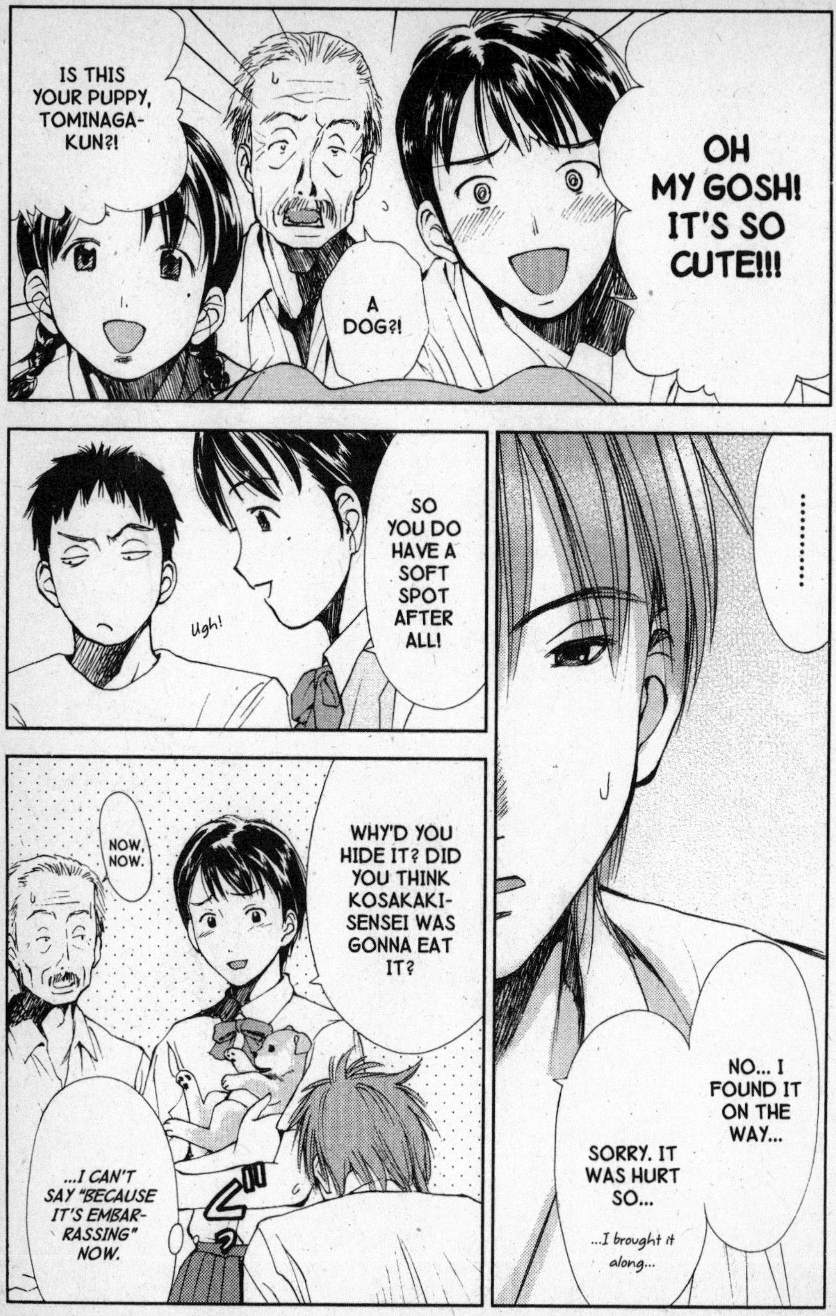
OH MY GOSH! IT'S SO CUTE!!!
A DOG?!
IS THIS YOUR PUPPY, TOMINAGA-KUN?!
......
NO... I FOUND IT ON THE WAY...
SORRY. IT WAS HURT SO...
...I brought it along...
SO YOU DO HAVE A SOFT SPOT AFTER ALL!
Ugh!
WHY'D YOU HIDE IT? DID YOU THINK KOSAKAKI-SENSEI WAS GONNA EAT IT?
NOW, NOW.
...I CAN'T SAY "BECAUSE IT'S EMBARRASSING" NOW.

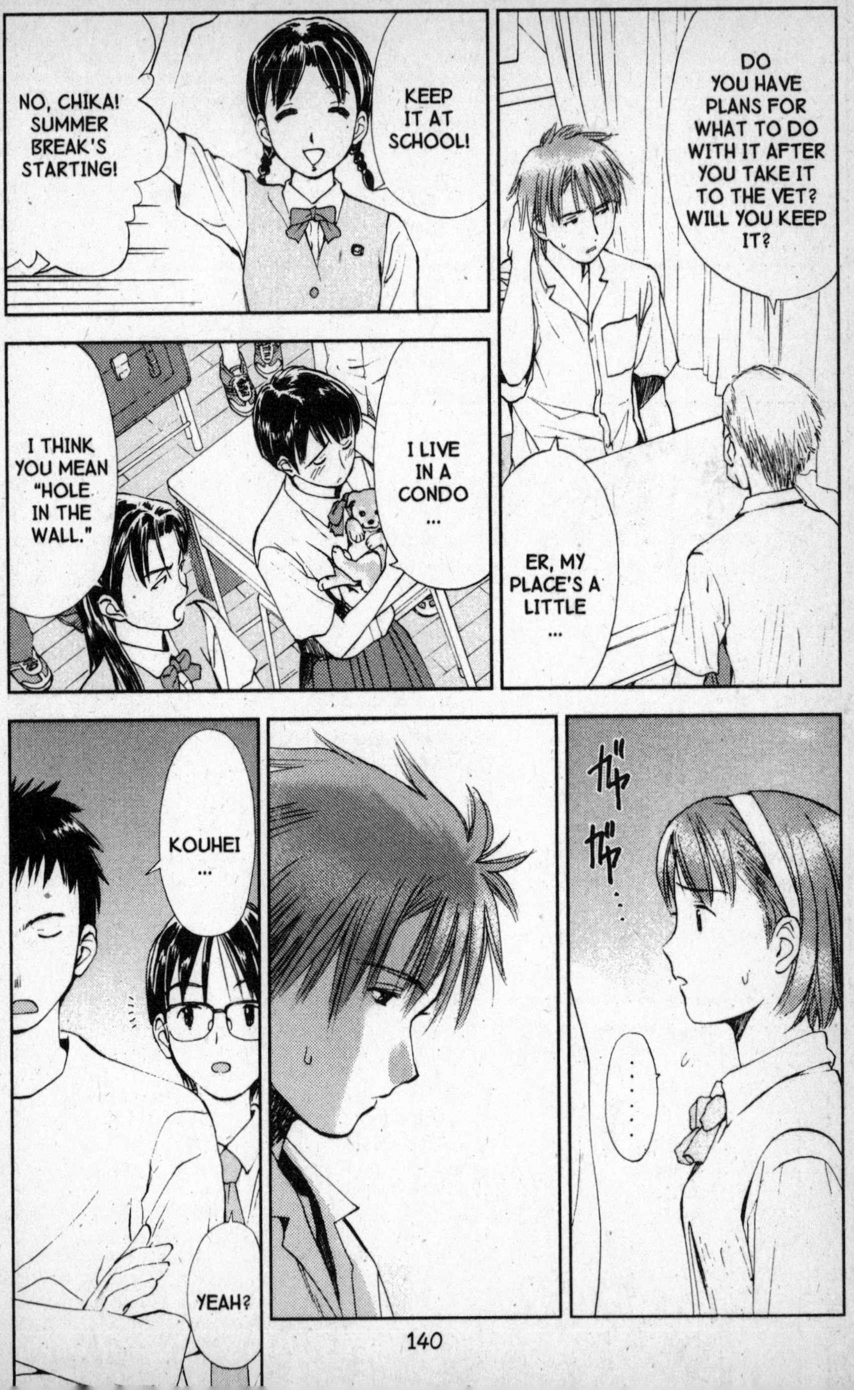
DO YOU HAVE PLANS FOR WHAT TO DO WITH IT AFTER YOU TAKE IT TO THE VET? WILL YOU KEEP IT?
ER, MY PLACE'S A LITTLE ...
KEEP IT AT SCHOOL!
NO, CHIKA! SUMMER BREAK'S STARTING!
I LIVE IN A CONDO ...
I THINK YOU MEAN "HOLE IN THE WALL."
ガヤガヤ...
......
KOUHEI ...
YEAH?

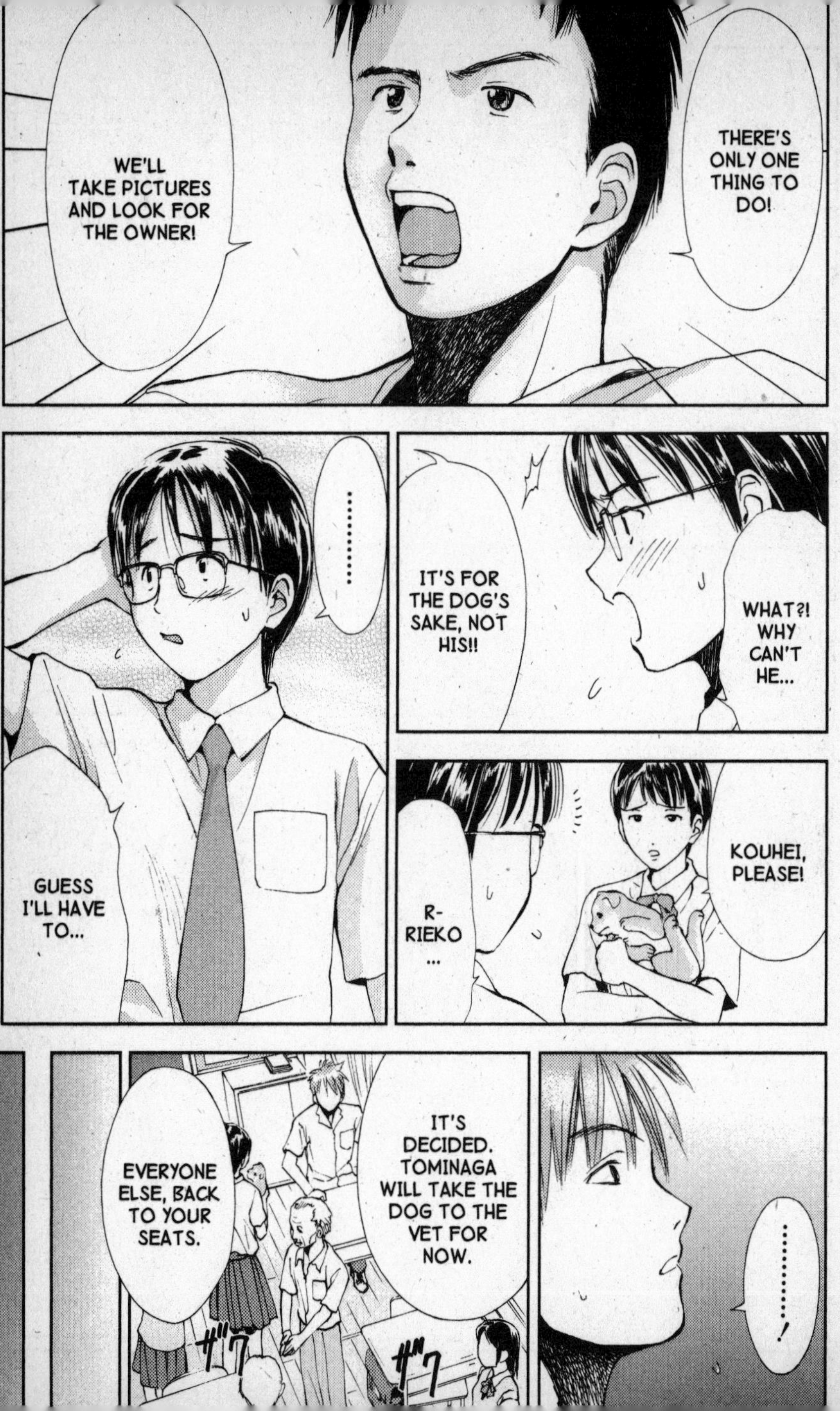
THERE'S ONLY ONE THING TO DO!
WE'LL TAKE PICTURES AND LOOK FOR THE OWNER!
WHAT?! WHY CAN'T HE...
IT'S FOR THE DOG'S SAKE, NOT HIS!!
KOUHEI, PLEASE!
R-RIEKO ...
......
GUESS I'LL HAVE TO...
......!
IT'S DECIDED. TOMINAGA WILL TAKE THE DOG TO THE VET FOR NOW.
EVERYONE ELSE, BACK TO YOUR SEATS.
ザワ
ザワ

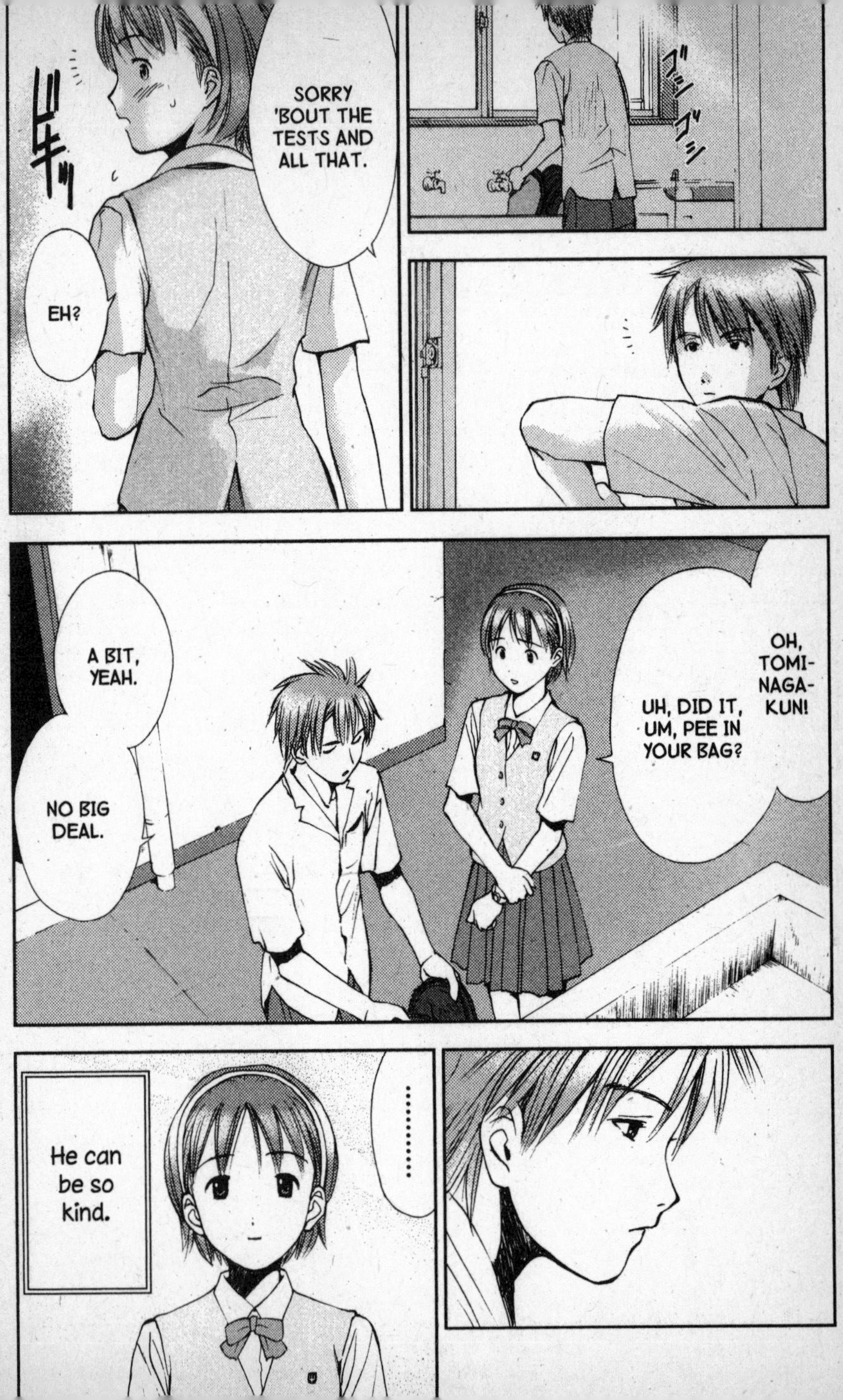
ゴシゴシ
SORRY 'BOUT THE TESTS AND ALL THAT.
ビキッ
EH?
OH, TOMI-NAGA-KUN!
UH, DID IT, UM, PEE IN YOUR BAG?
A BIT, YEAH.
NO BIG DEAL.
……
He can be so kind.

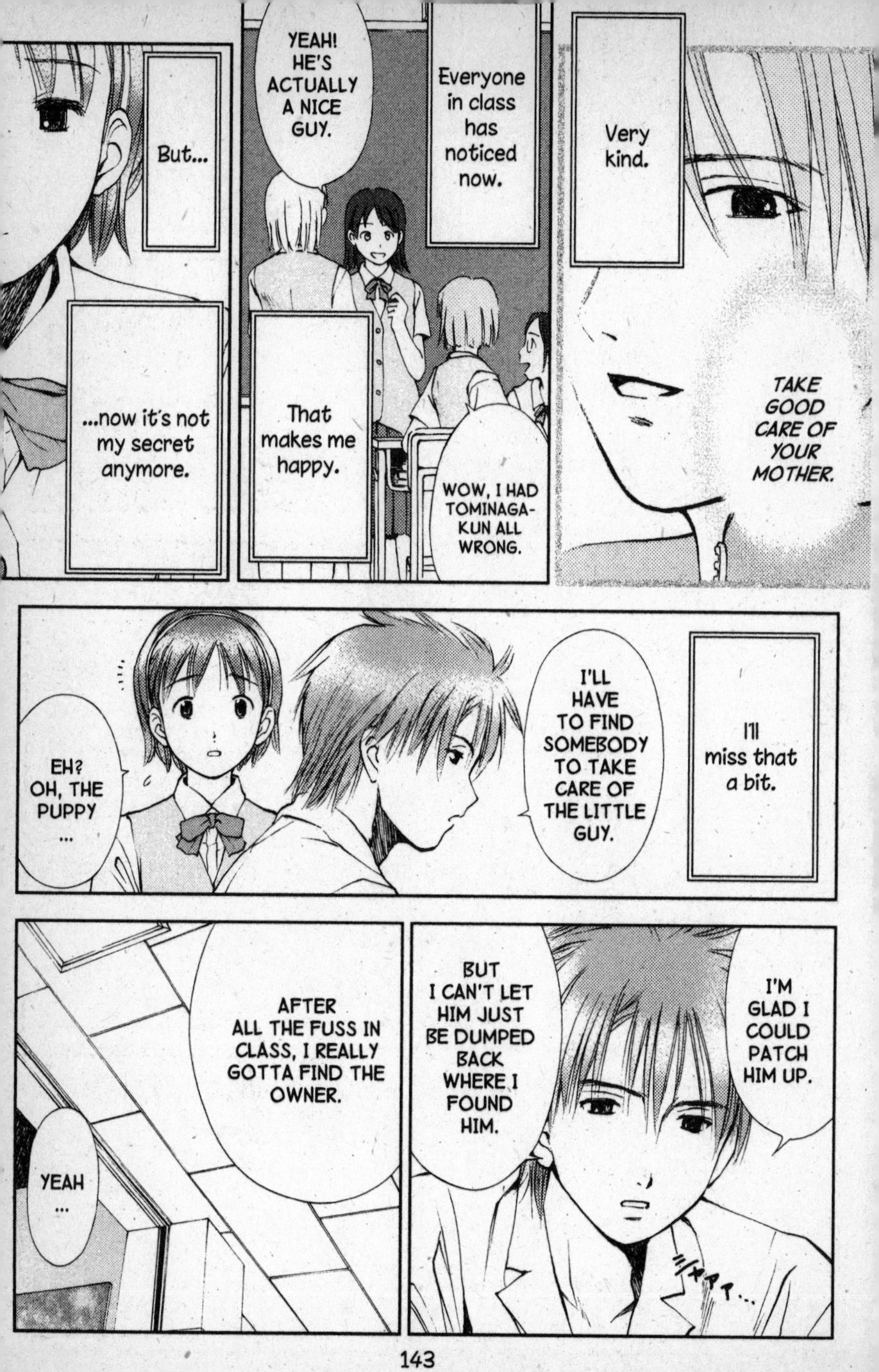
Very kind.
TAKE GOOD CARE OF YOUR MOTHER.
Everyone in class has noticed now.
YEAH! HE'S ACTUALLY A NICE GUY.
That makes me happy.
WOW, I HAD TOMINAGA-KUN ALL WRONG.
But...
...now it's not my secret anymore.
I'll miss that a bit.
I'LL HAVE TO FIND SOMEBODY TO TAKE CARE OF THE LITTLE GUY.
EH? OH, THE PUPPY ...
I'M GLAD I COULD PATCH HIM UP.
BUT I CAN'T LET HIM JUST BE DUMPED BACK WHERE I FOUND HIM.
AFTER ALL THE FUSS IN CLASS, I REALLY GOTTA FIND THE OWNER.
YEAH ...

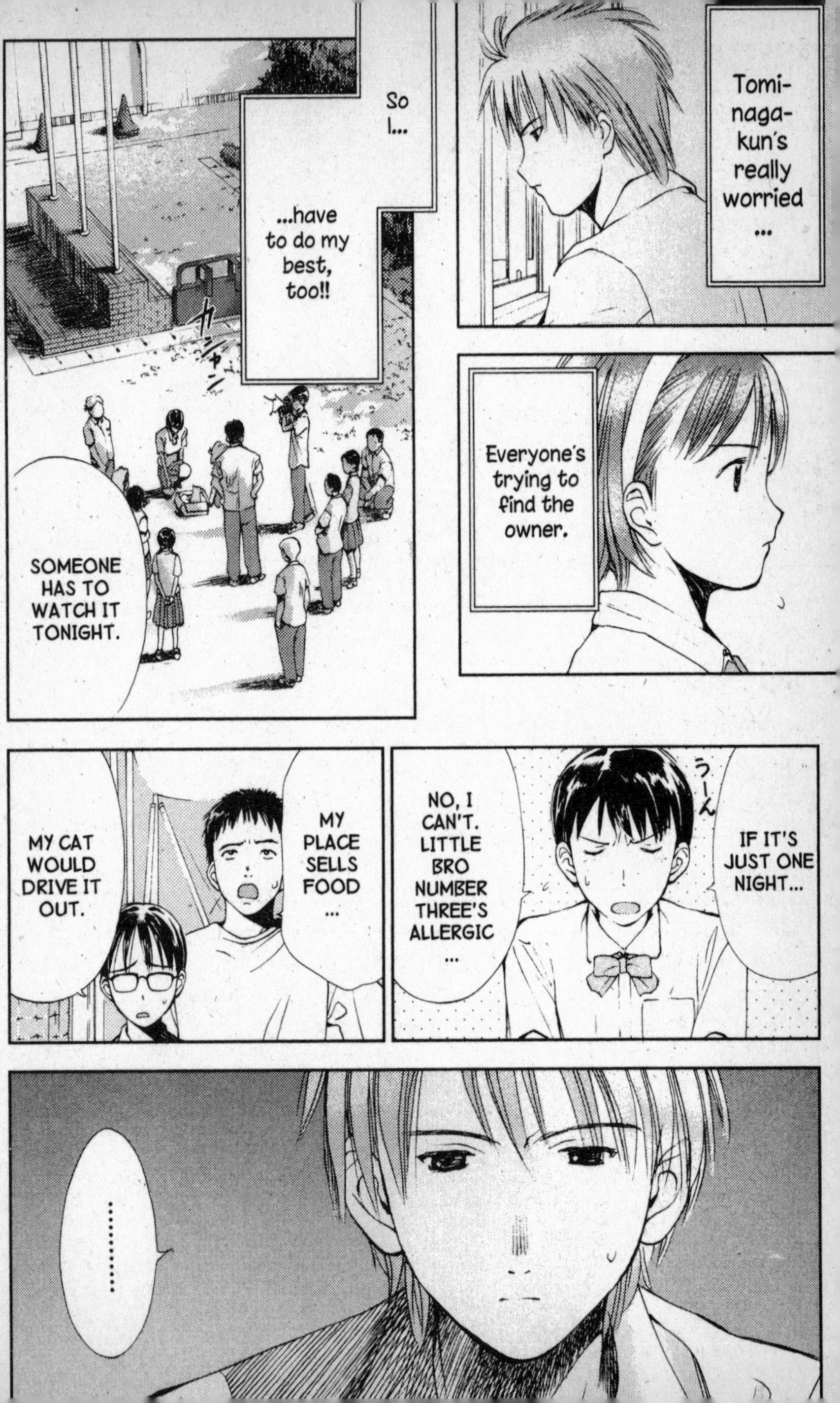
Tomi-naga-kun's really worried ...
Everyone's trying to find the owner.
So I...
...have to do my best, too!!
カシャン
SOMEONE HAS TO WATCH IT TONIGHT.
う～ん
IF IT'S JUST ONE NIGHT...
NO, I CAN'T. LITTLE BRO NUMBER THREE'S ALLERGIC ...
MY PLACE SELLS FOOD ...
MY CAT WOULD DRIVE IT OUT.
....

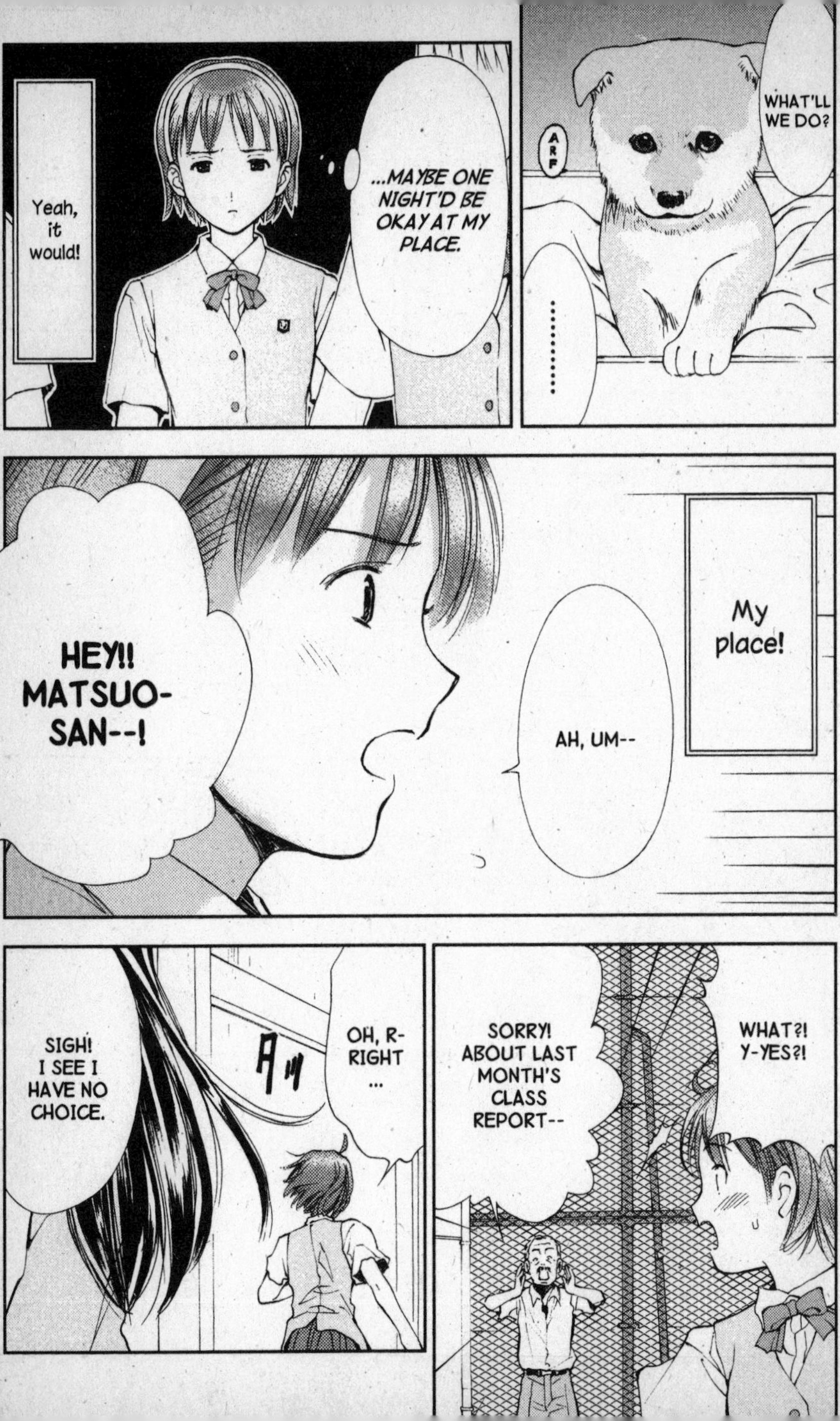
WHAT'LL WE DO?
ARF
......
...MAYBE ONE NIGHT'D BE OKAY AT MY PLACE.
Yeah, it would!
My place!
AH, UM--
HEY!! MATSUO-SAN--!
WHAT?! Y-YES?!
SORRY! ABOUT LAST MONTH'S CLASS REPORT--
OH, R-RIGHT ...
タッ
SIGH! I SEE I HAVE NO CHOICE.

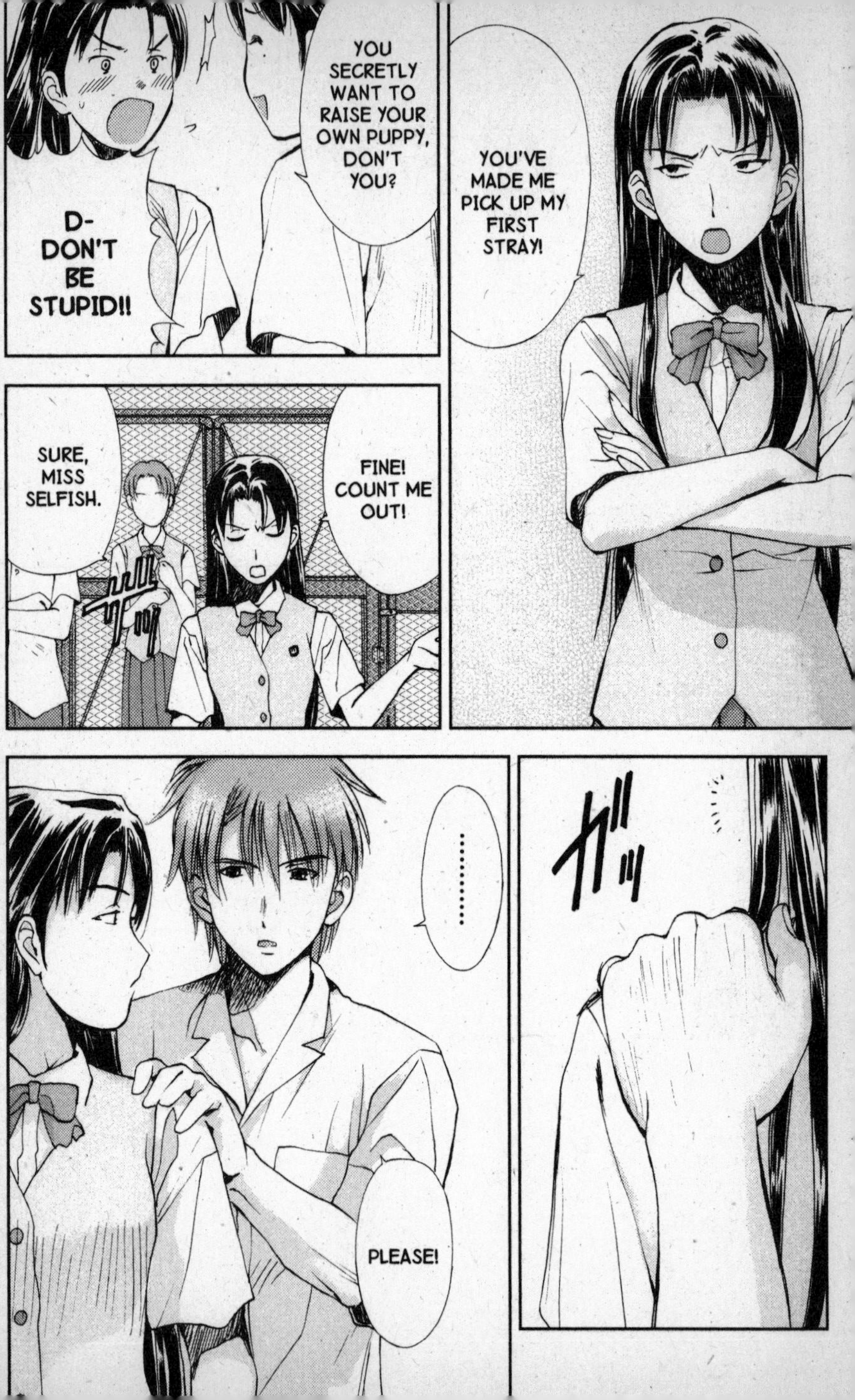
YOU'VE MADE ME PICK UP MY FIRST STRAY!
YOU SECRETLY WANT TO RAISE YOUR OWN PUPPY, DON'T YOU?
D-DON'T BE STUPID!!
FINE! COUNT ME OUT!
SURE, MISS SELFISH.
ガッ
......
PLEASE!

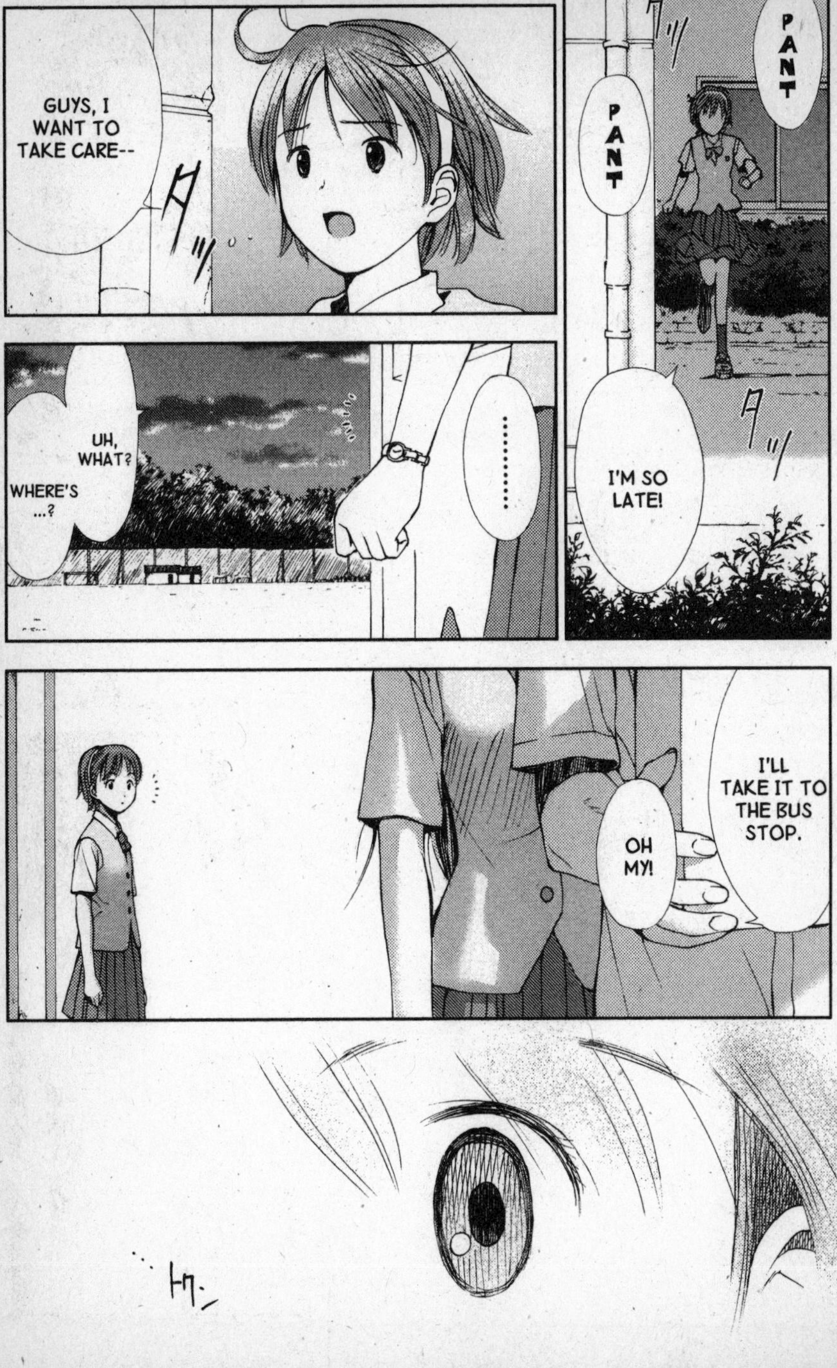
PANT
PANT
I'M SO LATE!
GUYS, I WANT TO TAKE CARE--
....
UH, WHAT?
WHERE'S ...?
I'LL TAKE IT TO THE BUS STOP.
OH MY!

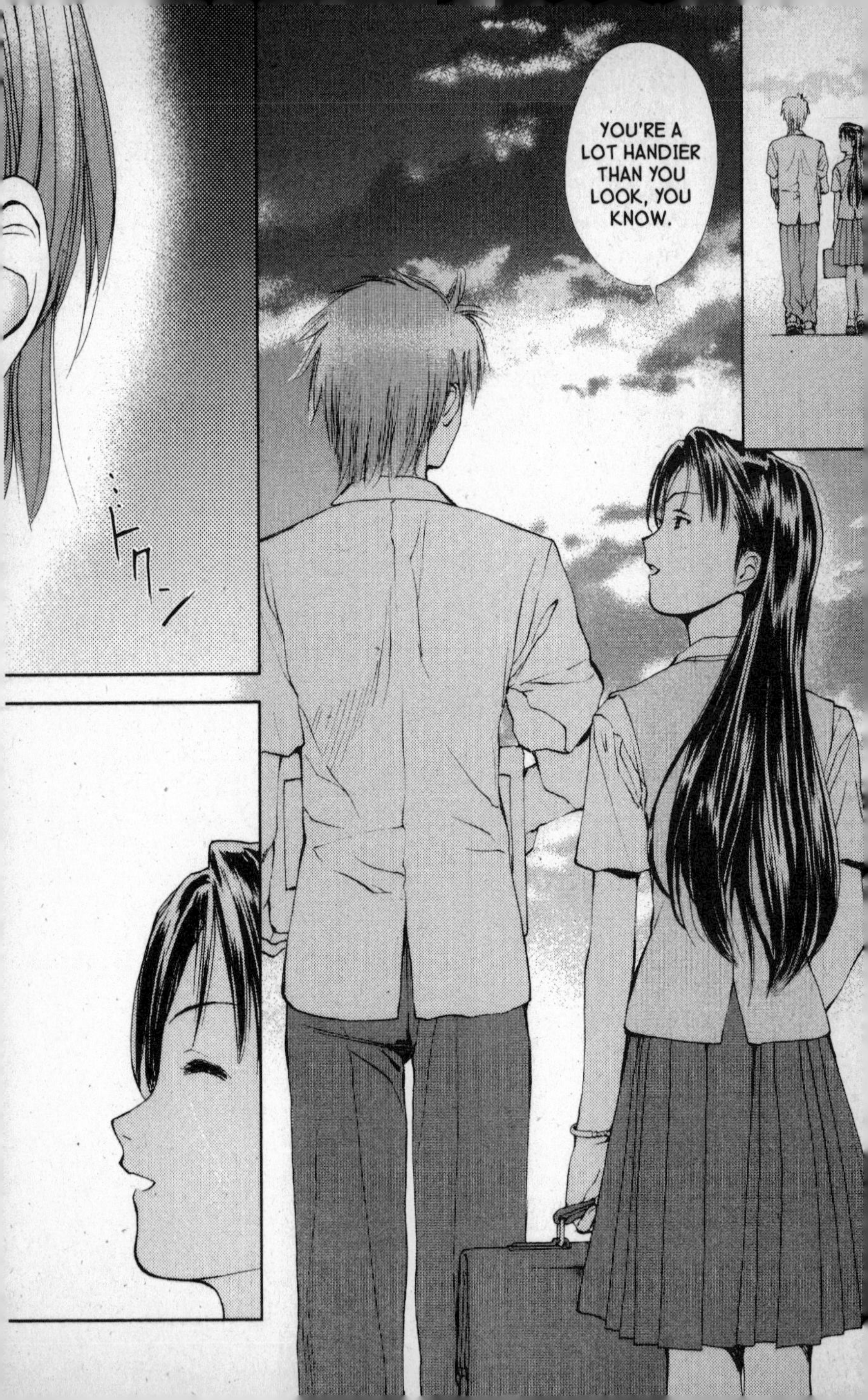
YOU'RE A LOT HANDIER THAN YOU LOOK, YOU KNOW.

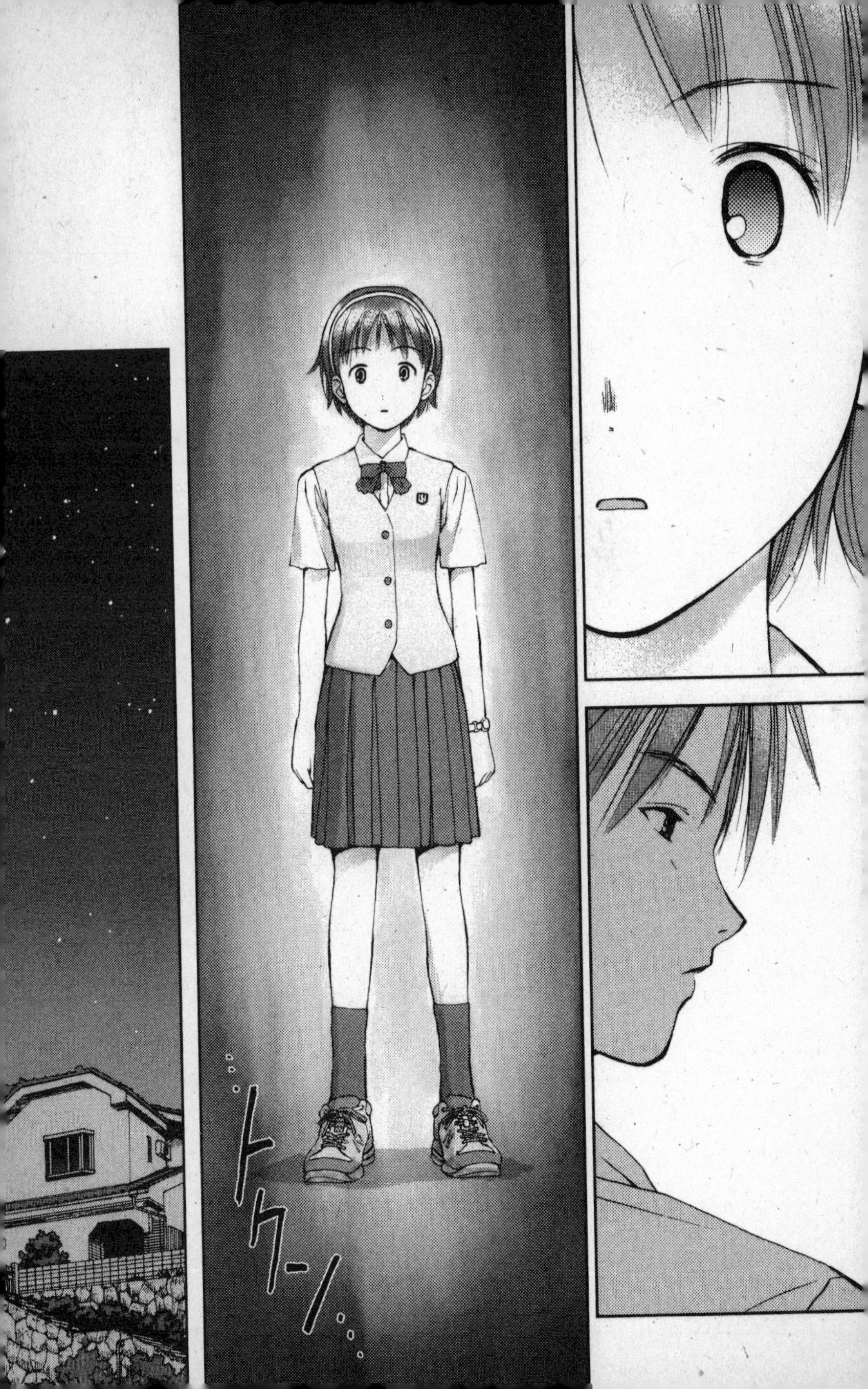
トクーン…

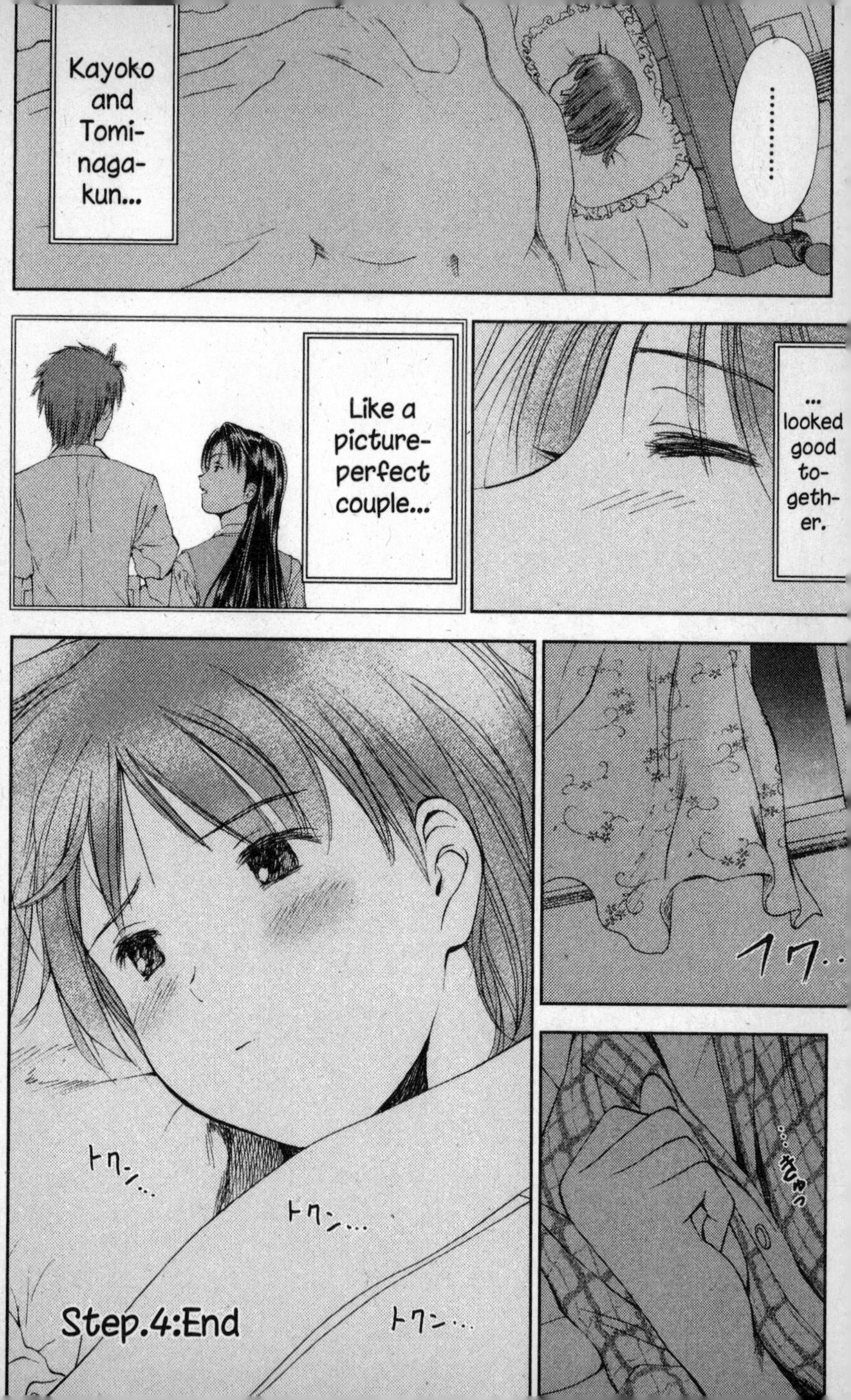
....
Kayoko and Tominaga-kun...
...looked good together.
Like a picture-perfect couple...
フワ...
トクン...
トクン...
トクン...
Step.4:End

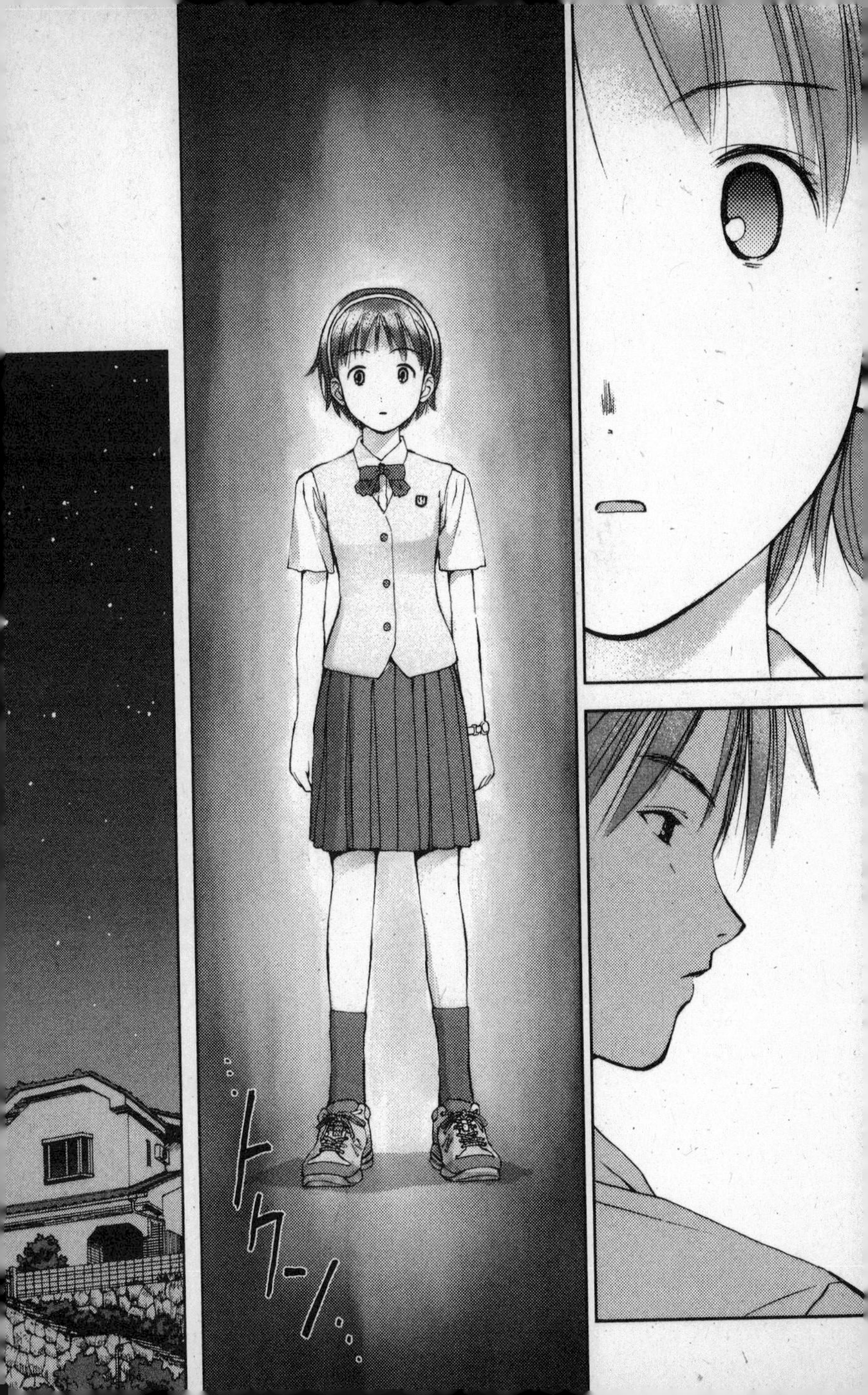
トクーン

Kayoko and Tomi- naga- kun...

Like a picture- perfect couple...

... looked good to- gether.

Step.4:End

ガチャッ

HELLO?
DAD?

AH,
I SEE.

RIIIIING
プルルル...

RIIIIING
プルルル...

LAWYER'S
IN YOKO-
HAMA FOR
A BIT...

WHAT?

ANO

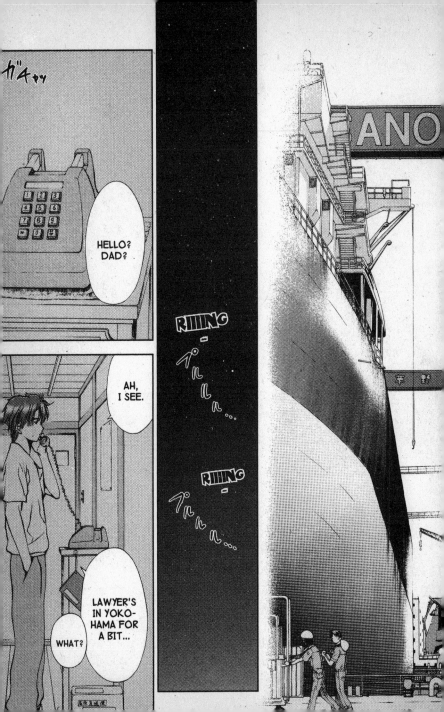

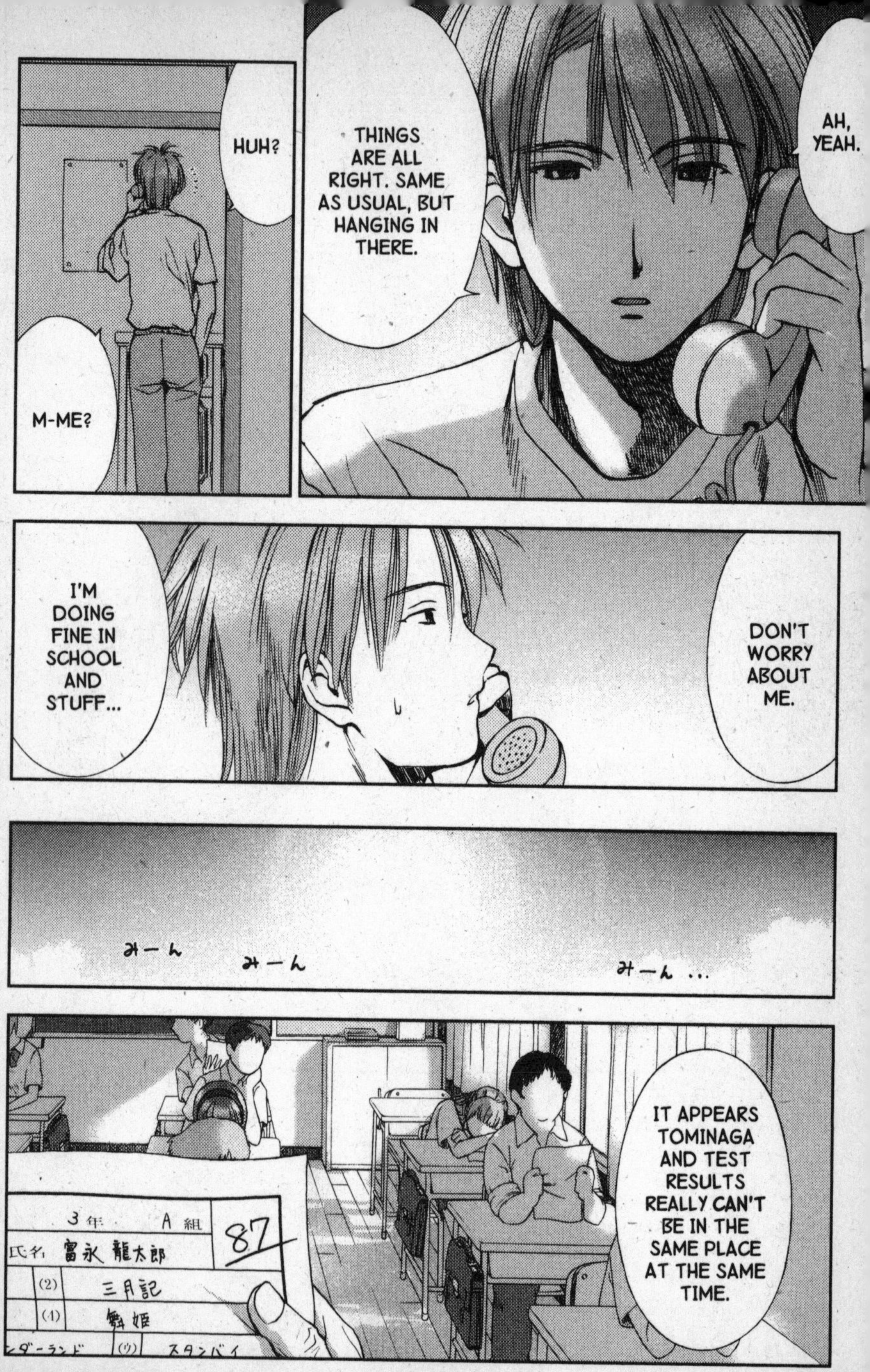
AH, YEAH.
THINGS ARE ALL RIGHT. SAME AS USUAL, BUT HANGING IN THERE.
HUH?
M-ME?
DON'T WORRY ABOUT ME.
I'M DOING FINE IN SCHOOL AND STUFF...
みーん
みーん
みーん…
IT APPEARS TOMINAGA AND TEST RESULTS REALLY CAN'T BE IN THE SAME PLACE AT THE SAME TIME.
3年 A組
87
氏名 富永龍太郎
(2) 三月記
(1) 舞姫
ンダーランド
(ウ) スタンバイ

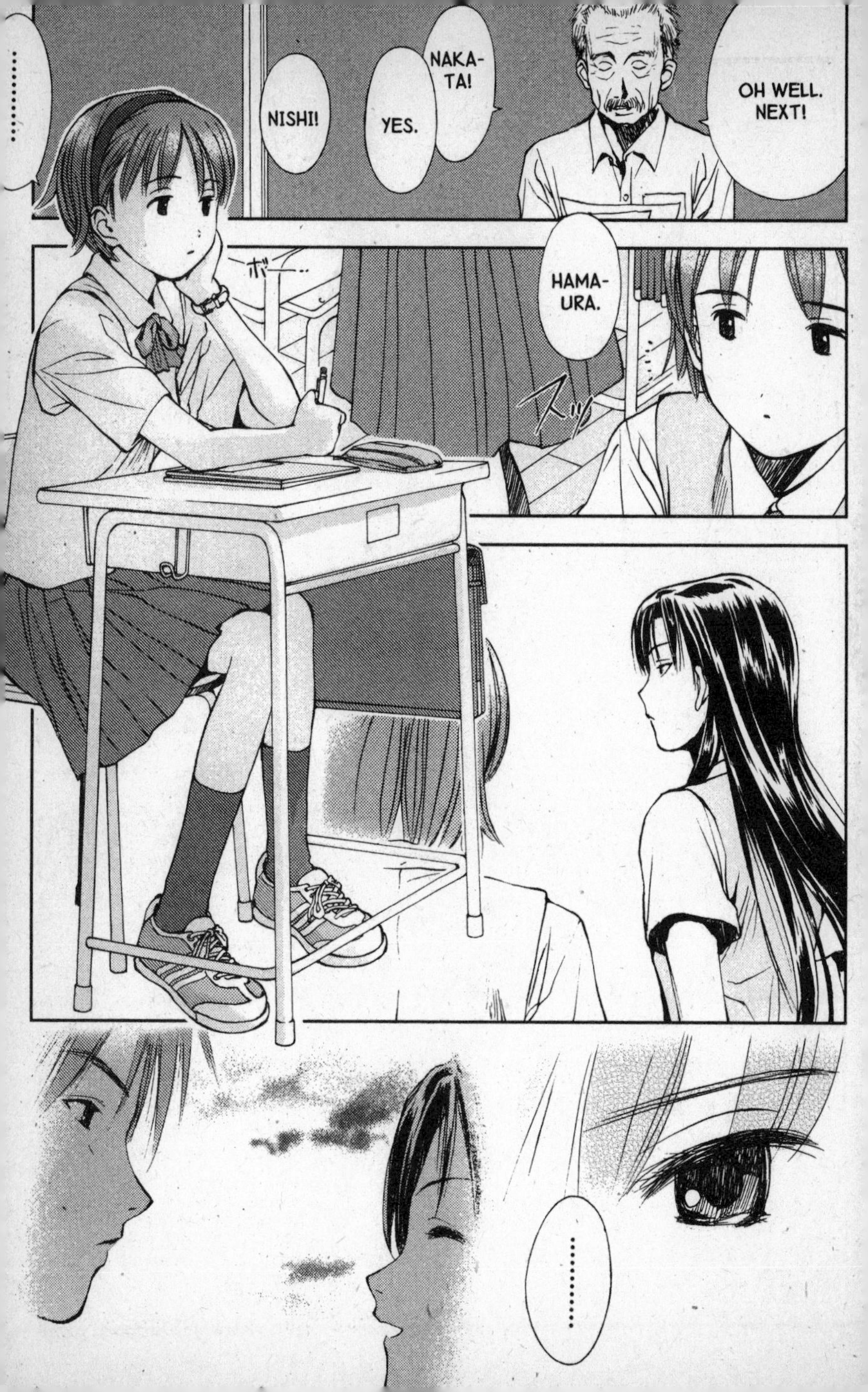
OH WELL. NEXT!
NAKA-TA!
YES.
NISHI!
......
HAMA-URA.
スッ
ボー…
......

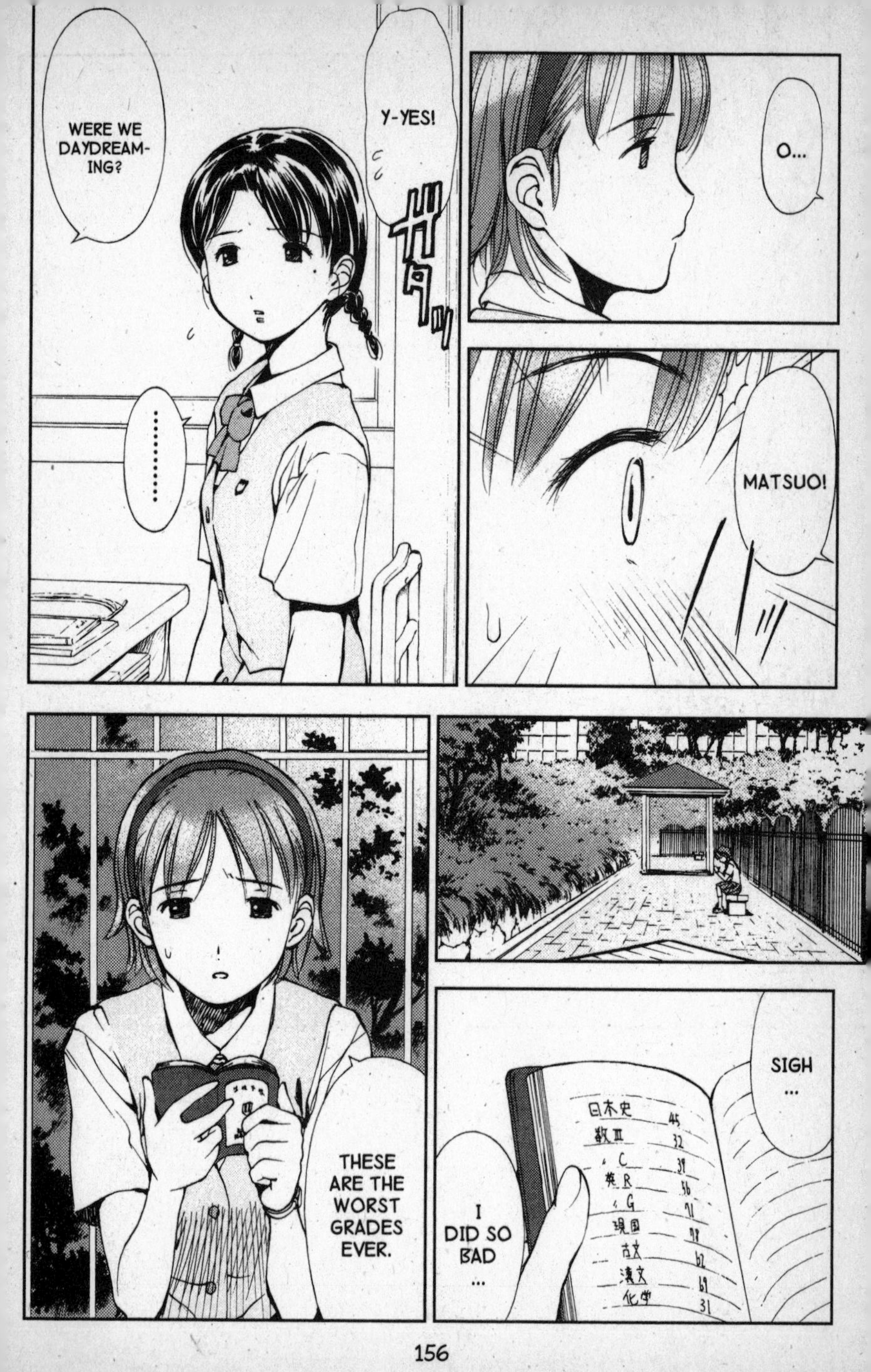
O...
MATSUO!
Y-YES!
ガタッ
WERE WE DAYDREAMING?
......
SIGH...
I DID SO BAD...
THESE ARE THE WORST GRADES EVER.

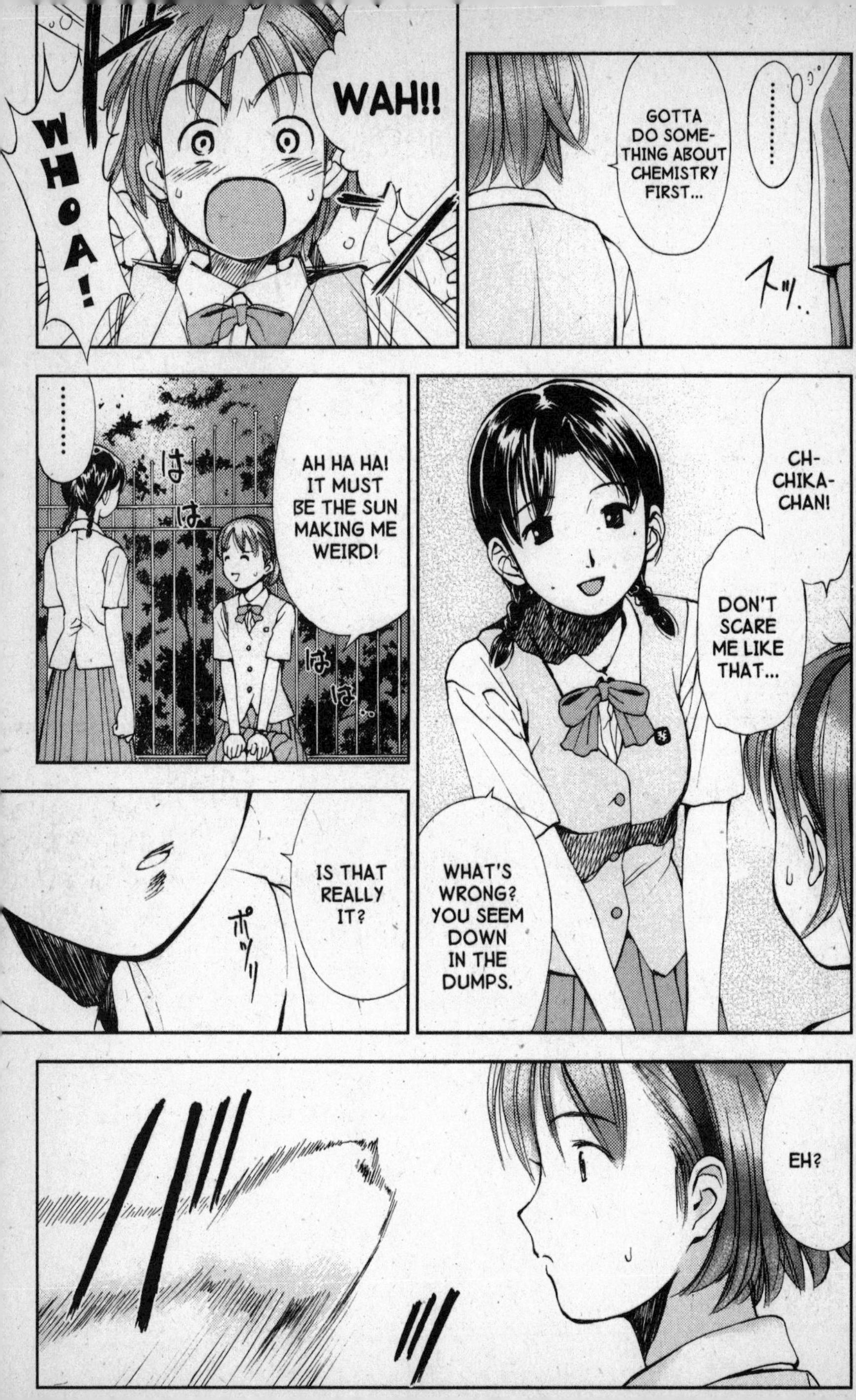
……
GOTTA DO SOME-THING ABOUT CHEMISTRY FIRST...
スッ..
WAH!!
WHOA!
CH-CHIKA-CHAN!
DON'T SCARE ME LIKE THAT...
WHAT'S WRONG? YOU SEEM DOWN IN THE DUMPS.
AH HA HA! IT MUST BE THE SUN MAKING ME WEIRD!
はは
はは..
……
IS THAT REALLY IT?
ポッ
EH?

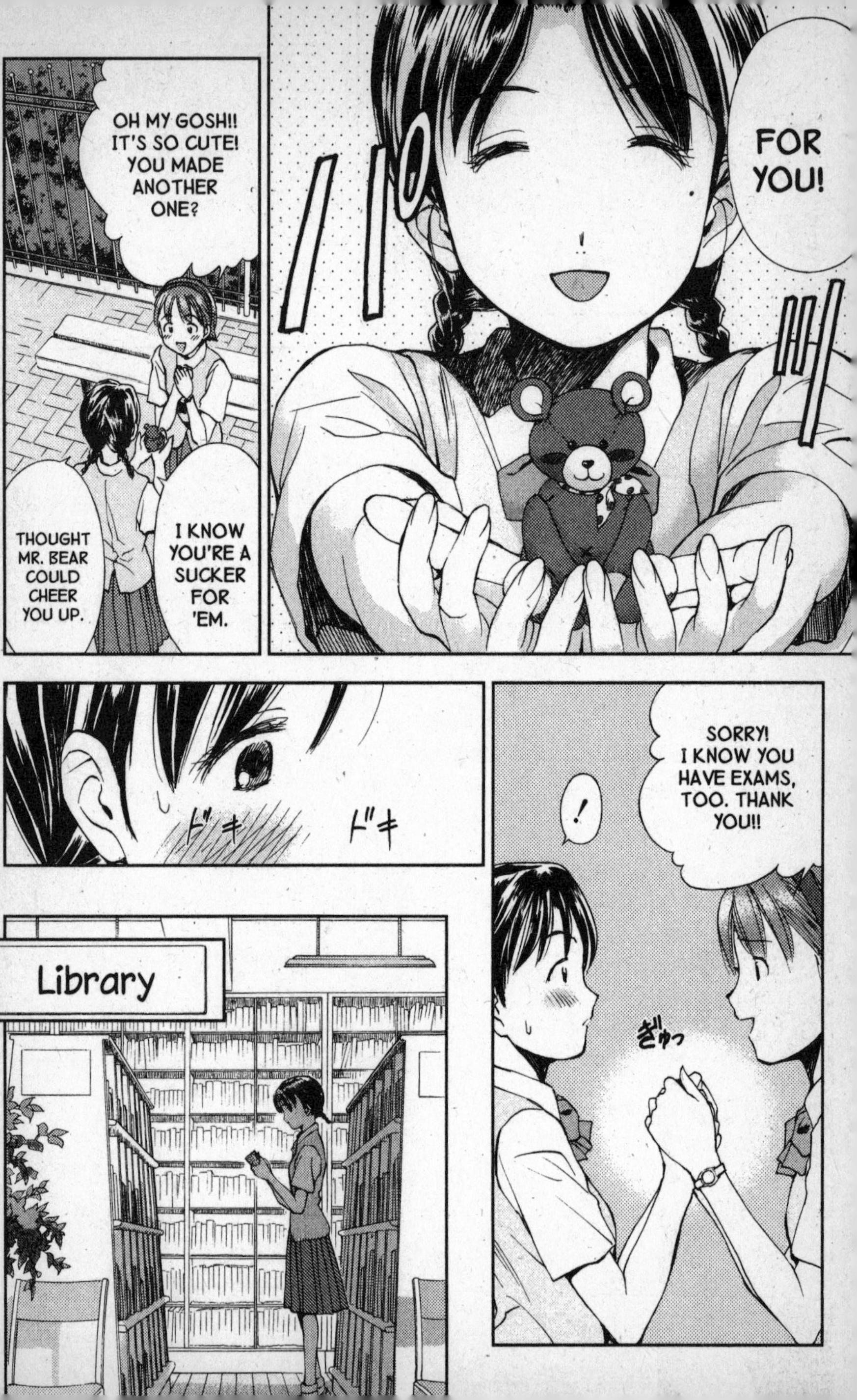
FOR YOU!
OH MY GOSH!! IT'S SO CUTE! YOU MADE ANOTHER ONE?
I KNOW YOU'RE A SUCKER FOR 'EM.
THOUGHT MR. BEAR COULD CHEER YOU UP.
SORRY! I KNOW YOU HAVE EXAMS, TOO. THANK YOU!!
!
ぎゅっ
ドキ
ドキ
Library

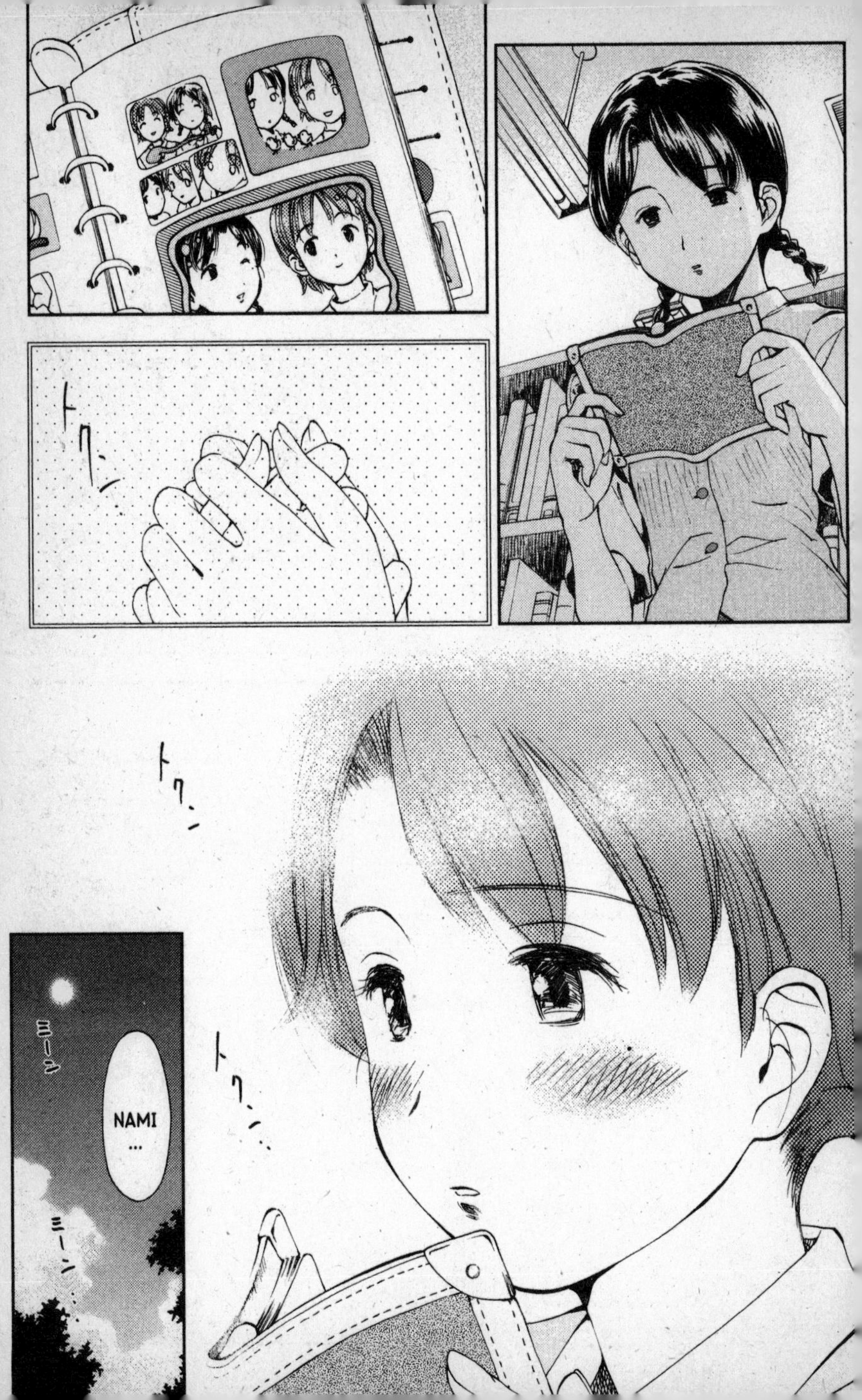
トクン…
トクン
トクン…
ミーン
NAMI ...
ミーン…

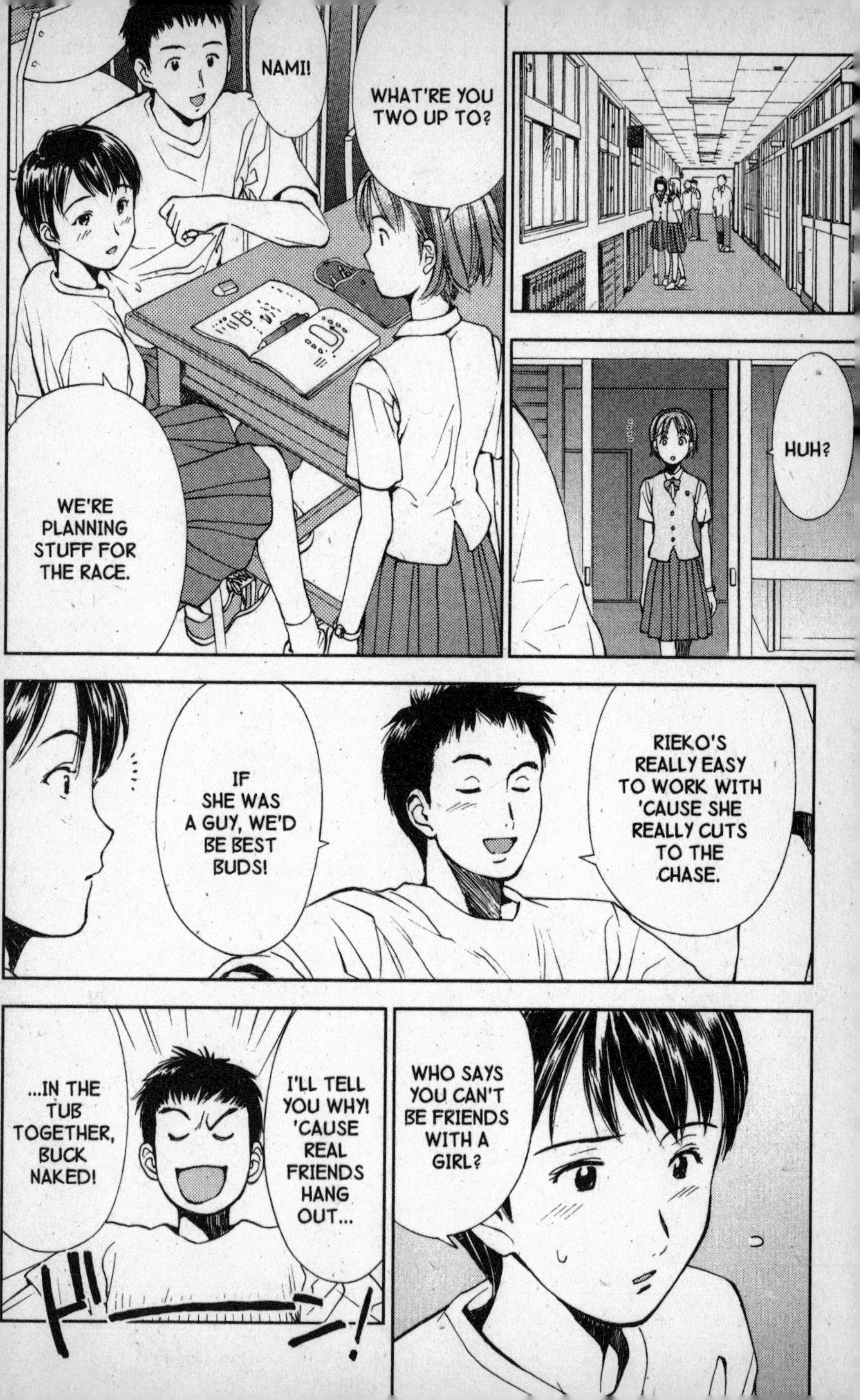
HUH?
NAMI!
WHAT'RE YOU TWO UP TO?
WE'RE PLANNING STUFF FOR THE RACE.
RIEKO'S REALLY EASY TO WORK WITH 'CAUSE SHE REALLY CUTS TO THE CHASE.
IF SHE WAS A GUY, WE'D BE BEST BUDS!
WHO SAYS YOU CAN'T BE FRIENDS WITH A GIRL?
I'LL TELL YOU WHY! 'CAUSE REAL FRIENDS HANG OUT...
...IN THE TUB TOGETHER, BUCK NAKED!

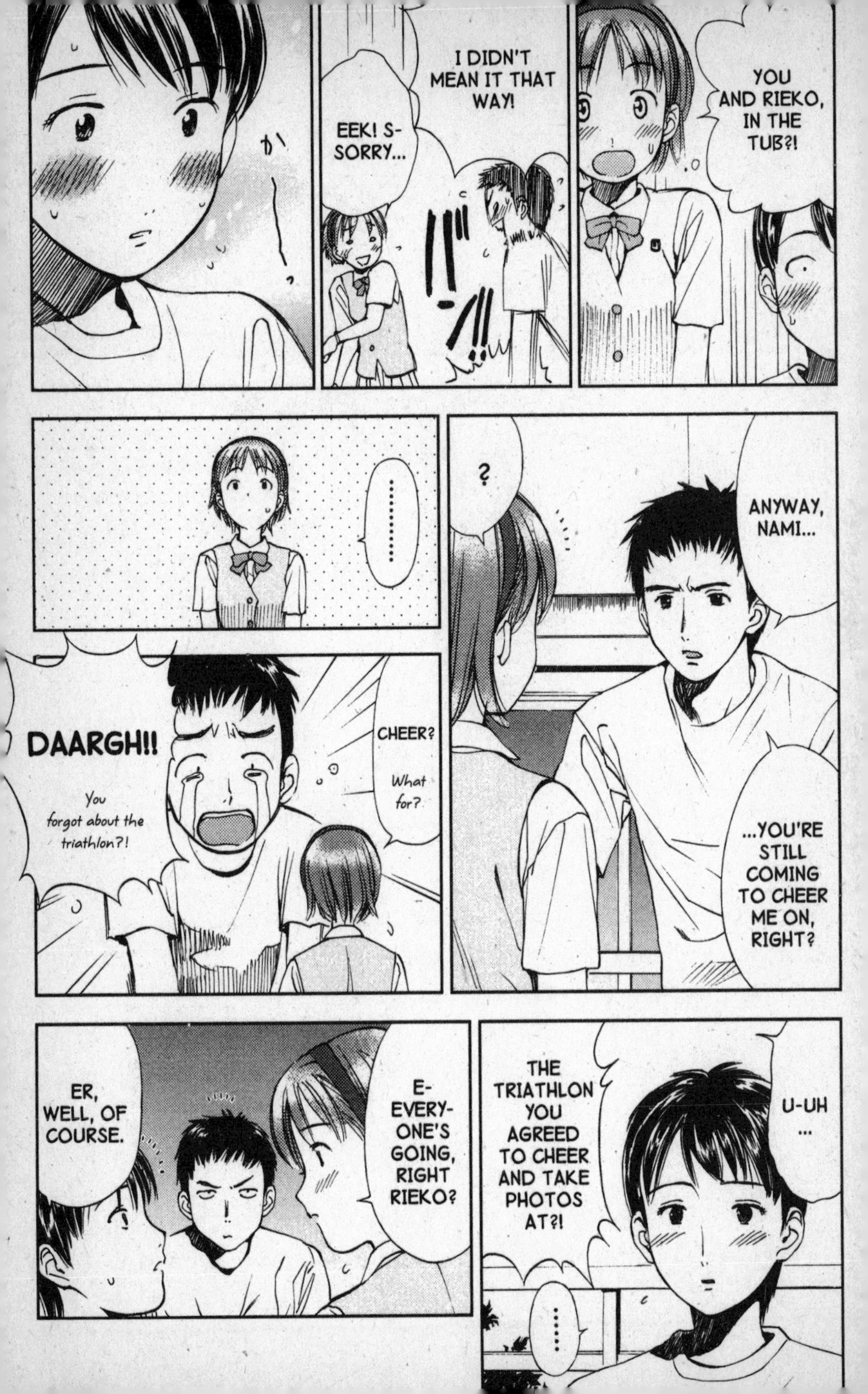
YOU AND RIEKO, IN THE TUB?!
I DIDN'T MEAN IT THAT WAY!
EEK! S-SORRY...
ANYWAY, NAMI...
?
...YOU'RE STILL COMING TO CHEER ME ON, RIGHT?
......
CHEER?
What for?
DAARGH!!
You forgot about the triathlon?!
U-UH ...
THE TRIATHLON YOU AGREED TO CHEER AND TAKE PHOTOS AT?!
......
E-EVERYONE'S GOING, RIGHT RIEKO?
ER, WELL, OF COURSE.

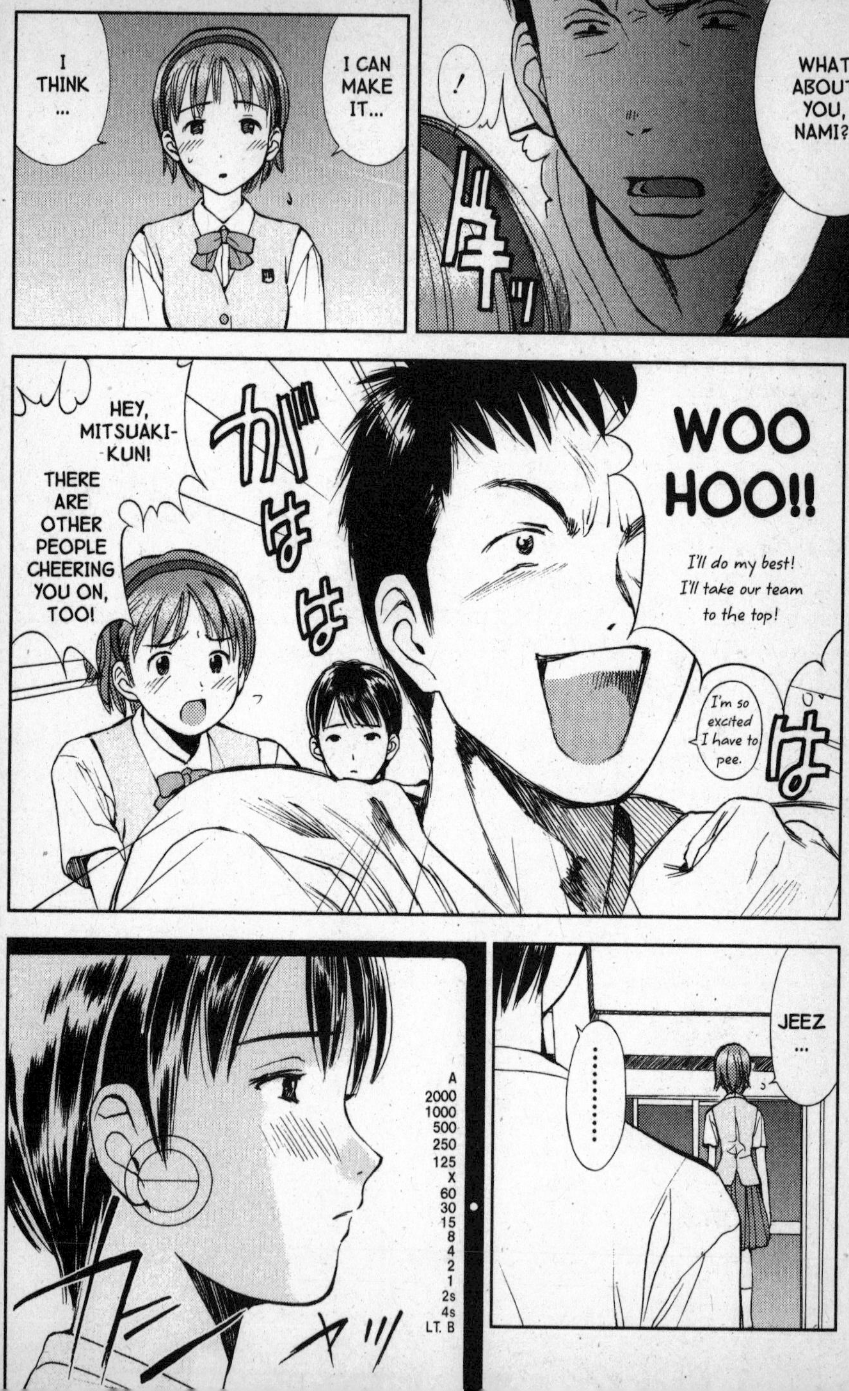
WHAT ABOUT YOU, NAMI?!
!
I CAN MAKE IT...
I THINK...
WOO HOO!!
I'll do my best! I'll take our team to the top!
I'm so excited I have to pee.
HEY, MITSUAKI-KUN!
THERE ARE OTHER PEOPLE CHEERING YOU ON, TOO!
JEEZ...
....

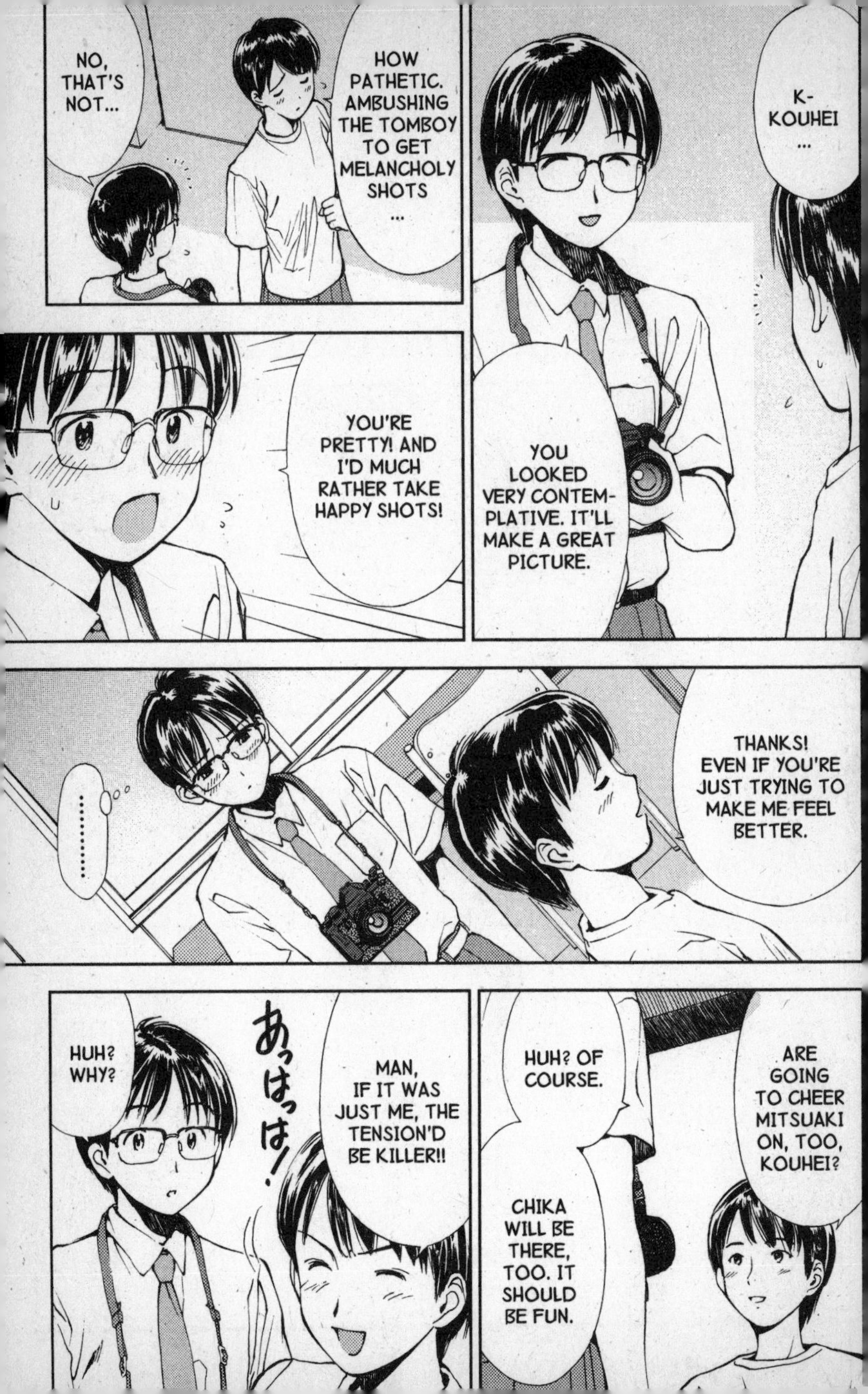
K-KOUHEI ...
YOU LOOKED VERY CONTEMPLATIVE. IT'LL MAKE A GREAT PICTURE.
HOW PATHETIC. AMBUSHING THE TOMBOY TO GET MELANCHOLY SHOTS ...
NO, THAT'S NOT...
YOU'RE PRETTY! AND I'D MUCH RATHER TAKE HAPPY SHOTS!
THANKS! EVEN IF YOU'RE JUST TRYING TO MAKE ME FEEL BETTER.
....
ARE GOING TO CHEER MITSUAKI ON, TOO, KOUHEI?
HUH? OF COURSE.
CHIKA WILL BE THERE, TOO. IT SHOULD BE FUN.
MAN, IF IT WAS JUST ME, THE TENSION'D BE KILLER!!
あっはっは!
HUH? WHY?

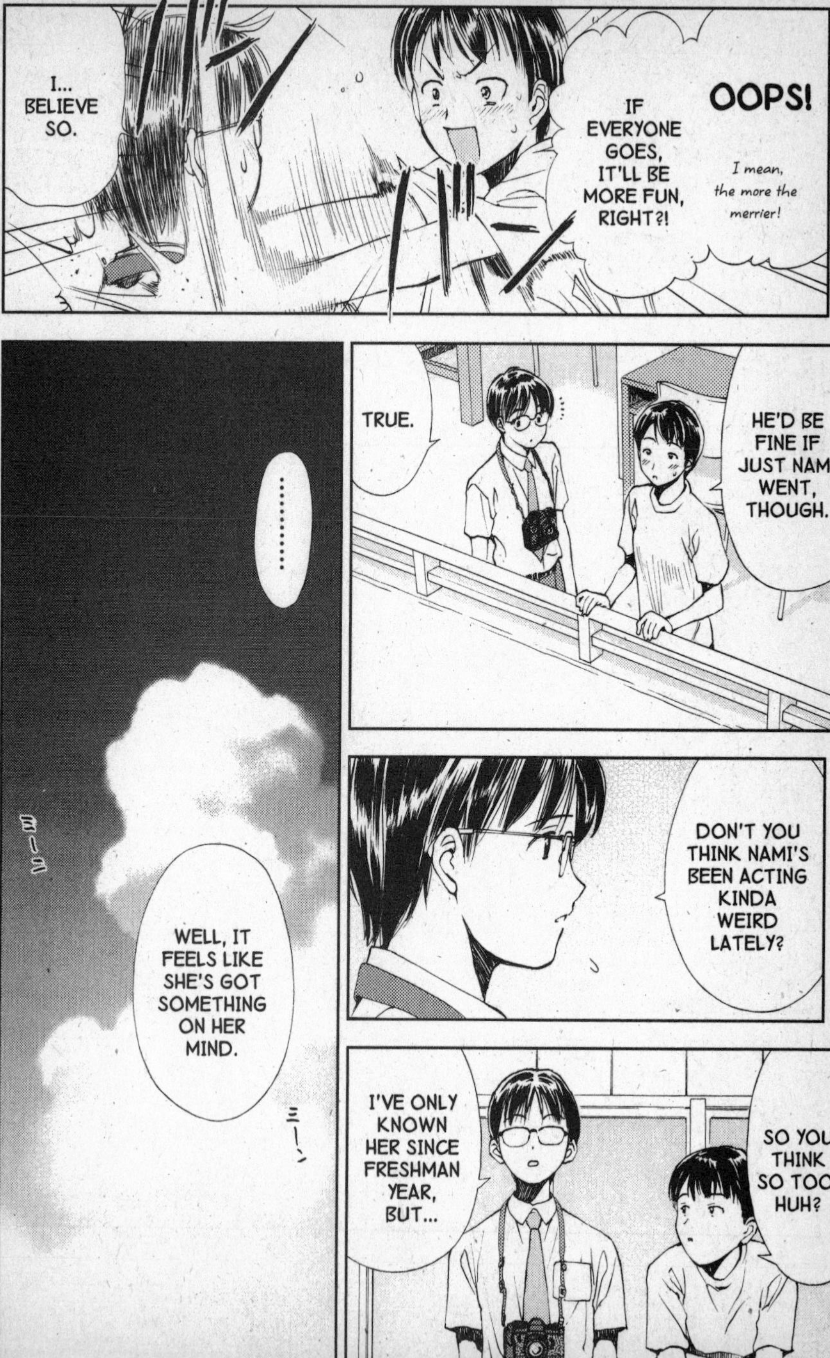
OOPS!
I mean, the more the merrier!
IF EVERYONE GOES, IT'LL BE MORE FUN, RIGHT?!
I... BELIEVE SO.
HE'D BE FINE IF JUST NAMI WENT, THOUGH.
TRUE.
DON'T YOU THINK NAMI'S BEEN ACTING KINDA WEIRD LATELY?
SO YOU THINK SO TOO, HUH?
I'VE ONLY KNOWN HER SINCE FRESHMAN YEAR, BUT...
......
ミーン
WELL, IT FEELS LIKE SHE'S GOT SOMETHING ON HER MIND.
ミーン

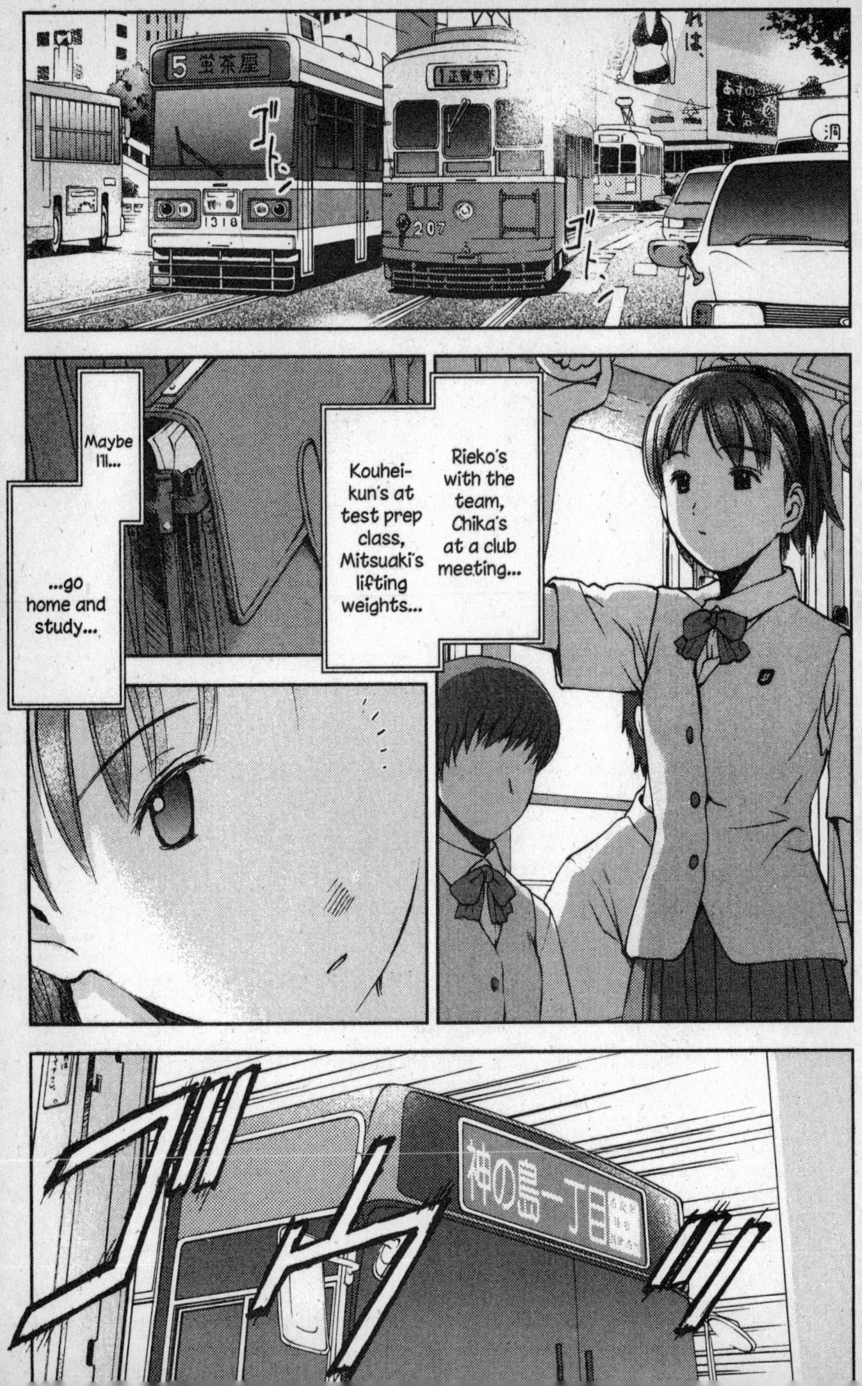
1318
207
Rieko's with the team, Chika's at a club meeting...
Kouhei-kun's at test prep class, Mitsuaki's lifting weights...
Maybe I'll...
...go home and study...
神の島一丁目

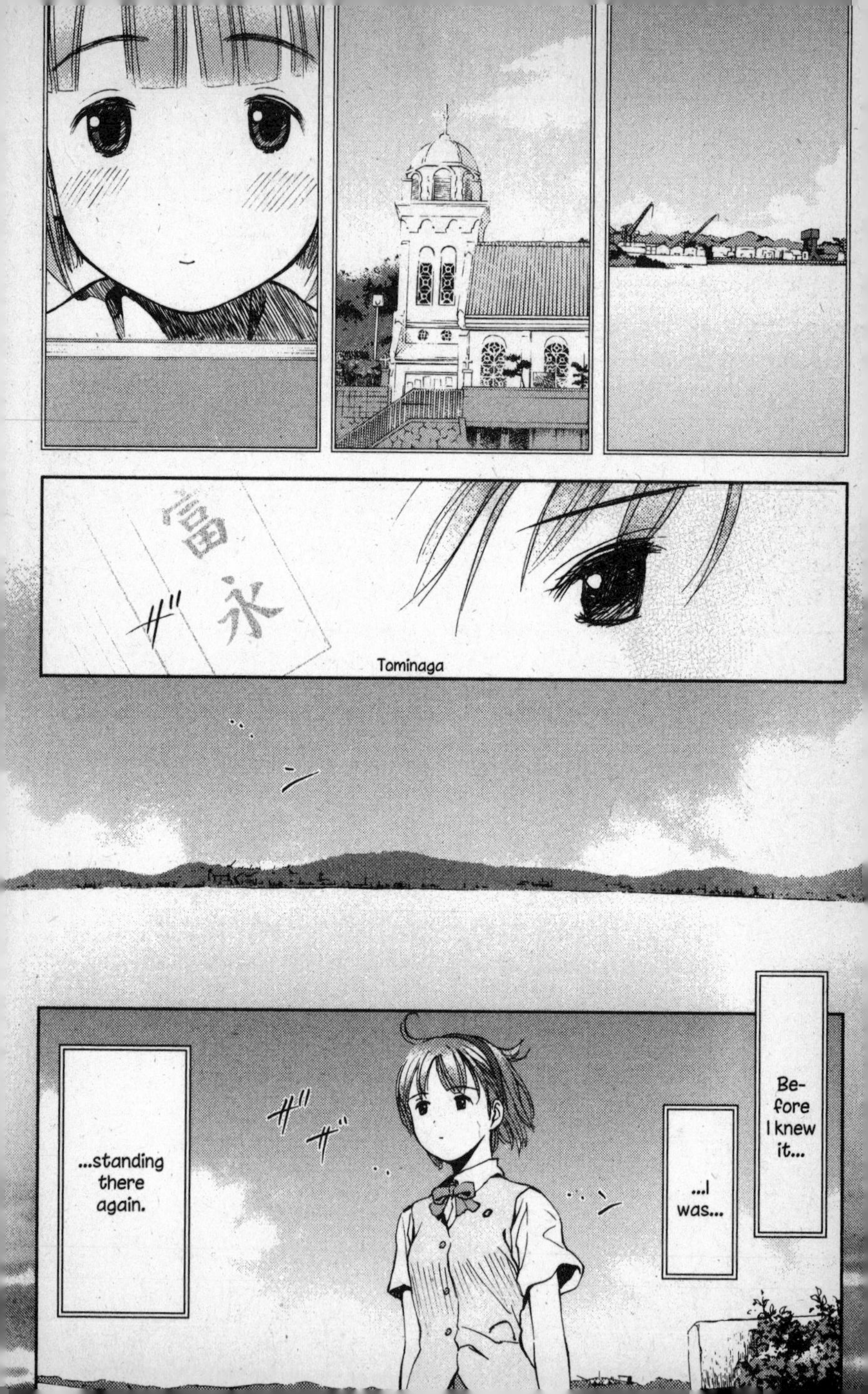
富永
ザ
Tominaga
Be-
fore
I knew
it...
...I
was...
ザザ
...standing
there
again.

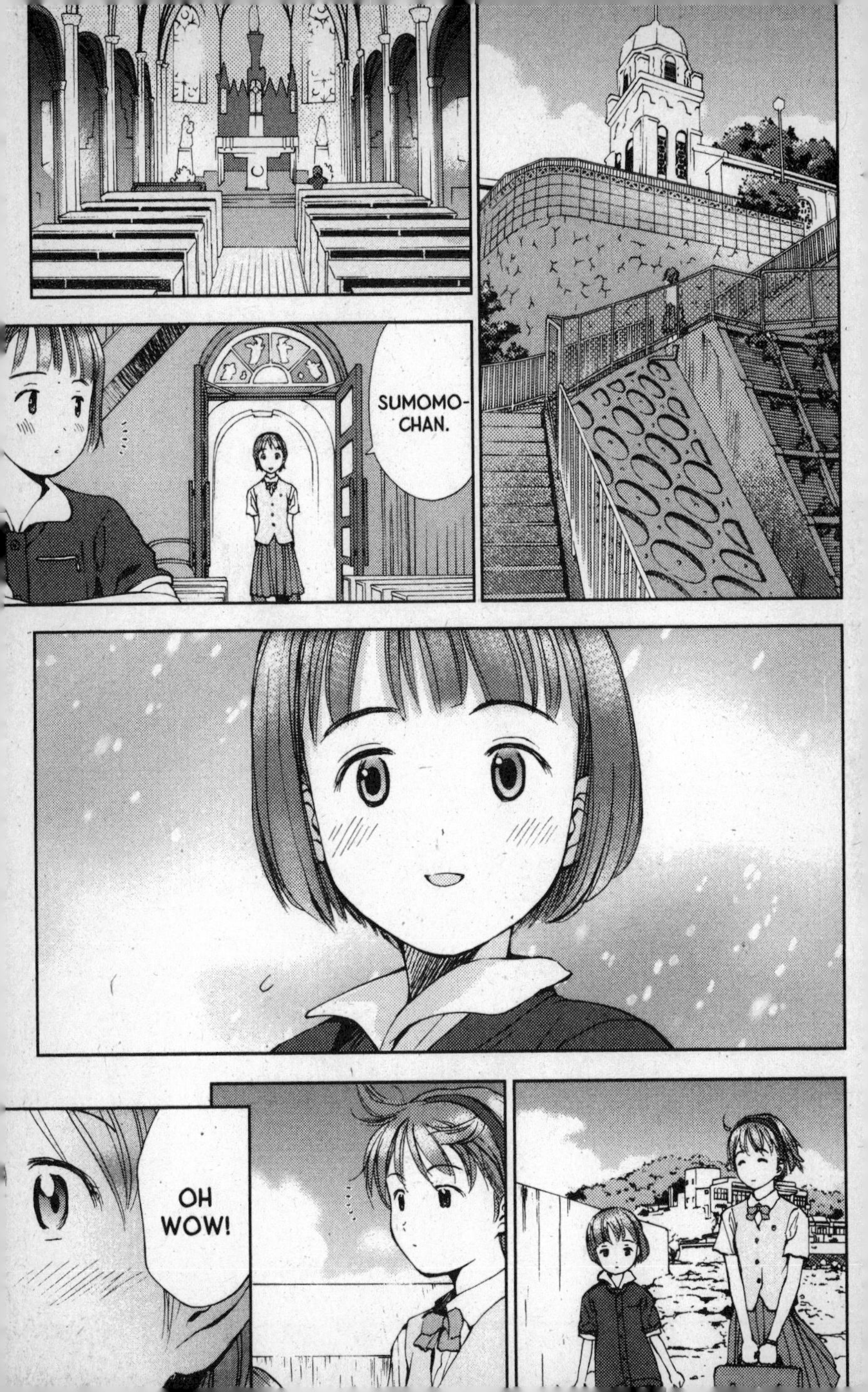
SUMOMO-CHAN.
OH WOW!

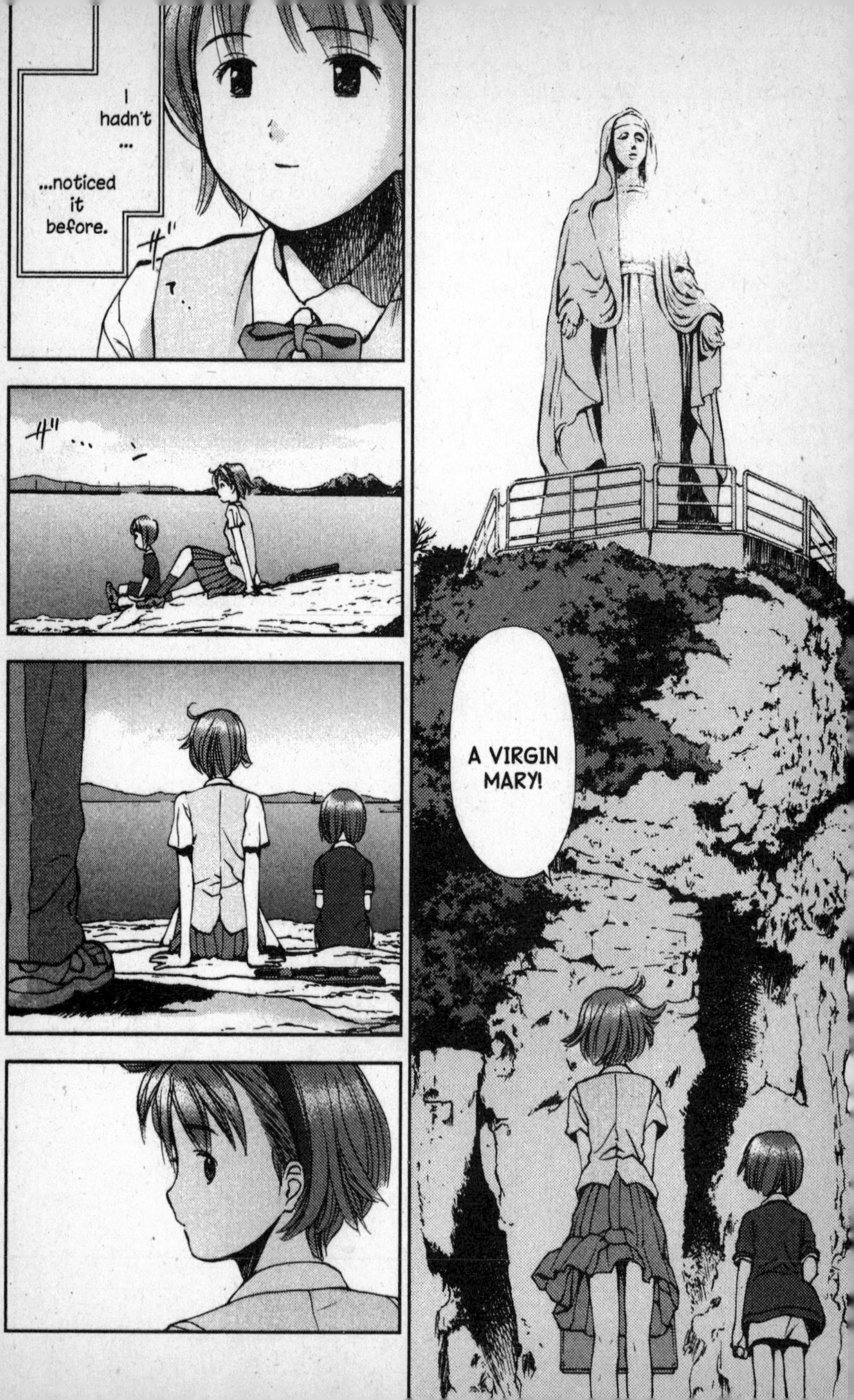
A VIRGIN MARY!
I hadn't ...
...noticed it before.

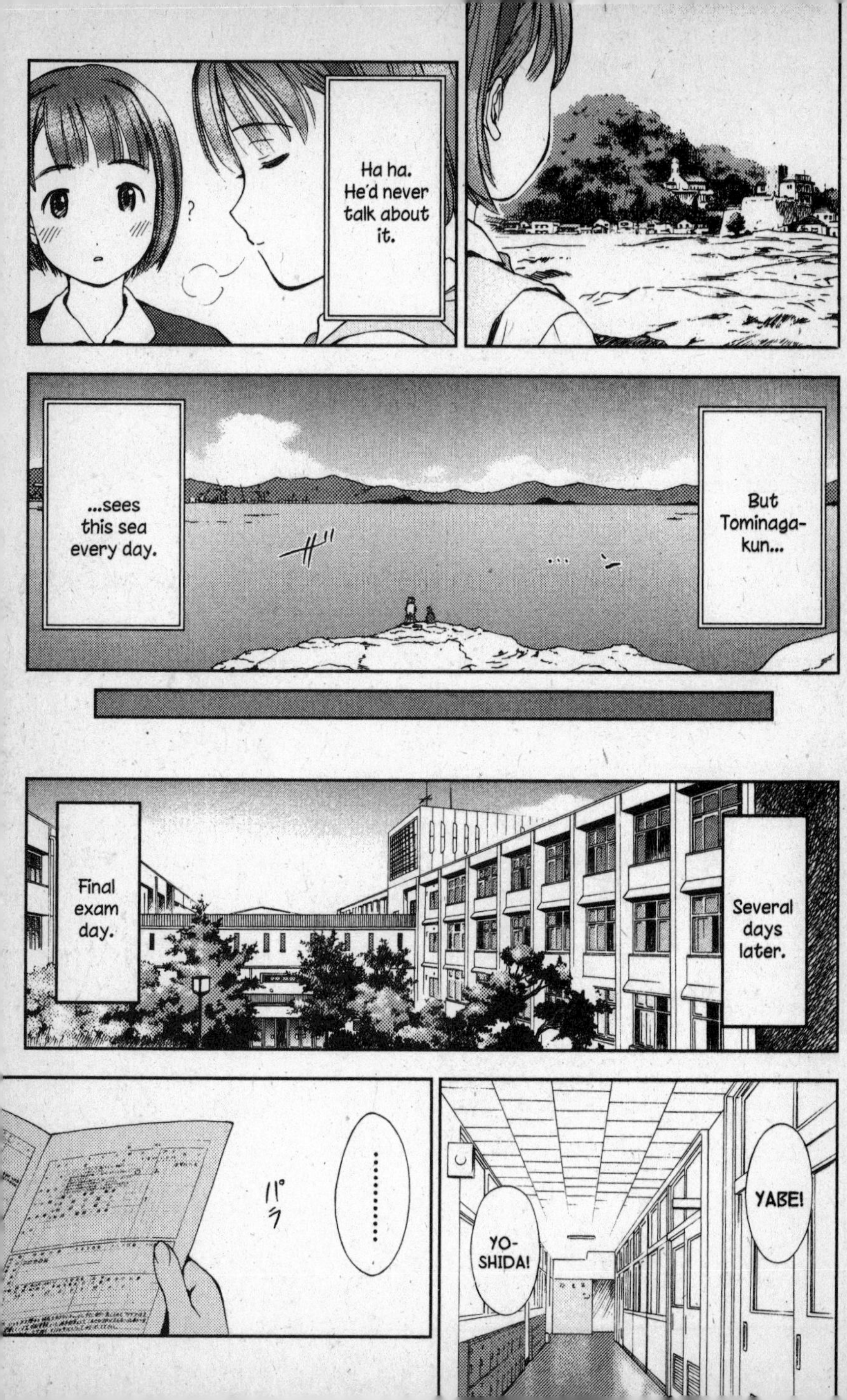

?
Ha ha. He'd never talk about it.
But Tominaga-kun...
...sees this sea every day.
Several days later.
Final exam day.
YABE!
YO-SHIDA!
......
パラ

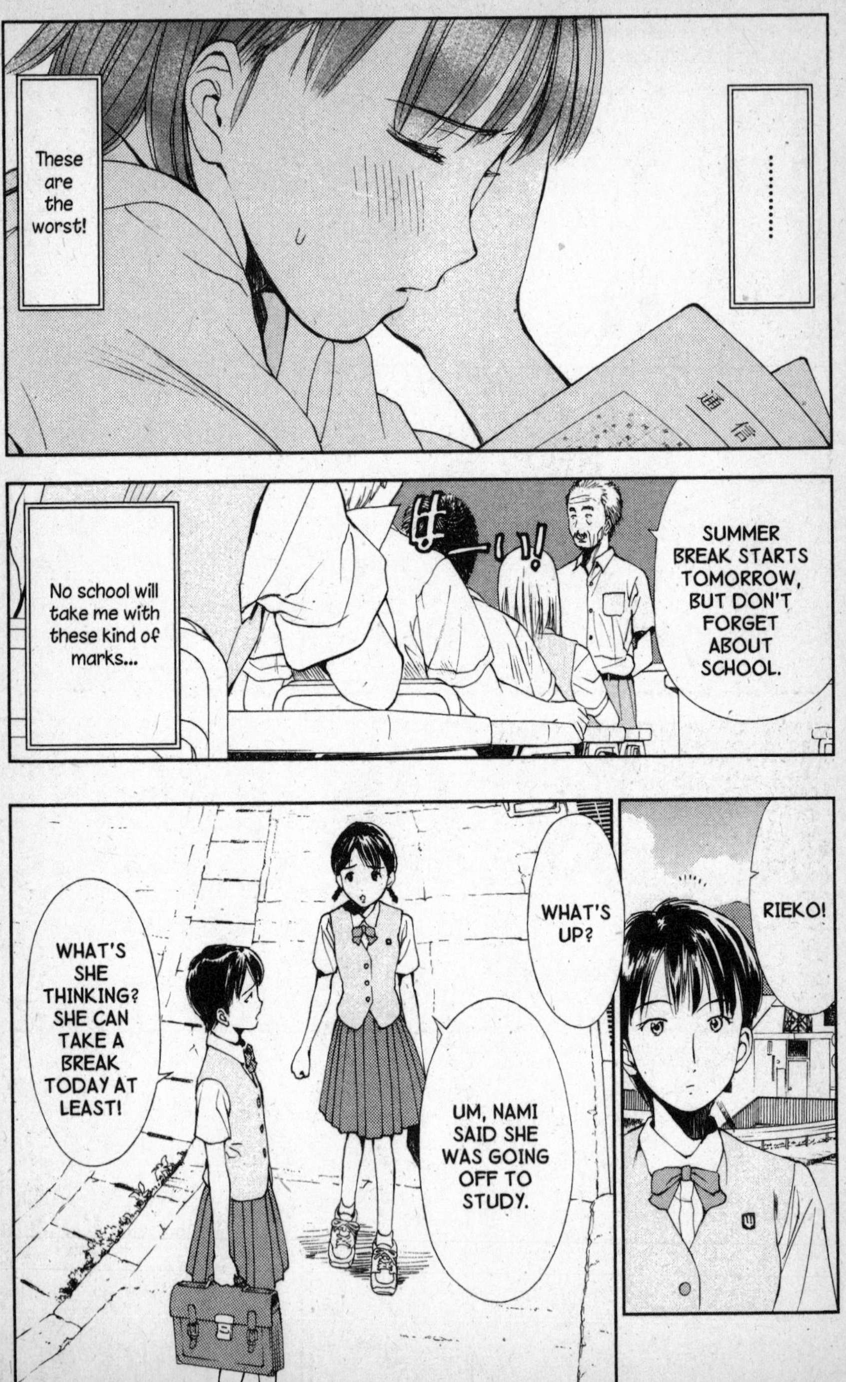
....
通信
These are the worst!
SUMMER BREAK STARTS TOMORROW, BUT DON'T FORGET ABOUT SCHOOL.
はーい!
No school will take me with these kind of marks...
RIEKO!
WHAT'S UP?
UM, NAMI SAID SHE WAS GOING OFF TO STUDY.
WHAT'S SHE THINKING? SHE CAN TAKE A BREAK TODAY AT LEAST!

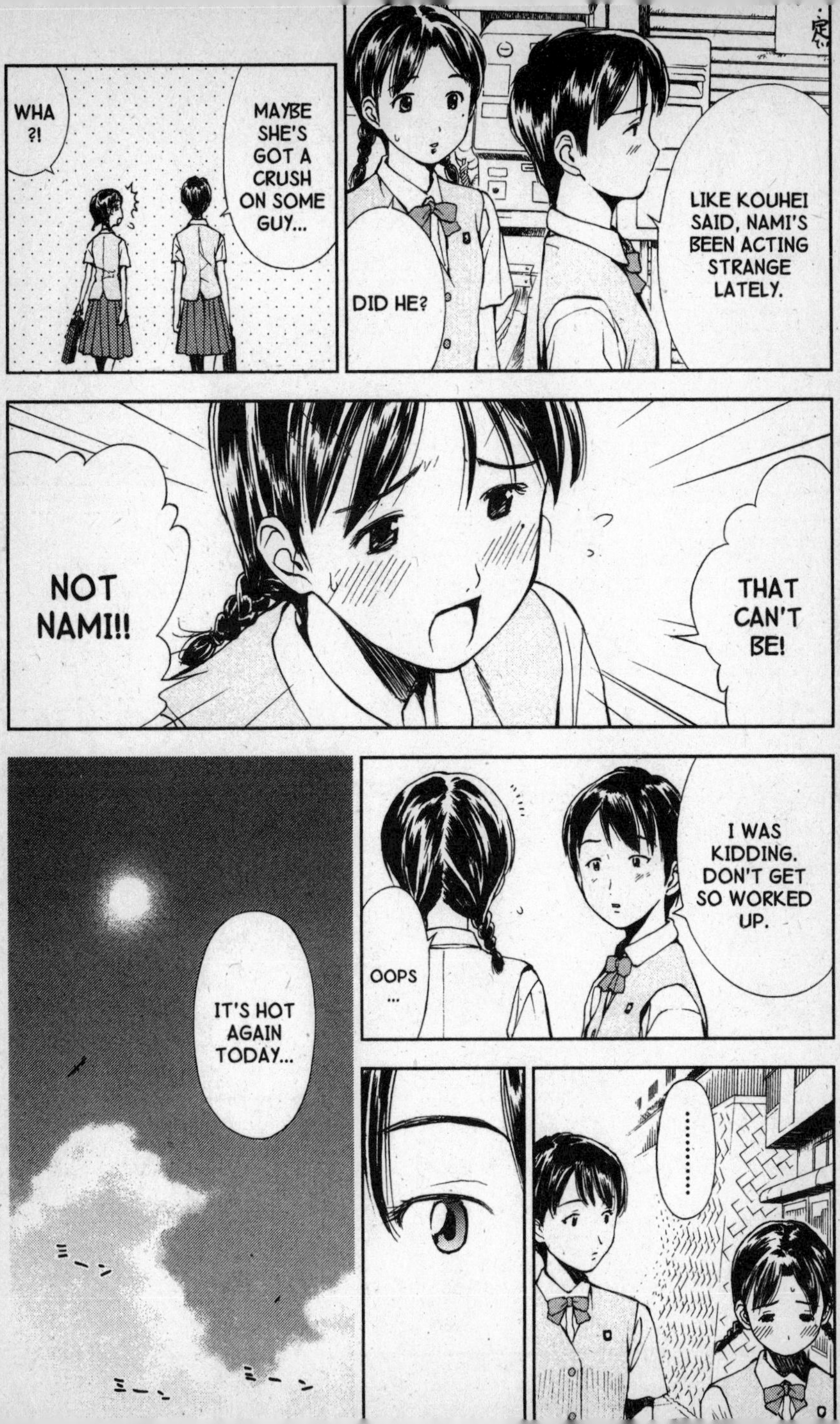
LIKE KOUHEI SAID, NAMI'S BEEN ACTING STRANGE LATELY.
DID HE?
MAYBE SHE'S GOT A CRUSH ON SOME GUY...
WHA?!
THAT CAN'T BE!
NOT NAMI!!
I WAS KIDDING. DON'T GET SO WORKED UP.
OOPS...
......
IT'S HOT AGAIN TODAY...

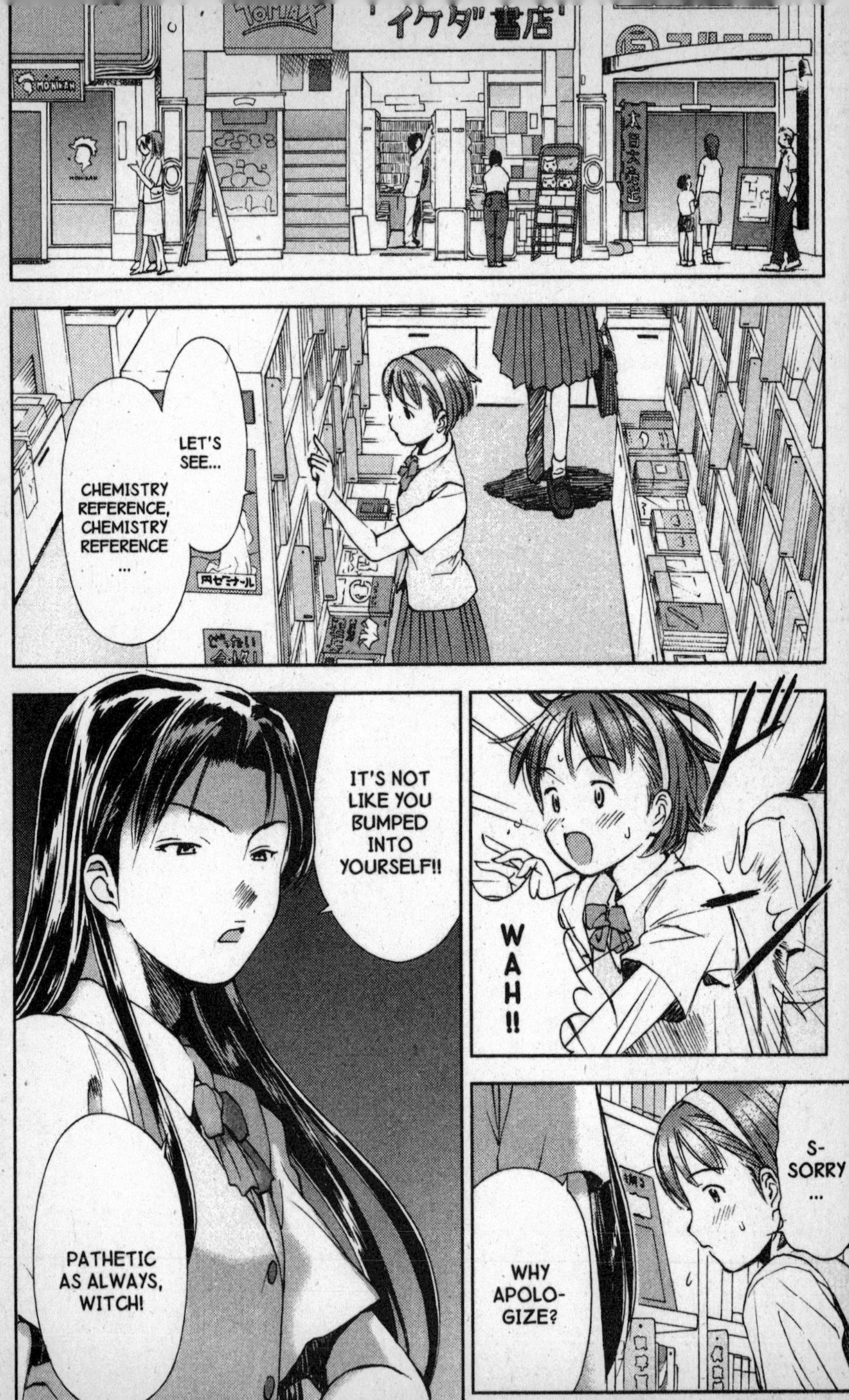

"イケダ"書店
LET'S SEE...
CHEMISTRY REFERENCE, CHEMISTRY REFERENCE ...
WAH!!
S-SORRY ...
WHY APOLOGIZE?
IT'S NOT LIKE YOU BUMPED INTO YOURSELF!!
PATHETIC AS ALWAYS, WITCH!

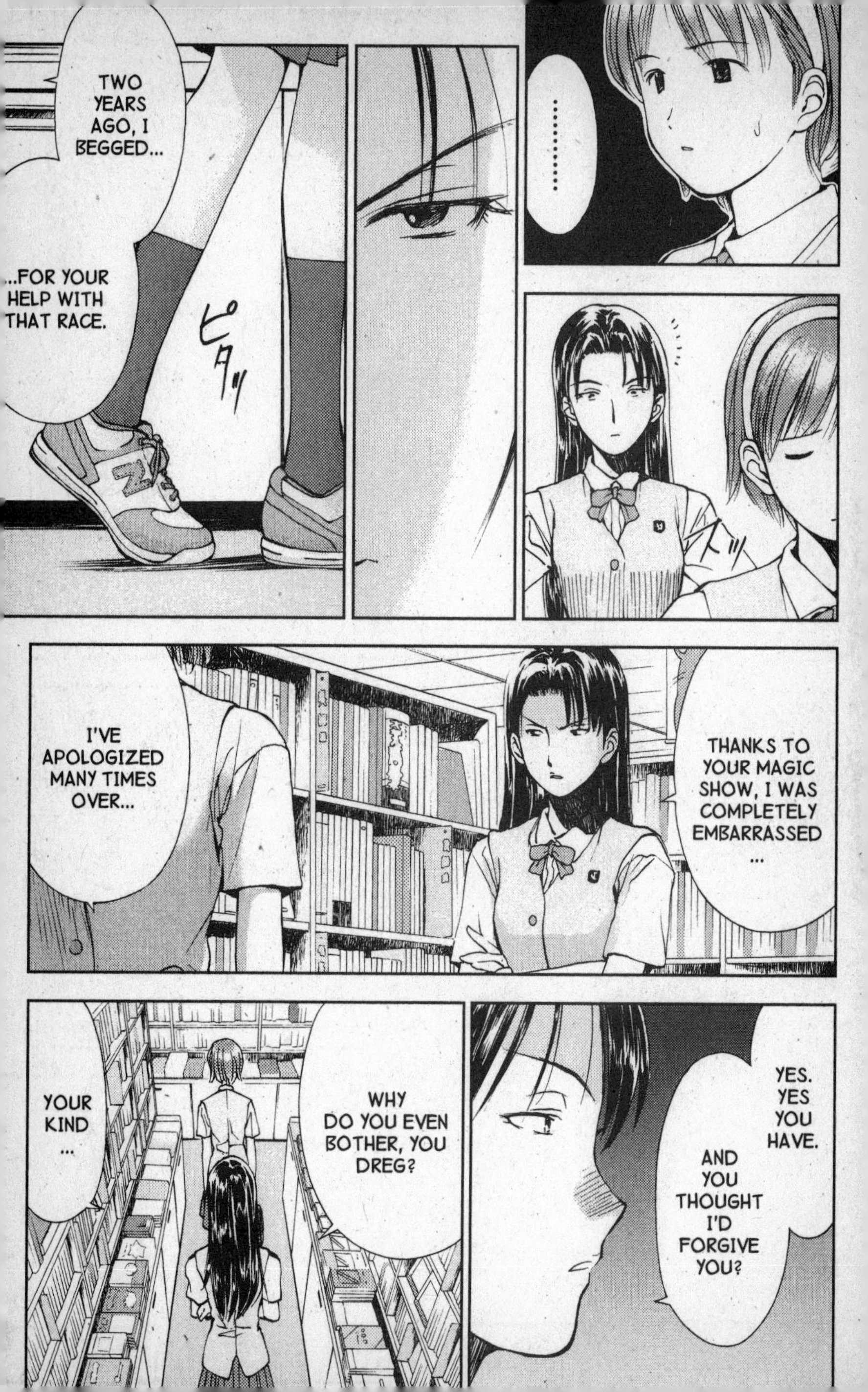
......
ズッ
TWO YEARS AGO, I BEGGED...
...FOR YOUR HELP WITH THAT RACE.
ピタッ
THANKS TO YOUR MAGIC SHOW, I WAS COMPLETELY EMBARRASSED ...
I'VE APOLOGIZED MANY TIMES OVER...
YES. YES YOU HAVE.
AND YOU THOUGHT I'D FORGIVE YOU?
WHY DO YOU EVEN BOTHER, YOU DREG?
YOUR KIND ...

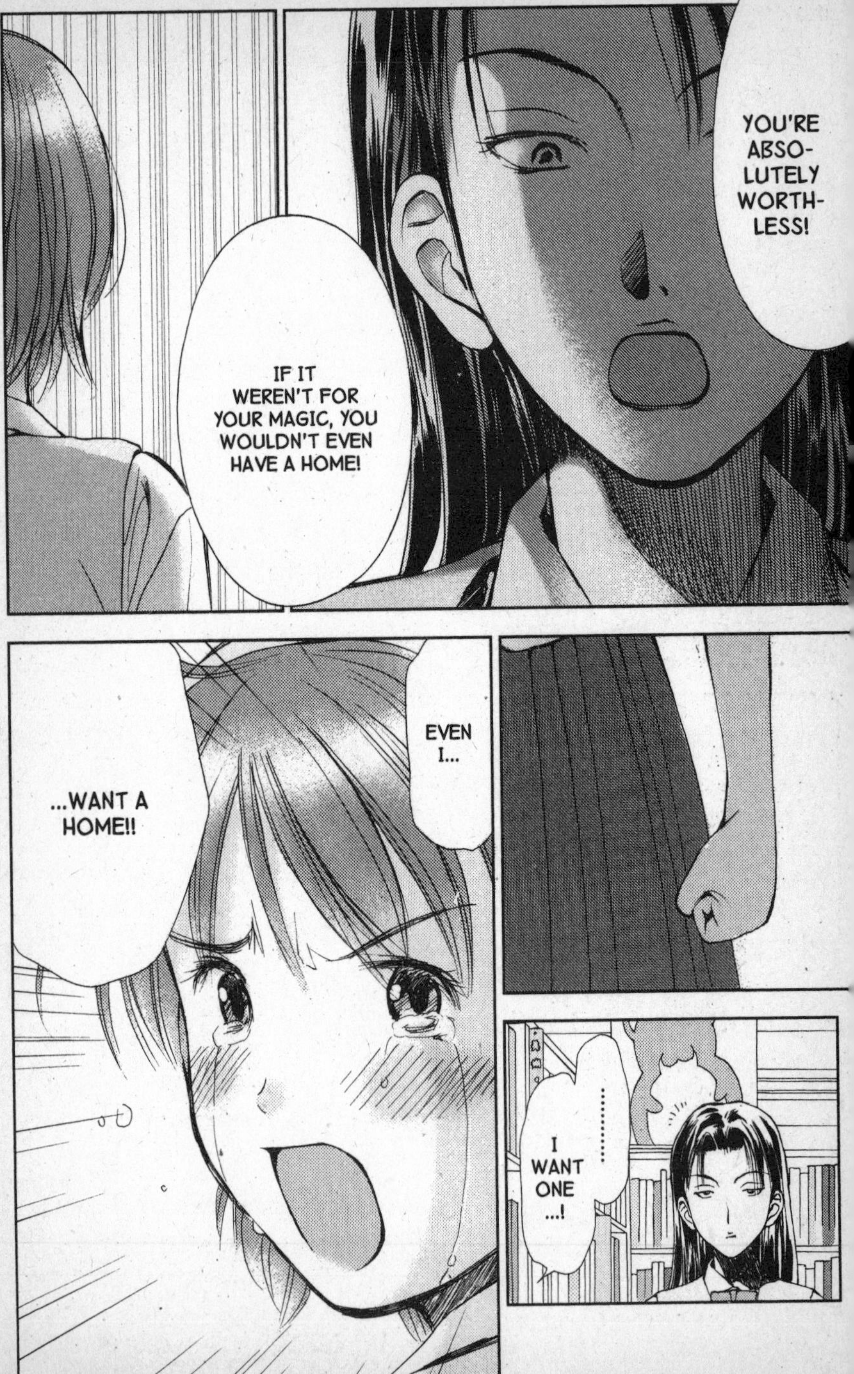
YOU'RE ABSO-LUTELY WORTH-LESS!
IF IT WEREN'T FOR YOUR MAGIC, YOU WOULDN'T EVEN HAVE A HOME!
...... I WANT ONE ...!
EVEN I...
...WANT A HOME!!

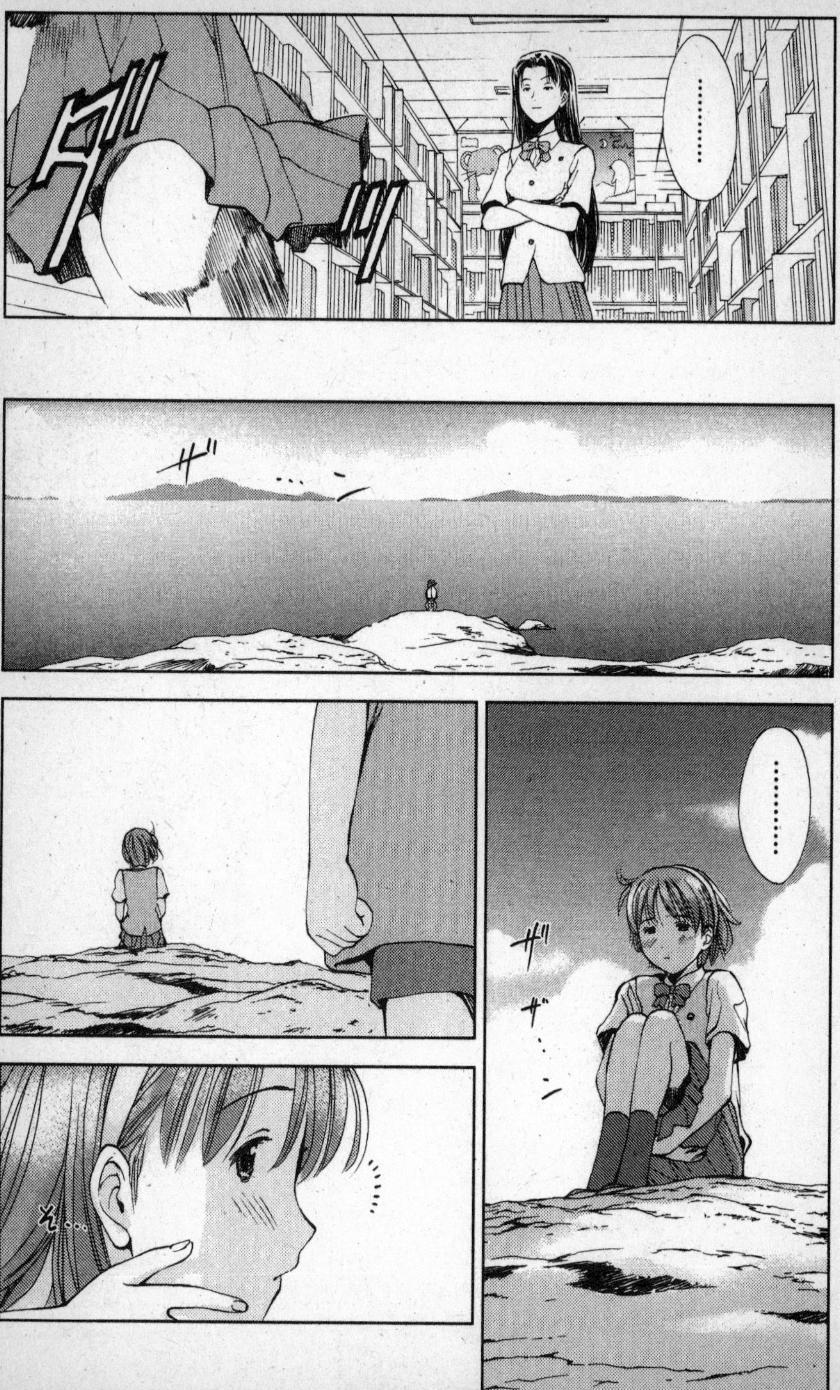
ダッ
……
ザ…ン
……
ザ
ザ…ン
…
そ…

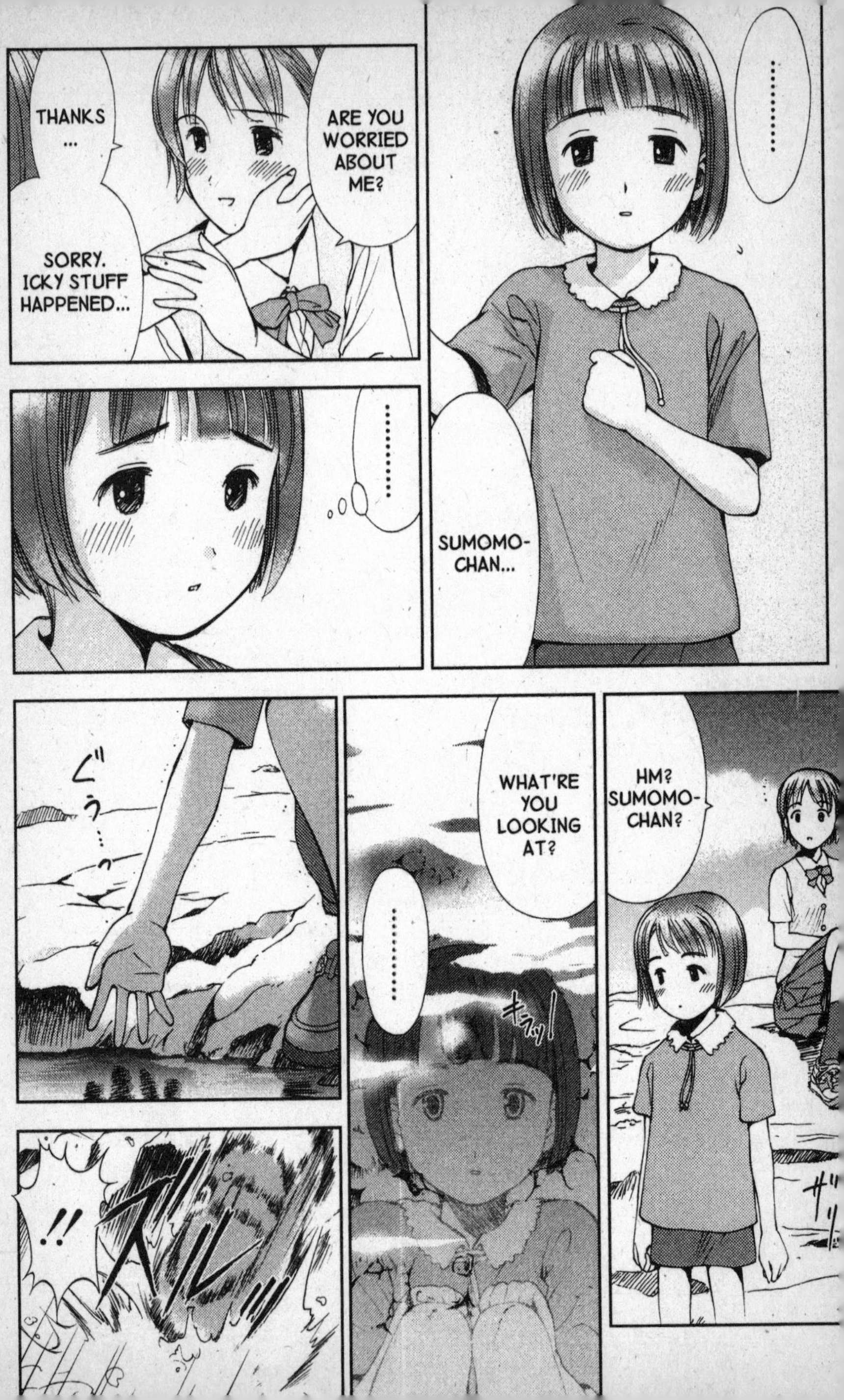
......
SUMOMO-CHAN...
ARE YOU WORRIED ABOUT ME?
THANKS ...
SORRY. ICKY STUFF HAPPENED...
......
HM? SUMOMO-CHAN?
ザリ
WHAT'RE YOU LOOKING AT?
......
キラッ
ぐう…っ
!!
ズル

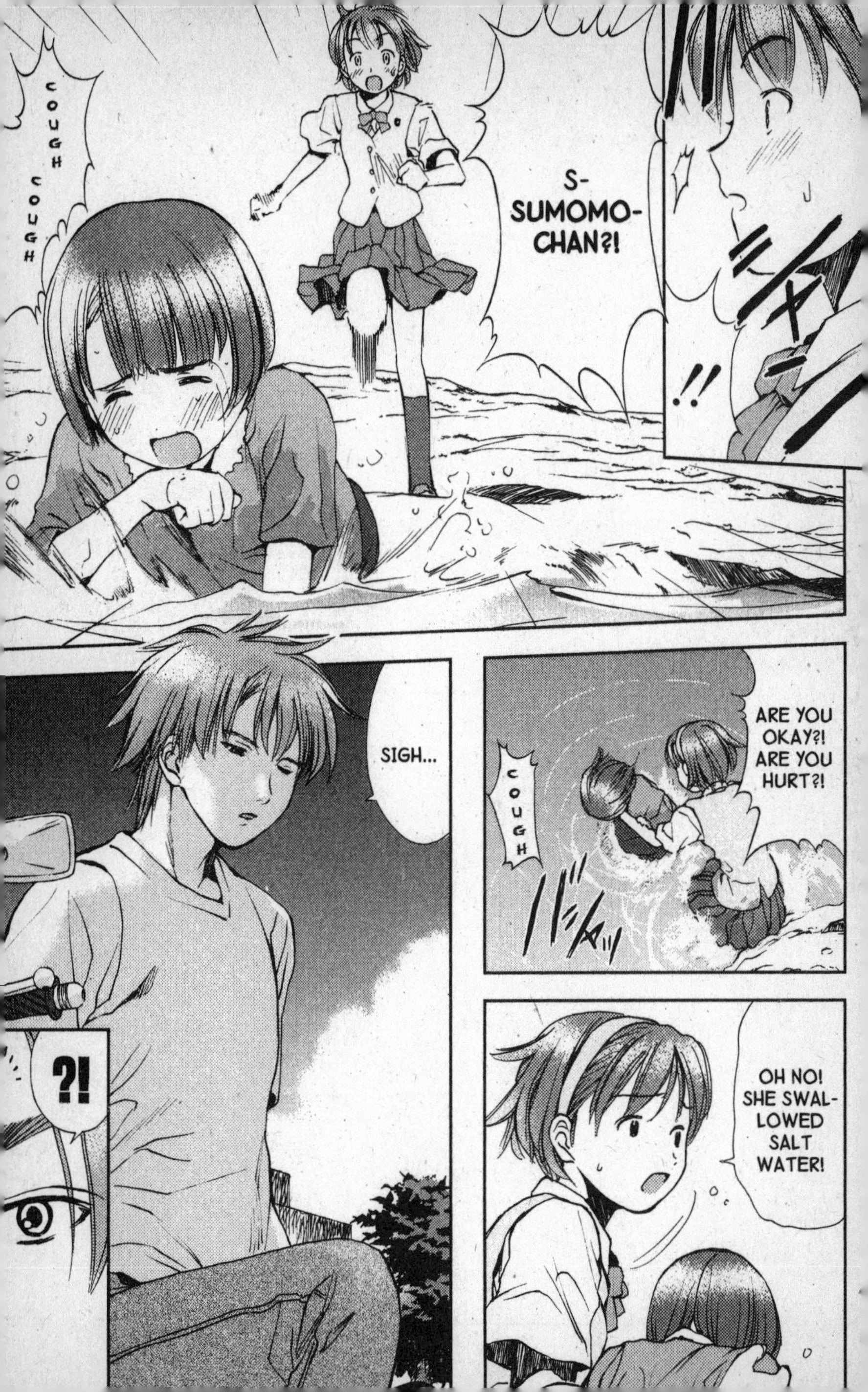
!!
S-SUMOMO-CHAN?!
COUGH COUGH
ARE YOU OKAY?! ARE YOU HURT?!
COUGH
OH NO! SHE SWAL-LOWED SALT WATER!
SIGH...
?!

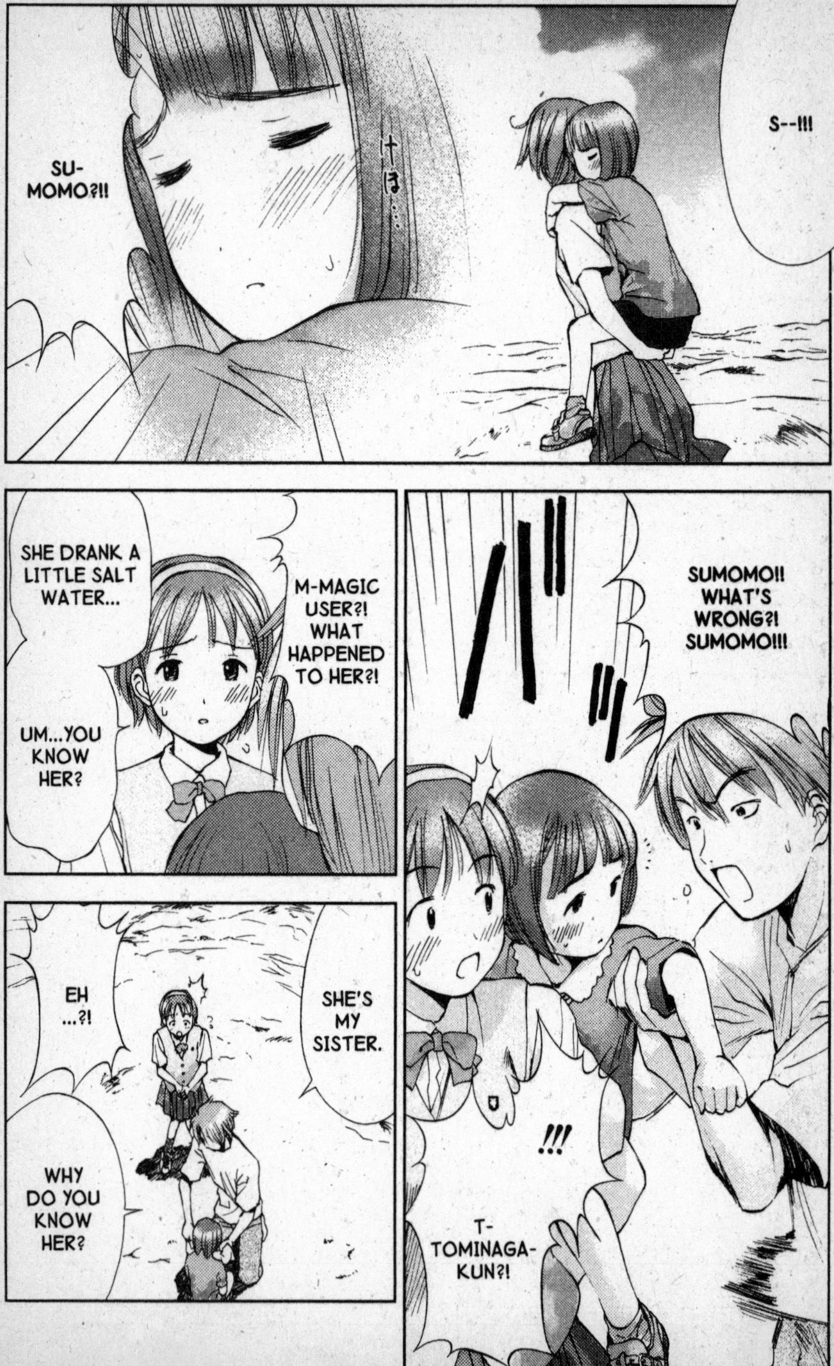
S--!!!
けほ…
SU-MOMO?!!
バッ
SUMOMO!! WHAT'S WRONG?! SUMOMO!!!
!!!
T-TOMINAGA-KUN?!
M-MAGIC USER?! WHAT HAPPENED TO HER?!
SHE DRANK A LITTLE SALT WATER...
UM...YOU KNOW HER?
SHE'S MY SISTER.
EH ...?!
WHY DO YOU KNOW HER?

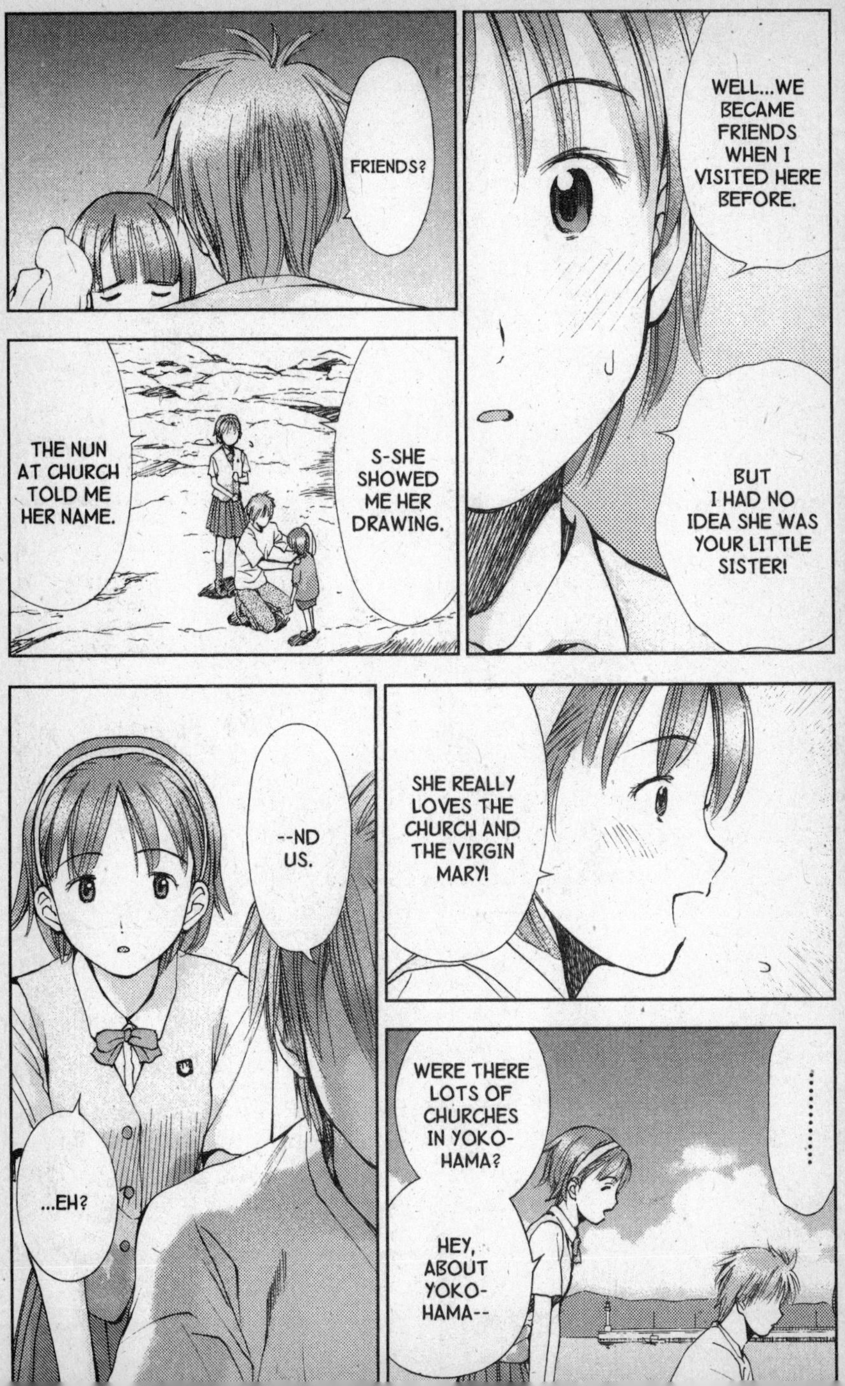
WELL...WE BECAME FRIENDS WHEN I VISITED HERE BEFORE.
BUT I HAD NO IDEA SHE WAS YOUR LITTLE SISTER!
FRIENDS?
S-SHE SHOWED ME HER DRAWING.
THE NUN AT CHURCH TOLD ME HER NAME.
SHE REALLY LOVES THE CHURCH AND THE VIRGIN MARY!
......
WERE THERE LOTS OF CHURCHES IN YOKO-HAMA?
HEY, ABOUT YOKO-HAMA--
--ND US.
...EH?

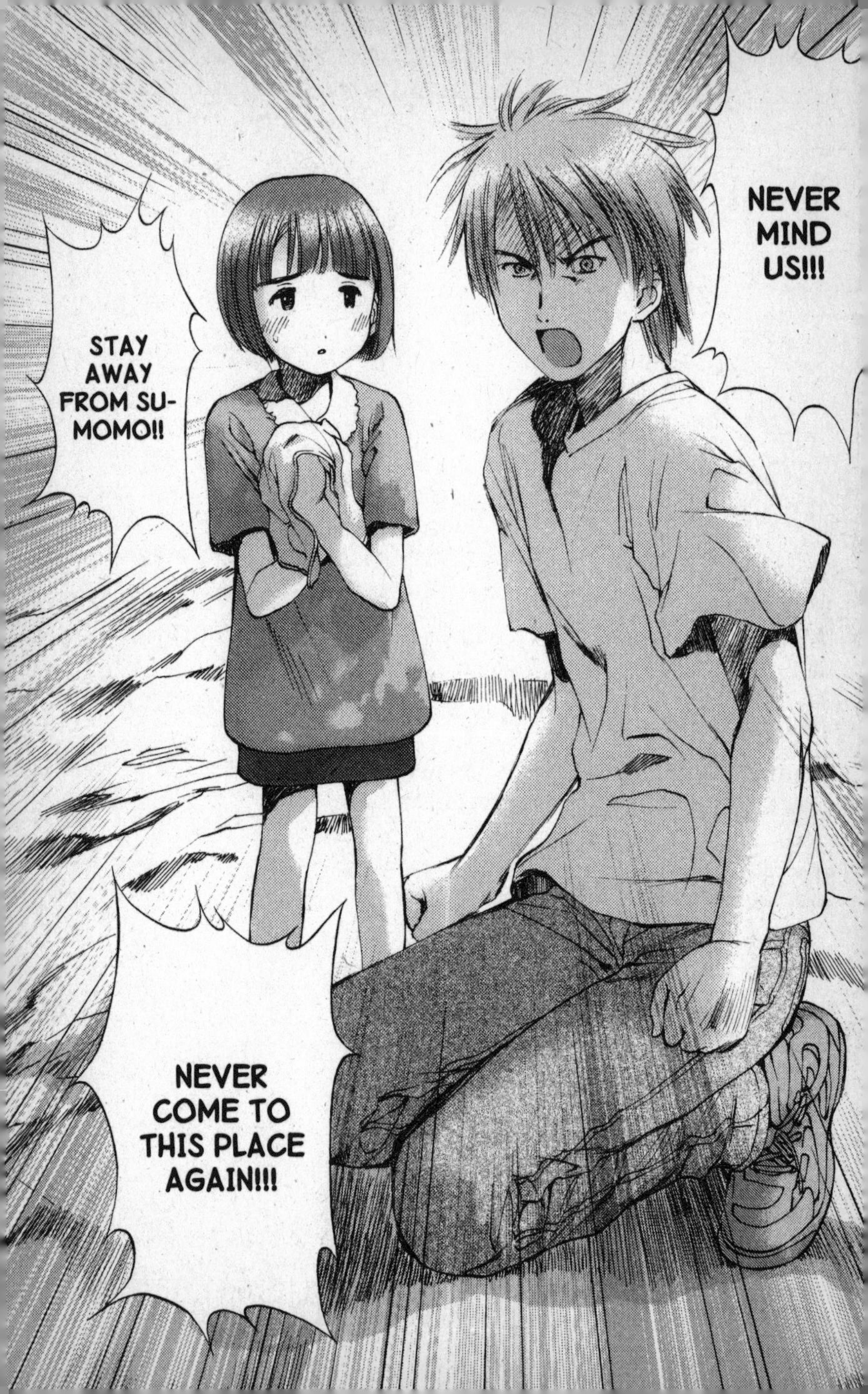
NEVER MIND US!!!
STAY AWAY FROM SU-MOMO!!
NEVER COME TO THIS PLACE AGAIN!!!

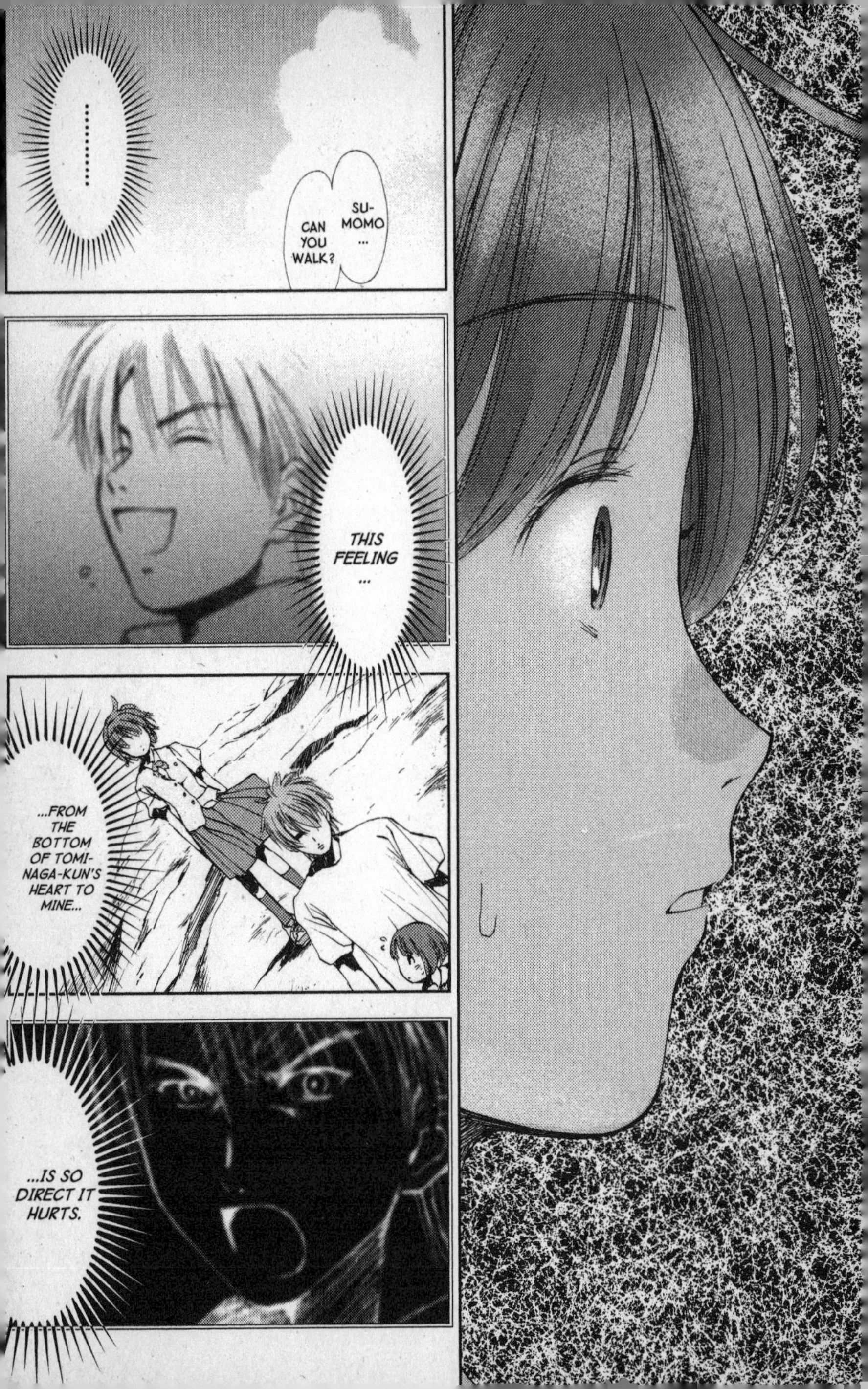
SU-MOMO ...
CAN YOU WALK?
......
THIS FEELING ...
...FROM THE BOTTOM OF TOMI-NAGA-KUN'S HEART TO MINE...
...IS SO DIRECT IT HURTS.

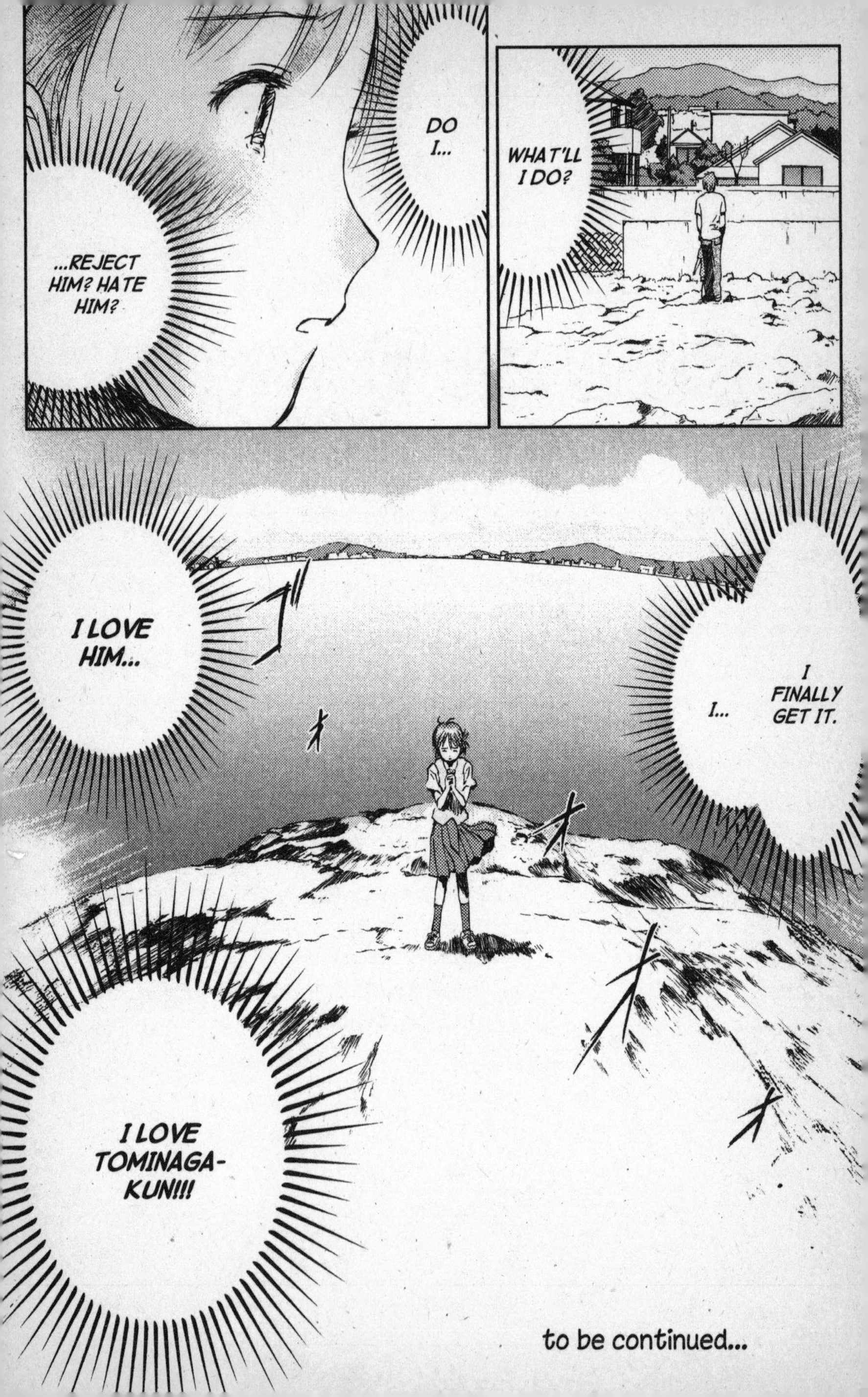
WHAT'LL I DO?
DO I...
...REJECT HIM? HATE HIM?
I... I FINALLY GET IT.
I LOVE HIM...
I LOVE TOMINAGA-KUN!!!
to be continued...

SOMEDAY'S DREAMERS SPELLBOUND™

Research Assistance
Nagasaki Tourism & Photography Support Center
Nagasaki Senior High
Ooshima Shipyard LLC
Kusano Landscaping LLC
"The Nagasaki" Editors
Natsuko Kogawa

Dialect Advisor
Jun Matsushita

Manga Assistants
Manami Satou
Hiroyuki Tanaka
Junji Ikeda
Shin Hasegawa

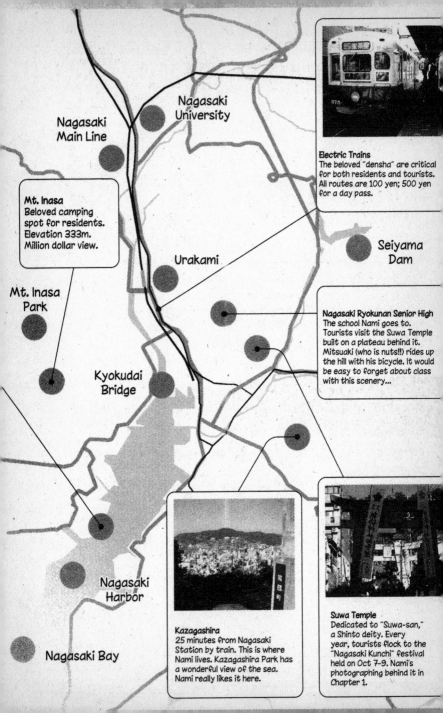

Nagasaki University

Nagasaki Main Line

Electric Trains
The beloved "densha" are critical for both residents and tourists. All routes are 100 yen; 500 yen for a day pass.

Mt. Inasa
Beloved camping spot for residents. Elevation 333m. Million dollar view.

Urakami

Seiyama Dam

Mt. Inasa Park

Nagasaki Ryokunan Senior High
The school Nami goes to. Tourists visit the Suwa Temple built on a plateau behind it. Mitsuaki (who is nuts!!) rides up the hill with his bicycle. It would be easy to forget about class with this scenery...

Kyokudai Bridge

Nagasaki Harbor

Kazagashira
25 minutes from Nagasaki Station by train. This is where Nami lives. Kazagashira Park has a wonderful view of the sea. Nami really likes it here.

Suwa Temple
Dedicated to "Suwa-san," a Shinto deity. Every year, tourists flock to the "Nagasaki Kunchi" festival held on Oct 7-9. Nami's photographing behind it in Chapter 1.

Nagasaki Bay

SOMEDAY'S DREAMERS SPELLBOUND™

Location Guide

This story takes place in Nagasaki, the Hill City. Let's traverse the city in which Nami and Ryutaro live.

Getting To Nagasaki

110 minutes from Tokyo by plane. 110 minutes from Hakata by bullet train. A long distance bus from Osaka is also available.

Yamada & Yoshizuki's Nagasaki Recommendations!

Yamada's Recommendations

I love the noodle plates and chanbon. I had some at the corner store in Chinatown near Nagasaki Station. Just remembering them makes me drool... Ikkoukou is honey-filled candy, I got mine at the airport. The liquor's good, too.

Yoshizuki's Recommendations

The view from Kazagashira's awesome! Excellent for strolling or taking pictures. The harbor side's especially nice. There are roads too narrow for cars with stone steps and pack horses right out of an old movie.

Kusano Shipyard
This is where Ryutaro works part-time. Actually, I used the Ooshima Shipyard, some two miles away by car, as my model. The sea's so beautiful from Ooshima Bridge.

* Photo from within city

Kami Island Church
Ryutaro lives right behind this beautiful white church. The "Kami Island Church" bus takes around 40 minutes from Nagasaki Station. A beautiful Virgin Mary prays for safe passage for ships nearby.

IouJi Island
About 20 minutes from Nagasaki Harbor with a fast boat. Pretty beach and coastline. Mitsuaki commutes from here daily.

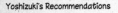

In the next volume of

SOMEDAY'S DREAMERS SPELLBOUND™

The summer break is in full swing, leaving Ryutaro time to visit his home town...and Nami time to wonder if she's the reason he left.

Meanwhile, Mitsuaki enters his first triathalon...though he may wish he hadn't insisted on inviting everyone to cheer him on.

Finally, Nami has an important revelation about magic using. Could this really be the first time she successfully works her charms?

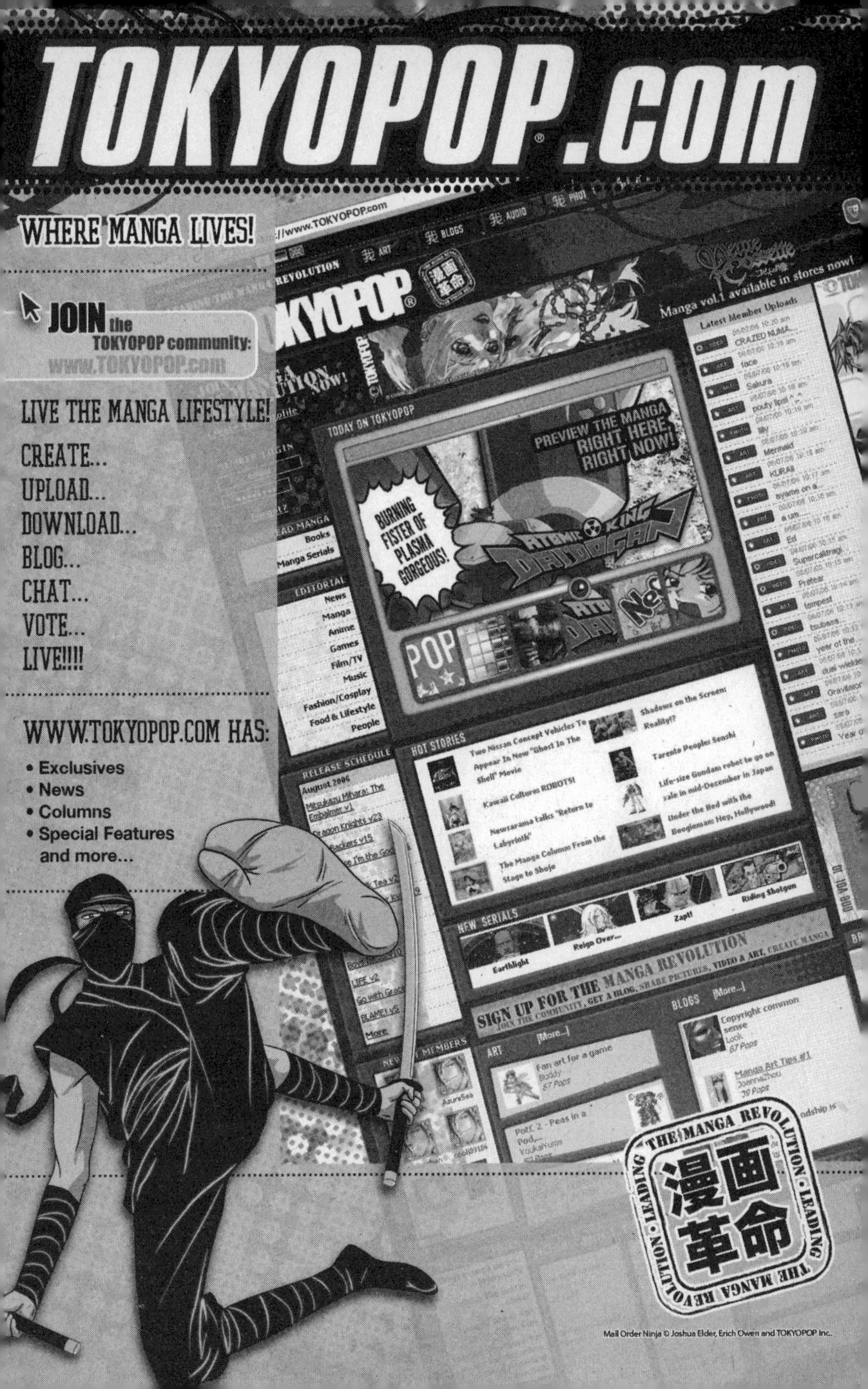
TOKYOPOP®.com
WHERE MANGA LIVES!
JOIN the TOKYOPOP community:
www.TOKYOPOP.com
LIVE THE MANGA LIFESTYLE!
CREATE...
UPLOAD...
DOWNLOAD...
BLOG...
CHAT...
VOTE...
LIVE!!!!
WWW.TOKYOPOP.COM HAS:
• Exclusives
• News
• Columns
• Special Features
and more...
TODAY ON TOKYOPOP
PREVIEW THE MANGA RIGHT HERE, RIGHT NOW!
BURNING FISTER OF PLASMA GORGEOUS!
HOT STORIES
RELEASE SCHEDULE
NEW SERIALS
SIGN UP FOR THE MANGA REVOLUTION
THE MANGA REVOLUTION • LEADING
漫画革命
Mail Order Ninja © Joshua Elder, Erich Owen and TOKYOPOP Inc.

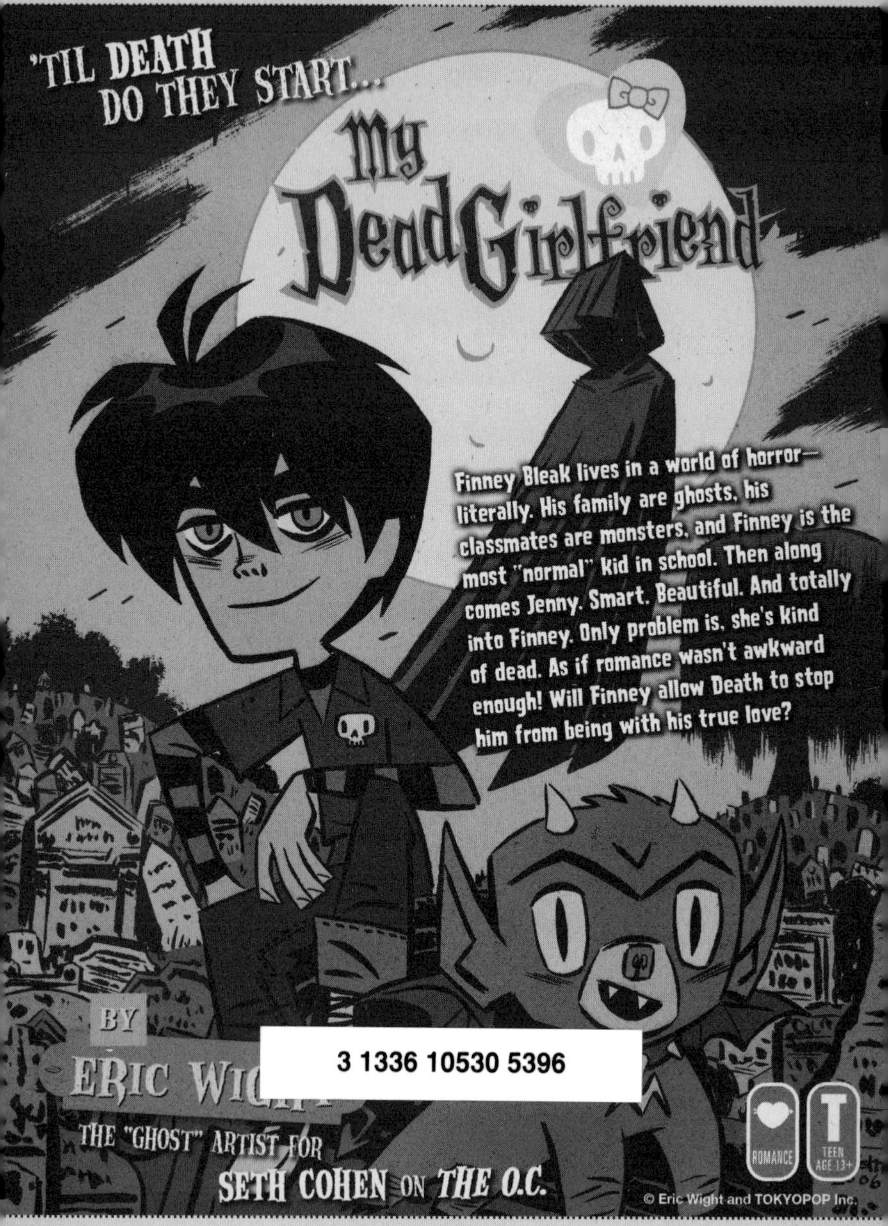
'TIL DEATH DO THEY START...
My Dead Girlfriend
Finney Bleak lives in a world of horror—literally. His family are ghosts, his classmates are monsters, and Finney is the most "normal" kid in school. Then along comes Jenny. Smart. Beautiful. And totally into Finney. Only problem is, she's kind of dead. As if romance wasn't awkward enough! Will Finney allow Death to stop him from being with his true love?
BY
ERIC WI
THE "GHOST" ARTIST FOR SETH COHEN ON THE O.C.
ROMANCE
T TEEN AGE 13+
© Eric Wight and TOKYOPOP Inc.

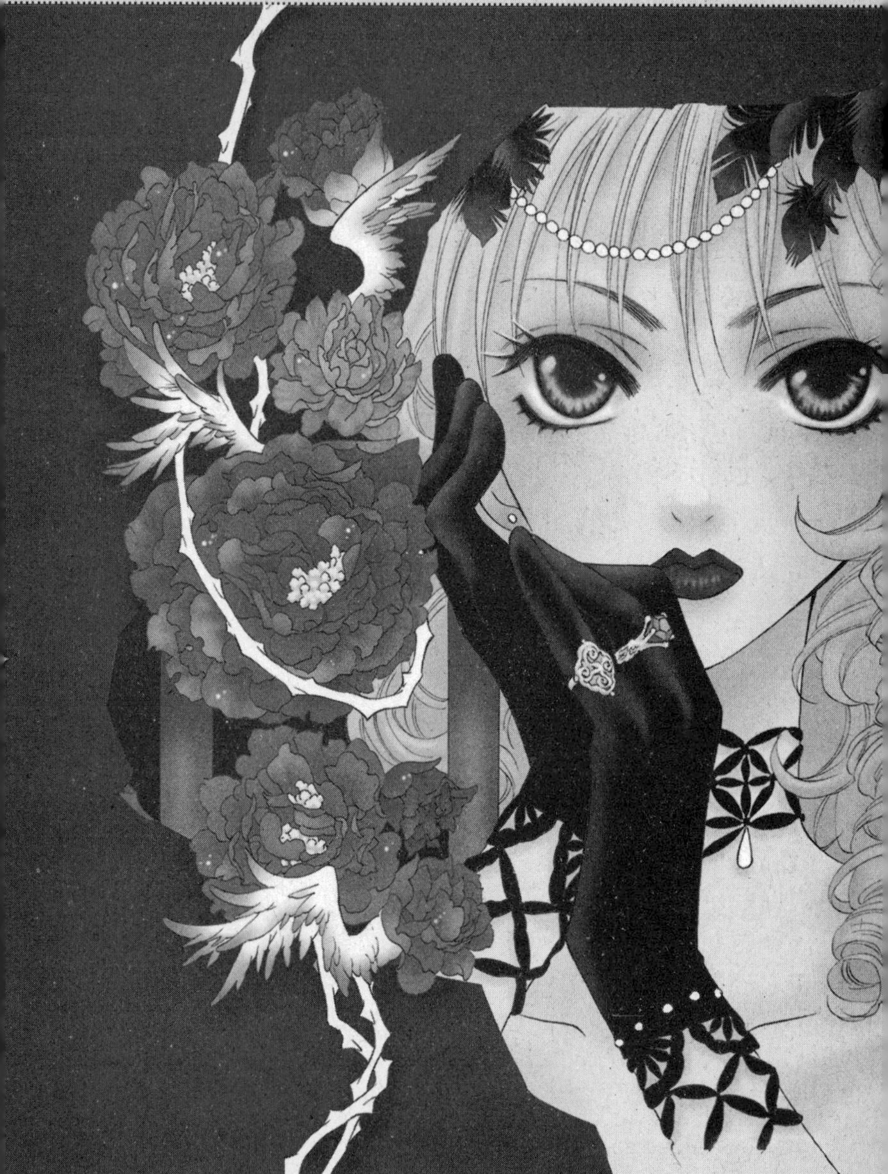

STOP!

This is the back of the book.
You wouldn't want to spoil a great ending

This book is printed "manga-style," in the authentic Japanese right-to-le format. Since none of the artwork has been flipped or altered, readers get to experience the story just as the creator intended. You've been asking for it, so TOKYOPOP® delivered: authentic, hot-off-the-press, and far more fun!

DIRECTIONS

If this is your first time reading manga-style, here's a quick guide to help you understand how it works.

1
2
3
4
5
6
7
8
9
10

It's easy... just start in the top right panel and follow the numbers. Have fun, and look fo more 100% authentic manga from TOKYOPOP®!

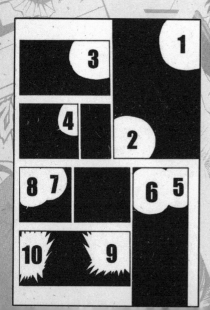